STUDIES IN
13TH CENTURY JUSTICE AND ADMINISTRATION

STUDIES IN 13TH CENTURY JUSTICE AND ADMINISTRATION

C.A.F. MEEKINGS

THE HAMBLEDON PRESS

Published by The Hambledon Press
35 Gloucester Avenue, London NW1 7AX

British Library Cataloguing in Publication Data

Meekings, C.A.F.
Studies in thirteenth century justice and administration
1. Common law – England – History and criticism – Addresses, essays, lectures
I. Title
344.2'009 KD606

ISBN 0–9506882–3–1

Printed by Unwin Brothers Limited
The Gresham Press, Old Woking, Surrey

History Series No. 3

This volume contains 342 pages

CONTENTS

ACKNOWLEDGEMENTS

The articles reprinted here first appeared in the following places and are reprinted with permission.

I	Bull. I.H.R., XXXII (1959), 209–21.
II	E.H.R., LXXI (1956), 615–8.
III	E.H.R., LXXII (1957), 260–9.
IV	Bull. I.H.R., XXVIII (1955), 173–88.
V	E.H.R., LXV (1950), 492–504.
VI	N. & Q., CCI (1956), 54–6.
VII	N. & Q. for Somerset and Dorset, XXVI (1951–4), 141–3.
VIII	Bull. I.H.R., XXXIV (1961), 1–15.
IX	Introduction to *Fitznells Cartulary* (Surrey Rec. Soc., XXVI, 1968), lviii–lxxv, clviii–clx.
X	Bull. I.H.R., XLI (1968), 132–8.
XI	Bull. I.H.R., XXVI (1953), 157–80.
XII	Bull. I.H.R., XLVIII (1974), 224–9.
XIII	Yorks Arch. Jnl, XXXVIII (1952–5), 465–73.
XIV	Arch. Aeliana, 4th ser., XXXV (1957), 100–28.
XV	Surrey Arch. Colls, LXXII (1980), 157–73.
XVI	Sussex Arch. Cols, CXVI (1978), 399–400.
XVII	Jnl Eccles. Hist., XXX (1979), 1–37.
XVIII	Surrey Arch. Colls, LVII (1960), 75–84.
XIX	Devon and Cornwall N. & Q., XXXII (1971–3), 168–70.
XX	*Studies Presented to Sir Hilary Jenkinson*, ed. J. Conway Davies (Oxford, 1957), 222–53.

INTRODUCTION

Cecil Anthony Francis Meekings, O.B.E., M.A., F.S.A., was born in Fulham in 1914. From his early life a strong patriot of London and its environs, he became particularly attached to the county of Surrey, for whose record society he later did some of his best work. He attended Latymer Upper School and Cambridge University, where he gained a first in history and won the George Williams Prize and a Lightfoot Scholarship. He continued his research until the outbreak of the Second World War, during which he served as an army officer in East Africa. After the war he was archives officer for the British Control Commission for Germany. In 1947 he became an assistant keeper at the Public Record Office, which he remained until his retirement in 1974. Among other posts, he held that of Office librarian, leaving countless annotations in his own distinctive hand in many of the volumes under his charge. An all too brief retirement left him with little of the time he needed to complete many of the projects he had begun, and he died in January 1977, leaving a mass of unpublished material, some virtually complete but most in the form of notes, to add to the relatively modest amount of work published during his lifetime. This volume reprints all the articles on Meekings's central interest, justice and administration in thirteenth-century England, which were published before the end of 1980. This introduction is intended to give some account of the main outlines of his work, official and private, both in that area and in the other fields in which he was involved, and to indicate in some detail the main unpublished material and its value. Articles reproduced here are referred to by the roman numerals by which they are identified in the contents list and index; other works are included in the bibliography and are referred to by the letters by which they are identified there.

Meekings's historical writing was founded essentially on an intimate knowledge of the sources for the subjects in which he became interested, documents with which he was in daily contact during a quarter of a century as an assistant keeper of the public records. Behind each piece of work he published lay a systematic study of all the sources which bore on the subject. The very exhaustiveness of his methods goes a long way towards explaining why he published relatively little. Where the sheer amount of matter available made it impossible for him to examine it all, an occurrence which his industry limited to a handful of occasions, he proffered his conclusions with a caution far greater than many others would have expressed. He was critical of historians who did not take account of all the evidence available on a given topic, or those who he considered had failed fully to understand the limitations of the sources they used. Further, he had the archivist's awareness of the documents which no longer survive, either because they were destroyed as soon as their immediate usefulness had passed, or because they had suffered from neglect during the intervening centuries. This made him a keen student of the activities of past generations of record keepers, whom he felt able to criticise or, more occasionally, to praise, from a standpoint of archival rectitude which few if any of them would have recognised. It was his concern to understand the intricate details of the judicial, financial or administrative processes, both as legitimate subjects for investigation in themselves and as a means of appreciating more fully the significance of the surviving documents and of the information they contain. Having examined and understood, the archivist blossomed into an historian whose sympathy with and appreciation of the people and places of the past now combined with his documentary knowledge to reveal, amid the unashamedly factual bedrock of his work, the occasional illuminating flash of insight into the preoccupations and concerns of people with whom, although they were long dead, one feels almost as if he had conversed.

During the years before he came to the Public Record Office, Meekings did research on the early modern period, producing a volume of abstracts of sixteenth-century feet of fines for Surrey (B) which remains the only treatment of those important documents for the post-medieval period and so retains its general as well as local importance. His main interest, however, came to be centred on the later seventeenth century, and in particular on the hearth tax. He made an exhaustive study of the history of its administration, but he was also concerned with the information that its records provide about local communities. He edited some assessments for Surrey (A) and provided an introduction to a Dorset volume whose text was prepared by others (D). For a brief account of the tax as a whole one has to turn to these volumes or to the introduction to the catalogue of an exhibition of hearth tax documents held at the Public Record Office in 1962-3 (L), because his major work on the subject, referred to in some of his published works, was only partially written; Dr. Helen Forde, an assistant keeper of public records, has undertaken to complete it. One chapter from it was rewritten as an article for inclusion in a festschrift dedicated to the former archivist of the city of London, Philip Jones (N). Meekings assembled folders of notes on the history of the tax in each county which, although difficult to use, are available on request at the Public Record Office. Two volumes of notes analysing all the surviving hearth tax documents among the public records, county by county and collection by collection, a valuable supplement to the official list of hearth tax records and more readily usable, have been reproduced and issued by the List and Index Society (Y).

When he became an assistant keeper, Meekings soon moved on to other work more germane to the subjects of the articles reprinted in the present volume, but he continued his interest in the hearth tax both by sorting and listing documentary miscellanea and by publishing occasional work on the subject; he wrote the sections on the tax for the Victoria County History of Cambridgeshire and the Isle of Ely, three of which have so far appeared (F). He left some other unpublished work which it is hoped will appear during the next few years. Mr. David G. Edwards is editing a volume of Derbyshire hearth tax assessments for the Derbyshire Record Society, and the introduction to his work will include a detailed account of the documents written by Meekings about 1947-8 for a projected edition which never materialised. His substantially complete edition of the unique Worcester city hearth tax collector's book for 1679-80 has been taken over by Dr. Ian Roy and Mr. Stephen Porter of King's College, London, and will appear in a future volume of the Worcestershire Historical Society's series; its publication was previously planned in the late 1930s and considered again in 1961. There is also an article on the politics of Worcester corporation in the 1680s called 'The Chamber of Worcester, 1679 to 1689', which Meekings wrote in 1949; it is to be included in the *Transactions of the Worcestershire Archaeological Society*.

Office lore has it that Meekings was unenthusiastic when, as a new assistant keeper but already well into his thirties and with an established line of research, he was put to work on early plea rolls. Lady Stenton, building on the foundations laid by F.W. Maitland, had illuminated the history of the central and itinerant royal courts of justice during the reigns of Henry II, Richard I and John and the very earliest years of the reign of Henry III; Professor Sayles had embarked on his study of the court coram rege, or king's bench, in what has eventually proved to be the century and a half following the accession of Edward I, at the same time shedding some light on the development of its more mundane counterpart, the common bench, or court of common pleas. Between them lay a period of fifty years whose vital importance in the history and development of law and judicial administration in England was widely recognised but whose records had received surprisingly little investigation. The publication of the *Curia*

Regis Rolls, mainly through the efforts of Sir Cyril Flower, meant that the texts of the plea rolls of the common bench for the earlier part of it were slowly becoming readily available, but by the time Meekings began his work they had only reached the early 1220s, the same point to which Lady Stenton had carried her editions of the eyre rolls. The publication of the pipe rolls of the exchequer, from which there was still much to be learned concerning judicial administration, had not yet reached the end of the reign of John; few of the feet of fines for the reign of Henry III were in print. The judicial records had many serious gaps and some of them were damaged, but they only required systematic attention to be persuaded to give up many of their secrets. It was from Cecil Meekings that they at last received their due.

Much of the obscurity surrounding the history of the central courts, and particularly the court coram rege, in the reign of Henry III was due to the creation in the late nineteenth century of the class of records called 'Curia Regis Rolls', which was grouped with the records of king's bench under the reference KB 26 but included the rolls of both courts. The plea rolls of the two courts after 1272 were clearly distinguished by being preserved in two completely separate classes; the inclusion of the earlier rolls in one undifferentiated grouping was conceived in ignorance and bred confusion. Meekings embarked on a thorough examination of the rolls and also of the related essoin rolls, paying close attention to the history of their custody and classification in the centuries since their creation. He similarly dealt with the rolls of the itinerant justices during the reign, particularly those who held the eyre for all pleas, what has now come to be called the general eyre. The few surviving writ files also received detailed attention, and he made a full examination of the thousands of feet of fines. Comprehensive use was made of the supporting evidence in the records of the exchequer and chancery, so that a full picture of the royal administration, and in particular of its judicial aspect, was built up. The detailed knowledge he had gained enabled him to identify and correctly place many pieces of unsorted plea roll miscellanea, as well as to rectify the errors of past generations of archivists who had interfered with the composition of the rolls. Users of the original rolls will be familiar with his manuscript introductory notes attached to those on which he worked, explaining in detail what he had done and the reasons for it. The minuteness of his instructions on how documents should be repaired is legendary among the more senior of the conservation staff of the Record Office. The editorial slips created for each roll still have great value and may be consulted upon request, but most of the fruits of this work are or will soon become available in more direct ways.

Detailed studies of the records of both central courts during the reign, incorporating new lists arranged by year and term and superbly illustrated with large numbers of photostats, and a similar separate treatment of the essoin rolls of the common bench from Edward I to George III, all completed between 1955 and 1957, have long been available in the Round Room at Chancery Lane. The lists and some of the other information from these works has been published (O). Detailed accounts of the history of the courts and of the surviving plea rolls for the earlier years of the reign have been published in the introductions to the continuing series of *Curia Regis Rolls* volumes (G), and similar material exists for four further volumes yet to be published. These introductions also contain details of eyres, taken from his 'General Eyres Henry III', an exhaustive list based mainly on the evidence of feet of fines, pipe rolls and chancery rolls because the majority of the plea rolls have not survived. The list, which has frequently been consulted by others, includes a long introductory note on the sources used. Meekings also examined the records of the eyres held after 1272, but they interested him much less. The Henry III list and the later note material have been used in the preparation of a forthcoming Public Record Office handbook, 'Records of the General Eyre', which will list all the records from 1194 to 1348 under the eyre for or during which they were created; work on the handbook has reached an advanced stage.

The eyre rolls comprise only about a third of the records in the class of 'Eyre Rolls, Assize Rolls, Etc.' (JUST 1), a miscellaneous grouping which has confused users of the records almost as much as the class of 'Curia Regis Rolls'. Meekings did not neglect the other kinds of documents it contains. They were subjected to the same systematic analysis and repair, and the editorial slips are available for consultation. He began separate lists of the large group of assize rolls and of the much smaller number of records of the proceedings of special commissions of oyer and terminer, the latter mainly from the fourteenth century; they will be completed when time permits, and in the meantime they are available in their incomplete form. Some attention was devoted to the records of general commissions of oyer and terminer, popularly known as trailbaston, but work on them did not proceed very far. It is hoped that an examination of them on what might be called Meekingsian principles will be undertaken in the not too distant future.

Three other classes of records exist within the Justices Itinerant group, and Meekings worked extensively on two of them. One (JUST 3) includes the rolls and files of the justices of gaol delivery, from the reign of Edward I to the middle of the fifteenth century. Meekings examined, listed and repaired them in the same way as the records already mentioned, and the editorial slips are available for consultation. A detailed list of them all, arranged by county and then chronologically, with the circuit files in chronological order at the end, and supplemented by separate lists of the records of gaol deliveries in rolls included in JUST 1 and in the plea rolls of king's bench, was compiled and later published (O). A long introductory account, illustrated with photostats on the lines of the studies of the common bench and court coram rege already mentioned, was incomplete at the time of his death. Dr. H.R.T. Summerson has undertaken its completion, and it will then become available in the Public Record Office search-rooms; in the meantime, the typescript of the completed sections can be made available to enquirers. Also available is a manuscript transcript of the commissions on the dorses of the patent rolls, 1232 to 1247, which were nearly all excluded from the *Calendar of Patent Rolls, 1232-47*; it was made in connection with the study of the early history of gaol delivery and assizes, and it is hoped that it will be published officially at some future date. Calendars of the commissions both for assizes and gaol delivery on the dorses of the patent rolls of Richard II, Henry IV and Henry V, including introductory formularies and brief histories of medieval assizes and gaol delivery, have already been published (T). Examination, listing and repair of the class of 'Eyre, Assize, Etc., Writ Files' (JUST 4) is proceeding. Meekings repaired a few of the earliest, for the reign of Henry III, including that of the 1248 Berkshire eyre which has been published in volume 90 of the Selden Society's series; he also made available a few assize files from the reigns of Richard II, Henry IV and Henry VI. He laid down the principles on which the files should be classified and repaired, and did much preliminary identification and sorting. The relatively few files from general eyres, about forty in all, have now been examined, listed and prepared for repair. With a few exceptions they have not yet been repaired and may be consulted only under special supervision; a few are too badly damaged to be examined at all before they are repaired. Work on making available the considerable number of assize files, particularly for the fourteenth century, will, it is hoped, be undertaken during the next few years.

During his last years as an assistant keeper, from 1966 to 1974, Meekings's main efforts were devoted to the sorting of the mass of files of the court of king's bench, kept at the Public Record Office's intermediate repository at Hayes, Middlesex. During that period he made great inroads into a task that will now have to be completed by other hands. He took his examination of most series down to the seventeenth century. He summarised the progress he had made in a special lecture delivered to a conference of legal historians (U). Some of the intact files are now available to readers, but lists of all the file series have not yet been compiled. Meekings also did a considerable amount of preliminary sorting work on the common pleas files, another task which it will take much further effort to complete.

The extent of Meekings's achievement in an official career which was not particularly lengthy and in which he had numerous other duties to perform is staggering. An account of his official work is, however, only part of the picture, as the contents of this volume show. It provided the basis for his private work, and the fruits of the latter in turn benefited his official work. The two cannot easily be disentangled in terms of subject matter but only by distinguishing whether particular projects were official or private, and even this can be misleading. His first encounter with medieval plea rolls was in producing the text for the calendar of the 1249 Wiltshire crown pleas (K), which was done in 1947-8 as an official training exercise, while the introductions to several *Curia Regis Rolls* volumes incorporate his private work on the courts, their records and their officials.

The history of the general eyre, particularly in the reign of Henry III, was the subject which Meekings illuminated most fully in his non-official publications. The volume on the 1249 Wiltshire crown pleas became the standard work on the subject (K), an unusual tribute to something which at first sight is of primarily local interest. The edition of the Chippenham veredictum of the 1281 Wiltshire eyre also remains fundamental to the study of crown pleas in eyre (H), and some of his early articles were concerned with detailed aspects of eyre administration (II, III). Meekings addressed the Anglo-American Conference of Historians on the subject of the general eyre in 1954, but the most comprehensive account of his views on it is to be found in his edition of the 1235 Surrey eyre roll, of which one volume has been issued and one is forthcoming (W); it deals with the civil as well as the crown pleas and has been revised to take account of recent work by himself and others. In view of his earlier interest in financial records, it is not surprising that he was particularly concerned with the financial issues of eyres, and he contributed a section on that subject to the introduction to the calendar of the London eyre roll of 1244 (P). It was this interest which led him into a detailed study of the alterations in exchequer procedures designed to cope with accounting for increasing numbers of small debts (XX), a study which demonstrates that he was as familiar with exchequer records as he was with those of the courts and which remains one of the most fundamental contributions yet made to our understanding of the exchequer in the thirteenth century. He had first become closely acquainted with the exchequer records of the period when, as one of his earliest official duties, he had prepared a scheme for calendaring the pipe rolls of Henry III's reign (C). Meekings was also closely interested in the forest eyre, and between his retirement and death was working on an introduction to the calendar of Surrey forest documents of the reign of Henry III which he had already completed. The introduction was fully planned but very little of it was written; sufficient material exists for the completion of the work when time allows.

In examining the records of the central courts and eyres for the reign of Henry III, Meekings became interested to know about the justices for whom they were made and the clerks who made them, not only in their official capacities but in their private lives. He followed them from Westminster and the eyre towns into the villages and hamlets where their personal interests were centred. The surviving evidence for the period is full of information about their official careers and property transactions, but it is not normally of a kind which gives insight into their thoughts and feelings. It is no coincidence that Meekings's first article on them, published in 1950, was based on a small group of personal letters by William of York, then an eyre clerk, to his patron, the chancellor Ralph Nevill, which were characterised by an 'engaging frankness' almost entirely lacking in the official chancery enrolments (V). From that point biographies of justices and clerks became the most characteristic feature of Meekings's writings. He was particularly concerned with the series of great justices who each worked as his predecessor's clerk and then succeeded him on the bench: Simon of Pattishall, Martin of Pattishall, William Raleigh and Henry Bracton (VII, XI, XII). He reacted to the criticism of H.G. Richardson, that the connections between them were not proved and that Bracton owed his legal training to the schools rather than to an apprenticeship as a clerk, by a long search for relevant documents. He finally proved his point with regard to the Martin of Pattishall–Raleigh connection (XII) and, while failing to find any clinching reference, established the strong possibility that Bracton was an official of the court coram rege when Raleigh was its senior justice (G). In direct terms some of this effort was wasted, since a charter showing that Raleigh was Martin of

Pattishall's clerk had long been available in print in the Oxfordshire Record Society's edition of the Sandford cartulary, but the search he undertook led him into fields that might otherwise have remained unexplored. Meekings intended to write a full biography of Raleigh, and collected a mass of material towards that end. A background examination of the history of the Raleigh family, mainly in Devon, from the reign of William the Conqueror to the thirteenth century was largely completed, and it is hoped to publish this in article form. Much of the other material related to Raleigh's dispute with the king over his election to the see of Winchester after his retirement from the court coram rege. It is hoped ultimately to produce a biography of Raleigh making use of this material; in view of the recent arguments of Professor Thorne that Raleigh rather than Bracton was responsible for most of the treatise 'De Legibus et Consuetudinibus Angliae', the need for a full account of Raleigh's life requires no further emphasis.

Meekings was also interested in Raleigh's successors as justices coram rege, and produced biographical accounts of them in an unpublished work entitled 'King's Bench Justices, 1239-58'; despite its title it also gives a less full account of the court's justices between 1258 and 1272, where it links up with the work of Professor Sayles. The justices dealt with include major figures like William of York and Henry of Bath, and the work contains what must be regarded as the definitive life of Bracton. It includes a calendar of the 110 coram rege feet of fines for the years 1240-58 and 1269-71 on which it is partly based. The work has already been summarised in published form (O) and details from the earlier part have been included in the introduction to volume XVI of *Curia Regis Rolls*. It is hoped to publish it as it stands. An almost complete biography of Robert de Briwes, who was senior justice of the court in 1268-9, exists in typescript and is to be published separately. Royal household stewards as well as professional justices sat in the court, and it was largely his need to know the chronology of their careers in connection with his study of it which led Meekings to remedy the omission of the witness lists from the published *Calendar of Charter Rolls* by drawing up tables of those attesting the king's charters from 1227 to 1272. They are available to enquirers at Chancery Lane, and it is hoped that it may be possible to publish them in some form at a later date.

Meekings did not restrict himself to the study of the great justices who had already attracted the attention of other writers, but dealt also with a number of much lesser-known figures whose careers helped to illustrate the development of judicial administration in the reign of

Henry III, including the men who served as justices of the Jews (V, VI, VIII, X, XIII, XIV). References were made in his works to biographies of other justices, such as William le Breton and William of Wilton, as being in the course of preparation. None of them was in fact completed; there are collections of notes made towards them which are of some value but which would take a considerable amount of work to turn into completed biographies. The summarised biographies appearing in the two eyre roll volumes (K and W) are drawn from these notes. Meekings did not restrict himself to biographies of justices, and one of his most impressive achievements was the collection of the huge amount of data which enabled him to append 120 biographies of knights, jurors and officials to the introduction to the 1235 Surrey eyre roll. His concern to correct errors in an old account of one of the more important Surrey families led to a full study of all its members who had lived since the late eleventh century in which his understanding of the legal records was of particularly crucial importance (XV). The discovery of some Sussex deeds relating to one of the gentry families led to another short paper published after his death (XVI). His interest in local society took him down to the lowest level for which early thirteenth-century sources provide biographical information, the freeholder active in local government; he dealt with a number of such men in Surrey, as well as Robert Carpenter, the Isle of Wight hundred juror whose doings were of particular significance for the history of the general eyre (III). His determination to place in their local context the people about whom he wrote is illustrated by the biography of Walter of Merton (IX). He was a great man, chancellor of England and the founder of the oldest Oxford college, but his life is dealt with in the introduction to the *Fitznells Cartulary* between the two parts of an account of Gilbert fitz Osbert of Ewell, a man of only local importance who happened to marry Walter's sister and so became enmeshed in the property transactions which were ultimately recorded in the cartulary. His knowledge of the biographical details of some relatively minor figures could be put to more general use, as when they enabled him to ascertain more closely than had previously been possible the date and significance of an early register of judicial writs used by chancery clerks (I).

Meekings, a devout Catholic, was not an ecclesiastical historian, but his work on the Chertsey cartularies for the Surrey Record Society (J) must have reinforced his appreciation of the role of ecclesiastical institutions in local and national life, and he naturally made full use of the available ecclesiastical sources. His article on the early history of

Sandon hospital set the house firmly in its local context and grew mainly out of his work on the Surrey gentry (XVIII). The local connection made him particularly interested in the records of the bishopric of Winchester, an interest heightened by William Raleigh's connection with the see. He collected material for biographies of lesser Surrey churchmen in the reign of Henry III, none of which was completed. He did produce an account of the early history of Netley abbey, in the diocese although not in Surrey, which was published posthumously, and was much concerned with a subject which has recently become of increasing interest to ecclesiastical historians, monastic patronage (XVII). A shorter piece resulted from the discovery of an unusual document dealing with the farming out of the tithes of a Cornish collegiate church (XIX).

Meekings's most recent writings derived mainly from his work on the king's bench files. The discovery of an oyer and terminer trial file elicited a typically detailed consideration of a treason trial of 1444 with implications for the state of England in the reign of Henry VI (R). His work on a fifteenth-century bill formulary compiled by William Jenney, a justice of king's bench, produced a lecture entitled 'A King's Bench Bill Formulary', given at Aberystwyth in 1975; its text is in the possession of Dr. J.H. Baker, who intends to secure its publication. He was able to bring his knowledge of philately to bear on the subject of Elizabethan king's bench stamps (Q). His interest in the filazers of king's bench led to a provisional biography of the author of a seventeenth-century tract on the details of the court's administration (S).

A full appreciation of Cecil Meekings's significance as an archivist and historian cannot depend on a study of his own writings alone. The number and extent of acknowledgments of his learning and personal help by others working in the same or related fields together amount to an equally enduring monument to him. As an archivist he was a provider of material for others; as an historian he did much to show them how to use it.

David Crook

BIBLIOGRAPHY
OF THE PUBLISHED WORKS OF C.A.F. MEEKINGS
NOT PRINTED IN THIS VOLUME

(A) *Surrey Hearth Tax 1664*, Surrey Record Society, XVII (1940)

(B) *Abstracts of Surrey Feet of Fines, 1509–1558*, Surrey Record Society, XIX (1946)

(C) *Prospectus for the Publication of a Calendar of Pipe Rolls, Henry III* (H.M.S.O., 1949)

(D) *Dorset Hearth Tax Assessments 1662–1664*, Dorset Natural History and Archaeological Society (1951). Introduction.

(E) 'Financial Problems of the Barset Record Society', *Archives*, I, no.7 (1952), 26-33

(F) *Victoria County History of Cambridge and the Isle of Ely*

i. 'Analysis of Hearth Tax Assessments, Isle of Ely, 1662, 1666 and 1674': IV (1953), 272-80

ii. 'Cambridge University and Borough Hearth Tax Assessments 1662–1674': III (1959), 500-4

iii. 'Analysis of Hearth Tax Assessments, Chilford, Radfield and Whittlesford Hundreds, 1662, 1666 and 1674': VI (1978), 277-82

(G) *Curia Regis Rolls*, XI–XVI (H.M.S.O., 1955–79). Introductions.

(H) 'The Veredictum of Chippenham Hundred, 1281', in *Collectanea*, ed. N.J. Williams, Wiltshire Archaeological and Natural History Society, Records Branch, XII (1956), 50-128. With R.E. Latham.

(J) *Chertsey Abbey Cartularies*, II, part I, Surrey Record Society, XII (1958). Introduction and Notes to the Text.

(K) *Crown Pleas of the Wiltshire Eyre, 1249*, Wiltshire Archaeological and Natural History Society, Records Branch, XVI (1961 for 1960)

(L) *The Hearth Tax 1662–1689: Exhibition of Records.* Public Record Office, 1962

(M) *Fitznells Cartulary: A Calendar of Bodleian Library MS. Rawlinson B 430*, Surrey Record Society, XVI (1968). With P. Shearman.

(N) 'The City Loans on the Hearth Tax, 1664–1668', in *Studies in London History presented to Philip Edmund Jones*, ed. A.E.J. Hollaender and W. Kellaway (1969), 335-70

(O) *List of Various Common Law Records*, P.R.O. Lists and Indexes, Supplementary series, I (1970)

(P) *The London Eyre of 1244*, ed. H.M. Chew and M. Weinbaum,

London Record Society, VI (1970). Section of introduction on eyre issues.

(Q) 'Early King's Bench Stamps, 1584–96', in *Journal of the Society of Archivists*, VI (1974–7), 90-3

(R) 'Thomas Kerver's Case, 1444', *English Historical Review*, XC (1975), 331-46

(S) 'John Trye (1634–after 1692)', in *The Irish Jurist*, New series, X (1975), 352-5

(T) *Calendar of the General and Special Assize and General Gaol Delivery Commissions on the Dorses of the Patent Rolls*

  i. *Richard II (1377–1399)* (Nendeln, 1977). With A.H. Watford.

  ii. *Henry IV and Henry V (1399–1413)* (Nendeln, 1979). With A.H. Watford and M.M. Condon.

(U) 'King's Bench Files', in *Legal Records and the Historian*, ed. J.H. Baker, London, Royal Historical Society (1978), 97-139

(W) *The 1235 Surrey Eyre*, I, Surrey Record Society, XXXI (1979); II (Text, Translation and Notes to the Text) forthcoming. With D. Crook.

(Y) *Analysis of Hearth Tax Accounts*

  i. *1662–1665* List and Index Society, CLIII (1979)

  ii. *1666–1699* List and Index Society, CLXIII (1980)

I

A Roll of Judicial Writs

IN AN ARTICLE in a previous number of the *Bulletin*, Mr. A. H. Humphreys described and summarized the contents of a register of judicial writs in a roll of three membranes that is preserved among the Miscellanea of the Exchequer with the call number E. 163/1/27.[1] He concluded: 'We have here a *registrum brevium* in roll form, which embodies the procedure current in the reign of Henry III. It dates in the main from some time after 1236–7.' The roll contains some sixty-nine writs, not reckoning separately those variants which are grouped under a common marginal heading or *regulum*. Of the total, fifty-eight are on the membrane's faces, all but the last two in the same hand and written apparently at the same time; eleven are on the dorses. In referring to the writs the numbers used are those assigned to them by Mr. Humphreys. The writs (H. 1–39) on membranes 1 and 2 are all pure forms: parties are A and B, places are N; all clauses of common form, such as the address, *et habeas* and *teste*, are much abbreviated or omitted. Also pure forms are five others (H. 43, 45–47, 50) on membrane 3 and a group, in the same hand as H. 1–56, on the dorse of membrane 2 (H., m. 2d, 1–2). In twelve writs on membrane 3 various initials are used for the parties, while sometimes there is a place name (H. 40–42, 44, 48–49, 51–56), suggesting that these writs had at some time been summarized from writs that issued in particular cases. The last two writs on membrane 3 (H. 57–58) and all those on the dorses except the group already mentioned (H., m. 1d, 1; m. 2d, 3–7; m. 3d, 1–3) are direct copies of writs that issued in particular cases. They generally have personal and place names in full, while three even retain their dating clause. These eleven writs are in various hands: perhaps as many as nine, certainly not fewer than seven. Thus out of the sixty-nine writs in the register there are forty-six pure forms but the other twenty-three have initials or names of parties and places and so hold out some possibility of identifying the particular action in which they issued. Mr. Humphreys did not attempt to identify any of these actions. Moreover, his account is not free from minor inequalities. A writ dated 24 November 28 Henry III is assigned to 1244 instead of 1243[2]; the hundred of Sherwell, co. Devon, is placed in Lincolnshire[3]; the church of Lancing, in Chichester diocese, becomes the church of Lanemos[4]; the rune 'wen' with the value 'gh' or 'w' in the word Laghidies (that is, Lawdays) is mistaken for a 'p', giving a mysterious Lapidies.[5]

[1] *Ante*, xviii (1940–41), 1–12.
[2] *Ibid.*, 3.
[3] *Ibid.*, 8.
[4] *Ibid.*, 9.
[5] *Ibid.*, 8.

By covering the material already available in the published Bench plea rolls and Chancery close rolls and by examining some of the unpublished *coram rege* plea rolls and various other sources it has been possible to identify with certainty the cases in which eleven of these writs issued and to suggest within varying limits, some quite narrow, the cases and dates of a further six. Nothing has been found about the remaining six, though one of them is dated. The picture that emerges from all this is much more definite than that drawn by Mr. Humphreys. It shows that behind our roll there lie two earlier registers. The first of these must have been compiled at the very beginning of Henry III's reign. It is represented by the pure forms H. 1–39 and, probably, H., m. 2d, 1–2. In the 1220's this register was in use by a clerk or clerks in the Bench, who added new writs that issued in particular cases. The register as left by them included all but the eleven direct copies in various hands. In the latter part of the 1230's it was copied for use by a clerk in the recently revived court *coram rege*. He and his colleagues, or assistants, added all the direct copies; no additions were made after 1247.

Before elaborating these conclusions it is necessary to give summaries of the twenty-three writs capable of identification, including all matter that has led or might lead to identification of writ with case; together with references to the certainly identified cases and notes on the rest.

H. 40: a writ for an inquest on a woman who is alleged to be falsely representing herself to be pregnant [*Rotuli Litterarum Clausarum*, i. 435b].

I. the relict of A. is said to be falsely representing herself to be pregnant, to the disinheritance of T. de N., brother of A.

Though there are a few cases of this sort in *Bracton's Note Book* and in the published Bench rolls of 1219–25, none of them fit these initials. Earlier than these is a writ of this sort which issued on 15 Feb. 1220 over the *teste* of Martin de Pateshull and which, perhaps because of its novelty, was entered on the close rolls. It must be the writ here given because the initials agree: Joan the relict of Adam de Aldham (a Surrey knight prominent in county affairs in John's reign) is representing herself to be pregnant, to the disherison of Adam's brother, Thomas de Aldham. The writ was returnable in the Lent vacation but there are no proceedings on it in the Bench rolls of 1220 Easter or later terms.

H. 41: a writ summoning coparceners. [Not found.]

R. has impleaded J. about three hides. J. will not answer without his coparcener, another R., who with him is joint heir of their grandfather F.

H. 42: a writ summoning anyone to show what right they claim in any land. [Not found.]

In a plea *de fine facto* between R. petant and A. tenant, A. complains that R. gave land to M., contrary to the form of the fine pleaded. M. is summoned to show what right he claims in 20 acres of land.

H. 44: a writ of attachment against a defendant where recovery of land has been awarded but has not been made. [Not found.]

Although this begins in the form A. *v.* B. about land at N., above N. has been inserted 'suburbs of Lincoln'. The account of the case goes on to say that the mayor of Lincoln and the bailiffs of the same county have testified to the recovery, by A. against G., presumably in the city court, before the justices at Westminster. No case has been found in the extant rolls of 1219–25 where representatives of the city of Lincoln so testified.

H. 48: a writ of *recordari facias* [*Curia Regis Rolls*, x. 267, 344–6; *Bracton's Note Book*, case 212].

The plea to be recorded by the sheriff and to be brought under his seal by six knights, other than the four who should have brought it, was one held in the county court about half a knight's fee, between S. petant and I. tenant. I. has complained of false judgment, saying that most of the knights present in the county court had risen and dissociated themselves from the judgment when it was made. At the end of the writ is the note: 'Hoc breve fuit inter Simonem de Berkestun' et Isabellam de Gerstun'.'

This writ was issued on the octave of Trinity (5 June) 1222, in the case between Isabel Guer and Simon de Bercheston' about a knight's fee at Sibford Gower, co. Oxford. It was returnable at Trinity one month. It is summarized in the record where it issued and given almost in full in the record of Trinity one month, when judgment was given: a normal practice of the Bench clerks when process involved a new or uncommon form of writ. The account given of what passed in the county court attracted Bracton's attention.

H. 49: a writ, issuable by chancery or justices itinerant, for the sheriff to summon an inquest to answer articles in an assize of mort d'ancestor. [Not found.]

This writ issued on a voucher to warrant. O., son of Norman, had brought an assize of mort d'ancestor against A. for a messuage in N. A. vouched to warrant E., the grandson of R., who had enfeoffed him with the messuage by a charter which he produced.

H. 51: a writ summoning four knights to elect a grand assize in a plea of customs and services [*Curia Regis Rolls*, x. 298–9; *Bracton's Note Book*, case 197].

A. petant had brought an action against B. deforciant about customs and services, described, which A. claims that B. should do to his hundred court of Shirewell in respect of both of his manors of Lint' etc.; whereupon the abbot put himself on the grand assize as to whether he had the greater right to hold quit of these services or by doing them as A. claims.

It will be noted that the impersonal B. in the first part of the writ gives way to 'the abbot' later on and that the name of one manor is omitted. The writ issued on the quinzaine of Trinity (12 June) 1222, in the action brought by Philip de Bello Monte against the abbot of Ford, about suit of court due in respect of the abbot's manors of Lynton and Countisbury, co. Devon, to Philip's hundred court of Sherwell. It was returnable at Michaelmas five weeks. As usual where the question that was to be put to the grand assize was not a simple one, it was summarized in the record. Bracton glossed his *Note Book* entry to show that he regarded this writ as a model for the clause *utrum . . . maius jus habeat* in a grand assize on customs and services.

H. 52: a writ of *habere facias ad valenciam*, against a warrantor who has not yet supplied a defendant with an equivalent estate to that lost [*Curia Regis Rolls*, x. 308; *Bracton's Note Book*, case 206].

W. had brought an action for a virgate at N. against master H., who vouched J. to warrant. The assize found against J., who was ordered to provide master H. with a valency, but has not yet done so.

This writ issued at Trinity three weeks (19 June) 1222. In the last Hampshire eyre (of 1219), William Berefray had brought an assize of mort d'ancestor against master Henry of Cerne, who vouched John de Compeny to warrant, about a virgate at West Dean, in West Tytherley. John lost, so William recovered against master Henry, to whom John was ordered to supply a valency. As he did not do this, master Henry now proceeds against him in the Bench. After the issue of this writ the action was concorded.

H. 53: a writ of mesne process against clerks, being a *venire facias* directed to the bishop, ordering him to cause the dean of St. Paul's and the archdeacon of London to appear to answer the plaintiff in a plea of *quare tenuerunt placitum in curia christianitatis* [*Curia Regis Rolls*, x. 330].

While the dean and archdeacon may often have been summoned to royal courts because of cases which they had held as ecclesiastical judges, the fact that the compiler has already taken three cases from 1222 Trinity term makes it certain that this writ is that which issued at Trinity three weeks (19 June) 1222 in the action brought against them by Walter de Turbervill'. The bishop of London was to produce them on the morrow of St. Martin.

H. 54: a writ summoning the witnesses in a charter and eight men of the neighbourhood [*Curia Regis Rolls*, x. 56–7].

W. has impleaded W. son of C. about 4 acres of land and has produced a charter whereby W. son of C. granted it to him. After pleading, both parties have put themselves on the witnesses to the charter. So the witnesses, the first of whom is Thomas, a knight, and a jury of eight neighbours are summoned to say whether W. son of C. made the gift and charter and whether W. was thereby put in seisin or not.

This writ issued at Easter three weeks (2 May) 1221 in the action of warranty of charter brought by William de Langham against William son of Clement about 80 (i.e. *quater xx*) acres of land in Hapton and Fundenhall, co. Norfolk. The record summarizes the contents of the charter and gives the witnesses, the first of whom was Thomas de Burgo, knight. The writ was returnable at Michaelmas one month; but for want of witnesses and jurors it was then (*Curia Regis Rolls*, x. 173) respited until the octave of Hilary 1222, the Hilary term roll being lost.

H. 55: a writ of attachment, with a clause for taking land into the king's hand. [Not found.]

In the last eyre at N., C. and an unnamed person by deceit made a final concord about a virgate at Y., in which K. relict of R. claims a third as dower. The unnamed person is to be attached to answer K. relict of R.; C. is summoned to be present to hear judgment; two-thirds of the virgate is to be taken into the king's hand.

No case matching these initials has been found but a case was proceeding in

1223 Hilary and Michaelmas terms (*Curia Regis Rolls*, xi, nos. 324, 683; *Bracton's Note Book*, case 1629) in which the circumstances were similar. In the 1221 Salop eyre, William de Witenesse had by deceit made a final concord with Hugh son of Henry about an estate in which Amice relict of Henry de Witenesse held dower, but in which she was neither impleaded nor summoned. But in view of the general agreement between the initials in the writs and the names in the cases it is not probable that this is the case in which the writ issued.

H. 56: a writ of summons in a special case [*Curia Regis Rolls*, xii, nos. 2243, 2667; *Bracton's Note Book*, case 247].

J. and his wife L. are summoned to answer W. to say why they are setting up a girl, *garcia*, named K. as their daughter and heir when she is not, and J. has no other heir than W.L.

The writ issued in the Sussex action brought by William de Monte Acuto against John de Monte Acuto and his wife Lucia, concerning their daughter Katherine: a famous case heard in Easter term 1227, where the record opens with a summary of this writ. The first summons seems to have been returnable at the beginning of Easter term 1226, probably on the quinzaine of Easter (3 May); there was then an attachment to the morrow of the Ascension when (*Curia Regis Rolls*, xii, no. 2667) there was a further adjournment to Michaelmas one month. By then, Bench sessions were suspended during an eyre visitation, so there was an automatic adjournment to the next Bench term, Easter 1227, the stage which is copied and glossed in the *Note Book*.

This writ concludes the register that was originally copied into our roll in the 1230's; that is, the register of the beginning of Henry III's reign with the additions of the 1220's. At this point, therefore, we may consider briefly that now lost register. The pure forms are nearly all judicial writs of the commonest sort; most of them would be issued in each return day period of every Bench term. They formed the basic equipment of any clerk whose business it was to pen judicial writs. It is clear that they come from before 1227 because, as Mr. Humphreys remarked, the writ *de mercato habendo* (H. 23) has the phrase *usque ad etatem nostram* which is characteristic of the minority, between 1216 and the resumption of the issue of royal charters in January 1227. By contrast, the additions are writs that issued in novel or uncommon cases. As we have seen, of those identified with their cases, one (H. 40) comes from 1220, one (H. 54) from 1221, four (H. 48, 51–53) from 1222, and one (H. 56) probably from 1226 but possibly from 1227. Like the direct copies from the 1240's on the dorses, these additions occur substantially but not quite strictly in chronological order. There was presumably a fair amount of vacant space in the lost register and the compiler entered his additions in it at his convenience. It therefore seems reasonable to assume that the pure forms represent the normal register required in the Bench before 1220 and the identifiable forms represent additions made, about 1220–27, of writs in novel and uncommon cases. The register must therefore have been one of those in use during the senior justiceship of Martin de Pateshull, 1217–29. How many clerks may have been at work in that period is uncertain. From the Bench and eyre rolls themselves we know the names of about a dozen. Judging by the hands in the extant plea rolls and final concords, as well as by the number of justices, it seems likely that during this period those who served at one time or another reached a total of at least fifty. The number of registers in use by them during the period was probably much fewer. It is unlikely that every clerk had one of his own and probable that those in use passed from clerk to clerk by sale and purchase. Still, there must have been a fair number in use during the period. There is nothing to associate the now lost register with any known clerk or justice. The only clue to ownership lies in the fact that the additions seem to be restricted to the years 1220–27. Several justices retired in or about the latter year; the one whose clerk might well have possessed a register like the lost register was Thomas de Heydon. Thomas began his career in the chancery; in 1198 he was Richard I's vice-chancellor in France and that king had presented him to royal livings.[1] Between 1218 and 1228 he served, almost continuously, on eyre and at the Bench; he ceased to act before he had reached the more senior positions, though he seems to have lived until about 1238.[2] His clerk or clerks would have needed a basic register of judicial writs in the first few years of the reign and would have had the opportunity of making all the additions in the course of their work. Their register might not have come on the market until the late 1230's which is the time when the earliest of the direct copies seem to have been made. This, however, is merely one among a very large field of possibilities.

One other point that calls for comment is the fact that four of the writs (H. 48, 51, 52, 56) issued in cases which Bracton included in his *Note Book*. It seems certain that if we had other registers of this period from the Bench we should find in them many more of Bracton's cases. The action which saw the issue of a writ that merited inclusion in the register of a clerk working in the Bench at the time of issue is just the action which would have attracted Bracton's attention as he worked through the rolls. Of all the registers, those kept by the two senior clerks of this period, William de Raleigh and William of York, and their assistants must have included the widest range of precedents. Nothing is more likely than that among the matter which Bracton acquired from Raleigh was a register which would have led him to many of the cases in the *Note Book*.

We may now return to our register, to list the direct copies which were added after the lost Bench register had been copied.

H. 57: a writ of *habere facias seisinam* following a special inquest. [Not found; ? *c*. 1234–9.]

[1] Brit. Mus., Additional Charter 11235(1): grant by the king to Reynold de Dammartin count of Boulogne dated 26 Oct. 10 Richard I, 'data per manum Thome de Haiden tunc gerentis vices cancelarii apud Rupem Andel'.'

[2] He had presumably not long been dead when in Hilary term 1239 an action of darrein presentment about the churches of Heigham Ferrers and Raunds, co. Northampton, was heard in the Bench (K.B. 26/119, m. 2). He was the last parson of these churches, having been presented by Richard I while the lands of Earl Ferrers were in his hands.

The Sheriff is to give Geoffrey de Bagshot[1] full seisin of his bailiwick, taking security from him for his relief, if any: since it appears by inquest that Geoffrey de Bagshot, Geoffrey's grandfather, granted half his bailiwick to his brother Peter de Bagshot, to hold of him for life; which half Lawrence Kokerel sometime held for the life of Peter, from Geoffrey and not in chief.

The case has not been found. Geoffrey, in whose favour the writ issued, was a minor on the death of his father Henry in 1221, but by 14 Nov. 1236 he had succeeded to the family's hereditary bailiwick of Bagshot in Windsor forest (*Close Rolls 1234–7*, p. 392). Lawrence succeeded his mother Maud in his own bailiwick on 13 July 1234 (*Excerpta e Rotulis Finium*, i. 258, and Fine Roll 18 Henry III, m. 3). Geoffrey and Lawrence are mentioned as foresters until May 1238 (*Close Rolls 1237–42*, pp. 22, 50, 81). We have found no later references to Lawrence, but Geoffrey continued in office until his death on 18 Jan. 1255. A date about 1238–9 thus seems the likeliest for this inquest and writ and certainly one after July 1234.

H. 58: a writ summoning coparceners. [Not found; ? *ante* 1239.]

G. is summoned to answer along with B. to the prior of Hereford [*sic*] why the same C. [*sic*] is exacting customs and services for the tenement which the prior holds in C., contrary to the charters of John de Lindesey, ancestor of G. and B.: whereon the prior has impleaded B., who will not answer without G. who is coparcener in the inheritance of John.

John de Limesi died before 1193 and, after the death of his male heirs as minors, was succeeded by 1213 by his sisters: Eleanor, wife of David de Lindsey, and Basilia, wife of Hugh de Odingsells. The history of the succession has been dealt with in numerous local histories, notably in *V.C.H. Warwicks.*, iv. 138 and vi. 125, and by Farrer, *Honors and Knights' Fees*, ii. 343–5. John was a benefactor of the priory of Hertford, not Hereford (*V.C.H. Herts.*, iv. 318–19). B. is apparently Basilia, the date of whose death is uncertain but would seem to be about May 1239, her son Gerard de Odingsells succeeding on 13 May 1239 (*Excerpta e Rotulis Finium*, i. 323–4). At that time the other coparcener would have been David de Lindsey, who was succeeded in May 1241 by his brother Gerard (*ibid.*, p. 342). Apparently, therefore, Basilia and the two Gerards were never contemporaneously joint heirs of John de Limesi. There are therefore two possibilities. 'B.' may be merely the usual convention for a party; in this case G. is one of the two Gerards and the date is after May 1239, while if 'B.' is Gerard de Odingsells and G. is Gerard de Lindesey the date must be between 1241 and 1246 when the latter died. Against this supposition is the fact that all writs of 1240–47 are on the dorses. If 'B.' is in fact Basilia, then G. may be either her son or Gerard de Lindesey, who may well have been enfeoffed with a lease of an estate by a family settlement. In this case the writ would have issued before May 1239.

H., m. 1d, 1: an original writ of *venire facias*, tested at Westminster, 24 Nov. 28 Henry III (1243) [*coram rege* plea roll, 1244 Hilary, K.B. 26/131, m. 10d].

This writ issued in the action brought by Sarah relict of Thomas de Polesdon and her son James against Gilbert de Fecham and his wife Alice and nine others for

[1] Some details of Geoffrey's career are taken from a short biography of him that will appear in a future volume of the Surrey Record Society.

intrusion into two virgates at Woodham, co. Surrey. It was returnable on the octave of Hilary in the court *coram rege*; the case occurs under that date in the plea roll.

H., m. 2d, 3: a writ *de idoneo persona admittendo*. [Not found; *ante* 1244.]

The writ issued to R[alph] bishop of Chichester [died 1 Feb. 1244] informing him that there had been litigation in the court *coram rege* between John de Gatesden, guardian of Ralph son of Maurice, plaintiff, and Ranulf de Broc, impediant, about the advowson of the church of Lancing, co. Sussex. Notwithstanding John's reclaim, the bishop is to admit a fit parson on Ranulf's presentation.

Lancing was held of the honor of Bramber which, *c.* 1231–45, was in ward to Richard earl of Cornwall. In 1242–3 Ranulf held two fees there and elsewhere while John de Gatesden, that insatiable purchaser of wardships, also held two fees there as guardian of the heir of Maurice Malesmains (*Book of Fees*, ii. 689). Nothing has been found of the action in the surviving *coram rege* plea rolls of 1240 Michaelmas to 1241 Long vacation and of 1242 Long vacation to 1244 Long vacation. From an assize of novel disseisin taken on 28 April 1248 we learn that John de Gatesden had held the wardship of the heir of Maurice Malesmains, otherwise Maurice de Ockley, by gift of John de Braose, from about 1231 until shortly before the date of the assize, when the heir Ralph died (Just. Itin. 1/870, m. 1). It is possible that the action took place between Michaelmas 1241 and Trinity 1242, a period for which there is no roll, but it is, perhaps, more likely that it took place in 1240 before Michaelmas because this writ and the next are in the same hand.

H., m. 2d, 4: a writ on a special matter [*coram rege* plea roll, 1240 Michaelmas, K.B. 26/121, m. 7].

This writ is addressed to Robert de Lexinton, informing him that in a plea in the court *coram rege* between Walter de Grendal and Sampson Baudechose and others about an estate at Barkby, co. Leicester, doubts have arisen whether the attorneys appointed by Sampson and others were appointed to act jointly or alternately. In the record which Robert has sent they are appointed jointly; but Walter claims that they were appointed alternately. Robert is to search his rolls and those of his fellows to find how they were appointed and to inform us, that is the court *coram rege*.

The case had originally been heard by Robert de Lexinton among the foreign pleas of his 1239 Northamptonshire eyre, in the period of the octave of St. Martin, and ended in an adjournment. The record referred to, like several others from eyres of 1240, is stitched up in the roll of the senior *coram rege* justice, Stephen de Segrave, about the period of the morrow of All Souls 1240. It is endorsed: 'Domino Regi. Recordum loquele inter Walterum de Grendal' . . . et plures alios' and contains the record of this and two other cases in which Walter was plaintiff. The record of this case ends with a *postea* showing that the case had been adjourned to the court *coram rege* for the octave of Michaelmas (6 Oct.) 1240. This writ must therefore have issued at or soon after that date.

H., m. 2d, 5: a writ of prohibition in favour of a patron. [Not found; after 1241–2.]

The writ prohibits Nicholas parson of Hale from suing in court christian about the church of Heckington, co. Lincoln, concerning which the abbot of Bardney complains that Nicholas is impleading the abbot's clerk, master Robert de Cadenai parson of Heckington, in court christian by papal letters.

Master Robert, a canon of Lincoln, was presented to Heckington by the abbot of Bardney and instituted by the bishop's official in the year 7 Bishop Robert Grosseteste (1241–2) (*Rotuli Roberti Grosseteste*, Lincoln Record Soc., vol. xi, p. 61). His presentation was conditional on his being able to hold it with his other benefices; if not, he was to receive the custody of it. Nothing has been found about the action in the extant *coram rege* rolls of the 1240's but it seems likely that it took place soon after the presentation, perhaps between 1241 Michaelmas and 1242 Trinity, for which period there is no roll.

This writ and the next are in the same hand.

H., m. 2d, 6: a writ for the arrest of those convicted of trespasses in parks and vivaries. [Not found; ? after 1240.]

The writ orders the arrest of Eudo de Hamel and A. and B. for trespass done in the park of Stephen Lungespeye, of which they have been convicted; they are to be brought to the court *coram rege* or before the justices itinerant.

Eudo de Hamel was a man of some prominence in Hertfordshire, where he held the manor of Tewin (*Book of Fees*, ii. 578). Stephen was the third son of the king's cousin, William Longespee; by a family arrangement he held the manor of Great Gaddesden, co. Herts, receiving royal gifts to stock his park there in 1241 and 1244 (*V.C.H. Herts.*, ii. 202; *Close Rolls 1237–42*, p. 332, and *1242–47*, p. 164). A distinguished courtier, he was with the king on his Gascon expedition of 1242–3 during which he secured for himself a magnificent Irish marriage, which took him several times to Ireland after his return from the expedition. His influence at court could have secured the issue of this writ at any time in the 1240's, whether or not he was in England. There is nothing about it in the *coram rege* plea rolls of 1240–41 and 1242–4, nor were any trespasses by Eudo in Stephen's park presented in the 1248 Herts eyre, though poaching offences were presented in that eyre as in the rest of the eyres of the visitation of 1246–9. This suggests that the offence may have been presented in the Herts eyre of July 1240, of which there is no roll; or that it was heard in the court *coram rege* at the time of a gap in the rolls, perhaps in 1241–2.

H., m. 2d, 7: a writ for a view in an action of waste. [Not found; in 1241–2.]

The writ is prefaced by the remark that if anyone complains of waste and the defendant seeks a view of the estate, he ought to have the writ which is as follows. At the end is a note that this writ issued in the case between Reynold de Cobham and Alan de Legh about an estate at Chitham, co. Kent, before William of York, who was then justice for the king's pleas wherever he was journeying in England. William of York became senior justice of the court *coram rege* in November 1241, on the death of Stephen de Segrave, and held office until he received the temporalities of the bishopric of Salisbury in February 1247. It is possible to narrow the date more closely than this. The *coram rege* plea roll of 1242–3, under the morrow of Michaelmas 1242, notes that the plea of waste between Alan de Legh plaintiff and Reynold de Cobham defendant was adjourned to the octave of Hilary 1243 at the parties' prayer, they having leave to concord meanwhile (K.B. 26/125, m. 8d). Such an adjournment could not take place until after a view. Presumably, therefore, the octave of Michaelmas 1242 was the date to which the parties had been adjourned when the view was reported. This writ must therefore have issued from the court *coram rege* between 1241 Michaelmas and 1242 Trinity terms, for which the roll is wanting.

H., m. 3d, 1: a writ for the recovery of a valency against a warrantor, tested by John de Lessinton at Reading, 11 June 1247. [Not found.]

This writ is in fact the last of the series on m. 2d, where its *regulum* occurs at the foot of the membrane, but there was not space enough to enter the writ there, so it was placed at the head of m. 3d. No record of *coram rege* pleas survive between the damaged remains of a roll for Easter and Trinity 1245 and of a roll for Michaelmas 1249: hence the case has not been found. It issued following an action brought by the king for one-fifth of 100*s*. worth of land at Twyford, co. Bucks, as an escheat of Bretons' lands. William de Rye, the defendant, vouched to warrant John de Munchesny and his coparceners, heirs of Walter Marshal late earl of Pembroke. John lost the action by default, so by this writ the sheriff of Worcestershire is ordered to assess a valency of 20*s*. worth for William from John's lands in that county.

Following on the retirement of William of York as senior justice of the court *coram rege* in February 1247, no professional justices were appointed to sit with the puisne justice, Jeremy de Caxton, until the promotion in October 1247 of Henry de la Mare and Bracton. In the meantime Jeremy's colleagues were, as usual, the household stewards: of whom John de Lexington had already served on several occasions as keeper of the seal and was to do so again. It would seem therefore, although he was not the senior steward, that he attested *coram rege* writs during the summer of 1247. There is some evidence which suggests that he acted in a similar capacity again in the summer of 1249 and in 1250–51 when the court *coram rege* was also without a senior justice of the first rank. As household steward he appears in thirty-one *coram rege* feet of fines between July 1246 and September 1255. Mr. Humphreys, in commenting on this writ, failed to realize the capacity in which John was testing and repeated the common error, derived from a mistake by the Nottinghamshire historian Thoroton, that John was the elder brother of Robert de Lexinton the Bench justice, who was in fact the eldest of the five distinguished Lexinton brothers.[1]

H., m. 3d, 2: a writ *de seisina habenda de advocacione ecclesie* [*coram rege* plea roll, 1244 Easter, K.B. 26/131, m. 18].

This writ is addressed to the archdeacon of Richmond: it informs him that the king had impleaded the prior of Dutton and Walter Muton in the court *coram rege* to answer why they do not permit the king to present a parson to the church of Ribchester, by reason of the king's wardship of the son and heir of Edmund [de Lacy], whereupon the prior said he claimed no right and Walter did not prove his right; and it commands him, notwithstanding these reclaims, to admit a fit parson on the king's presentation.

This episode has been admirably described in *V.C.H. Lancs.*, vii. 40–41. On 25 Feb. 1244 letters of presentation to Ribchester issued in favour of Guy de Russelon a kinsman of the king. This presentation was opposed by the prior and

[1]These and other details about the court *coram rege* are taken from a study of it which it is hoped to publish elsewhere.

Walter who were thereupon impleaded, the action appearing in the Easter term roll under the period of Easter one month (1 May) 1244, which is therefore the date of this writ.

H., m. 3d, 3: a writ to give seisin of common of pasture, following a concorded action, tested by Stephen de Segrave at Gloucester, 8 June 1241 [*Placitorum Abbreviatio*, p. 113, from the *coram rege* plea roll of 1241 Trinity, K.B. 26/121, m. 25d].

The writ explains that William de Burgo parson of Peachurch, co. Northampton, had impleaded the abbot of Croyland in the court *coram rege* for common of pasture in Peachurch, of which his predecessor Amisius had been seised, and that the abbot, by his attorney, concorded the action; the terms of the concord being given.

The case occurs in the plea roll under the period of the quinzaine of Trinity (9 June) 1241. The concord was entered in the roll, hence there is no foot of fine; its terms are just as set out in the writ. The text of the *coram rege* plea roll for Michaelmas 1240–Long vacation 1241, which was that of the senior justice Stephen de Segrave, was printed in the *Abbreviatio* from abstracts made in February 1633 by the deputy chamberlain of the exchequer, Thomas Fauconberg, whose note that he made the abstracts appears on m. 22d. Segrave tested the writ in his capacity as senior justice.

We may now consider these direct copies. We have seen that seven of them issued following litigation in the court *coram rege* and that another, about poachers in parks and vivaries, was returnable either in that court or before the justices itinerant. It is, therefore, a reasonable supposition that the other three writs were also judicial writs issuing from the court *coram rege*. The inquest whose return led to Geoffrey de Bagshot's writ is certainly most likely to have been ordered following a claim by the king in the court *coram rege*; the actions brought by the prior of Hertford and abbot of Bardney are as likely to have been brought *coram rege* as in the Bench. The dates of the main run of six writs seem to be between 1240 and 1247; the dates of the other three writs on the dorses fall within this period, being 1241, 1243 and 1244. The dates of the two cases on the foot of m. 3, which must have been the first to be entered, seem to be a little earlier, but probably not much earlier than 1238–9. The conclusion seems to be inescapable: between 1238 and 1247 the register was in the possession of one or more persons connected with the court *coram rege*, who had the bulk of it copied from a register used by a clerk or clerks in the Bench in the 1220's and who added to that these direct copies. There are at least seven hands in the direct copies. Except for the hand responsible for a writ of 1240, and another (H., m. 2d, 3 and 4), which resembles a hand found in Jeremy de Caxton's roll of 1241 (K.B. 26/122), none of these hands are found in the extant plea rolls of the court; in particular, the writs of 24 Nov. 1243 and of 1244 (concerning Ribchester church) are in hands quite unlike those of the relevant plea roll entries. The number of hands does not mean an equal number of possessors, but it does make it likely that the roll did change its ownership in the period. This probability is heightened by the facts that the writ of 24 Nov. 1243 was entered upside down to the rest on m. 1d—being a longish writ m. 1d alone furnished space enough for it; that when the writ of May 1244 was added it was put above that of 8 June 1241; and that when the last writ, of 11 June 1247, was added, it was fitted into the main sequence of m. 2d.

There are, however, no clues in the writs to associate the register with any of the justices or stewards of the royal household, who together formed the court for most of the reign of Henry III from its revival, either by William de Raleigh in May 1234 or by Stephen de Segrave between 1230 and 1234. The senior justices during the period concerned were: Raleigh, to between February and May 1239; Segrave, from between those dates to about September 1241; William of York from November 1241 to February 1247. The only assistant justice was Jeremy de Caxton, who served from January 1241 until his death about December 1249, though Henry of Bath served briefly in the winter and spring of 1241–2. The household stewards were more numerous.[1] Between 1239 and the summer of 1247 there are some thirty-five surviving *coram rege* feet of fines; the extent to which the stewards are named in them gives a rough guide to their attendance in the court. William de Cantilupe was in office throughout the period and for most of it was the senior steward, a position recognized by his appointment as one of the regents in 1242–3; he is present in thirty fines. By contrast, his companion throughout the period, Bertram de Cryoll, is present only in twelve. One steward, Aumary de St. Amand, left England in 1240 to go on the journey to the Holy Land on which he died; he was present in both the fines made before then. The rest were men who were either appointed within the period or engaged much overseas. Paulin Peyvre, a Buckinghamshire knight who began his career as a steward of the Cantelupes, seems to have become a household steward about January 1242; he is present only in fourteen of thirty-two fines from that date. John de Lexinton, whom we have already mentioned, does not appear until July 1246; he is present in seven of the ten fines between then and the summer of 1247. Ralph fitz Nicholas does not appear until March 1246 and is present in ten of eleven fines between then and the summer of 1247. John fitz Geoffrey and Geoffrey Despenser appear only casually. No justice or steward died or retired soon after June 1247, the date of the last writ.

Of the other officers of the court very little is known. Lawrence del Brok, who in August 1247 was appointed king's attorney, had been active in the courts since 1234 or earlier.[2] The most reasonable interpretation of Bracton's earlier career is that he became a clerk of the court some time before Raleigh retired in 1239 and continued until his own promotion to be a justice in it in October 1247. Nicholas de Turri, who replaced Bracton as a justice in the autumn of 1251, seems to have been connected with the court from 1241. There is nothing in the register to connect any of them with it. Very little

[1]The information given about the stewards in Tout's *Chapters in the administrative history of medieval England* (1920–33), vi. 39–40, is very incomplete.

[2]List of Coram Rege Plea Rolls and Writs, Henry III (P.R.O. Round Room), Photostat 32.

is known about the staff of the court *coram rege* in the 1240's, though it seems probable that it was connected quite closely with the chancery. For the present it does not seem possible to make any conjecture about the ownership of the register.

Nor do we know how the register came to be preserved. The collection in which it now exists is no more than a residue of nineteenth-century methodization among the records of the Offices of the King's Remembrancer and the Augmentation and the four Westminster treasuries that were known latterly as the Chapter House. It is from the last that the register came. Strachey, in 1739, mentions it as being at the Chapter House and describes it well enough as 'A Roll or Register of Writs about the year 1240'.[1] George Rose, with characteristic inaccuracy, in 1800 described it as 'Register of Writs, a Roll of 1140'.[2] It was apparently still reckoned a treasury of the receipt document in 1853.[3] It bears only one archival endorsement: the words *Rotulus Brevium Regis*, obscured and mutilated by the sewing on of a guard in the present century, at the top right-hand corner of m. 1d. The hand seems to be of the seventeenth century. It is not Agarde's but might well belong to one of his successors who used a hand derived from the italic, such as John Bradshaw or the Fauconbergs. Le Squyer and Le Neve may be ruled out. The position of this endorsement, coupled with the defacement of the first writ on the other side of the membrane and the perfect preservation of the bottom of the last membrane, suggests that the roll was always, as now, rolled up from the bottom so that the top of the first membrane was outermost. Probably for a long time it was rolled with the faces outside so that the top of the first membrane became badly rubbed. The seventeenth-century endorsement made it possible to roll it up with the dorses outside while the nature of its contents could readily be seen.

[1] *Index to the Records* (1739), p. 95.
[2] *Report on the Records* (1800), p. 40.
[3] F. S. Thomas, *Handbook to the Public Records*, pp. 256–7.

II

The Rutland Eyre of 1253: a Correction

In reviewing a work by Lady Stenton in *History* for January 1928 Professor Jacob mentioned 'an Assize Roll of late Henry III, where some of the judges are discovered holding the Assizes and juries, while others are in a room apart "amercing the county" (*in quadam camera . . . ubi amerciaverunt comitatum*). This must, I think, be an unconsciously cynical reference to the pleas of the Crown . . .' he added.[1] Subsequently, Professor Treharne made use of these remarks;[2] but, as often happens when matter is cited at a remove, there was elaboration, inference being turned into fact for, he writes: 'one clerk, drawing up an Assize Roll, actually described the hearing of the Crown pleas as "amercing the county".' Behind the remarks of Professors Jacob and Treharne there lies, one feels, that extraordinary conception of the eyre, and especially of the crown pleas side of the eyre, that was popularized with more vehemence than scholarship by the late Dr. Bolland and which has misled too many scholars. A more balanced understanding of the eyre would have prevented Professor Jacob from a misquotation and Professor Treharne from crediting a clerk of the courts from a heading that was never penned.

The passage to which Professor Jacob referred occurs in the record of a Rutland case in the roll of pleas heard by Hugh le Bigod the justiciar in 1258.[3] It is repeated *verbatim* in the record of the final stage of this case on the King's Bench plea roll for Michaelmas 1260.[4] The case concerned the outlawry of Geoffrey de Rockingham and is of considerable interest; here the bare outlines only need be sketched in order to explain why the record of the case included a description of the way in which the justices sat at Oakham in the autumn of 1253. Geoffrey was born about 1226 and about July 1251 he succeeded his father, another Geoffrey, in the small family estates in Rutland and Northamptonshire, which included a virgate held in chief by the serjeanty of collecting Rockingham castle-guard rents.[5] In 1251 he also killed one Peter le Escot, was imprisoned, bailed by writ dated 10 October 1251 and then pardoned by patent dated 26 May 1252, for which he paid a gold mark.[6] The pardon was read in the Rutland county court in 1252;

[1] Vol. xii. p. 348.

[2] *Baronial Plan of Reform*, p. 42.

[3] Justices Itinerant Roll 1/1187, m. 14.

[4] K.B. 26/168, m. 17d.

[5] *Calendar of Inquisitions post mortem, Henry III*, nos. 210, 246; *Book of Fees*, ii, 1398.

[6] *Cal. Close Rolls, 1247–1251*, p. 512; *Cal. Pat. Rolls, 1247–1258*, p. 140; *Excerpta e Rotulis Finium*, II, 131.

no one, he later claimed, appeared then or afterwards to prosecute an appeal of homicide against him. On 30 September 1253 the Rutland eyre was opened at Oakham by Roger de Thurkelby, Gilbert de Preston, William Trussel and Baldwin de Paunton. Geoffrey's homicide was apparently presented among the Crown pleas and then, notwithstanding his pardon and its due publication, he was, at the king's suit, ordered to be exacted and outlawed. At this time he seems to have been in Gascony, serving under Henry III; but his brother-in-law, master Henry of Lutterworth, who held the pardon, heard of the order made by the court and thereupon went to Oakham while the eyre was still in session, on a certain Friday (probably 3 October), and exhibited the pardon in court before the justices, who were sitting in two divisions, one for Crown and the other for civil pleas. Nevertheless the order for exaction stood and in due course Geoffrey was outlawed. He heard of this in France, for on 3 June 1254, on his complaint to the king there, letters close which show considerable redrafting were sent to the regent and chancellor at home, commanding them to investigate the matter.[1] But the inquests then summoned were unfavourable —Geoffrey alleged in 1258 that they had been packed by his enemies —and all he got was a pardon, dated 23 February 1255, conditional on his making peace with Peter's relations and stood his trial if any wished to implead him; while the escheat of his fees to the king and other chief lords was reserved.[2] As the king's year and a day ran out orders for the return to their lords of his various estates at North Luffenham, Morcott and Pilton, all in Rutland, were issued on various dates between 18 May 1255 and 12 February 1256.[3] If Geoffrey was no longer an outlaw he had lost most if not all of his estates, though some of his former lords may have re-enfeoffed him for a consideration. Then came the reforms of 1258, the visitations made by the justiciar to redress grievances, the informal procedure of plaint. Geoffrey had a last chance to secure annulment of his outlawry and so, when Bigod sat at Oakham on 1 September 1258, a full gathering of Rutland, except for representatives of the townships, came before him to testify to the facts of Geoffrey's case. Gilbert de Preston, who was sitting with Bigod, was able to confirm that part of the story which concerned the Rutland eyre of 1253. Bigod adjourned the case into the King's Bench for Thurkelby's testimony. If that testimony was ever given it does not seem to have been recorded. At the end of Michaelmas term 1260 the case was concluded: the outlawry was annulled, while on 21 November 1260 new letters patent of pardon were issued from chancery.[4]

[1] *Cal. Close Rolls, 1253–1254*, pp. 294–5.
[2] *Cal. Pat. Rolls, 1247–1258*, p. 400.
[3] *Cal. Close Rolls, 1254–1256*, pp. 86, 143–4, 148–9, 271–2.
[4] *Cal. Pat. Rolls, 1258–1266*, p. 129.

It is with the account of master Henry of Lutterworth's visit to the eyre at Oakham in 1253, as described by the representatives of the county to Bigod and entered on his roll in 1258, that we are concerned. On a certain Friday, they say, master Henry came with the letters patent of pardon and appeared *coram Gilberto de Preston' et Baldewyno de Paunton' et easdem litteras exhibuit in quadam grangia castri de Okham in qua idem Gilbertus et Baldewinus placita corone comitatus istius placitabant. Et postea in aula eiusdem castri ubi brevia eiusdem comitatus placitabantur set dicunt quod predictus Rogerus de Thurkelby et Willelmus Trussel' qui eadem placita tenebant tunc non fuerunt ibi, immo in quadam camera ubi amerciaverunt comitatum predictum.* So it was not Gilbert and Baldwin whom Henry found in a chamber apart amercing the county; on the contrary, they were still holding the Crown pleas in open court in an outbuilding of Oakham castle, no doubt a roomy barn which could accommodate the presenting jurors, the representatives of the townships, the accused and their sureties, the finders of corpses, witnesses, appellors and appellees, the county and hundred officials and the rest, all of whom, even in the smallest English county, must have made quite a crowd as the two justices proceeded, hundred by hundred, with the Rutland Crown pleas. But Thurkelby and Trussel, who had been holding the pleas of writs, that is the assizes and juries or civil pleas, in the great hall of Oakham castle, had finished or adjourned their proceedings and withdrawn to a chamber apart to amerce the county or, as we may fairly say, to hold a taxing session in chambers. Nor is there anything remarkable in their so doing. In the course of hearing the civil pleas various parties and their sureties would be put in mercy or cast in damages, would agree to pay fines to compose real litigation or merely to register a conveyance by a fictitious action. The amount of fines were sometimes, but not always, settled during pleading; the amount of an amercement was always left to be fixed at the taxing sessions at the end of pleadings and at this date is never to be found in the plea roll of a royal court but only in the separate amercements roll. Pleadings being finished or adjourned, all these details had to be settled, the clerks' share of damages allotted, the sureties for the payments of fines and amercements accepted and all this matter enrolled. By long custom each county—that is, all those by custom owing suit to the court—had, in eyre, to pay a common fine variously described—at this date 'a fine before judgement' was the usual term—which covered all the county's errors and omissions since the last eyre and was spread in traditional proportions among all those who owed suit to the county court; this matter had also to be settled. So it was while Thurkelby and Trussel were engaged on some of this normal routine work, no doubt with the leading men of the county and the persons concerned, in the comparative calm of chambers, that master Henry found them. Perhaps there was some doubt whether the pardon thus produced in chambers in the civil pleas division, after being produced in open court in the Crown pleas division, could properly be held to have been published in eyre; on those grounds Thurkelby may have forborne to annul the order for exaction and outlawry. We cannot be sure about this, but in describing events to Bigod in 1258 the county must have felt that the precise way in which the pardon had been produced in each division in 1253 was relevant to the case. So far as is known this description provides the earliest account of the way in which justices sat in two divisions, though the practice can be inferred from the eyre rolls of the previous half-century.

Geoffrey's story tempts further investigation, for it poses a number of unanswered questions. Why, despite publication of the pardon, was the exaction and outlawry ordered in 1253? Preston, in 1258, said that he was amazed when he heard that this had been done, since he understood that the clerks had been strictly enjoined not to put Geoffrey's name in the exigent roll. Preston, moreover, must have known all there was to know about the affair, for not only was he a leading landowner in Northamptonshire but for years he had been the justice who took most of the district's assizes. Why was Thurkelby's testimony apparently never given, or at least not recorded? Was Geoffrey a young man involved in an unfortunate accident which his envious neighbours turned to their advantage when he was overseas? Or was he something of a young ruffian, whom his more respectable neighbours were determined to see punished; but who was quick to take advantage of the disturbed conditions of 1258 and the very informal procedure of the plaint? Either interpretation seems possible, for the judgement in 1260 did not end matters. In the next Rutland eyre, of 1263, we find Geoffrey bringing many actions of entry against persons whom he alleged had occupied his lands because of his outlawry.[1] In some of these actions he obtained judgement in his favour but in the majority the record ends abruptly before the juries were called. An explanation for this may perhaps lie in a Crown plea in which a Geoffrey de Rockingham is indicted and convicted of robbery, only to escape secular judgement by successfully pleading his clergy.[2]

[1] Justices Itinerant Roll 1/721, ms. 2, 2d, 3, 3d.
[2] *Ibid.* m. 10.

III

More about Robert Carpenter of Hareslade

In his article, *Robert Carpenter and the Provisions of Westminster*, Mr. Denholm Young pursued one of Maitland's discoveries and attempted 'to show who Robert Carpenter of Haresdale was and what he did'.[1] He showed that Robert 'was probably a free-tenant of William de Lisle's manor of Shorwell in the West Medina of the Isle of Wight' and that Robert's family was probably associated with what is now the farmstead of Haslett in that parish, lying on the southern slopes of the downs at the head of a valley whose stream breaks through the cliffs into the sea two miles away. He suggested that in the late 1250s Robert was acting as bailiff and man of business for Sir William de Lisle, mesne lord of Shorwell and other fees in the Isle, who was at that time a knight in Philip Basset's household; that in the summer of 1259 Robert passed from this work to act as clerk to Roger de Thurkelby until that distinguished judge died suddenly at the end of the first week of Trinity term, about 13 June 1260; and that about 1261–2 Robert, out of employment, used his leisure to compile the book which is now Gonville and Caius College MS. 205, and well known to scholars through the descriptions of Mr. Denholm Young and Dr. M. R. James.[2] This book contains: a Glanvill brought up to date; various tracts on procedure in ecclesiastical and royal courts, on the making of deeds and the preparation of manorial accounts; copies of such basic legal texts as Magna Carta, the provisions of Merton, the articles of the eyre and the provisions of Westminster; and, of first importance for the identification of the compiler, a calendar and brief annals that include many references to the Carpenter or de Hareslade family and to events in the Isle of Wight and Hampshire. Maitland did not know of this book but only of another, written in a hand of Edward I's time, that is now Cambridge University Library MS. Mm. I. 27. This contains copies of much that is in Robert's own book, including the highly personal calendar and annals, as well as matter that is not in the older book. Among such matter is a statement that at Whitsuntide 1265 Robert le Carpenter was in St. Edward's chapel at Westminster when he

[1] *Eng. Hist. Rev.*, l (1935), 22–35; reprinted in *Collected Papers*, pp. 96–110.

[2] *Op. cit.* and *Catalogue of Gonville and Caius College Manuscripts*. My thanks are due to Mr. Philip Grierson, the College Librarian, for an opportunity to inspect it. Following convention it will be cited as *S*.

copied some passages into a small roll. Maitland, unaware of the existence of the earlier book, conjectured reasonably enough from this and from what is in the calendar, annals and other matter copied from the earlier book that the later compilation was made by this Robert le Carpenter.[1] Mr. Denholm Young, by a detailed comparison of the two books, has shown that this conjecture is untenable and that the later book was probably written in Edward I's reign by Robert's son, another Robert who was born on 1 January 1258, in part being compiled from his father's book and in part from other material including matter left by his father. The statement about Robert in 1265 is thus merely the heading of a small roll in which Robert then entered some chronologies and which his son eventually copied. It tells us nothing about the copier or author of anything else in the later compilation except what we know already, that the compiler worked from matter left by Robert le Carpenter. One of the texts in the later work is a copy of the tract *Placita Corona* in which several opinions of Roger de Thurkelby are cited, as Maitland noticed. Subsequently, Professor Jacob, believing that Robert le Carpenter not only compiled the book but was the author of this tract, concluded that Robert must have been Thurkelby's clerk.[2] But in the older book, which Mr. Denholm Young has shown was probably written about 1261–2, there is no copy of the *Placita Corona*. Mr. Denholm Young, therefore, could not admit Professor Jacob's argument for believing that Robert le Carpenter had been Thurkelby's clerk. His son may have found a copy of the tract among the matter left by his father; but there is nothing to show that his father was the author of the tract. We may, indeed, note in passing that there are many copies of the tract in manuscript the earliest of which seem (from the dates of the supposed crimes in them) to have been composed shortly after 1272; that the copy in Mm. I. 27 is a little later than this; and that although it is longer than any of the others it has, by comparison with the others, several *lacunae* the biggest of which makes nonsense of its account of an appeal of rape: hence whoever wrote the version in Mm. I. 27 was a copyist, not an author. Nevertheless Mr. Denholm Young was reluctant to abandon the conclusion, which he seems to have felt attractive as an explanation of the way in which a small freeholder from the Isle of Wight may have obtained prompt access to the documents of the provisions of Westminster and how he came to be at Westminster in the summer of 1265. So he adduced other evidence for the belief that Robert

[1] *Glanvill Revised*, *Harvard Law Review*, April 1892; reprinted in *Collected Papers*, ii. 266–289. Dr. M. R. James first drew attention to the relationship between the two manuscripts.

[2] *Oxford Studies in Social and Legal History*, vol. viii, no. xiv, *Studies in the period of Baronial Reform and Rebellion, 1258–1267*, p. 79.

served Thurkelby, namely, the facts that Robert's own book includes copies of two writs that issued over Thurkelby's *teste* and a copy of the articles of the great fiscal enquiry of 1255 as used in Thurkelby's circuit.[1]

Since then, Professor W. H. Dunham, in his edition of Ralph de Hengham's *Summae*, and Mr. H. G. Richardson and Professor Sayles, in editing one of the legal tracts found in Carpenter's book, appear to have accepted this suggestion.[2] There is thus some likelihood of the connexion between Carpenter and Thurkelby being regarded as established. The purpose of the present note is to show that this evidence will not support such a conclusion. Rather, the contents of Robert Carpenter's book can be accounted for sufficiently by Mr. Denholm Young's major premise, that Robert was a freeholder in the West Medina, who may at times have served William de Lisle.

In general it may be said that the men whom Henry III's justices took into their service as clerks came from districts in which the justices had lay or ecclesiastical interests. A typical example concerns Giles de Erdington, a Bench justice in 1251–5, who, for over a decade after his retirement, continued to act as a commissioner for possessory assizes and other special commissions. Giles's main interests were in the western midlands but through his mother, Rose de Cockfield, he had interests and connexions in East Anglia. It was from East Anglia that he took as clerk the man who was to become the most famous lawyer of the later thirteenth century, Ralph de Hengham.[3] Indeed, in the year in which Carpenter is supposed to have entered Thurkelby's service, in Hilary term 1259, we first find Hengham acting for his master in a plea in the Bench.[4] Roger de Thurkelby had a career of some thirty years as clerk and justice in the Bench or on eyre. In the course of this career he added to the small estates which he had inherited in his native East Riding to build up a network of holdings in the upper Derwent valley and in the wolds to the south. His marriage with the widow Letice de Roscelin, who in her own right was heiress of her father Peter de Edgefield, gave him life interests in Norfolk to which he added by lease and purchase. Like his colleague Henry of Bath he also acquired interests in the rich lands of the parts of Holland south of the Wash, which were then being reclaimed from the fens. He had minor interests in the midlands, town houses in Bury St. Edmund's and Westminster; but no interests in southern England.

[1] *S*, pp. 15, 195, 227–8. [2] *Op. cit.* p. lxvi; *Selden Society*, vol. lx. p. cxciv.

[3] *Ancient Petition*, no. 4340: a petition by the prior and convent of Tickford, to the parliament of 1320, concerning the advowson of Yardley, alleged to be a chapel of ease to their church of Aston by Birmingham. Its detailed statements can be controlled.

[4] K.B. 26/162, m. 41: a plea of darrein presentment concerning the advowson of Yardley.

Feet of fines, recognizances in plea rolls and his widow's actions for dower in Michaelmas term 1260, all show that his main interests lay in the East Riding, Norfolk and the parts of Holland. It is reasonable to assume that it would be from one of these districts that he would take an able man into his service as a clerk; and when, in December 1257, we find him securing the gift of a robe from the royal wardrobe for his clerk, that clerk is Robert of Beverley.[1] If we assume that Robert Carpenter became Thurkelby's clerk in 1259 we have to believe that Thurkelby, at the height of his career, took into his service a man who came from a part of England with which he himself had no connexion; who had had no previous experience as a clerk in royal courts; and who had reached his thirtieth year without acquiring any great proficiency as a Latinist or lawyer. We have further to believe that from a year's work under Thurkelby, Robert carried away only the text of three documents whose connexions with Thurkelby were mere routine but whose connexions with Robert's own part of England were intimate.

If we are to believe that Robert ever served as a justice's clerk a far less improbable case might be made out for his having served one of Thurkelby's colleagues, John de Wyvill. Unlike Thurkelby, Wyvill's career takes use beyond the latest dated document in Robert's book, for Wyvill was at the Bench continuously from Hilary term 1259 until his sudden death at the beginning of Michaelmas term 1263. Unlike Thurkelby, Wyvill's interests were not merely in southern England: his principal residence was at Whitefield in the Isle of Wight, which lies north of the downs, halfway between Brading and Quarr. Like William de Lisle he held from the main Lisle fee of Carisbrooke castle.[2] Like William's wife, Juliana de Lisle, he enjoyed gifts of royal buck from Porchester forest.[3] In 1258 Wyvill was William de Lisle's colleague in the special commission to investigate the revenues of the bishopric of Winchester in which, Mr. Denholm Young persuasively argues, Robert accompanied William, learnt the rules for drawing up Winchester accounts and made the copy of the account for Merewell manor that he later entered in his book.[4] The example which Robert gives of the writ which issues to the sheriff when anyone recovers seisin by a possessory assize before an assize commissioner is the writ that issued in an action concerning an estate at Rockley, three miles from Shorwell, that Wyvill had tried at Newport, the

[1] *Cal. Close Rolls, 1256–1259*, p. 178.

[2] *Calendar of Inquisitions post mortem, Henry III*, p. 175; *V.C.H., Hampshire*, v. 159 and *cf. ibid.* pp. 160, 164, 181, 191 n.

[3] *Cal. Close Rolls, 1256–1259*, pp. 236, 411; *Cal. Close Rolls, 1261–1264*, pp. 66, 255.

[4] *Cal. Pat. Rolls, 1247–1258*, p. 644. Appointed on 3 August to ascertain and safeguard the revenues of the see following the exile of the bishop elect Aymer de Valence, the assignment presumably ended with the appointment of Nicholas de Hadlow as keeper on 24 December, *Cal. Pat. Rolls, 1258–1266*, p. 7.

island's chief town, and which was tested by Wyvill at his home at Whitefield during the long vacation on 4 September 1260.[1] One might easily believe that Wyvill knew something of Robert Carpenter as a fellow islander before 1258; that he saw more of him when Robert was serving William de Lisle in the affairs of Winchester bishopric; that when this assignment came to an end, Wyvill took Robert into his service and so gave him the opportunity of being much at Westminster and of following affairs of state until October 1263; and that in the summer of 1265 Robert was making use of his old Westminster connexions in order to make a few extracts, probably from Westminster chronicles. But one does not have to believe this in order to explain why certain documents are in Robert's book.

As to the articles of the fiscal eyre of 1255 pleaded by Thurkelby, of which Robert gives a truncated version in his book: Robert probably attended this eyre either as William de Lisle's representative or as a hundred juror from the West Medina, for Thurkelby held the Hampshire sessions.[2] Immediately before these articles, Robert gives a copy of the articles of an eyre *ad omnia placita* which is said to have been held in 40 Henry III.[3] At the end of the copy of the tract on procedure in various courts Robert gives a copy of the summons of the eyre. This summons supposes an eyre for the county of C. to open on the morrow of Hilary, 40 Henry III, before G., R., W. and H., justices.[4] On the morrow of Hilary, 40 Henry III (1256), the Hampshire eyre was opened by Gilbert de Preston, Roger de Whitchester, William de Cobham and William de Englefield. The abbreviation C. is a normal one for a place in legal tracts. The alteration of the initial of the junior justice's Christian name is a minor matter, and seems to have been done to avoid putting 'W' twice. There can be no doubt that these articles of the eyre which Robert copied into his book were those used in the Hampshire eyre of 1256. As with the articles of the fiscal eyre, the copy is imperfect: six articles are omitted which were generally pleaded at this date and to some of which presentments were made in this eyre. Did Robert attend at Southampton, where the civil and crown pleas for the Isle were taken? Fortunately the eyre roll of Gilbert de Preston himself survives and includes the calendar or list which contains the names of over 600 jurors of hundreds, boroughs and other privileged districts which were represented before the justices. Carpenter is not an uncommon name. Nevertheless there is but one Carpenter among these many Hampshire men, Robert le Carpenter, a juror for the West Medina in the Isle of Wight.[5] In the civil and crown pleas of the Isle there are matters which concern him or his family, to

[1] *S*, p. 200.
[2] *Cal. Pat. Rolls, 1247–1258*, p. 438.
[3] *S*, pp. 222–7.
[4] *S*, p. 430.
[5] J.I. 1/778, m. 63d.

which we will return. Meanwhile we may conclude that Robert came by his copy of the articles and summons of the Hampshire eyre of 1256 because he attended it as a hundred juror and litigant. Moreover, the Annals in his book contain a note of the opening date of the Hampshire eyres of 1249, 1256, 1263, 1271, and 1280:[1] this suggests that one of the family attended these Hampshire eyres, possibly as a hundred juror for the West Medina. The calendar of the eyre of 1249 also survives; six of the jurors for the West Medina bear the same names, though they may not have been the same men, as those who served in 1256: Robert le Carpenter is one of these six and again the only Carpenter in over 600 Hampshire jurymen.[2] In January 1249, when this eyre opened, our Robert was not yet nineteen and his father, also Robert, was still alive. The juryman of 1249 must therefore have been Robert's father. The county pleas for the eyre of 1263 are wanting. The plea rolls for the eyre of 1271 are the rather scrappy rolls of junior justices and do not include a calendar of jurors. The eyre of 1280 was held just after our Robert's death. Once again there is only one Carpenter among the jurors, Robert le Carpenter, who serves for Titchfield hundred, just across the Solent from the Isle.[3] However, among those returned in default for non-appearance on the first day of the eyre in the crown pleas of the West Medina is a Robert le Carpenter.[4] This must certainly have been our Robert's son; it is not impossible that he had acquired interests on the mainland and was also the juror for Titchfield hundred. It seems reasonable to conclude that the family owed suit to the hundred court of West Medina and also provided one of the hundred's representatives before the royal justices in eyre. Since Robert attended the eyre in 1256 as a hundred juror it seems likely that he did the same in the fiscal eyre which Thurkelby held a few months previously, and that as a juryman he came by a copy of the articles which he later copied, incompletely, into his book.[5]

We may now consider the writs tested by Thurkelby. Of the thirty-one complete Bench terms between Michaelmas 1252 and Easter 1260, Thurkelby was senior justice in all but eight, when he was on eyre or engaged in the deliberations at Westminster and Oxford in 1258. The chances that any judicial writ from the Bench in this period will bear his *teste* are therefore about three to one. The first writ is headed *extractum de Rotulis justiciariorum* but is undated.[6] It is a writ *quare implacitavit in curia christianitatis*, concerning the advowson of the chapel of Kingston, in Shorwell; Geoffrey, the parson of Shorwell, has been impleading Jordan de

[1] *S*, pp. 251–2. [2] J.I. 1/776, m. 38d. [3] J.I. 1/784, m. 1. [4] *Ibid.* m. 39d.
[5] *S*, pp. 227–8. It ends at the foot of a page, omitting the last ten articles given by the Burton annalist in *Annales Monastici* (Rolls Series), i. 337–9.
[6] *S*, p. 15.

Kingston in court christian and by this writ Jordan takes the matter into the king's courts, Geoffrey being summoned to answer in the Bench on the octave of Hilary. We may assume from this that Thurkelby tested the writ during a Michaelmas term and that the most likely dates for its return are the Hilary terms of the years 1253–6 and 1259–60. The series of Bench plea and essoin rolls is very defective for this period. After a fairly exhaustive search nothing has been found of the case in the plea rolls for Hilary 1259 and 1260; the plea rolls for the Hilary terms 1253–6 are wanting. But the advowson of Kingston chapel is obviously a local matter in which Robert would be greatly interested and he has another writ about it. For as his example of a writ of prohibition he takes one dated 14 June 45 Henry III (1261), which forbids John, vicar of Shorwell, to plead in court christian concerning the advowson of Kingston chapel, to which he had been presented by William de Lisle; Jordan de Kingston having presented Peter de Kingston to this chapelry.[1] It seems, therefore, that the right to the advowson was in dispute between William de Lisle and Jordan de Kingston. Perhaps Robert did some business for William in the matter and when the later action was afoot he secured a copy of the writ in the earlier action from the files. Jordan de Kingston, like William de Lisle, was a tenant of Baldwin de Lisle and had served with Robert on the West Medina jury in 1256.[2]

The second writ is dated 6 November 44 Henry III (1259).[3] It is Robert's example of a summons by better pledges, in an action *de fine facto* brought by Richard de la Lee and his mother Eve against Robert de la Mare concerning the third part of a knight's fee at Cnabwell (in Stanton St. Quinton), in Wiltshire. The final concord in question had been made in Trinity term 1250 after litigation on warranty of charter.[4] The writ was returnable at Hilary three weeks 1260 but a further stage of the action has not been found in the roll for that term; [5] possibly Robert de la Mare essoined. At first sight there is nothing to show why Robert Carpenter should have seen this writ. However, we find that William de Lisle had connexions with both parties to the action. Robert de la Mare is shown by litigation in 1258–62 to have held from William's overlord, Baldwin de Lisle; [6] when William was summoned to the royal army at Oxford in March 1264 he occurs in the list of knights within a few names of Robert de la Mare.[7] Richard de la Lee, like William de Lisle, was a member of Phillip Basset's household; for in July 1260 William and Richard, at Basset's instance, mainperned for another member of the household who was in Winchester gaol on a charge

[1] *S*, p. 221. [2] *S*, p. 194; J.I. 1/778, m. 63d. [3] *S*, p. 195.
[4] C.P. 25(1), 251/17, no. 5; K.B. 26/141, m. 7; /142, m. 2. [5] K.B. 26/164.
[6] Bench plea rolls for Mich. 1258, Trinity 1260, Easter 1262: K.B. 16/160, m. 45; /220, m. 6d; /166, m. 35. [7] *Cal. Close Rolls, 1261–1264*, p. 381.

of trespass of venison.[1] There are, therefore, many possible ways whereby Robert Carpenter can have known about this action and obtained a copy of the writ.

The three pieces of evidence which have been supposed to show that Robert was Thurkelby's clerk thus fit into place, with so much else in his book, as evidence only of his activity as a freeholder of the West Medina and of his connexions with William de Lisle.

We may now turn to the civil and crown pleas of the Isle from the Hampshire eyre of 1256 which concern Robert or his family; following the customary practice in Hampshire eyres, the Isle pleas were taken at Southampton towards the close of the eyre, in the middle of February. The first action is a plea of novel disseisin brought by Roger Horri and his wife Hawys against Hawys who was the wife of Robert le Charpenter, Nigel de Standen and his wife Dulcia, and Sciencia, daughter of Hawys.[2] The tenement in dispute is a messuage and eighteen acres at Whitwell, some five miles south-west of Shorwell. Nigel, who pleaded for the defendants, began with the exception to the writ that he had no wife named Dulcia but only one named Maud. However, he went on to plead to the writ, probably because he knew he had an excellent case, for his plea was confirmed by the jury in much the same terms as he had narrated. Hawys Horri had been a widow and in her widowhood she had enfeoffed Maud and Sciencia; upon her marriage, Roger Horri and she had confirmed the enfeoffment, to Maud, Nigel, and Sciencia. Judgment was accordingly given for the defendants and the plaintiffs were put in mercy. The second action is another plea of novel disseisin brought by Robert le Charpenter against Nigel de Standen and his wife Maud.[3] There is no detailed narration, merely a bare plea by Robert and a bare verdict by the jury that he was disseised; so judgment was given for Robert. The tenement in dispute was half a curtilage and ten acres at 'Sord', which is probably to be identified with Shorwell.[4] Then in the crown pleas of the West Medina a woman with the uncommon name of Phina, who is described as the wife of Robert le Carpenter, appeals Roger Hurri of beating her and causing her to miscarry a baby.[5] Phina did not prosecute her appeal, for the jurors say that at that moment she lay in childbirth. Roger denied the charge and was acquitted. No action was taken against Phina. But at the bottom of the preceding membrane, unrelated to any plea, there is a note that Robert le Carpenter is in mercy for an offence.[6]

[1] *Cal. Close Rolls, 1259–1261*, p. 78.

[2] J.I. 1/778, m. 22. Standen house is in Arreton, some five miles north-east of Shorwell; Great and Little Standen lie a mile farther away.

[3] *Ibid.* m. 23d.

[4] In a crown plea, *ibid.* m. 56, a place name was written *Sholde* and corrected by the clerk who seems to have prepared the amercements roll to *Shorwell'*.

[5] *Ibid.* m. 57.

[6] *Ibid.* m. 56d.

Such laconic and unexplained notes are often entered at the bottom of membranes both of crown and civil pleas. Robert's offence may have been an error or omission on his part as a juror; or it may have been for what, in technical terms, was his wife's false appeal. Although the appeal was unsuccessful there seems plainly to have been ill feeling between the Horri or Hurri family and Robert's family, possibly arising from the disputed estate at Whitwell.

The details in these pleas enable us to suggest some revisions in Mr. Denholm Young's pedigree of the family and to notice some examples of a latterday snobbery in the family that seems to have called itself ' de Hareslade ' under Edward I but in 1256 was simply ' le Carpenter '. In the Annals of Robert's book, under 1253 we find that R *de Hareslad' senior* died on 30 January and under 1268 that *Hawys uxor* R *de Hareslad'* died on 17 November.[1] In each case *de Hareslad'* has been written over an erasure. If we turn to the Calendar, at the beginning of Robert's book, we find under 30 January that *Robert Hares'* died in 1253: *Hares'* has been written over an erasure.[2] But the entry against 17 November is simply *Obiit H. Carpenter*.[3] *H. Carpenter* is thus an alias for *Hawys wife of Robert de Hareslad'*. We are entitled to assume that at some time in the later thirteenth century a member of the family, possibly our Robert himself in old age, possibly his son, went through Calendar and Annals erasing *Carpenter* and inserting *de Hareslade*; but he forgot to do so with this entry of the death of Hawys in the Calendar under 17 November. Mr. Denholm Young assumed that this Hawys was our Robert's wife. But we have seen from the pleas of 1256 that a widowed Hawys was then alive whose husband had been a Robert le Carpenter, whereas our Robert's wife seems then to have been Phina. It seems reasonable to conclude, therefore, that the Hawys of the Calendar and Annals is Robert's mother. The following is a suggested correction of the first two generations of the pedigree:

Robert le Carpenter I [4] = Hawise, living Feb. 1256,
died 30 Jan. 1253 | died 17 Nov. 1268 [5]

?		?	?
Phina =	Robert le Carpenter II [7]	Sciencia [8]	Maud = Nigel de Standon
living Feb. 1256 [6]	born 24 Apr. 1230 died 19 June 1280	living 1256	both living 1256 [9]

It must have been on his father's death in 1253 that Robert, in his twenty-third year, began to assume those public responsibilities which the head of his family was bound to discharge. Among such

[1] *S*, p. 251. [2] *S*, p. 1. [3] *S*, p. 11. [4] *S*, pp. 1, 251.
[5] *S*, pp. 11, 251; J.I. 1/778, m. 22. [6] J.I. 1/778, m. 57. [7] *S*, pp. 6, 252.
[8] J.I. 1/778, m. 22. [9] J.I. 1/778, m. 22; cf. *ibid.* m. 23d.

obligations must have been attendance at William de Lisle's seignorial court, a share in the work of the West Medina hundred court (including service as one of its representatives before royal justices), and, possibly, service in Isle of Wight assize and jury cases. There were several thousands of men in England like Robert, who took a leading part in the affairs of their hundred, free manor or borough and represented it before royal justices. Many were knights or men possessing the property qualification for knighthood; of Robert's fellow jurymen in 1256 Adam de Barnevill, Adam de Compton, Adam de Gotten and Jordan de Kingston seem to have been of such rank. The majority were freeholders of substance, some richer and perhaps more accomplished than Robert while many, especially in the smaller hundreds and free manors of southern England, had no greater advantages than his. Not all were lettered; few may have shared Robert's acquisitive curiosity. But they all had the same round of public responsibilities to discharge; they needed to know the sort of things that were in the tracts and other matter of Robert's book. Some of the tracts are old enough for it to be possible that Robert inherited copies of them from his father. Then, in the early years of his own public responsibilities, Robert seems to have collected anything relevant that he came across in his discharge of those responsibilities: the articles of the fiscal eyre of 1255, the articles of the eyre *ad omnia placita* of 1256, the accounts of Shorwell and Merewell manors, various writs, and the provisions of Oxford and Westminster which represented a definition of law without parallel since Magna Carta. The resulting book seems to be unique now. In Robert's day, however, there must have been many such compilations. The legislation of parliaments and changes in judicial procedure would make them largely obsolete by the beginning of the fourteenth century. Robert's book would have been of little use to either the professional lawyer or the 'sisoure', the man who made money out of his jury obligations, in Langland's day. For it is a typical collection of a mid-thirteenth century hundred juror and it is as such, and not as the work of a justice's clerk, that its materials should be considered; even if Robert Carpenter's service with a household knight of a justiciar of England and his probable acquaintance with a Bench justice who lived in his district gave him exceptional opportunities.

IV

JUSTICES OF THE JEWS, 1218–68: A PROVISIONAL LIST

In the course of tracing the careers of some of Henry III's justices the present writer has often felt the need of a list of the justices of the exchequer of the Jews more reliable than the alphabetical list which Dr. Gross published in 1888.[1] The list which follows is a limited attempt to supply this need. Gross covered, most thoroughly and systematically, the published sources then available and the unpublished plea rolls and other records of the exchequer of the Jews. But for the reign of Henry III the only chancery rolls then fully published were the close rolls down to October 1227 (with *liberate* entries to 1226). So for most of this reign Gross had to rely on extracts from, or references to, the chancery rolls in Prynne's *Short Demurrer*, Madox's *History of the Exchequer* and the *Foedera*. As a result of this want of published record sources, Gross's list omits the names of some men who were justices, includes others who were not justices and is defective on various points of dating. The publication of the calendars of chancery rolls for Henry III's reign had only made a modest beginning when J. M. Rigg was at work on his Selden Society volume.[2] So although Rigg attempted a narrative history of the exchequer of the Jews in his introduction, he was content to use Gross's list of justices without significant criticism. Since then, no attempt seems to have been made to incorporate the material of the published chancery rolls in a revision of Gross's list. Hence, when scholars like Herbert Loewe, Michael Adler and Cecil Roth have dealt with the justices of the Jews we find inaccuracies of both fact and interpretation.

It would be invidious to catalogue the inaccuracies into which these and others writing on the medieval English Jewry have fallen when dealing with its justices under Henry III, for nearly all such inaccuracies can be traced back to the sources which Gross had to use and to the fact that the matter in the chancery rolls since published has not been made readily available. A few typical examples may be given. Loewe, in dealing with the careers of the three justices, Robert de Fuleham, Hugh of Bath and William le Breton, confuses them with three other men who were not justices, respectively Robert Fukes or Fulconis, Henry of

[1] *Papers read at the Anglo-Jewish Historical Exhibition, 1887*, pp. 216–19.

[2] *Select Pleas, Starrs and other Records . . . of the Exchequer of Jews, 1220–1284* (Selden Society, vol. 15, 1902).

Bath and another William le Breton.[1] Adler, in dealing with the events of 1234, assumes that Stephen de Segrave and Peter de Rivaux were justices.[2] Roth believes that the justices about 1252–8 were Philip Lovel, Simon Passelewe and Henry of Bath and that they were removed from office in 1259 by the baronial reformers.[3] In fact, Lovel had resigned his justiceship in February 1256; Passelewe did not become a justice much before 1255 and the autumn of 1259 saw him reappointed as a justice after a short interval which may have been due to his employment on urgent business elsewhere in the royal service; Henry of Bath was not a justice of the Jews at all but the senior justice *coram rege*, who retained the confidence of both royal and baronial parties until his death in 1260. Roth also has Lovel and Passelewe in office 'at the close of the reign':[4] but Lovel died in 1259 and Passelewe seems never to have acted after 1262.

The present list covers the published charter, close, *liberate* and patent rolls.[5] A few other sources have been used; but no others have been systematically examined except for the plea rolls published by J. M. Rigg in his *Select Pleas* and in his *Plea Rolls of the Exchequer of Jews*, volume one, which add hardly anything to the chancery sources since the few rolls surviving from the period covered contain only casual references to justices already known to have been in office at the time. The charter rolls supply only a few references indicating that an inquest has been held or evidence given by certain named justices of the Jews. The matter in the other rolls falls into two main divisions. The first consists of letters of appointment, directed to the treasurer; of writs of *liberate* for the payment of salaries, addressed to the treasurer and chamberlains; and of orders for the gift of robes, addressed to the keeper or keepers of the wardrobe. In 1218 and 1265 appointments were made by patents; otherwise they were made by letters close. We do not know if such letters were issued for all appointments; if they were, many were not enrolled in the chancery. Even so, such enrolments are more numerous than in the case of appointments of justices of the Bench or of exchequer barons; they form the backbone of this list. The enrolment of writs of *liberate* for the justices' salaries begins about 1240 but, as with the justices of the Bench, not all the justices of the Jews received such salaries. Authorities for the issue of robes to the justices do not seem to be enrolled much

[1] *Starrs and Jewish Charters preserved in the British Museum*, vol. ii, notes 1016, 1160, 1161.

[2] 'The Testimony of London Jewry against the Ministers of Henry III' in *Transactions of the Jewish Historical Society of England*, vol. xiv.

[3] *A History of the Jews in England*, pp. 51, 60.

[4] *Ibid.*, p. 60, note 2.

[5] The *Calendar of Liberate Rolls* has been published only to 1251; but use has been made of the complete (though unindexed) sheets of the volume for 1251–60 which are available on the shelves of the Round Room at the Public Record Office. The other rolls have been published for the whole reign; but the *Calendar of Patent Rolls* from 1232 omits commissions for assizes and gaol deliveries and (by accident) a few other matters which are on the dorses of the rolls, while the *Calendar of Charter Rolls* omits the names of witnesses.

before the baronial reformers in 1258–9 exercised control over the royal household. The second main division consists of mandates to, or concerning, the justices which mention one or more of them by name. They are mostly commissions for special Jewish business. As with the mandates addressed to the treasurer and barons or to the justices of the Bench, the majority of mandates addressed to the justices of the Jews or referring to them are addressed or refer to them impersonally.

The list is divided into two parts. The first sets out in chronological order references to the appointment of justices, or of their acting or removal. The second lists the justices in alphabetical order, with the date of their appointment or retirement so far as these are known; where either date is uncertain an attempt has been made in most cases to supply some biographical information from about the time when they are likely to have been in office but such information makes no pretence to completeness and is usually confined to evidence from the published chancery rolls. It will be readily understood that a list whose sources are limited, in the main, to the published chancery enrolments cannot be regarded as a definitive list of the justices. The list cannot even be said to exhaust the main chancery enrolments, since the fine rolls and the names of witnesses in the charter rolls are unpublished. It neglects the memoranda rolls of the exchequer and the plea rolls of all other courts apart from that held by the justices themselves. To have produced anything more definitive would have demanded both a thorough investigation of many unpublished records and a detailed examination of the careers of many of the justices, which it was foreign to the compiler's purpose to attempt. Nevertheless it will be seen from the facts assembled that the succession of justices is tolerably clear from 1234 onwards, except about 1239–40 and 1262–4. The loss of the close roll for 1238–9 and of the patent rolls for 1238–40 may be partly responsible for the earlier gap; the later gap seems to some extent to reflect administrative weaknesses whose causes were political.

Nine persons included in Gross's list as justices under Henry III will not be found in this list. 'John de Pynkesden' is a fictitious creature, compounded out of a misreading by Prynne and a misreading of Prynne's text by Gross.[1] The real person was master Thomas de Pyuelesdon. William de Thurlaeston is shown by the memoranda rolls to be identical with William de Orlaveston.[2] Philip Basset, Henry of Bath, Hugh Bigod, Peter de Rivaux, Stephen de Segrave and Roger de Thurkelby were not justices. The mistake over each of them is the same, that of failing to understand that the high officials who on occasion

[1] *Demurrer*, ii, f. 51v (giving text of letters close of 20 October 1262, cf. *Close Rolls, 1261–4*, p. 91). Prynne gives 'Thomas de Pynkesden'; Gross was responsible for 'John'. In the same extract, Prynne converts Nicholas de Turri to 'de True'.

[2] See note on *Orlaveston, William de*.

acted with the justices of the Jews were not justices themselves; except for Thurkelby, the mistake can be traced back to Prynne's misinterpretation of passages in the chancery rolls or in a *coram rege* roll. To give an example not copied by Gross: Prynne must have known well enough from the chronicles and chancery rolls that the archbishop of York and the senior household steward William de Cantelupe were two of the regents in England during the king's Gascon expedition in 1242–3. Yet when he came across a mandate to them on Jewish affairs from Henry III, in Gascony, he jumped to the conclusion that they 'were then Commissioners or justices for the Jews affairs'.[1] If Prynne could make this sort of mistake it is not surprising that he erred elsewhere when there was less to guide him. As to Segrave and Rivaux: after Martin de Pateshull's retirement in February 1229, Segrave was the senior common law justice, a position reflected in his being one of the regents during the king's absence overseas in 1230 and in the fact that after the king's return he seems mostly to have been holding pleas in the king's train, apart from eyres in the summers of 1231 and 1232. It was natural that he should have been appointed justiciar of England when Hubert de Burgh was disgraced. It was as justiciar that he took part in exchequer affairs between August 1232 and May 1234. Peter de Rivaux held the guardianship of the English Jewry[2], but this was an office superior to that of justice of the Jews and was one of the many through which he controlled affairs. From the well-known proceedings against Segrave, Rivaux and Robert Passelewe which followed the baronial reaction of 1234 and which are recorded on William de Raleigh's earliest *coram rege roll*, Prynne saw that all three were involved together and so mistakenly concluded that all three were justices of the Jews; but his citations, the basis of all later assertions, show only that Robert was a justice.[3] The mistakes over Basset, Henry of Bath and Thurkelby can be examined together. Henry of Bath during his second period in office as the senior justice of the court *coram rege*, from June 1253 to his death about November 1260, was naturally called upon from time to time to act as legal adviser in matters affecting various government departments. The common law justice next in seniority to him, Roger de Thurkelby, who for much of this time was senior justice of the Bench, was sometimes called upon likewise. For example in 1255 both Bath and Thurkelby assisted the treasurer and exchequer barons in dealing with the city of London's attempt to evade payment of tallage.[4] The Jewish matters in which Bath was called upon to act included the action between Thomas de Charlecote and Licoricia of Winchester, matters arising from the murder of Hugh of Lincoln,

[1] *Demurrer*, f. 31, giving text of letters close of 3 February 1243, cf. *Close Rolls, 1242–7*, p. 12.

[2] *Calendar of Charter Rolls, 1226–57*, p. 163.

[3] *Demurrer*, ii, f. 23v, citing what is now K.B. 26/115B, ms. 1d, 10, 11, 17, 20 (seventeenth-century ink numbers).

[4] *Close Rolls, 1254–6*, pp. 157, 160.

the affair of Kok son of Aaron and the affair of the high-priest of the London Jewry.[1] In the first two matters Thurkelby was also called on to assist. In the last Philip Basset, a prominent member of the king's council who happened to be a close personal friend of Henry of Bath, also acted. In the formal acts of the matters mentioned the names of these three precede the justices of the Jews, who are so styled in some cases. The letters patent of 20 July 1257 and the charter of 24 February 1258 have contributed most to these errors, the latter even misleading the indexers of the *Calendar of Charter Rolls*. The error over Hugh le Bigod arose in similar fashion from the fact that as justiciar of England in 1258–1260 he naturally acted at times with the exchequer barons or with the justices of the Jews. In the extract which Prynne gives, the sheriffs, who had been ordered to answer for an instalment of a Jewish tallage before the exchequer barons, are instead commanded to answer *coram Hugone le Bigod Justiciario Anglie et justiciariis regis ad custodiendum Judeorum assignatis*: Prynne and Gross read *justiciario . . . assignato*.[2]

The last error concerns Simon de Pateshull. Gross here followed a reference given by Madox, from the Hilary *Communia* in the treasurer's remembrancer's memoranda roll for 25 Henry III.[3] The enrolment is of an exchequer mandate to the mayor and sheriffs of London. It says that after inspection of the roll of Jewry for the fifteenth year it appears that Geoffrey fitz Peter and his heirs are quit of a debt of 80½ marks exacted on houses which belonged to Robert fitz Walter in the Jewry in St. Leonard's, London, which houses Geoffrey deraigned as his right before S. de Patteshull and his fellows *then* justices of the Jews. It goes on to say that whoever holds these houses is also quit of this debt and that Matthew Bukerel and his heirs are likewise quit. The word 'then' has been interpolated. Madox assumed from this passage that the roll inspected, of pleas *anno regni regis xv*, was that of Pateshull and his colleagues. But this assumption is only possible if we further suppose that the roll was one of pleadings in the fifteenth year of John, not of Henry III, and that Pateshull was a justice of the Jews in 1212–13. Both these suppositions are possible, but not very probable. Simon de Pateshull was a justice of the Jews about 1198[4]; but under John his service, of the greatest distinction, was as a common law justice at the Bench or *coram rege*. He died in 1217. Geoffrey fitz Peter died in October 1213. It

[1] Rigg, *Select Pleas*, p. 27; *Close Rolls, 1254–6*, pp. 214, 319, 322, 424; *Close Rolls, 1256–9*, p. 415; *Calendar of Patent Rolls, 1247–58*, pp. 570–1 (letters patent of 20 July 1257); *Calendar of Charter Rolls, 1257–1300*, p. 8 (charter of 24 February 1258).

[2] *Demurrer*, ff. 48, 48v. Prynne's reference is faulty and incomplete. It runs: *Fines 42 H. 3, m. Pro communitate Judeorum* (i.e. omitting the membrane reference), yet it concerns an instalment due at Michaelmas 44 Henry III. The mandate was tested at Woodstock on 15 August, which suggests 1258; but there is no such entry in the fine roll of 42 Henry III. The above extension is common form.

[3] *E. 368/13*, m. 4d.

[4] *Pipe Roll, 10 Richard I* (*Pipe Roll Society*), p. 125.

seems reasonable to conclude that Pateshull and his fellows heard this case nearer 1198 than 1213; that the estate came afterwards to Matthew Bukerel, who was being charged with a Jewish debt in 1229[1]; and that there was some litigation about the houses at the exchequer of Jews in 1230-1, in the course of which Pateshull's judgement was pleaded and the position clarified. We may note that another house which Geoffrey fitz Peter acquired in the Jewry, by the tilting ground, had by the early 1220's came into the possession of master Alexander of Dorset, one of the justices of the Jews.[2] There is no evidence that a Simon de Pateshull of a younger generation was a justice of the Jews under Henry III. The *Dictionary of National Biography* in the article on a younger Simon credits him with being a justice in 1257, but this is because the *Foedera* gives Pateshull in error for Passelewe in its text of the letters patent of 20 July 1257.[3]

It will be seen that there were few common lawyers among the justices. Apart from Ralph of Norwich, whose claim to be considered as a justice rests on a single ambiguous passage, the most distinguished of these few was John de Wyvill, who followed a decade at the Jewish exchequer with eight years as a justice in eyre and at the Bench, where in 1261 he acted as senior justice in the absence of Gilbert de Preston on eyre. William of St. Edmunds came to the Jewish exchequer after some years as a justice in eyre and at the Bench. Adam de Greynvill, the only other man to serve at the Bench, did so only for a term in emergency. His main legal work, like that of Hugh of Bath, William le Breton and Geoffrey of Lewknor, was done as an assize or eyre commissioner or in forest eyres. The great majority of the justices were experts in administrative matters or in fiscal or financial affairs. Three were men of outstanding ability: the brothers Robert and Simon Passelewe and Philip Lovel. The standing of many of the others may well increase when biographical investigation makes the course of their careers plainer. One general point may be made. There seems to be current among scholars a view of the justices of the Jews and their administration under Henry III which may be summed up as chronic corruption tempered by occasional dismissals. This view seems to be due simply to a failure to apply to the evidences for the justices' careers and their administration the same criticism that has been accorded to the evidences, for example, of crimes and atrocities committed by Jews. Like any other office which concerned the titles to estates and the receipt of money, the office of justice of the Jews exposed the holder to temptations. The royal policy from the 1230's also exposed the office to some obloquy and made it a target in political manoeuvres. The general evidence of this list suggests that most of the justices withstood the

[1] *Close Rolls, 1227–31*, p. 185.
[2] *Starrs and Jewish Charters*, i. 26–30; ii. notes 351, 354–5.
[3] *Foedera*, i. 362.

temptation, though several were the victims of political or palace manoeuvres. In contrast to the current view, their standing and integrity as a whole seems to have been as high as that of other royal servants under Henry III, whose reign, in this respect, will bear comparison with any other.

In the Lists the following abbreviations are used for published texts or calendars of chancery rolls: *ClR*, *Close Rolls; CLibR*, *Calendar of Liberate Rolls; CPR*, *Calendar of Patent Rolls.*

List

18 May 1218 Richard de Dol, master Alexander of Dorset and Elias de Sunninges are appointed: *CPR 1216–25*, p. 154.

All three occur as witnesses, after the Bench justices, in a charter enrolled in the Bench plea roll about 18 November 1219: *Curia Regis Rolls*, viii. 168. Mandates were addressed to Richard and master Alexander as keepers or justices on 20 July and 19 August 1218 and 7 January 1221: *Rotuli Litterarum Clausarum*, i. 366, 370b, 445b. No later references of this sort have been found for Richard. A mandate of 22 June 1222 implies that master Alexander was still in office, *ibid.*, p. 462b. On 8 December 1222 he was appointed keeper of exchanges in company with Henry of St. Albans, *ibid.*, 359; thenceforward there are many mandates to him in this capacity but none to him as justice, though the two offices could have been held in conjunction. Elias remained in office for over twenty years.

3 July 1225 A *liberate* for 10*s*. is made in favour of Ralph of Norwich and Elyas de Sunning, for paying workmen who had put a window in the Jews' chamber: *Rotuli Litterarum Clausarum*, ii. 47.

It is on the authority of this entry that Foss (followed by the *D.N.B.*) describes Ralph as having been a justice of the Jews.

21 Jan. 1231 The appointment of Henry de Cern is cancelled: *ClR 1227–31*, p. 473.

At the same time Henry vacated his guardianship of St. Mary's, Winchester or Romsey abbey on the election of an abbess: *ibid.*, p. 473 and *CPR 1225–32*, p. 421. His appointment as justice had perhaps been temporary.

About 1232–4 Robert Passelewe in office as senior justice.

Robert is not styled justice in the sources covered. In the charges made by the London Jews after his disgrace, which are recorded in the *coram rege* roll for 1234–5 (K.B. 26/115B, ms. 13–14, printed by Michael Adler in *Jewish Historical Society's Transactions*, vol. xiv) the London community mention a present made to Robert when he became justice: *op. cit.*, p. 141. In view of the history of Peter de Rivaux's administration this is not likely to have happened before August 1232 and may have been as late as January 1233, when Robert became deputy treasurer. He was removed from all offices at the council of Gloucester, which opened on 23 May 1234; on 30 May the London Jews were commanded to be no longer intendant to him: *ClR 1231–4*, p. 438.

6 July 1234 Hugh of Bath and Elyas de Sunninges are in office: William le Breton (Brito) is associated with them: *ClR 1231–4*, p. 569.

Hugh of Bath can have been appointed at any time after Michaelmas 1228, when he seems to have ceased to act as deputy sheriff of Berkshire. He is addressed as senior justice in a mandate of 3 October 1235: *ClR 1234–7*, p. 198.

2 Feb. 1236 Philip de Ascellis is appointed in place of Hugh of Bath, removed: *ClR 1234–7*, p. 237.

William le Breton is addressed as senior justice in a mandate of 13 August 1236: *ibid.*, p. 302.

26 Dec. 1237 Master William le Brun is appointed: *ClR 1237–42*, p. 17.

28 July 1238 William le Breton, Elias de Sunninges, Philip de Ascellis and Philip le Brun are in office: *CPR 1232–47*, p. 228.

It seems that Philip le Brun is an error for William le Brun, since nothing else is known of a Philip. William le Breton had left office some time before February 1241, when a *quo warranto* action was brought against him in the court *coram rege* about the manor of Sporle, Norfolk. In this, Robert Passelewe, prosecuting, pleaded that Ranulf le Breton had gained seisin of this manor (which he later conveyed to his brother William and William's son John) by a lease from a Jew 'and thus it was enrolled in the exchequer of the Jews and is there yet enrolled unless it may have been removed by William le Breton while he was a justice of the Jews': K.B. 26/121, m. 15d. Elias of Sonning must by now have been rather elderly and probably died or retired soon after 1238. Philip de Ascellis can hardly have acted after his appointment as sheriff of Warwick and Leicester about 24 June 1240. William le Brun can hardly have acted after his appointment as guardian of Durham bishopric in 1240.

23 Jan. 1241 Writs of *liberate* issue for 20 li. each to Thomas de Newerk and William of St. Edmunds, justices of the Jews: *CLibR 1240–5*, p. 23.

These payments were presumably in respect of the year 25 Henry III (commencing 28 October 1240). There are authorities for the payment of Thomas's salary up to 28 Henry III: *ibid.*, pp. 98, 190; *ClR 1242–7*, p. 34, 227. On 20 June 1244 a mandate was addressed to him as justice, *ibid.*, 253. In June or July 1244 Thomas and William, styled justices of the Jews, witnessed a charter in favour of the treasurer which is dated 28 Henry III but which the names of the Bench justices and exchequer barons, so styled, who also witness, enable to be dated as made in Trinity term 1244: P.R.O. Ancient Deeds, A. 734. On 1 May 1245 a mandate was addressed to both William and Thomas as justices: *ClR 1242–7*, p. 307. The decision to keep the Bench in session in the summer of 1245 while a visitation of the eyre was in progress in two circuits caused a shortage of justices; so William, who had had service in the Bench or on eyre between September 1232 and July 1238, was recalled to sit in the Bench for Easter and Trinity terms 1245.

28 Jan. 1246 A *liberate* for 10 marks issues in favour of John de Wyvill, justice of the Jews: *CLibR 1245–51*, p. 23.

During the ten years that he was in office, 1246–55, John's yearly salary was 40 marks; his first half-yearly instalment of it was for 30 Henry III Easter, on 10 May 1246: *ibid.*, p. 51. This payment would therefore seem to be for one quarter's salary, in respect of Hilary term 1246, so he must have begun to act in January 1246.

23 Apr. 1246 John de Wyvill and master Roger de Gosebec are appointed; Thomas de Newerk is relieved of office: *ClR 1242–7*, p. 416.

The language of the letters close about Thomas '*quem ab officio illo dimisimus*' does not necessarily imply that Thomas was being removed for unsatisfactory conduct as Cecil Roth *A History of the Jews in England*, p. 50, suggests.

3 Nov. 1249 Philip Lovel is appointed: *ClR 1247–51*, p. 234.

It is possible that Lovel took precedence over Wyvill and Gosebek.

31 [*sic*] Sep. 1250 Robert de Ho is appointed in place of master Roger de Gosebek: *ClR 1247–51*, p. 330.

c. 29 Sep. 1251 Philip Lovel is accused of corruption while tallaging the Jews in the north in company with his clerk Nicholas of St. Albans; he is not convicted but is removed or suspended from office and makes a fine for the restoration of royal favour: Matthew Paris, *Chronica Majora*, v. 261.

Lovel had been commissioned for this tallage in May 1250: *CPR 1247–58*, pp. 63–4. On 5 February 1252 he was granted remission of the king's rancour and indignation for all offences committed up to 25 December 1251, for a fine of 10 gold marks paid to the wardrobe on that day: *ibid.*, p. 128. He had probably been suspended rather than removed, for on 26 August 1252 a mandate issued to him and his fellow justices of the Jews: *ibid.*, p. 149. Next day he was appointed treasurer but retained his office of justice.

c. 16 Nov. 1251 to *c.* 17 June 1252 — Between these dates mandates are addressed to William le Breton as justice of the Jews: *ClR 1251–3*, pp. 9, 15, 61–2, 110, 200, 226.

It seems possible that William's recall was a temporary measure which lasted while Lovel was suspended.

c. 28 Oct. 1252 — Robert de Ho is accused of falsifying a charter; he is imprisoned but apparently acquitted and fined four gold marks for restoration of favour: *Chronica Majora*, v. 345.

On 2 November 1252 Robert de Ho was ordered to be removed from the Tower and delivered to the custody of Philip Lovel, who was to cause him to be bailed for appearance *coram rege*: *ClR 1251–3*, p. 270. About 26 December 1252 he paid three gold marks for his fine for the remission of the king's indignation: Fine Roll, 37 Henry III, m. 20.

19 Feb. 1255 — Reference is made to a recent occasion when John de Wyvill and Simon Passelewe, justices of the Jews, gave evidence on a matter *coram rege*: *ClR 1254–6*, p. 42.

On 20 February 1255 Lovel, Wyvill and Passelewe authorize letters close on a Jewish matter: *ibid.*, p. 45.

5 Feb. 1256 — Adam de Greynvill is appointed in place of Philip Lovel: *ClR 1254–6*, p. 269.

On 20 June and 6 July 1256 and on 27 June 1257 mandates were addressed to Simon Passelewe, Adam de Greynvill and Thomas Esporun, justices of the Jews: *ClR 1254–6*, pp. 322, 426; *ClR 1256–1259*, p. 70.

27 Apr. 1258 — A royal charter of this date refers to an inquest taken some time before by Simon Passelewe, Adam de Greynvill, Thomas Esporun and Ralph de Hotot, justices of the Jews: *Calendar of Charter Rolls, 1257–1300*, p. 10.

A charter of 21 June 1258 refers to a similar inquest made by Passelewe, Esporun and Hotot only: *ibid.*, p. 12. Ralph de Hotot's salary as justice was 20 li. yearly; the *liberate* for the 42 Michaelmas instalment issued on 29 December 1258 and for the 43 Easter instalment on 14 April 1259: *CLibR 1251–60*, pp. 444, 457. The *Liberate* roll for 42 Henry III is split in two; the first part ends in January 1258, with one membrane missing; the second part runs only from January to May, the rest of the year to October being missing. It seems probable that a *liberate* for Ralph de Hotot for 42 Easter was on a membrane now lost.

6 June 1259 — John de Swyneford, Geoffrey de Leukenore and Roger de Scaccario are appointed: *ClR 1256–9*, p. 392.

This appointment is enrolled among the Trinity *Communia* in L.T.R. Memoranda Roll 43 Henry III, m. 13.

30 Sep. 1259 — There being at present none to attend to business, Simon Passelewe is summoned with all speed to act until more permanent arrangements can be made when the king reaches London about 13 October: *ClR 1256–9*, p. 442.

This appointment must have been made for the opening of Michaelmas term 1259. A royal charter of 11 September 1259 refers to evidence given by John de Wyvil and Simon Passelewe, justices of the Jews; but this evidence may have been given before 1256: *Calendar of Charter Rolls, 1257–1300*, p. 21.

23 Oct. 1259 — Simon Passelewe and Roger de Scaccario are to have their robes as justices of the Jews: *ClR 1256–9*, p. 454.

Their appointment must have been the more permanent arrangement settled when the king reached London.

JUSTICES OF THE JEWS, 1218–68: A PROVISIONAL LIST

10 June 1260 Roger de Scaccario, Simon Passelewe and William de Hasilbech are in office: *ClR 1259–61*, p. 55.

On 4 August 1260 an order was made for William de Hasilbech to receive his robe as a justice; on 6 December 1260 a similar order was made in favour of all three justices: *ibid.*, pp. 93, 312. On 5 December 1260 a *liberate* was issued for the salary of all three for 44 Michaelmas, each receiving 25 marks half-yearly: Liberate Roll, 45 Henry III, m. 16. A royal charter of 15 February 1261 refers to evidence given by John de Wyvill and Simon Passelewe, justices of the Jews, but perhaps this, like the previous example, refers to something done before 1256: *Calendar of Charter Rolls, 1257–1300*, p. 33. Another charter, of 22 August 1261, refers to evidence given by Passelewe alone: *ibid.*, p. 38. Passelewe and Hasilbech were among those commissioned to investigate the *arche* of Jewry on 17 July 1261: *CPR 1258–66*, p. 186. Passelewe may still have been in office on 3 February 1262, when he tested letters close on Jewish matters: *ClR 1261–4*, pp. 103–4.

In July 1262 Master Thomas de Pyuelesdon' and John de Weston are in office and a charter of the Jew Samuel de Staunford is delivered to them: Trinity *Communia* in L.T.R. Memoranda Roll, 46 Henry III, m. 16d.

Letters patent of about August 1262 show that master Thomas and John were in office while Nicholas de Turri was holding the Essex eyre (which lasted from 11 June to about 29 July), when they issued a prohibition against a Jew answering to a writ by which he had been impleaded, as a result of which judgement had been given against him: *CPR 1258–66*, p. 235. On 20 October they were commissioned to hear the action with Nicholas: *ClR 1261–4*, p. 91. Both justices were presumably nominated by prince Edward, to whom the Jewry had been committed, *cf.* the instructions issued to the chancellor of the exchequer in July 1262: L.T.R. Memoranda Roll, 46 Henry III, ms. 17, 17d. Entries in the *Communia* for Michaelmas 1262 and Hilary 1263 show master Thomas in office: L.T.R. Memoranda Roll 47, Henry III, ms. 11, 19d. In a charter of Robert Walerand, enrolled about 1 February 1263, John and master Thomas occur as witnesses after the justiciar, William de Wilton (then senior justice *coram rege*) and Gilbert de Preston and John de Wyvill (then the Bench justices): *ClR 1261–4*, p. 280. The political situation caused the exchequer, like the Bench, to be suspended from the end of Hilary term to the opening of Michaelmas term 1264.

8 Jan. 1265 Hamo Hauteyn and William de Haselbech are to receive their robes as justices of the Jews: *ClR 1264–8*, p. 11.

On 4 February 1265 the justices were instructed to resume sessions at the exchequer as customary; on 15 March the sessions were suspended at the instance of prince Edward, to whom the Jewry had been committed. These orders reflect Simon de Montfort's attempts to re-establish the Jewish administration and to conciliate prince Edward: *ClR 1264–8*, pp. 19, 32.

3 May 1265 Robert de Crepping and Adam de Winton are appointed, on the nomination of prince Edward: *ibid.*, p. 52.

30 May 1265 William de Haselbeche is appointed in place of Adam de Winton, *ibid.*, p. 62.

Since Adam's appointment was made near the end of Easter term and William's was made before the opening of Trinity term there may be a doubt whether Adam ever acted. The Jewry had been taken into the king's hand following prince Edward's escape.

5 Dec. 1265 John le Moyne and Robert de Fulleham are appointed: *CPR 1258–66*, p.517.

These appointments represent the final re-establishment of the exchequer of Jews after the troubles. On 28 September 1266 an *allocate* issued in favour of John le Moyne to credit him against his crown debts with 25 marks for his expenses lately in sitting for half a year at the exchequer of Jews: Liberate Roll, 50 Henry III, m. 2. This suggests that he sat in Michaelmas term 1265 and Hilary 1266.

17 Feb. 1266 Robert de Folham and Thomas Esperun, justices of the Jews, are to receive a yearly salary of 40 marks each, payable half yearly at Easter and Michaelmas: *ibid.*, m. 9.

This *liberate* is a standing order for payment, not an order for the payment of a particular instalment.

JUSTICES OF THE JEWS, 1218–68: A PROVISIONAL LIST

27 Oct. 1266 William de Orlaveston is to have his robe as a justice of the Jews as long as he is in office, according to past custom: *ClR 1264–8*, p. 277.

On the same date a *liberate* issued for a half-yearly payment of his salary of 40 marks yearly; the term is lost in a defective margin of the roll: Liberate Roll, 50 Henry III, m. 1. Presumably he entered office at the beginning of Michaelmas term 1266.

20 Jan. 1267 William de Watford is appointed in place of Thomas Esporun: *ClR 1264–8*, p. 286.

26 July 1267 An enrolment in the plea roll of the exchequer of the Jews is made on the morrow of St. James 51 Henry III before William de Orlaveston, Robert de Fulleham and William de Watford: Rigg, *Plea Rolls of the Exchequer of Jews*, i. 157.

A similar enrolment was made on the Tuesday before the Purification 52 Henry III (31 January 1268): *ibid.*, 209. On 10 July 1272 a mandate issued for William de Watford to be mainprized to stand trial *coram rege* on 25 July for an offence committed in office: *ClR 1268–72*, p. 492. His colleagues were removed at the same time and all three were ordered to account on the morrow of St. Thomas Martyr (8 July 1272), being thence adjourned to the quindene of Michaelmas (13 October) and thence to the morrow of Purification (3 February 1273): L.T.R. Memoranda Rolls, 56 Henry III, ms. 7, 7d; 1 Edward I, m. 3. Meanwhile, on the Saturday before St. Margaret (16 July 1272) the treasury of the exchequer of Jews was officially investigated and an enrolment made of the charters found there; this shows that Fulk Peyforer and Ralph of St. Osyths had succeeded as justices and that they were apparently still in office on the vigil of St. Nicholas following (5 December 1272): Exchequer K.R., Accounts Various, Jews [E. 101] no. 249/11. On 27 January 1273 Hamo Hauteyn and William de Ludham were appointed justices: *ClR 1272–9*, p. 6.

Alphabetical List of Justices

Ascellis, Philip de. Appointed 2 Feb. 1236; in office 28 July 1238; cannot have acted after 24 June 1240 about which time he was appointed sheriff of Warwick and Leicester, holding office till 28 March 1246.

Bath, Hugh of. In office 6 July 1234; removed 2 Feb. 1246. Hugh had estates in Buckinghamshire and Berkshire. His earlier career, 1216–26, seems to have been spent in the administration of the honor of Berkhamsted, during which time he undertook various public duties in Bedfordshire and Buckinghamshire. During 1226–32 he was more concerned with Berkshire, acting successively as sheriff and under-sheriff from 23 October 1226 to Michaelmas 1228 and being commissioned regularly to take assizes from August 1229 to June 1232. He then seems to have returned to his Buckinghamshire estates, for in the pipe roll for 16 Henry III the crown debts arising from his period in Berkshire were transferred from the account of that county to the Beds. and Bucks. account, while in September 1235 he held an assize session at Bedford whose issues were given the unusual distinction of a separate heading in the pipe roll of 20 Henry III. On the whole it seems likely that he was appointed as justice at some time between the autumn of 1228 and the summer of 1232; in June 1231 he was commissioned, along with the senior Bench justice, Thomas de Muleton, to survey the earl Marshal's lands, which might suggest that he was then already working at the exchequer. The foregoing facts are taken from an account of his career which it is hoped to publish elsewhere.

Breton, William le. Appointed 6 July 1234; in office 28 July 1238; ceased to act before the end of 1240. Recalled about Nov. 1251 and served till about June 1252. Since William was one of Hubert de Burgh's supporters who lost office in 1232 the original appointment would seem to be due to the political changes of 1234 and it is not impossible that

Hubert's second disgrace in 1239 also affected his career. Between 1239 and 1247 he held hardly any public appointments but from the latter year until shortly before his death in 1261 he was active in many capacities: as an assistant justice in eyre, as a commissioner for special enquiries, as a guardian of various estates temporarily in the king's hand, as an assize commissioner and as a senior justice for forest eyres. He died shortly before 3 April 1261 and on 14 January 1263 his son and heir John delivered to the exchequer fifteen *forule* of pleas taken before him for deposit in the treasury; two of these *forule* contained pleas of the Jewry and were handed over to master Thomas de Peuelesdon, justice of the Jews: L.T.R. Memoranda Roll, 46–7 Henry III, m. 11. Contemporary with him were two members of the Le Breton family who held at Badingham and Sternfield, Suffolk and who were also named William; the indexes of several calendars of chancery enrolments confuse them with him. It is hoped to publish an account of his career elsewhere.

Brun, master William. Appointed 26 Dec. 1237; probably in office 28 July 1238; cannot have acted after his appointment as guardian of Durham bishopric, which office he held 24 June 1240–10 Feb. 1241: Pipe Roll, 25 Henry III, rot. 6d. In the summer of 1241 he undertook a mission to Ireland, while between May 1242 and May 1244 he was joint guardian with Hugh Giffard of the young prince Edward. He had an estate in Camberwell, Surrey, Surrey 1235 eyre roll [J.I. 1/864], m. 18d.

Cern, Henry de. Appointment cancelled 21 Jan. 1231. The order cancelling his appointment refers to a previous order by which he was appointed; but this is not enrolled. At the same time he vacated office as guardian of Romsey Abbey, but this was normal since an abbess had been elected. His appointment as keeper of the abbey of St. Mary's, Winchester, was also cancelled at this time but the entry is marginated as if it concerned Romsey abbey: *CPR 1225–32*, pp. 420–1. There does not seem to have been a vacancy at St. Mary's at this time and it may be that both this mandate and that about his justiceship of the Jews show the chancery correcting its own mistakes. Henry acted as an assistant justice in forest eyres in 1229 and 1232: *ClR 1227–31*, pp. 238, 382; *ClR 1231–4*, p. 137. He was a Dorset man: *ibid.*, pp. 125, 140; *CPR 1225–32*, p. 450.

Crepping, Robert de. Appointed 3 May 1265; if he acted at all it can only have been for a short time in the summer of 1265.

Dol, Richard de. Appointed 18 May 1218; in office 7 Jan. 1221; date of retirement uncertain. Richard was a Surrey man and his holding of estates there at Battersea and Wandsworth, as well as having rents in Westminster, suggest tenancies or connexions with Westminster abbey which seem to be typical of a career exchequer official: *Surrey Feet of Fines* (Surrey Arch. Soc.), pp. 4, 6, 7; *Surrey Arch. Soc. Trans.*, x. 240; *V.C.H. Surrey*, iii. 6; iv. 12. He also had an estate at Loseley. He took some part in Surrey affairs, as a leading member of the county court, and as a tallage and assize commissioner, between 1219 and 1233: *Curia Regis Rolls*, viii. 142; x. 310; *CPR 1216–25*, pp. 172, 409, 485; Patent Roll, 17 Henry III, m. 7d. There are notices of his acting as an attorney in the Bench in 1219 and 1221: *Curia Regis Rolls*, viii. 46; x. 16. Since exchequer officials often acted in this capacity the publication of further volumes in this series may provide some guide to the length of his possible connexion with the exchequer. His appearance in 1227 as a witness to a private charter of the Justiciar, Hubert de Burgh, might suggest that he was still employed there: *CPR 1225–32*, p. 164. The fact that we find no reference to his colleague Elias of Sonning as justice of the Jews between 1221 and 1234, when he was still in office makes it possible that Richard was in office for some years after 1221.

Dorset, master Alexander of. Appointed 18 May 1218; in office June 1222; date of retirement uncertain. From Dec. 1222 to Dec. 1228 he was keeper of the mints with the

Londoners Henry of St. Albans and Richard Renger. By inheritance from his mother he held an estate at Weston, Somerset, of the barony of the bishop (later of the prior) of Bath: *Somerset Fines* (Somerset Record Society), vi. 366; *Somerset Pleas* (Somerset Rec. Soc.), xi, nos. 301, 308. Nevertheless by 7 Oct. 1230 he had obtained a canonry of Bridlington and the rectory of East Cowton (York diocese): *Gray's Register* (Surtees Society, vol. 56), p. 40. This northern preferment may explain his acting as taxation commissioner for Yorkshire in 1225 and a commission to take an assize at Newcastle on Tyne in Sept. 1228: *CPR 1216–25*, pp. 566, 571; *CPR 1225–32*, p. 221. In July 1227 he held Robert Passelewe's lands at farm from a merchant of Sens who held them as security for debts owed him by Robert: *ibid.*, p. 136. He died about March 1233, leaving estates at four places in Yorkshire, at Rampton in Notts., Winterbourne in Dorset, Weston in Somerset and Bagshot in Surrey: Fine Roll 17 Henry III, m. 6, given incompletely in *Excerpta e Rotulis Finium*, i, p. 239.

Esporun, Thomas. In office by 20 June 1256 and still in office about June 1258, retiring between then and 6 June 1259. Reappointed about Feb. 1266; replaced 20 Jan. 1267. He may have retained some connexion with the Jewish administration since on 20 Feb. 1273 he was one of the four commissioners (two of whom were justices) appointed to inspect the *arche* in the provinces.

Fulham, Robert of. Appointed 5 Dec. 1265; removed about July 1272. He was a career exchequer official having served successively as constable and remembrancer. A special payment to him on 7 Nov. 1259 for having composed and written charters in English and French which were sent through all the counties of England suggests that he was responsible for the well-known proclamations of 15 Oct. 1258: *CLibR 1251–60*, p. 440. His own or his wife Joan's landed interests seem to have been mainly in Essex, at Buttsbury, Chelmsford, Ginges Mountnessing and Runwell: Kirk, *Essex Feet of Fines, 1182–1272*, pp. 172, 185, 207, 343.

Gosebek, master Roger de. Appointed 23 April 1246; replaced 30 Sept. or 1 Oct. 1250. He was apparently a career exchequer official, for he took part in the Jewish inquiry of 1243 along with the exchequer baron John le Franceys: *CLibR 1240–5*, p. 206. After 1250 he was for some years marshal of the exchequer. He presumably came from the Suffolk family which held at Brightwell and Gosbeck.

Greynvill, Adam de. Appointed 5 Feb. 1257; in office until Michaelmas 1258 or Hilary 1259. His salary was 40 marks yearly: *CLibR 1251–60*, p. 331. From about April 1257 to after April 1258 he was responsible for arranging very large sales of crown timber under the direction of the treasurer Lovel and the most prominent household steward Robert Walerand: *CPR 1247–58*, pp. 550, 591, 624; *CLibR 1251–60*, pp. 375, 415, 417, 430 etc. But he retained his office meanwhile and was litigating in a Somerset action in that style at the exchequer in Hilary 1258; L.T.R. Memoranda Roll, 41–2 Henry III, m. 10. On 10 Jan. 1259 a *liberate* issued for his salary as justice of the Jews for 42 Easter and Michaelmas terms: *CLibR 1251–60*, p. 446. He continued to draw this salary for 43 Easter to 44 Michaelmas terms, *ibid.*, pp. 468, 530, but simply as a justice, having become a leading assize and special commissioner for the south-western counties, in which capacity he continued until the end of the reign; he also served as an assistant justice in Nicholas de Turri's eyre circuit, 1261–3, in Richard de Middleton's circuit, 1268–9, in Roger de Seyton's circuit, 1271–2, and in the Bench for Hilary term 1267.

Hasilbech, William de. In office 10 June 1260; probably still serving when commissioned to inspect the *arche* and enrol charters on 17 July 1261; replaced by about June 1262. From 18 July 1262 to 3 August 1263 he was joint guardian of the Honor of Clare: Pipe Roll Edward I, rot. 7d. His name is unfortunately not indexed in *CPR 1258–66*.

In office again 8 Jan. to 15 March or 3 May 1265; reappointed 30 May 1265 serving (if there were any sessions) in the summer of 1265 only. He presumably came from the family which held at Haselbech and Yelvertoft, Northamptonshire.

HAUTEYN, HAMO. In office 8 Jan. to 15 March or 3 May 1265. A Norfok man, he seems at this time to have been a follower of the earl of Gloucester; his career at the exchequer of Jews belongs properly to the next reign.

HO, ROBERT DE. Appointed 30 Sept. or 1 Oct. 1250; removed about 28 Oct. 1252 for alleged misconduct in office.

HOTOT, RALPH DE. In office by 27 April 1258, probably to June 1259. On 28 May 1258 the treasurer was ordered to give him one of the three keys to the *arche* at Westminster: *CPR 1256–9*, p. 226. On 14 June 1259 he was presented to a prebend in the collegiate church of Steyning, Sussex, which may have been intended to make good the loss of his salary as justice consequent on the appointments of 6 June 1259: *CPR 1258–66*, p. 28. He was a household official who received various grants and preferments, after a temporary disgrace in 1256, up to 1268; he was also an executor of Peter Chaceporc, keeper of the wardrobe: L.T.R. Memoranda Roll, 46–7 Henry III, m. 14. In July 1260 he took office for a short time as clerk of the works at Gillingham, Dorset, in place of Adam de Greynvill, who was too busy to act: *CLibR, 1251–60*, p. 514.

LEUKENORE, GEOFFREY DE. Appointed 6 June 1259; probably acted only in Trinity term 1259. His previous service had been as an assistant justice in William le Breton's forest eyres and as an assize and special commissioner, since about 1256; he was a member of the Oxfordshire family.

LOVEL, PHILIP. Appointed 3 Nov. 1249; probably suspended from Michaelmas term 1251 to Hilary or Easter term 1252; replaced 5 Feb. 1256, having since 27 Aug. 1252 held the office with the treasureship.

MOYNE, JOHN LE. Appointed 5 Dec. 1265; probably acted till the end of Hilary term 1266, leaving office on becoming guardian of Worcester bishopric, which appointment he held 15 Feb.–18 June 1266, *CPR 1258–66*, pp. 553, 607, and for which he was allowed 25 marks expenses in the same allocate as that which allowed him the same sum for half a year as justice of the Jews: Liberate Roll, 50 Henry III, m. 2. His principal estate was at Shelford, Cambridgeshire; there is an imperfect summary of his career in C. Moor, *Knights of Edward I (Harleian Society)*.

NEWARK, THOMAS OF. In office 23 Jan. 1241; replaced 23 April 1246. A gift of wine to him and William of St. Edmunds on 15 Oct. 1240 suggests that they may have been in office from Michaelmas term 1240: *ClR 1237–42*, p. 231. His career had previously been in the household and he was controller of the wardrobe, 23 Oct. 1236–3 Feb. 1240. The preferment he obtained included the perpetual vicarage of Aughton, in 1228, and the rectory of Leake, in 1238 (both York diocese) and the rectory of Blickling (Norwich) in 1237: *Gray's Register* (Surtees Soc. 56), pp. 19, 20, 84, 86; *CPR 1232–47*, pp. 204, 211. It seems likely that his retirement in 1246 was normal, since his only later royal appointment was as joint guardian of Durham bishopric with Peter Chaceporc, 10 Feb.–20 Oct. 1249. While in office he took part in the important forest inquest in the summer of 1244.

NORWICH, RALPH OF. Possibly in office about July 1225. Ralph was engaged on a number of missions to Ireland between 1217 and his return from one in March 1230. On 29 April 1230 he was appointed a justice of the Bench and he served continuously in the Bench or on eyre until Hilary term 1237, returning to Ireland about the following May to spend almost all the rest of his long life there. In 1222 he returned from an Irish mission undertaken with Geoffrey de Crowcombe concerning the royal castles and he may have remained in England until August 1227 when he went to Ireland on a mission concerned with the clerical sixteenth: *CPR 1216–25*, pp. 316, 317, 342, 351; *CPR 1225–32*, p. 138; *Rot. Litt. Claus.*, i. 477b, 584. If he ever was a justice it would seem that it must have been between these dates. The account of his career in *D.N.B.* requires some correction and addition.

ORLAVESTON, WILLIAM DE. In office 27 Dec. 1266; removed July 1272. In the entry referring to his removal and to his being mainprized to account he is called both de Orlaveston and de Thurlaeston: L.T.R. Memoranda Roll, 55–6 Henry III, m. 7. He came from Orlestone, Kent and there is a brief summary of his career in Moor, *Knights of Edward I.*

PASSELEWE, ROBERT. In office from some time between August 1232 and January 1233 to May 1234.

PASSELEWE, SIMON. In office by 19 Feb. 1255 to after June 1258, possibly until the fresh appointments of 3 June 1259. Reappointed temporarily 30 Sept. 1259, appointment confirmed by 23 Oct. 1259; in office probably till some time between February and June 1262.

On 18 May 1255 he was granted an annual salary of 40 marks as a royal clerk by *liberate* patent, in which case subsequent instalments are not recorded and we have found none for him as justice during his first period of office: *CLibR 1251–60*, pp. 218–19. His service was constantly interrupted by diplomatic missions: in December 1257 and again in the early part of 1260 he went to France, while in August 1260 he was one of the negotiators for a Welsh peace: *CLibR 1251–60*, p. 412; *CPR 1258–66*, pp. 74, 81, 88–9. In July 1262 he accompanied the king to France and remained there as his proctor in various litigation until after March 1263: *ibid.*, pp. 222–3, 240–1, 243, 258. He had no further connexion with the exchequer of the Jews but in the Recognizances of Trinity 1268 and Trinity 1269 he occurs as an exchequer baron: L.T.R. Memoranda Rolls, 51–2 Henry III, m. 15d; 52–3 Henry III, m. 17. His earliest connexion with Jewish affairs seems to be his acting as assistant to the Bench justice Gilbert de Preston in the inquiry of 1243: *CLibR 1240–5*, p. 206.

PYUELESDON, MASTER THOMAS DE. In office July 1262 until after Hilary term 1263. In 1256–7 master Thomas was concerned in the collection of money for the crusade; in November 1261 and February 1262 he was acting as the king's proctor in France: *CPR 1247–58*, pp. 461, 552, 605; *CPR 1258–66*, pp. 189, 198. Meanwhile he had been concerned in the administration of prince Edward's estates: *Staffs. Historical Collections* (William Salt Arch. Soc.), iv. 150–1. He seems to have been appointed on the committal of the Jewry to prince Edward. However, he became one of the most notable of Montfortians, being one of a small group, the rest of whom were trading citizens, who secured London's adhesion to earl Simon. He was elected constable of London by popular vote at the beginning of 1264, led the citizens' attack on Isleworth manor, was at the head of affairs until the submission of October 1265 and was then singled out for loss of all property and for detention at Windsor at prince Edward's pleasure: *Liber de Antiquis Legibus* (Camden Society), pp. 61, 79, 98, 114, 120, 149; *CPR 1258–66*, pp. 416, 419–20, 460, 462, 532. He was still in prison, at Dover, in 1272: Eyton's *Shropshire*, viii. 123. On him and his family, which originated at Pilson, in Shropshire, and held also at Flashbrook in Adbaston, just across the boundary in Staffordshire, see R. W. Eyton, *Antiquities of Shropshire*, viii. 95–8 and *Staffs. Historical Collections*, iv. 284–5. His career seems to merit exhaustive research.

ST. EDMUNDS, WILLIAM OF. In office 23 Jan. 1241 to about May 1245. Between the summers of 1232 and 1238 William acted as an assistant justice in eyres and in the Bench as well as a commissioner for assizes and gaol deliveries. Little is known of him in 1238–40 except that he went with Alexander le Seculer (later an exchequer baron) on a mission to

Rome in the summer of 1239: *CLibR 1226–40*, pp. 384, 438. In the summer of 1240 he took part in an investigation of *arche* with Peter Chaceporc: *ibid.*, p. 482. On 16 Oct. he received a gift of wine along with Thomas de Newerk, which makes it likely that he was then already a justice of the Jews. Throughout his time at the exchequer of Jews he and Thomas were commissioned for assizes in the home counties. After leaving the exchequer to sit in the Bench for Easter and Trinity terms 1245 it seems possible that he died, since no more is then heard of him. He had an estate at Sherington, Bucks., and interests elsewhere in that county: *Bucks. Feet of Fines* (Bucks. Record Soc.), iv. 65, 74; Bucks. 1240 eyre roll (J.I. 1/55), m. 5d.

Scaccario, Roger de. In office 23 Oct. 1259 to Dec. 1260 or later. He was the senior member of the family which held the well-known exchequer fee at Lewknor and Stokenchurch, Oxfordshire, and died before 2 April 1271: *Cal. Inquisitions Post Mortem Henry III*, no. 763. There is a brief account of his career in Moor, *Knights of Edward I.*

Sonning, Elias of. Appointed 18 May 1218; in office, apparently continuously, until after 28 July 1238.

Swyneford, John de. Appointed 6 June 1259; probably acted only in Trinity term 1259. He was a career household official who served for some years on the supply side as a buyer, especially of wines; in this capacity he received a yearly salary of 20 li. but the writs of *liberate* for the instalments of 43 Easter and 44 Michaelmas of this salary do not style him as justice of the Jews: *CLibR 1251–60*, pp. 485, 511.

Watford, William de. Appointed 20 Jan. 1267; removed about July 1272 for alleged misconduct in office.

Weston, John de. In office by July 1262 to about Hilary term 1263 or later. John was a Somerset knight who was in prince Edward's service by 1262 and who seems to have been appointed on the committal of the Jewry to prince Edward; at the outbreak of the troubles in 1264 he was acting as steward to the princess Eleanor and was in the garrison of Windsor castle: *CPR 1266–72 (1262 addenda)*, p. 727; *CPR 1258–66*, pp. 324–5; *ClR 1264–8*, p. 8. He remained a devoted follower of Edward and there is a full, though confused, account of his career in Moor, *Knights of Edward I.* He retained some interest in Jewish affairs after the baron's war, for in 1268 we find him lending money to Robert of Fulham, while in May 1269 he was at the head of the commission to examine the *arche* of London: *ClR 1264–8*, p. 524; *CPR 1266–72*, p. 382.

Winton, Adam de. Appointed 3 May, replaced 30 May, 1265. He may never have acted. It seems likely that he was a subordinate official of the exchequer or of the exchequer of Jews, for in February 1273 he was one of the four commissioners (two of whom were justices) appointed to examine the *arche* while on 9 June 1276 he succeeded to the office of keeper of the writs and rolls of Jewry: *CPR 1272–81*, pp. 6, 148.

Wyvill, John de. In office 28 Jan. 1246 though letters close of appointment were not issued until 23 April 1246; retired about December 1255. The first warrant for his full half-yearly salary issued on 10 May 1246 in respect of Easter 30 Henry III; the last issued on 5 Nov. 1255 for 39 Michaelmas: *CLibR 1245–51*, pp. 51, 89, 127, 151, 209, 232, 256, 288, 308, 353, 384; *CLibR 1251–60*, pp. 39, 78, 127, 150, 184, 219, 249. From January 1256 to his death in the early part of Michaelmas term 1263 he served continuously as an assistant justice of the Bench or in eyre and as an assize commissioner. He was one of the seven justices appointed to take assizes and other special commissions under the restrictive order of August 1259 and he took the special eyre under the Provisions in the south-west, having successfully excused himself, in a letter still extant, from his original assignment to the five northern counties: *Ancient Correspondence*, v. 85. He held in mesne of the de Lisle fee in the Isle of Wight.

V

Six Letters concerning the Eyres of 1226-8

'The said M[artin of Pateshull] is energetic, and so conscientious and thorough in his work that he has overwhelmed all his fellows, especially W[illiam] of Ralege and myself, with the most exacting labour. No wonder, for everyday he starts work at sunrise and does not stop till night.' This passage has been frequently quoted or referred to for its vivid picture of the way the business of an eyre was conducted by that Martin whose judgements, above all others, Bracton revered. Its writer has not hitherto been identified, though in his own day he became as eminent a judge as Martin had been and his career earned him richer preferment than the archdeaconry of Norfolk, or the deanery of St. Paul's and a tenure of it happier than Raleigh's episcopate of Winchester. For our present purpose is to show that the letter in which this passage occurs is the first of an incomplete series of six which were written by William of York to his patron Ralph Neville, the chancellor, between October 1226 and May 1228.[1] The texts of three of them were given in Shirley's *Royal Letters*. These are undated and the writer names neither himself nor his correspondent, though one is endorsed ' W. de Eboraco ' ; Shirley misdated them and, failing to discover by and to whom they were written, did not establish their relationship.[2] A fourth, also undated, in which the writer calls himself William, was published without comment by Jacques Boussard in his brief study of Neville.[3] The other two, hitherto unpublished, are undated but in one, the last of the series, the writer does name both himself and his correspondent.

It was the above passage and the letter from which it comes which supplied the initial clues to the identity of writer and correspondent. A study of Pateshull's eyres showed that the letter must have been written in October 1226. At that time

[1] The letters are here numbered I–VI for convenience in reference.

[2] His suggestions were : I, A Justice Itinerant [to Hubert de Burgh, Justiciar ?], about 1228 ? ; II, A Justice Itinerant to Walter of Merton, Chancellor ?, autumn 1262 ? ; IV, A Justice Itinerant to William of York, 22 September 1233 ?. It is unnecessary to say more about these and the editorial notes supporting them than that the quantity of published records then available (though much less than now) was sufficient for more precise dating and ascription.

[3] *Revue Historique*, clxxvi, p. 222.

Raleigh had not sat as a justice in the bench or in eyre so that, as Lady Stenton has suggested, by 'all his fellows' the writer intended both the justices and their clerks : pre-eminent among the latter Raleigh and himself.[1] Since Raleigh became a justice not long afterwards it was not impossible that the writer also reached that dignity soon after the autumn of 1226. He was anxious to visit a living he had recently obtained in Yorkshire, near his other rents there, and, within the narrow field of those who sat for the first time as justices in eyre or in the bench soon after 1226, this seemed appropriate only to William of York. William of York and William of Raleigh were, indeed, contemporaries whose careers followed a similar pattern ; we find them both as clerks in a royal court in 1219, both rose to become senior justices in the decade 1230–40, both obtained bishoprics. Furthermore, we know on good authority—that of Henry III himself, reported by Matthew Paris—that in the early stages of his career William of York had also been a Chancery clerk : 'you were the scribbler of my writs '.[2] The remains of the official and semi-official correspondence of Ralph Neville, the chancellor, bulk large in the earlier part of the collection of Ancient Correspondence in which the letter is preserved, and it might be hazarded that Neville was the unknown but influential correspondent whom the writer regarded as his patron and with whom he was so intimate that he could write with engaging frankness.

In the course of testing this hypothesis the relationship of this letter to the other five was established. That relationship might be maintained on stylistic grounds alone. The author of all these letters writes as a favoured client to an influential and well disposed patron : 'God knows, I have such fellowship and your providence has so loaded me that it behoves me in all things to bear the heat and burden of the day '.[3] He employs a set of similar or identical phrases to emphasize this relationship. 'I your devoted servant ' ; 'ready and willing to obey your commands' ; 'I beg by all our friendship ' ; 'I thank you as much as lies in my power ' and, as a farewell, 'long, long may your lordship flourish ' ; these are phrases which stud his letters.[4]

[1] *Selden Society*, vol. 53, p. xviii, where 1226 is also suggested as the date of the letter but it is taken as a plea to avoid going with Pateshull *to* Yorkshire, which does not accord with the general sense of the letter or with the specific wording : *supplico . . . si consulatis et velitis ut ulterius itinerem . . . quam in partibus Ebor* '. I was unaware of Lady Stenton's suggestions when beginning my study.

[2] *Chronica Majora* (*Rolls Series*), v. 374 ; the English is Maitland's : *History of English Law*, i. n. 5 to 205 on 206.

[3] Letter III.

[4] (1) *Ego vester penitus :* all letters. (2) *In omnibus et per omnia paratus :* I ; *promptus enim . . . et paratus in omnibus et per omnia :* II ; *me paratum invenietis ad ea facienda qua vestre sederint beneplacito voluntatis :* III ; *promptum enim et paratum*

The relationship of the letters might also be upheld on the grounds of the writer's personal interests. Most of the letters are written when the writer is on royal service and he is anxious for his patron to secure that the expenses of such service are met by a royal allowance.[1] He is equally anxious for his patron to permit him to combine the course of royal business with his own private affairs.[2] He is fond of little jokes, calling an expense allowance 'a fat blessing', promising to come 'on any day you appoint . . . without essoin' and asking for fixed instructions in case 'having finished this Eyre, the leisure tempts me to go on a spree'.[3] He is refreshingly frank about himself. We have already seen him implying a dislike of long hours and hard work; later, a couple of very short eyres, for the business of one of which he coins the super-superlative *paucissississima*, weary him unutterably.[4] The climate of Cumberland, where he must go on public business, does not agree with him but he finds Holderness, where he has private interests, very refreshing.[5] He is equally candid about others: 'When I arrived in the bishopric of Durham the poor cried out, in a lamentable way, that they were fleeced and afflicted enough by Stephen de Lucy, the Keeper, without my coming to ruin them completely'. 'Moreover, since the Archbishop [Walter de Gray, of York] takes the greatest delight in the gossip and news of how things stand at Court, it would be a good idea, if it suits you, to gratify him by writing often to him in this way and then, if you want him to do any of your friends a favour, slip in a word about it at the end of your letter.'[6] Martin of Pateshull himself liked to have the gossip and news of the court from Neville, but his letters are those of an older man, more respectful, less indiscreet.[7] These six letters all come from the mind of one man, a rising protégé, addressing a patron of great influence such as we know Neville to have been: popular, accessible, competent.[8]

As the use made of the reference to Pateshull has already shown, the letters have an individual value because of their frank and lively manner. They deserve study as a whole, however, for they show us a clerk of the Curia Regis at the

me invenietis ad ea facienda in omnibus que vestre sederint voluntati: IV; *faciam autem in omnibus secundum quod michi mandastis*: V; *prompto et parato in omnibus ad ea facienda que vestre sederint beneplacito voluntatis*: VI; (3) *Omni qua possum affectione supplico*: I, II, IV and VI; *Supplicans omni qua possum affectione*: V. (4) *Ad quantas sufficio assurgo graciarum actiones*: IV and VI; (5) *Valeat dominus meus* [*dominatio vestra*: II and IV] *per tempora longissima*: I, II, IV, V and VI.

[1] Letters II, IV and VI. [2] All letters except IV. [3] Letters IV, VI and III.

[4] Letter VI. [5] Letters II and VI. [6] Letters VI and V.

[7] Ancient Correspondence, vi. nos. 75, 76 (August 1225), 127 (September 1227), and 128; Neville is always *paternitas vestra*.

[8] *Chronica Majora*, iii. 90, 226 and iv. 287; cf. Powicke, *King Henry III and the Lord Edward*, i. 86.

critical stage in his career when he first sits as a justice, they sketch the world in which he lived and throw light, or tempt questions not, it is true, on the outstanding events but on aspects of the routine royal administration of the period for which we have usually only official records as sources. Since a good text of four of the letters is available, the contents of those is here summarized in the first person; the text of the two unpublished letters is given, with some modifications of punctuation and paragraphed.[1] Summaries and texts are followed by the conjectural dating, with a short account of the circumstances in which the letters were written and of passages which can be controlled from other sources.

I. Ancient Correspondence, xi. no. 50 [2]

My Lord, please let me, your devoted servant, know by return of messenger if you want me to go on eyre with Martin of Pateshull farther than to Yorkshire. If I do go farther with him it will be a great nuisance, because of the heavy expense and enormous labour, for Martin works from sunrise to nightfall and has worn out all his fellows, above all William of Ralege and myself. Don't doubt, however, that I am ready to obey your command, even to my own cost and hurt. Your excellency might like to know that I've recently been presented to a living in Yorkshire, which suits me very well since it is near to another of my rents. The Archbishop has just committed it to my custody: he estimates its value at £20 a year. I'd like your advice about getting a dispensation for it, since I intend to send to Rome about it this Christmas. Long may you flourish.
[October 1226]

On 27 May 1226 the opening programme for the second general eyre of Henry III's reign was published.[3] There were to be two Circuits, one headed by Stephen Segrave and the other by Martin Pateshull who, with other professional justices and magnates, was to hold the eyres for Lincolnshire, Yorkshire, Northumberland, Cumberland, Westmorland, and Lancashire, opening at Lincoln on 1 July. On 7 June, the sheriff of Lincoln was ordered, by letters close, to allow 'our trusty and well beloved William of York, clerk, £10 to keep him in our service with our trusty and well beloved Martin of Pateshull and his fellows our Justices in their Eyre'.[4] The council advised the king to postpone the opening of the eyre, perhaps on account of the harvest, and this postponement, to 15 September, was published on 25 June.[5] Meanwhile, on Whit Sunday,

[1] I take this opportunity of thanking my colleagues, Mr. L. C. Hector and Mr. H. C. Johnson, who have been generous in their advice and assistance in the preparation of these texts and summaries.

[2] Formerly Royal Letter 317; calendared in *Deputy Keeper's IV Report*, appendix ii, p. 161. Text in Shirley, *Royal Letters* (*Rolls Series*), i. no. 281 (pp. 342–3).

[3] *Rotuli Litterarum Clausarum, 1224–7*, pp. 151a and b.

[4] *Ibid.* p. 119b; the sheriff paid out of the issues of Robert Lexington's 'Eyre' of 1225, *Pipe Roll*, 10 Henry III, rot. 4.

[5] *Ibid.* p. 153b.

7 June, the archbishop of York granted William of York a charter for the living of Dicton' [Kirk Deighton], on the presentation of William d'Albany.[1] According to the *Taxatio* the old value of this living was £20.[2] The other rents which William held at this time are not known precisely but they may have been at Hemsworth, near Wakefield.[3]

The Lincoln eyre opened on 15 September, as arranged, and closed on or after 13 October; the Yorkshire eyre opened at Doncaster on 20 October.[4] At the date of writing this letter William has had a disagreeable taste of work under Martin, does not yet seem to have gone to Yorkshire but has excellent reasons for wishing to go there and thoroughly dislikes the idea of accompanying Martin to the four northern counties. This suggests very strongly that he wrote to Neville either towards the end of the Lincolnshire eyre or in the brief interval between the end of business at Lincoln and the opening of the Yorkshire eyre at Doncaster. As chancellor, Neville can perhaps arrange more congenial work for William elsewhere in his own or the royal service, and this is the most pressing question. There is another: since 1220 William has held the living of [King's] Ripton, in Huntingdonshire,[5] and so will need a dispensation to hold in plurality if he is to keep it now that he has a second benefice. So he slips in a question about that at the end.

The Yorkshire eyre moved to York about 3 November and, with a short recess for Christmas, continued there until about 7 January. It was probably in the January sessions that an agreement was made, dated simply 1227, to which the archbishop of York was a party and which was witnessed by 'Martin de Patishill, William de Insula, Richard Duket, then justices itinerating in Yorkshire, Richard Abbot of Selby, William Raleia, William de Eboraco' and four others.[6] Pateshull, de l'Isle, and Duket, the three professional justices, then went to Lancaster, to hold the Lancashire eyre (about 14–20 January) and on to Appleby, for the Westmorland eyre (about 27 January—3 February) and the probability is that, in spite of his plea, William went with them. Pateshull himself left Appleby before the end of the eyre to hold a final session of the Yorkshire eyre at York about 9 February; but de l'Isle and Duket went up to Newcastle to hold the Northumberland eyre (11 February and a few days following). It seems that William accompanied them as their senior clerk, for two years later, when the matter of prise of herrings by the constable of Newcastle was being discussed, William de l'Isle and William of York refer to a decision of theirs made when they were 'Justices in eyre in Northumberland'.[7] Moreover, an estreat of those portions of the Crown Pleas Roll of this eyre which dealt with answers to enquiries about royal rights (later incorporated in the *Book of Fees*) carries an

[1] *Archbishop Gray's Register* (*Surtees Society, vol. 56*), pp. 224–5.

[2] *Record Commission* edition, p. 323b.

[3] See remarks on Letter V, below.

[4] The dates of eyres are based on an exhaustive list of them which I have prepared for the reign of Henry III.

[5] *Rolls of Hugh de Welles* (*Lincoln Record Society*), vol. iii; he had been presented by Pandulf.

[6] *Gray's Register*, p. 232, n.

[7] *Calendar of Close Rolls, 1227–31*, p. 152; the next Northumberland eyre was in 1235.

endorsement to the effect that William of York delivered it, presumably to the exchequer, on 18 May 1227.[1]

Although in exceptional circumstances, as in 1219, judicial sessions might be held in Lent up to Passiontide, it was the normal practice to finish or adjourn business about Ash Wednesday, which this year fell on 23 February. At this date Pateshull's programme had not been completed: neither the Cumberland eyre nor the Durham eyre (added to the programme, *sede vacante*, on 1 January [2]) had been held. The need for postponing the Cumberland eyre was seen as early as 13 January, when 9 May was fixed for its opening.[3] It seems likely that, because of the postponement of the opening of the circuit from July to September, Pateshull was forced at Lincoln to work against time in a vain effort to complete his programme before Lent and that this, as well as his natural energy, was what made life so disagreeable to William.

We have seen that William visited the exchequer in May. This suggests that he had only then arrived from the north, where he had spent Lent and Eastertide. All that is certainly shown of his movements during the rest of the summer is that he was due to take two assizes of novel disseisin at Lincoln on 1 August.[4]

II. Ancient Correspondence, vii. no. 142 [5]

My Lord, I implore you to arrange that I do not have to go on Eyre in Cumberland. It would mean a long journey and the climate there disagrees with my constitution. I have discussed it with the Bishop of Carlisle [Walter Mauclerk] and told him that I won't go, even if I have a royal mandate, unless I get a special order from you. If the Eyres are beginning again, and if you want me to go on them, please let me go to Cambridge and Huntingdon, with a grant for expenses. I've got a good store of provisions in that district. If there are any fresh troubles, please let me know by letter if I ought to return to Court or to await better times in my home country, at Scarborough or Knaresborough castles or on one of my rents. For God's sake don't forget to tell me how things go with you and the Court. Long may you flourish. If you have to stay in London and war breaks out, there are three casks of wine at my lodgings, near yours, which you can have. Again goodbye.
[August 1227.]

Mr. Denholm Young has recently recounted the crisis of 1227, when Richard of Cornwall, five earls and a great body of supporters gathered at Stamford in late July, threatened civil war if their grievances were not redressed and forced the king to meet them at the 'armed Parliament' of Northampton, on 10–13 August.[6] These are the recent events which form the background to this letter. William, who perhaps left court for the harvest, has had difficulty in getting accurate and up to date news

[1] Exchequer Serjeanties [E. 190] 2/11, membrane 3 dorse, printed in *Book of Fees*, i. 372.

[2] *Rot. Litt. Claus.* p. 152.

[3] *Ibid.* p. 206a.

[4] *Calendar of Patent Rolls, 1225–32*, pp. 157–8.

[5] Formerly Royal Letter 2507. Text in Shirley, *Royal Letters* (*Rolls Series*), ii. no. 583 (pp. 222–3).

[6] *Richard of Cornwall*, pp. 10–13.

of fast-moving and threatening events and still fears that war may break out.

The first stage of the general eyre planned in the summer of 1226 ended soon after Easter 1227 with the completion of Segrave's circuit. For some reason, probably because the king hoped to lead an expedition to Gascony, no further stage took place in the summer of 1227; but at the time of the Northampton meeting, or very soon after, a further stage in the General eyre was published.[1] There were to be three circuits, headed by Muleton, Pateshull, and Segrave. Segrave's programme comprised Northamptonshire, Bedfordshire, Buckinghamshire, Cambridgeshire, and Huntingdonshire, opening at Northampton on 21 September. But Cumberland still remained over from the first stage and to this small eyre were appointed two northern magnates with Simon of Hales and William of York: his first eyre as a justice. However, if he was to sit as a justice, Segrave's circuit was far more attractive. He still held his living of King's Ripton; he may have had an interest in one of the Ramsey Abbey estates nearby.[2] From these he could draw bread, beer, meat, and other provisions. His uncertainty about the future suggests that, to contemporaries, the success of the peace-making at Northampton was not immediately apparent. His two refuges are obvious enough, for he had himself acted as clerk to the commission which examined the state of Scarborough castle when Robert of Cockfield was appointed to hold it in March 1226,[3] while Knaresborough, a few miles from Kirk Deighton, was held by the archbishop of York.[4] We know nothing of the precise whereabouts at this time of Walter Mauclerk, treasurer, bishop of Carlisle and, whence his interest in this eyre, sheriff of Cumberland.

III. Ancient Correspondence, v. no. 100

Domino suo salutem et se totum.

Precepto vestro condescendens paratus sum ire ad partes Cumberland' et ibidem itinerare in forma quam michi mandastis et vos cum locus et tempus affuerint expensas ad opus meum in Itinere illo si placet procuretis. Non autem vos super hoc sollicitarem si in servicio vestro alicubi moram facerem nec in posterum deo dante sollicitabo quamdiu in servicio vestro morabor. Et si placet consideretis distanciam patrie et moram meam ibidem et respondeant[5] stipendia mea laboribus sudoribus et expensis meis. Non enim cederet vobis ad honorem si ego vester penitus tam amplis beneficiis ditatus ob servicium alterius aliena medicarem. Societatem habeo qualem deus scit et sic me oneravit vestra providencia quod in omnibus sustinere me oportebit pondus diei et estus.

Cum igitur Iter illud Cumberland' cito per graciam dei erit perfectum, supplico dominacioni vestre quod me vestrum adiungi faciatis Justiciariis

[1] *Rot. Litt. Claus.* p. 213a; the undated notes of the commissions and circuits immediately follow the enrolment of the summons for the Forest enquiry, dated Northampton, 13 August, and are themselves followed by an enrolment of 17 August.

[2] *Ramsey Cartulary* (*Rolls Series*), i. 331.

[3] *Patent Rolls*, p. 22; cf. *Close Rolls*, p. 20.

[4] *Patent Rolls*, p. 254.

[5] Original has *respendeant*.

itinerantibus in Comitatibus Canteber' et Huntd' cum providencia expensarum, ne forte itinere meo Cumberland' perfecto otiositas prestet michi occasionem vagandi.

Valeat dominacio vestra semper in domino.

Voluntatem vestram michi vestro penitus significate et me paratum invenietis ad ea facienda qua vestre sederint beneplacito voluntatis.

Iterum et bene et diu valeat dominacio vestra in domino.

[Late August or early September 1227]

The tone of this letter, soberer than any of the others, suggests that Neville had written a strongly worded 'No' in answer to Letter II. William's plea to be let off the Cumberland eyre has failed and he must carry it out with as good a grace as possible; but he has not given up hopes of joining Segrave in the Midlands at a later date. Segrave's intention, as we can gather from a letter written by William of London, one of his colleagues, was to complete his circuit before Christmas.[1] On 1 September, letters close were sent to the sheriff of Yorkshire ordering him to allow William of York £10 for the expenses of his Cumberland eyre,[2] which suggests that Neville knew him to be in Yorkshire on his estates; but William himself cannot have known of the allowance yet, or he would not be so insistent in his plea for it.

IV. Ancient Correspondence, vi. no. 162 [3]

My Lord,

On Saturday after the Exaltation of the Cross [18 September 1227] I left Carlisle having finished all the King's business. We were there nine days and obtained 40 marks a day for the King, the total of the Eyre being 360 marks or more. We did not make any summonses since I had not got those instructions I asked for in my letter sent you by Ranulph fitz Henry. As you wrote by Thomas the clerk that, at the end of this Cumberland Eyre, I should hurry to wherever S[tephen] Segrave and his fellows are on Eyre, to assist them, and as I don't expect to be in those parts again for some time, I ought to pay a visit to my Yorkshire estates on my way back. Let me know if you want me to come back straight to you or to go to them first. If you want me to go to them, send me letters of admission to their Eyre. My thanks for getting me my Cumberland expenses; please get me a fat blessing if I go on Eyre with Segrave.

The bearer leaves on the Morrow of St. Matthew [22 September] leaving your servants Thomas de Lasceles and Thomas de Burnham with me. They will follow by the direct route but more slowly, because Lasceles has been ill with stomach trouble. I'll let you know how he gets on.

Long may you flourish.

[1] Ancient Correspondence, vi. no. 121.

[2] *Calendar of Liberate Rolls, 1226–1240*, p. 48.

[3] Formerly Royal Letter 708; calendared in *Deputy Keeper's V Report*, appendix ii, p. 75, which suggests that it was written to the chancellor, a suggestion ignored by Shirley. The *List of Ancient Correspondence* (*P.R.O. Lists and Indexes, No. XV*) correctly understood the endorsement as a note by the recipient of the writer's name and not, as Shirley did, an address. Text in Shirley, *Royal Letters* (*Rolls Series*), i. no. 350 (pp. 421–2).

I send my Rolls, so that William of London and his fellows can find out about Pleas which were in the Bench.

Again goodbye.[1] *Endorsed* W. of York.

[19/22 September 1227]

William slightly overestimated the net yield of the fines and amercements of this, his first eyre, for the Pipe Roll shows that those leviable by the exchequer came to £235 2s. 4d., or just under 360 marks.[2] With Cumberland behind and the prospect of at last joining Segrave in the Midlands, William still wishes to combine the course of business with his own affairs. The direct route south lay west of the Pennines: missing Yorkshire. He may not be north of the Trent again for some time and therefore does not want to miss the chance of visiting Yorkshire, but this means a long detour and coming down east of the Pennines. If, after this detour, he goes on to Westminster (where the court was until November) before joining Segrave the latter's circuit will be far advanced for, as far as he knew, it was Segrave's intention to complete his programme before Christmas. Lasceles disappears from the story but Thomas de Burnham, one of Neville's trusted servants who acted at times as a chancery messenger,[3] had already reached Northampton, by the direct route, when William of London wrote from there to Neville about the end of September.[4] William of London's main object in writing was to inform Neville that, on account of heavy business at Northampton and known also to await them at Newport Pagnel and Bedford, their circuit would take much longer than had been anticipated: they could not hope to hold the eyres at Huntingdon and Cambridge before Christmas. He was also anxious about William of York's Rolls, which Thomas de Burnham told him had been sent to Neville for forwarding to Northampton. As we might expect, these were Rolls of the bench, for Easter Term 1227, which William of York had taken to Carlisle for the continuation of such civil pleas of Cumberland and other northern counties as had been in the bench during the summer. At this time, and until 1249, it was the practice to suspend sessions of the bench while a general eyre (absorbing all or most of the professional justices) was in progress; thus, since the summer of 1226 the bench had sat only in the Easter and Trinity terms 1227 and did not sit again until Hilary term 1228. Each circuit of a general eyre acted as an itinerant bench for the civil pleas of a roughly defined geographical area as well, of course, as for those counties in which it sat. It seems likely that each circuit had a copy of the recent Bench Rolls and that William of York, for his isolated Cumberland eyre, had the set later to be used by Segrave, who had fixed a week from Michaelmas [6 October] as the day for hearing pleas begun in the bench. This date was now near and William of London was accordingly perturbed that the Rolls had not yet come, for any adjournment of these pleas will cause great damage to the litigants and congest an already heavy programme.[5]

[1] The ink in which this postcript was written is now very much lighter than that of the rest of the letter; for *certificare* in Shirley read *certificari*.

[2] Pipe Roll, 12 Henry III, rot. 15 dorse.

[3] *Liberate Rolls*, pp. 101, 103.

[4] Ancient Correspondence, vi. no. 121. He writes after the opening of the Northampton eyre (21 September) but at a sufficient distance from 6 October to hope for Neville to send the Rolls to him, in reply to his letter, by that date.

[5] *Non dum autem recipimus rotulos placitorum de Banco a proximo preterito termino Pasche, quos W. de Ebor' vobis iam transmisit, sicut Thomas de Burnham michi narravit, quorum quidem copiam necesse esse nos habere in octabis Sancti Michaelis die videlicet ad talia placita tenenda prefixo. Et erit eorum expectatio ultra diem illum multis dampnosa.*

The letters close admitting William to Segrave's eyre had been issued on 10 September,[1] before Neville knew that Cambridge and Huntingdon could not be visited until 1228. William's return south was therefore not urgent; indeed he probably stayed in the north all that autumn and winter, as Letter V suggests, for the court came north in November and the king kept Christmas at York.[2]

V. Ancient Correspondence, vi. no. 159[3]

My Lord, from his servant William.

In that business about Simon de Nevill', your relation and nephew of N[icholas] de Nevill' your colleague, I explained to the Archbishop of York that Simon was the son of the last incumbent. The Archbishop, after a little consideration, most kindly answered that that would not be an obstacle if he thought it was what you desired, adding that you could not make a request which he would not hear; so Simon's business was advanced. Since the Archbishop delights in gossip and news of the Court, it would be a good idea, if it suits you, to gratify him by writing often in this way, and then, if you want him to do any of your friends a favour, slip in a word about it at the end of your letter.

Please let me, your devoted servant, have news of you by the bearer of this letter and let me know if you think the King will come north before Easter, if I shall be obliged to sit in the Bench all this summer so that I can provide for it, if you know anything for certain about Stephen, the papal nuncio who was in England last year, especially about his powers, and if you advise me to resign Ripton' and Hymeleseworth before I have a talk with you. I'll be guided by you in everything.

I send you the writ in which the name of my clerk Thomas has been inserted. It has been no use to him. I beg by all friendship that you would put, in place of Thomas, the name of a certain poor scholar and relative of mine, who has spent all his life in the Schools and whom I support there: Master John Paulin. You will be rewarded in heaven for this.

Long may you flourish.

[January 1228]

William held an inquiry at Grimsby in January,[4] which, with this letter, suggests that he remained in the north when the court came south after Christmas. Simon de Neville's business is not reflected in the archbishop's Register[5] and it is William's own affairs which help to date the letter. For the writ in which the name of Thomas the clerk appeared—he has so far defied identification—must have been concerned with his presentation to King's Ripton. Neville approved William's suggestion and on

[1] *Rot. Litt. Claus.* p. 213a, entered later at the end of the notes of commissions and circuits made in August.

[2] *Close and Patent Rolls*, November 1227 to January 1228.

[3] Text in *Revue Historique*, vol. 176, p. 222.

[4] *Liberate Rolls*, p. 63; cf. *Patent Rolls*, p. 176, and *Close Rolls*, p. 20.

[5] He appears first in *Gray's Register*, p. 61, on presentation to Tiverington by a relation in July 1233; Nicholas de Neville is apparently the chancellor's clerk in the exchequer (*Close Rolls*, p. 263).

1 February 1228 letters of presentation for John Paulin, on the resignation of William of York, were issued.[1] Stephen, the papal chaplain, had visited England in the autumn of 1227 in connexion with the negotiations for the French treaty,[2] a visit much less noticed by the monastic annalists than when he came in 1229 as a papal tax collector ; since William writes of the visit as taking place ' last year ' he must be writing after Christmas or after 1 January but plainly before his relation received his appointment. William has not yet obtained his dispensation to hold in plurality but apparently has some hopes of enlisting Stephen's help in the matter. This is the first, and only, reference we have to his holding yet another benefice, at Hemsworth. It is noteworthy that in 1245, when William de Wenrevill, the patron of Hemsworth, died, it is William of York who obtains the wardship of his estates and heir and, in this capacity, soon afterwards presents to the living.[3] It may well be, therefore, that there were old ties of friendship or relationship between the two families and that William had once held the living or at least received a rent from it.

It is not clear what Segrave did in January, nor is there any formal postponement of the opening of the eyre at Huntingdon, but in fact this eyre did not take place until after Easter. It opened on 3 April and the full sessions seem to have lasted only a week.[4] It was, perhaps, the occasion of William's farewell visit to King's Ripton, for the jurors, in returning the living as being in the king's gift, mention him and not John Paulin as the incumbent.[5] Segrave and his fellows went on to Cambridge but William must have ridden north rapidly, for the Durham eyre had been summoned (on 30 March) to open on 16 April.[6] Two northern barons and Master Stephen de Lucy, Keeper of the See since Bishop Marsh's death in May 1226, were the other members of the commission. William's expense allowance of £10, payable by de Lucy from the issues of the See, had been granted on 11 April.[7]

VI. Ancient Correspondence, vi. no. 161

Reverentissimo domino suo domino R[adulpho] dei gracia Cicestrensi Episcopo domini Regis Cancellario suus devotus clericus W[illelmus] de Eboraco Salutem et devotam in omnibus ad obsequia voluntatem.

Noverit dominacio vestra me die mercurii in vigilia Ascenscionis [3 May 1228] a partibus Dunelm' omnibus negociis domini Regis rite peractis recessisse, ubi in adventu meo et sociorum meorum placita paucississma et pauperrima tam de corona quam alia invenimus placitanda sicut perpendere poteritis per rotulum de finibus et ammerciamentis quam vobis transmitto. Eo eciam pauciora quod ultimo anno Pontificatus domini R[icardi] Episcopi itineraverunt Justiciarii sui ad omnia

[1] *Patent Rolls*, p. 177.

[2] *Ibid.* p. 150 ; cf. *ibid.* pp. 213–15.

[3] *Excerpta e Rotulis Finium*, i. 431–2 and *Patent Rolls, 1232–47*, p. 448 ; *Gray's Register*, p. 102.

[4] Final concords were levied on the morrow of the Close of Easter (3 April) and on the quindene (10 April) and William's names appears on them all as the junior ; but the Roll (J.I. 1/341) has notes of adjournments to Huntingdon for 20 April, as well as to Cambridge for the same date.

[5] J.I. 1/341, mem. 1 ; printed in *Book of Fees*, ii. 1351.

[6] *Close Rolls*, pp. 96–7.

[7] *Liberate Rolls*, p. 76.

placita et post ejusdem decessum placitaverunt ballivi Episcopatus inquantum potuerunt omnia placita qui postea emerserunt ante adventum nostrum in partibus illis.

Cum igitur tam de itinere apud Huntind' quam de hoc itinere apud Dunelm' ultra modum tedio affectus sim vellem si dominacioni vestre placeret animum meum modicum refocillare et spiritus meos in partibus Holdirness commorando ante reditum meum ad curiam parumper recreare. Hinc est quod dominacioni vestre omni qua possum affectione supplico quatinus si placet moram meam in partibus Borialibus habere velitis excusatam et quamcitius vobis placuerit quod ad curiam redeam michi vestro si placet significetis. Prompto et parato in omnibus ad ea facienda que vestre sederint beneplacito voluntatis quia diem quem michi prefigere curaverit vestra dominacio deo dante vita comite sine essonio ubi vobis placuerit observabo.

Valeat dominus meus in eternum et ultra.

De decem marcis quas michi vestra gratia habere fecistis vobis ad quantas sufficio assurgo gratiarum actiones. Valeat dominus meus per tempora longissima.

Placeat dominacioni vestre quod ad vos veniam ad quindenam sancti Trinitatis [4 June] vel cito post. Et si opus fuerit clericum meum ad vos premittam qui vices meas usque ad terminum illum supplebit.

Cum primo intravi Episcopatum Dunelm' quasi lamentando clamaverunt pauperes quod satis excoriati et afflicti fuerunt per Magistrum S[tephanum] de Lucy custodem si ego . . .[1] venirem ad eos penitus confundendos. In recessu vero meo omnes refocillati tam maiores quam minores cum gaudio et exultacione processum nostrum in omnibus commendaverunt. De statu domini Regis et vestro me vestrum penitus si placet certificetis.

Iterum et bene et diu valeat dominacio vestra per tempora diutina.
[Shortly after 3 May 1228]

The Durham eyre, like those at Huntingdon and Carlisle, can hardly have lasted longer than ten days.[2] We should, therefore, beware of treating William's weariness too seriously and may, indeed, wonder whether he was really so hard pressed by Pateshull at Lincoln as his isolated sentence has caused many to believe. In the years ahead, when he himself headed a team of justices in eyre, he covered county after county at a rate comparable with that of Pateshull himself. As in Letters I and IV, the end of official business is a good excuse for visiting places in Yorkshire. At this date he held no ecclesiastical preferment in Holderness, that stronghold of the earls of Albemarle, but he may have had a lay fee or rents there. In the immediate future he received the Albemarle living of Easington, near Spurn Head (4 March 1230) and the Percy living of Nafferton, just outside Holderness (18 February 1232).[3] Later, about the beginning of November 1239, he obtained that perquisite of great royal

[1] One or more words illegible.

[2] This eyre may have opened later than the day on which it was summoned since of the ten final concords levied in it (C.P. 25(1), 180/6) nine are dated one month from Easter (23 April) and the other five weeks from Easter.

[3] *Gray's Register*, pp. 33, 54.

servants, the provostship of Beverley.[1] While provost he granted his brother Nicholas his manor of Esk, just north of Beverley.[2] It is possible that he already held this manor, or some interest in it, at this date, though perhaps more probable that he obtained it later.

It is a long coincidence that a visit to Holderness and Beverley prompted William Cobbett to a defence of the 'hardness and sharpness ascribed to Yorkshiremen' in language not inappropriate to William's character as revealed in these letters.[3] That William gained a reputation for 'hardness and sharpness' from some of his actions in his career as a justice is plain from Matthew Paris.[4] These three short eyres were only the prelude to that career which began when he first sat in the bench in Easter Term 1231. On the transfer to Raleigh to the court *Coram Rege* in 1234, William became, next to Robert Lexington, the senior justice of the bench and retained that position until the end of 1241. Thereafter, until he became bishop of Salisbury in December 1246, he sat *Coram Rege* and was one of the most intimate circle of royal advisers.[5]

How he was employed between 1228 and 1231 we do not at present know precisely. In addition to Easington he obtained in this period a canonry at York [6] and, though he presumably worked as a clerk in the bench, it seems likely that he was still in Neville's service and perhaps much in the north. He had no need to make an essoin on the quinzaine of Trinity 1228 for Neville, taking him at his word, conveniently appointed that day for him to hold an assize of novel disseisin: at York.[7]

[1] The precise date of this promotion may never be known, since the Patent Roll is lost; in the final concords levied in Michaelmas term 1239 he is first so styled in those dated the morrow of All Souls (3 November).

[2] Poulson, *Holderness*, i. 476–7; the charter is undated. He held the provostship until his elevation to Salisbury. On 14 July 1244, among the witnesses to the grant of a market to that extraordinary character, Lambert de Multon (Charter Roll 28 Henry III, m. 2), were: *William of Cantilupe, William of York Provost of Beverley*, a temptation to haplography to which the clerk of a 'Quo Warranto' enquiry in Edward II's reign succumbed when he copied the original charter and wrote *William of Cantilupe Provost of Beverley*. On the authority of this copy (British Museum, Harleian Charter 58/1/3), which contains other mistakes like *de Huscegros* for *de Muscegros*, A. F. Leach, in *Beverley Chapter Act Book*, ii. xxv–xxvi, introduced Cantilupe as provost for 1244-6 and went so far as to attribute the presentation to Hemsworth (above, p. 502, n. 3) to him, in spite of the testimony of all the Chancery and Exchequer Enrolments and *Gray's Register* that it was William of York who obtained the Wenrevill wardship. Leach's error has been copied by others, e.g. C. T. Clay, *Early Yorkshire Charters*, vii. 250, n. 9, and would not have gone so long undetected had the *Calendar of Charter Rolls* not misconceivedly omitted the names of witnesses.

[3] Letter of 19 April 1830 in *Rural Rides*: 'that quickness, that activity, that buoyancy of spirits, which bears them up through adverse circumstances and their consequent success in all the situations of life . . . you get to the bottom of their hearts in a minute. Everything they think soon gets to the tongue, and out it comes, heads and tails, as fast as they can pour it.'

[4] *Chronica Majora*, iv. 34, 587; v. 534, 545.

[5] He appears in the few final concords levied *Coram Rege* in this period,

[6] *Gray's Register*, p. 51, n.

[7] *Patent Rolls*, p. 216.

VI

SIR WILLIAM BONQUER
(cc. 324, 418)

It may be useful to add a little precision to Mr. J. B. Whitmore's account of Bonquer's service as an eyre commissioner in 1262-3 and as a Bench justice in 1264-5 and again in 1266. That Bonquer was called upon to serve was due largely to a number of unexpected deaths and retirements since 1255 which had considerably thinned the judicial ranks.

In January 1262 government was able to resume the eyre visitation which had been halted by political opposition in the preceding summer. There were two circuits, one of which was led by Nicholas de Turri, the only one of Bracton's former *coram rege* colleagues still serving. It was with Turri that Bonquer served. He began as the most junior of five justices in the Bedford eyre which lasted from Easter three weeks until after the morrow of the Ascension (20 April-19 May 1262) with the usual main sessions at Bedford and a subsidiary session at Dunstable, from which a civil and foreign plea roll, an amercements roll and 28 feet of fines survive. After Whitsun the same five justices held the Essex eyre, from the octave of Trinity to about St. John five weeks (11 June-29 July) with the usual main sessions at Chelmsford and a subsidiary session at Rayleigh for the liberty of Rochford, from which the remains of Turri's heavily damaged roll and 99 feet of fines survive. In these fines Bonquer now takes precedence over two of his colleagues, William de Englefield and Adam de Greynvill; though both had been prominent for more than a decade in the royal service, the former as an eyre and assize commissioner, the latter as a justice of the Jews and forest administrator. Bonquer occurs in only a few of the 19 fines made at the Rayleigh session, which took place at the very end of the eyre; his absence from this was probably caused by his impending visit to

France. The circuit was resumed after the long vacation with the Hertford eyre. The justice next in seniority to Turri, Robert de Brywes, had now left to conduct a third circuit in his own western counties so the chirographers now place Bonquer in second position. The main session of the eyre lasted from the octave of Michaelmas to the morrow of Souls (6 October-3 November) at Hertford, then at St. Albans and then again at Hertford. Afterwards there was a session at Berkhamstead, for pleas from the Honor, at which Bonquer was not present. A damaged civil and foreign plea roll and 36 feet of fines survive. Next came the Kent eyre, which ran from the octave of St. Martin to about St. Martin three weeks (18 Nov-2 Dec. 1262) when it was adjourned for Advent and Christmas, resuming on the morrow of Hilary one month (14 Jan.-10 Feb. 1263). There were the usual main sessions at Canterbury and Rochester and the special session at Tonbridge for the liberty of the lowy which on this occasion was conducted by Bonquer alone. As well as the 78 feet of fines and a main foreign pleas roll Bonquer's own roll for the eyre survives (Justices Itinerant etc. roll No. 363). It is a typical subsidiary roll of a puisne justices and contains the civil pleas for the lowy of Tonbridge, the attornies, the essoins, the foreign pleas and the civil pleas taken at Canterbury and Rochester. After Lent the circuit resumed with the Hampshire eyre, which opened on the quinzaine of Easter (15 April). The usual Winchester sessions were completed before Whitsun and the Southampton sessions began afterwards, on the morrow of Trinity (28 May) but on the same day the eyre was prorogued by letters close and the next eyre, for Wiltshire, abandoned. The troubles on the Welsh border which heralded Simon de Montfort's armed demonstration against London had begun. Nevertheless the justices had to tidy up the outstanding civil business against a possible resumption and they continued at Southampton until about the quinzaine of Trinity (10 June) and then moved to Wilton for a brief session devoted wholly to civil pleas until about the morrow of St. John (25 June). With that the eyre visitation ended, the eyres planned for the autumn and winter being abandoned. There is a foreign pleas roll for the Hampshire eyre and the Wilton sessions and 53 feet of fine survive from the former.

The Liberate roll for 46 Henry III (*ms.* 11, 3) shows that Bonquer's £20 instalment of salary for the Easter half year 1262 was payable from the issues of the Bedfordshire eyre as his Michaelmas instalment was payable from the Kent eyre. The roll for the next year is heavily damaged but no doubt he was assigned on the issues of the Hampshire eyre.

His first period of Bench service began after Lewes and was continuous from Michaelmas term 1264 to Michaelmas 1265. There are no plea rolls for any of these terms, in the first four of which Bonquer was junior to Gilbert de Preston, Nicholas de Turri and Harvey de Borham, an Essex man and former steward of Westminster abbey who seems to have been a pronounced supporter of the earl of Gloucester and the baronial side. For Michaelmas 1264 there are only seven feet of fines dated between the morrow of Souls and the quinzaine of St. Martin (3-25 November), suggesting that term opened late and that much less than normal business was done. For Hilary term there are 25 fines dated between the octave of Hilary and the octave of Candlemas (20 Jan.-9 Feb. 1265); for Easter term there are 37 fines dated as usual between the quinzaine of Easter and the morrow of the Ascension (19 April-15 May). Trinity term was cut short as the political situation deteriorated rapidly and only four fines survive, all dated on the usual opening date of the octave of Trinity (7 June). All four justices are named as present in all the foregoing feet of fines. After Evesham Nicholas de Turri left the Bench to re-establish his old court *coram rege* with his colleagues the stewards of the royal household; there was no place for Harvey de Borham; so Gilbert de Preston and Bonquer sat together for Michaelmas term 1265, the 24 fines being dated on the octave and quinzaine of Michaelmas and again from Michaelmas one month to the quinzaine of St. Martin (6-13 Oct. and 27 Oct.-25 Nov.).

During Bonquer's absence on diplomatic affairs for the first three terms of 1266 the perennial Gilbert de Preston had the assistance of the Kent and Dorset knights Walter de Bearstead and John de la Lynde. Bonquer rejoined the court for the opening of Michaelmas term; he and de la Lynde are named along with Preston in all 30 feet of fines for the term, dated between the octave of Michaelmas and the morrow of St. Andrew (6 Oct.-1 Dec.). However it is plain that the presence of Bonquer and de la Lynde during the later dates of the term is a fiction. For apart from what we know of their mission to France from the chancery enrolments Preston's plea roll for the term survives (*Curia Regis Roll* 7176) and among the business of the octave of St. Martin it carries the enrolment of a chancery order dated 4 November at Kenilworth associating the treasurer, master Thomas de Wymondham, with the Bench justices in hearing an important action between the bishop of Bath and Wells and the abbot of Glastonbury. To this is added the note that when the mandate was received only Preston and the treasurer were present in the Bench because Bonquer and de la Lynde were then busied in parts beyond the seas but their return was expected before the opening of Hilary term, so the parties were adjourned to the octave of Hilary (*m.* 33 *d.*). But Bonquer never returned to the Bench, nor did de la Lynde.

VII

HENRY DE BRACTON, CANON OF WELLS

HENRY DE BRACTON, CANON OF WELLS. The associations of Henry de Bracton, England's greatest medieval legal writer, with Devonshire and the Exeter Chapter are well known; less well known is the fact that for some twenty years he was also a Canon of Wells, holding the prebend of Whitchurch, in Binegar. The earliest evidence for Bracton's holding this preferment is a copy of a deed, in the second volume of the Wells *Liber Albus*, which can be dated as between October 1247 and February 1249.[1] By this deed, William Longespee, earl of Salisbury in all but name, granted Bracton the right to enclose a rabbit warren on the north side of his prebendal mill at Whitchurch. The witnesses show that the deed must have been made in the court *coram rege*, of which Bracton had become a justice about October 1247; for five of them are officials of this court. Two are Bracton's fellow justices, Jeremy of Caxton and Henry de la Mare; two are stewards of the royal household who also sat regularly in this court, John of Laxton and Geoffrey le Despenser; the fifth is the King's attorney, Lawrence del Brok, who since August 1247 had been responsible for prosecuting actions on the King's behalf. Before becoming justice of this court, at the same time as Bracton, Henry de la Mare had been closely associated with Longespee, acting for some years as his steward; in February 1249 he retired from the court in order to look after Longespee's affairs while the latter was preparing to go on his last crusade, on which he left in July 1249. The deed must therefore date from the seventeen months or so during which Caxton, Bracton and de la Mare were all three justices of the court *coram rege*. The only witness not connected with the court was de la Mare's kinsman, Pain de la Mare. It is possible that Bracton had but recently obtained his Canonry, perhaps about the time of his promotion to be a justice *coram rege*, for in 1247 two royal officials, William of York and Silvester de Everdon, each vacated Wells Canonries on receiving the royal confirmation of their election as Bishops; the former had been senior justice *coram rege* 1242–7. Bracton held the Canonry till his death, in the late summer of 1268. The first mention of the endowment of his *obit* as a charge on Barlynch priory estates, occurs in a deed of December 1273.[2] The *obit* was remembered until the end of Mary's reign.[3]

This Canonry explains Bracton's activity as an assize justice in Somerset. The practice of holding sessions for possessory assizes regularly at one or two towns in a county, as part of a fixed circuit, did not develop until the very end of the thirteenth century. In Bracton's days assize commissions were usually issued to justices of the central courts, household stewards or a few other royal officials for counties in which they held lay estates or ecclesiastical benefices. The justices heard the cases when their duties in the central courts or elsewhere allowed them to visit their property ; they often sat at or near their manor or benefice. So we often find Bracton sitting in the neighbourhood of Wells or Whitchurch, while from his first recorded commission in February 1248 down to October 1257, his assize commissions on the dorse of the close and patent rolls show some 131 for Somerset against some 144 for Devon and only 80 for ten other counties, which were those in the south-west or on the road to London and Lincolnshire, where he also had a benefice. In 1250 dame Agatha de Meysey endowed two chantry priests in Wells cathedral ; Bracton heads the witnesses to the deed.[4] Two recognizances of charters by dame Agatha are enrolled among the records of assizes taken by Bracton in 1250 ; one of them is said to have been made before him and others, Somerset knights and Wells clerks and citizens, some of whom also occur as witnesses to the chantry deed.[5] In the summer of 1254 we find Bracton bringing an assize of novel disseisin concerning his tenements at Wells against John de Hereford, and arranging for it to be heard by Nicholas de Turri, a Dorset man who was then his fellow justice in the court *coram rege*.[6] In the spring of 1258 he brought similar actions about his property at Whitchurch and Emborrow against Bartholomew of Emborrow, arranging for them to be heard by Robert de Brewys, then senior justice of the court of Common Pleas who held considerable estates in Somerset.[7] Bartholomew was a leading knight in the district ; once, at least, when Bracton took Somerset assizes at Shepton Mallet in August 1255, he chose Bartholomew as one of his fellows.[8] Twice during the years 1250-7 for which we have a nearly complete record of the pleas heard by Bracton on commission we find him sitting at Binegar itself, in October 1254 and April 1257.[9] All this suggests that during the two periods when Bracton was a *coram rege* justice, namely from October 1247 to about July 1251 and again from June 1253 to about July 1257, he regularly visited both his prebend and Wells. It must have been in these years that he became interested in Witham Charterhouse. In 1256 his friend and senior justice *coram rege*, Henry of Bath, had been appointed to hold an inquest on the metes and bounds of this house, but in fact it was Bracton who took the inquest, sitting at Ashwick in October 1256.[10] In November 1260 Bracton was appointed protector and defender of this royal foundation[11] and in succeeding years was occasionally commissioned to take assizes to which the house was a party. But after 1261, and especially after 1264, when he became successively Archdeacon of Barnstaple and Chancellor of Exeter, Bracton no longer took any considerable share of Somerset commissions. His last recorded commissions, three in December 1267 and one in June 1268, were for Devon and Cornwall.[12]

---

1 *H.M.C. Calendar of Wells Dean and Chapter Mss.*, i, 487.
2 *Ibid.*, i, 110.
3 *Ibid.*, ii, 10, 11, 26, 286.
4 *Ibid.*, i, 450.
5 *Somerset Pleas* (*Somerset Record Society*), ed. Chadwyck Healey, pp. 422-3, translating *Justices Itinerant Roll* [*J.I.*1], 1178 *ms.* 20, 20d. This edition of the Somerset portions of Bracton's two assize rolls needs to be used with caution so far as the dates of some sessions are concerned. The earlier roll (No. 1178) runs from about August 1250 to September 1253, with one record of a case from June 1257, but the earliest proceedings in it are on the last three membranes. It includes a membrane from Bracton's *coram rege* roll for Hilary term 1251. The later roll (No. 1182) runs from June 1254 to October 1256 for commissions, ending with a membrane from Bracton's *coram rege* roll for Hilary term 1257. The membranes of both rolls have been renumbered since Chadwyck Healey's edition.
6 *Patent Roll* 38 *Henry III*, *m.* 4d.
7 *Patent Roll* 42 *Henry III*, *m.* 11d.
8 *Somerset Pleas*, p. 444 = *J.I.* 1:1182, *m.* 7.
9 *Somerset Pleas*, pp. 426, 400 = *J.I.* 1:1182, *m.* 5d, *J.I.*1:1178, *m.* 8.
10 *Somerset Pleas*, p. 449 = *J.I.* 1:1182, *m.* 9.
11 *Calendar of Patent Rolls*, 1258-66, 125; *cf. Close Rolls*, 1259-61, 135-6, 458.
12 *Patent Roll* 52 *Henry III*, *ms.* 37d, 36d, 34d, 13d.

VIII

Adam fitz William (d. 1238)

ADAM FITZ WILLIAM was a Hertfordshire knight who, after being active in that county's affairs for well over a decade, became a justice of the Bench in Hilary term 1232. He continued to serve as a justice in the Bench or on eyre until his sudden death about the middle of May 1238; from June 1234 to about May 1236 he was also one of the two joint escheators for the counties south of Trent. A tenant, and apparently a close confidant, of Robert fitz Walter, the leader of the baronial opposition to King John; a knight of good estates who played a prominent part in his county's affairs; a justice who seems to have earned the regard of William de Raleigh, Bracton's master; an administrator who helped to found the system of escheators; one whose chief executor was a great friend of Robert Grosseteste: such a man might seem to represent the knightly class of thirteenth-century England at its best. But Adam's chief seat at Hatfield made him a close neighbour of the monks of St. Albans. Few of their knightly neighbours were beloved of that house. Moreover Matthew Paris and his immediate successor as chronicler observed a simple canon in dealing with royal justices. Those whose decisions had pleased the house received honourable obituaries. Those who had caused offence to the house, and insulted the protomartyr, had to be shown suffering for their ill deed; their deaths became the occasion for tracing the hand of the outraged protomartyr in their fate either temporal, as when they died suddenly and unprepared or miserably while travelling overseas, or eternal, as when they seemed to die full of years and honour. So Adam comes first in a group that was to include two senior justices of the court *coram rege*, William of York and Henry of Bath, and several puisne justices, notably Henry de la Mare and Roger de Whitchester. The obituary which Paris accorded Adam and his wife in the *Gesta Abbatum* merits a high place among the least charitable to come from a gall-steeped pen.[1] In the *Chronica Majora* Adam's death was merely mentioned, five years after the event, in company with that of an archdeacon, as a suitable pendant to the equally sudden though more

[1] *Gesta Abbatum*, ed. T. Walsingham (3 vols., 1867–9), i. 306–7, in *Chronica Mon. S. Albani*, ed. H. T. Riley (Rolls Ser.), iv.

dramatic death of another neighbour and enemy.[1] Foss, covering the Record Commission publications thoroughly, noticed that Adam was on the baronial side in 1215–17, mistakenly suggested that his career as a justice lasted from 1225 to 1237 and noted that in 1234–6 he was an escheator. The *Dictionary of National Biography* omitted him. The following account of his career has been confined to the main printed or readily workable unprinted sources[2] and is intended to serve only until such time as more unpublished matter appears in print or unpublished sources can be examined more exhaustively. The largest unused source is local deeds, since few of those for Essex, Herts and Kent from the first half of the thirteenth century are in print or readily accessible in collections.

Adam's family, which may have descended from Adam son of Hubert de Ryes, the Domesday Book mesne tenant of several of their Hertfordshire manors, did not acquire a toponymic surname. His grandfather was Simon fitz Adam; his father was William fitz Simon; his son was Simon fitz Adam; his grandson was John fitz Simon. Thereafter the family retained the name fitz Simon and remained of some standing in Hertfordshire until it ended with co-heirs some years before 1428.[3] The family's chief estate was a half fee in Hatfield, known from the time that the family became the fitz Simons as the manor of Symondshyde; it was held of the bishop of Ely's head manor of Hatfield.[4] But their greater interests were in fees held in Adam's day by Robert fitz Walter. Two of these were Herts fees which had passed before 1198 from the Valoynes by the marriage of Gunnora de Valoynes to Robert fitz Walter: Almshoe, in Ippolitts, near Hitchin, and Radwell, near Baldock.[5] Adam joined in making presentations to Radwell in 1219 and 1223 and in 1221 successfully defended an action for dower there.[6] From fitz Walter he held three of the castleguard fees of Dover castle: Graveley, near Stevenage, in Herts, Downe, in Shelve in Lenham, and Hartanger, in Barfreston, the last two in Kent.[7] In 1225 Trinity term Adam intervened in a darrein presentment brought in the Bench by John fitz William of Graveley against Ralph fitz

[1] *Chronica Majora*, ed. H. R. Luard (7 vols., Rolls Ser.), iv. 263.

[2] All references to unpublished material are to documents in the Public Record Office.

[3] Details of the descent are given in *V.C.H. Herts.*, iii. 26, 245. There is a fuller account in *East Herts. Arch. Soc. Trans.*, vii. 398–401; see also W. Farrer, *Honors and Knights Fees*, iii. 294–5.

[4] *V.C.H. Herts.*, iii. 106.

[5] *Ibid.*, pp. 26, 245.

[6] *Rotuli Hugonis de Welles* (Canterbury and York Soc.), i. 161, iii. 427; *Curia Regis Rolls*, iv. 32, 153.

[7] *Red Book of the Exchequer*, ed. H. Hall (3 vols., Rolls Ser.), ii. 615, 722; *Book of Fees*, ii. 664, 677. Hall misidentified Downe as Lydden and Graveley as Graveney, co. Kent. F. W. Hardman, 'Castleguard service of Dover Castle', *Archaeologia Cantiana*, xlix (1938), 96–107, usefully corrects the traditional account of the castleguard fees but is insufficiently critical of Hall's dating and place identification and fails to trace the 12th-cent. descent of the fitz William fees.

William, a minor, about the church of Graveley.[1] When the assize was taken the jurors said that Adam's grandfather, Simon fitz Adam, had presented the last parson, recently deceased, and that neither John's nor Ralph's ancestors had ever presented.[2] So Adam recovered the church and thereupon made a presentation to it.[3] In 1232 Michaelmas term he successfully defended a darrein presentment about the church of Chesfield, a chapelry of Graveley, which was brought by Robert de la Haye who held another manor there.[4] His lesser interests in Herts included rents at Waterships, in Hatfield just across the Lea valley from Symondshyde. In the 1235 Herts eyre he secured for five marks the grant of 10*s.* 10¼*d.* rent there and at Radwellhead, in Radwell, and Titburst, in Aldenham, from Robert de Cranmere and his wife.[5] In November 1236, by a conveyance with his fellow escheator Richard de la Lade, he obtained a grant of 7*s.* 2¾*d.* rent in Waterships and a further 2*s.* 1*d.* rent there and in Bygrave.[6] In Michaelmas term 1233 he was vouched to warrant in a widow's claim for dower at Harpsfield, in St. Peter's, a little south of Symondshyde.[7] In Kent he also held ¼ fee and $\frac{1}{20}$ fee and 20*s.* rent at Wateringbury, in the Medway valley, and was engaged in litigation about the latter holding in 1236.[8] He obtained the lease of a virgate at Bearsted from Leeds priory but in litigation in 1225 successfully pleaded that he had never gained seisin of it.[9] He probably held the estate at Royton, in Lenham, from St. Augustine's abbey, Canterbury, which in April 1250 was the subject of a settlement between his son Simon fitz Adam and the abbey.[10] But there is nothing to show that he interested himself much in Kent affairs, while in February 1252 the family's connexions with Kent were practically severed when Simon fitz Adam and his wife Fina surrendered to Richard de Rokele the services due to them from their tenants in Downe, Shelve, Hartanger and Wateringbury in exchange for estates in several places in Essex.[11] One of the towers of Dover castle was known as Fitzwilliam's Tower and was presumably the tower guarded by the knights of his fees;[12] but it is not clear whether the name is traditional. His Essex interests are

[1] *Curia Regis Rolls*, xii. 445, also in *Bracton's Note Book*, ed. F. W. Maitland (3 vols., 1887), ii, case 706. *V.C.H. Herts.*, iii. 90, badly garbles this case.

[2] *Curia Regis Rolls*, xii. 670.

[3] *Rotuli Hugonis de Welles*, iii. 50.

[4] *Curia Regis Rolls*, xiv. 2124, also in *Bracton's Note Book*, ii. 864.

[5] C.P. 25(1), 85/16, no. 218: this is discussed in *East Herts. Arch. Soc. Trans.*, x. 159–61.

[6] C.P. 25(1), 85/17, no. 233.

[7] K.B. 26/113, m. 11d.

[8] *Book of Fees*, ii. 683; *Close Rolls, 1234–7*, p. 352.

[9] *Curia Regis Rolls*, xi. 2046, xii. 293.

[10] *Calendar of Kent Feet of Fines to 1272* (Kent Arch. Soc., Records Branch, xv), p. 231; cf. *Black Book of St. Augustine*, ed. G. J. Turner and H. E. Salter, p. 479.

[11] *Kent Fines*, p. 409.

[12] S. P. H. Statham, *History of the Castle, Town and Port of Dover* (1899), p. 270, and plan (no. 16) facing p. 244.

less certain, and since Adam fitz William was a not uncommon name we cannot be sure of his identity in all cases. It is possible that it was he who in 1224 Trinity term was defending an action over a carucate at one of the Colnes;[1] and who in 1225 Michaelmas term appears as the tenant of an estate at Sible Hedingham.[2] When Robert fitz Walter's widow Rose was allocated dower in 1236 her portion included Adam's fee at Almshoe and another at Shelewe, which has been identified as Shellow Bowells;[3] but it is possible that his Kentish fee at Shelve was intended. In 1233 Michaelmas term Henry de Cornhill, as keeper of the lands of Robert de St. John, was litigating against William de Wiggehale for a moiety of the custody of the lands of William de Thorp.[4] In the pleadings it emerged that Adam fitz William and his (unnamed) wife had been coparceners with Robert but had released all their interests in the wardship to the defendant. It would seem from this that Adam's wife was by birth a St. John.

Adam's grandfather, Simon fitz Adam, appears among the bishop of Ely's knights in Herts in the survey of fees in 1166.[5] Since the clerk whom he presented to Graveley apparently lived until about 1224 it seems probable that he himself lived until the closing years of Henry II or the early years of Richard I. His son, William fitz Simon, appears active in county affairs as soon as legal records begin. He was among the knights serving on five Herts grand assize panels between the 1198 Herts eyre and Michaelmas term 1207;[6] in 1200 he was on the panel about Robert fitz Walter's claim to Hertford castle.[7] His Hatfield fee is among those in the list of the bishop of Ely's fee in the survey of 1210–12.[8] He presumably died between then and 1215. In the 1198 Herts eyre, like many other prominent men of the county, he had essoined of the common summons.[9] His essoiner was Adam of Hatfield, who may well have been a tenant, but it is just possible that the essoiner was his son, in which case Adam would have been born about 1175 and have been in his sixties when he died.

Matthew Paris's account of the dispute between St. Albans and Robert fitz Walter over the right to appoint the prior of Binham, co. Norfolk,[10] a dispute which began after Robert's return from the Irish expedition of 1210 and which was being litigated in the court *coram rege* between

[1] *Curia Regis Rolls*, xi. 1693.
[2] *Ibid.*, xii. 1344.
[3] *Close Rolls, 1234–7*, p. 231.
[4] K.B. 26/113, m. 23d.
[5] *Red Book*, i. 364.
[6] *Rotuli Curiae Regis* (Record Comm.), i. 158; *Curia Regis Rolls*, ii. 142, iii. 5; iii. 307, iv. 258, 288; iv. 144, 205; v. 51.
[7] *Ibid.*, i. 116.
[8] *Red Book*, ii. 525–6.
[9] *Rotuli Curiae Regis*, i. 171.
[10] *Gesta Abbatum*, i. 228.

1210 Michaelmas and 1212 Easter terms,[1] makes Adam the only one of Robert's associates who was privy to the burial of an allegedly forged charter. Paris's dates are vague but the burial seems to have taken place before the death of Abbot John on 17 July 1214 and probably when Robert fled the country at the end of 1212. Many years later, after Robert died, Adam surrendered the charter to the abbey.[2] We cannot be sure that Paris did not introduce Adam in the story at an early date merely as part of the general blackening of his memory. However, nothing is more probable than that while his father was still alive and active in local affairs, Adam should have entered the service of his family's overlord and the most powerful magnate of the district. He was presumably on the baronial side throughout the troubles. Orders issued for the confiscation of his land at Shelve in September 1215 and at Hatfield in January 1216.[3] Order for the restoration of his Kentish lands on his return to fealty issued on 9 August 1217.[4]

Thereafter he was prominent in Hertfordshire affairs. He was commissioned for three Herts assizes in the summer of 1220;[5] in Michaelmas term 1220 he was one of four knights who bore the record of a case in the Herts county court to the Bench.[6] In 1222 he was commissioned for an assize at St. Albans.[7] In March 1225 he was one of the taxation commissioners in Essex and Herts for the administration of the fifteenth.[8] Later in the year there was a limited eyre for assizes and gaol delivery throughout the country; Adam was among those commissioned to sit with the circuit justices Hale and Duket for the sessions at Chelmsford and Hertford in June.[9] Between about 24 October and 16 November 1227 the first Essex eyre since 1218 was held by Martin de Pateshull and his colleagues, with William de Raleigh among the clerks.[10] As with most counties administered by a single sheriff, Essex and Herts had four coroners between them and Adam is in the list of those sworn at the end of the eyre.[11] In this eyre he was concerned as elector or juror in seven

[1] *Curia Regis Rolls*, vi. 52, 55–6, 133–4, 273, 284.
[2] *Gesta Abbatum*, i. 230.
[3] *Rotuli Litterarum Clausarum* (Record Comm.), i. 229, 245.
[4] *Ibid.*, i. 318.
[5] *Calendar of Patent Rolls, 1216–25*, pp. 261–2.
[6] *Curia Regis Rolls*, ix. 345.
[7] *Cal. Pat. Rolls, 1216–25*, p. 344.
[8] *Ibid.*, p. 563; *Rot. Litt. Claus.*, ii. 74b, 147.
[9] *Rot. Litt. Claus.*, ii. 76b; cf. *Curia Regis Rolls*, xii, p. xiii.
[10] Justices Itinerant etc. roll 229, m. 30. In dealing with Raleigh's career as a clerk (*ante*, xxvi. 168) the writer mentioned that Raleigh was present as a clerk in the Kent eyre which immediately preceded that of Essex but said that so far no reference to clerks had been found in the Essex roll. This reference has since been discovered. It is a note that on St. Martin's day (11 Nov.) William de Ralegh' received 20 marks from Osbert Giffard de Luddesdun', being payment due for a fine made by Osbert at Westminster with his nephew; and is thus of a piece with numerous other evidences of Raleigh's presence in courts held by Martin de Pateshull.
[11] *Ibid.*, m. 18.

grand assize panels and in a grand jury of thirty-six Essex knights which enquired into the liberties of Rochford.[1] One of his fellow coroners, Simon fitz Richard, had like him served as a commissioner in the visitation of 1225 and it is possible that both had held office as coroners for some years before 1227. In 1228 Adam was commissioned for an assize at St. Albans;[2] in 1230 he was commissioned for four Herts and one Essex assize.[3]

At the beginning of Hilary term 1232 the holding of a Kent eyre had drawn away several of the regular Bench justices from Westminster and Adam was appointed as junior justice of the Bench. He is named in ten of the fourteen fines of the first return period, the octave of Hilary, covering 20–26 January, and in all those of the term thereafter. On 25 January letters close issued for the election of a new coroner for Herts in his place.[4] He was at the Bench throughout Easter term 1232. He then accompanied William de Raleigh in the latter's eyre circuit in cos. Leicester (7–20 June), Warwick (23 June–3 July) and Northampton (8 July–4 August). Along with his two other junior colleagues, Richard Duket and Ralph fitz Reynold, he was granted an expense allowance of £10 for his circuit work on 26 July.[5] In the Long vacation he was commissioned to take Essex assizes at Colchester and Chelmsford on 16 August.[6] In the autumn he resumed his service with Raleigh in the eyres for cos. Bedford (23 September–6 October) and Buckingham (6–27 October), he and Duket being granted an expense allowance for this of ten marks on 13 November.[7] The political situation created by Peter de Rivaux's coup d'état caused the eyre visitation to be abandoned at this point and Adam returned to the Bench for the remainder of Michaelmas term 1232; in November he was commissioned along with one of Martin de Pateshull's protégés, the Northants knight William de Insula, to deliver Colchester and Hertford gaols at Hertford.[8] In Hilary term 1233 Adam did not reach the Bench until some time between 27 January and 2 February, being present in eight of the ten fines of the quinzaine of Hilary and all thereafter. In the Lent vacation he and Ralph of Norwich were commissioned to take a Sussex assize at Horsham.[9] On the Monday in Low week (11 April) Raleigh and he sat for Norfolk assizes at Lynn; the record of this session is in Raleigh's plea roll for Hilary and the first period of Easter 1233 that was used by Bracton.[10] They then returned to Westminster to take part briefly in the business of Easter term before journeying to Launceston to hold the first Cornish eyre since 1201, which lasted, with the usual Whitsun adjournment, from 24 April to 31 May and attracted the attention of the chroniclers because of the

[1] Justices Itinerant etc. roll 229, ms. 2, 3, 7, 12d, 14.
[2] *Cal. Pat. Rolls, 1225–32*, p. 217.
[3] *Ibid.*, pp. 353, 368, 446.
[4] *Close Rolls, 1231–4*, p. 24.
[5] *Calendar of Liberate Rolls, 1226–40*, p. 91.
[6] *Cal. Pat. Rolls, 1225–32*, pp. 521–2.
[7] *Cal. Lib. Rolls, 1226–40*, p. 189.
[8] Patent Roll 17 Hen. III, m. 9d.
[9] *Ibid.*, m. 7d.
[10] *Ibid.*; K.B. 26/163, m. 10.

apprehension of the Cornishmen, who had no doubt come to believe that there might never be another eyre in their county.[1] He received an allowance of ten marks for this work.[2] Raleigh and he did not arrive back at Westminster until Trinity term was well under way, being present in thirteen of the fourteen fines of the quinzaine of Trinity (12–18 June) and all thereafter. With the appointment of William of St. Edmunds, Adam had now ceased to be the junior Bench justice. When grants of buck were made to the justices on 15 July 1233 Adam was granted one from the forest of Essex.[3] In the Long vacation Raleigh and he were commissioned to take Essex assizes at Colchester on 4 August.[4] On 9 September, with local knights, he was to take a Norfolk assize at Norwich and he was appointed sole justice with power to choose his colleagues for a Bucks assize at Dunstable on 6 October.[5] At this time assizes for Surrey, Kent and Essex were often heard by Bench justices on a day during term time at such places within easy distance of Westminster as Lambeth, Greenwich and Stratford Langthorne. During Michaelmas term he and William of St. Edmunds were thus commissioned to take Kent assizes at Greenwich on 10 November and Essex assizes at Stratford on 12 November.[6] He left the Bench a few days before the end of Michaelmas term, probably to take another Bucks assize at Dunstable on 25 November for which he had again been commissioned alone with power to choose his associates.[7] He was present at the Bench throughout Hilary term 1234 and with Raleigh was commissioned to take Essex assizes at Stratford on 16 February.[8] This was his last known commission with Raleigh; during the preceding two years Raleigh had been far more often associated with Adam than with any other justice. Adam also received commissions to take an Oxford assize at Oxford on 2 February along with local knights, to take Norfolk assizes and deliver the gaol at Norwich with William of St. Edmunds on 9 February and to deliver Canterbury gaol with two Kentish knights on 28 February; but whether the first two commissions, which fell within term time, were carried out on the appointed dates or at some later time in the Lent vacation is not certain.[9]

For the next two years his associate in commissions was usually William of St. Edmunds, a man who served as Bench and eyre justice on various occasions between 1232 and 1245, was a justice of the Jews between 1240 and 1244 and served on some diplomatic missions at other times. In the Lent vacation 1234 Adam and he were commissioned to visit the countess of Essex at Pleshey to hear a Bucks plea that had been brought against her.[10] In Low week 1234 they were to take assizes at Cambridge on 1 and 2 May, to take Suffolk assizes at Catteshull on 4 May and to take

[1] *Annales Monastici* (Rolls Ser.), i. 90, iii. 135.
[2] *Cal. Lib. Rolls, 1226–40*, p. 208.
[3] *Close Rolls, 1231–4*, p. 240.
[4] Patent Roll 17 Hen. III, ms. 4d, 3d.
[5] *Ibid.*, m. 3d.
[6] *Ibid.*, m. 2d.
[7] Patent Roll 18 Hen. III, m. 17d.
[8] *Ibid.*
[9] Patent Rolls 17 Hen. III, m. 2d, 18 Hen. III, m. 17d.
[10] *Close Rolls, 1231–4*, p. 550.

Herts assizes and deliver the abbot of St. Albans' gaol at St. Albans on their way back from Suffolk.[1] During Easter term the two were commissioned to take Surrey assizes at Lambeth on 14 May.[2] Meanwhile the political movements that broke the regime of Peter de Rivaux reached their climax in the Council of Gloucester, which opened on 23 May. The Bench stood adjourned for the whole of the period of Easter five weeks, covering 28 May–1 June, and probably a few days longer. But both Raleigh and Adam left Westminster before their colleagues for they are named in only ten of the fifteen fines of Easter one month, covering 21–27 May. Raleigh took his Bench plea roll with him; although that roll is lost we know from Bracton's extracts from it that it contained the record of the judgment reversing the outlawry of Hubert de Burgh's rescuers, a judgment which Raleigh delivered at Gloucester in the name of their peers on 27 May.[3] From then until some time between February and May 1239 Raleigh was to be the senior and only professional justice of the court *coram rege*, with the household stewards as his colleagues. In a list concerned with another act of the Council of Gloucester Adam appears with his Bench colleagues Robert de Lexinton, William of York and Ralph of Norwich.[4] Unlike them he did not return to Westminster for the short concluding session of Easter term.

The last days of May and the beginning of June 1234 saw a considerable number of changes made in appointments in the royal service as part of the reaction from the de Rivaux regime. Among these was the appointment on 6 June of Adam and Richard de la Lade, an official from the great Clare estates, as escheators for the counties south of the Trent.[5] The effect of the appointment was to continue the central control of escheats and wardships, introduced under Peter de Rivaux, by permanent officers alone responsible for this business. Richard de la Lade was one of those who had worked under the de Rivaux regime and seems to have been the administrative expert of the partnership. Adam seems to have been joined with him as one of the leading legal experts who was acceptable to the earls and barons. During the two years in which he was active most of the mandates which Adam received as escheator were addressed to him and Richard jointly.[6] Those addressed to Adam alone appear to have been mandates concerned with two special keeperships which he held during this time.[7] From 11 June 1234 to 11 June 1235 he was keeper of

[1] Patent Roll 18 Hen. III, m. 16d.

[2] *Ibid.*

[3] *Bracton's Note Book*, ii, case 857; *Chronica Majora*, vi. 74.

[4] K.B. 26/115B, m. 2.

[5] *Cal. Pat. Rolls, 1232–47*, p. 54.

[6] *Close Rolls, 1231–4*, pp. 463, 471, 481–3, 492, 497–8, 503, 507–9, 514, 518, 521, 529, 535–9, 579, 588; *Close Rolls, 1234–7*, 12; 17, 45; 26; 47; 56, 224; 57; 78; 80; 91; 105; 106; 114; 209; 223; 226, 230; 249 (the related entries are grouped); *Cal. Pat. Rolls, 1232–47*, pp. 62, 70, 100–1, 131–2, 134.

[7] *Close Rolls, 1231–4*, p. 580; *Close Rolls, 1234–7*, pp. 50, 58, 130, 205, 251–2, 257, 278, 406.

the honor of Rayleigh and of Hadleigh castle, co. Essex, until that former possession of Hubert de Burgh was returned to its owner; for this he received an allowance of £10.[1] When the fitz Walter lands came to the Crown's keeping on the death of Robert fitz Walter on 9 December 1235, Adam, probably because of his former position in the baron's household, was more concerned with their administration than his fellow escheator and received a special allowance for his clerk who was responsible for looking after them.[2] By contrast, Richard de la Lade received many mandates addressed to himself alone and since he had no other duties he must have been the officer principally concerned with organizing the business of the escheateries.

One episode of Adam's escheatorship is nowhere reflected in the records. On the death of Abbot William on 24 February 1235 the monks of St. Albans decided to make a composition for the right to have the custody of their abbey during the vacancy.[3] Their fine of £200 for this purpose was accepted on 3 April, half to be paid at Easter and half at Michaelmas;[4] the payments were made by the stipulated dates.[5]

The monks [writes Matthew Paris] rejoiced that they were not to be enmeshed in the nets of royal satellites. But there was a knight, Adam fitz William by name, rich but desirous of being richer, lord of Hatfield (not far from Sandridge) and then the king's escheator. In complete ignorance of the suing out [of their privilege] he came to St. Albans, dragging with him a great horde of his rustics whom, on turning out the existing officers, he proposed to put into all the abbey's bailiwicks. On arriving, mightily puffed up, he bellowed out; but on inspecting the king's letters, and assuring himself of the truth of the matter, he went away, sad and silent, like one struck by the hammer of contradiction. This we insert here so that posterity may know what misery and servitude it is to lie under the will of such satellites who, while they are reputed to be the king's faithful servants, seek their own profits by fair means and foul. For we know from what is given below how much harm of various sorts this impostor—a neighbour, well known and on familiar terms with us—tried to heap on this church.[6]

In 1234 Trinity term Adam left early, being present in only nine of the fifteen fines of Trinity three weeks, covering 9–15 July, and in none of those of Trinity one month. In Trinity week before term began, on 23 June, he was commissioned for assizes at Cambridge with local knights and was similarly commissioned to take an Essex assize at Stratford on 2 August.[7] In the autumn the fourth eyre visitation of the reign began. It lasted two years and during the first of these there were no Bench sessions at Westminster, the business normally transacted there being, as usual, conducted as foreign plea business in the eyres. Adam accompanied

[1] *Close Rolls, 1231–4*, p. 454; *Cal. Lib. Rolls, 1226–40*, p. 258.
[2] *Cal. Lib. Rolls, 1226–40*, p. 258.
[3] *Gesta Abbatum*, i. 306–7.
[4] Fine Roll 19 Hen. III, m. 10.
[5] Pipe Roll 19 Hen. III, rot. 7d.
[6] *Gesta Abbatum*, i. 306–7.
[7] Patent Roll 18 Hen. III, ms. 16d, 11d.

Thomas de Muleton and Robert de Lexinton in their eyres of Norfolk (15 September–5 November) and Suffolk (10 November–14 December 1234 and 14 January 1235). He continued under Lexinton in the eyres of Essex (14 January–9 February 1235), Herts (11–29 April), Middlesex (6–12 May), a special session at St. Albans (17–18 May), Cambridge (10–17 June) and Huntingdon (1–15 July). On 3 January 1235 he was granted a yearly salary of £20 and does not seem to have received any additional expense allowances during the circuit.[1] On 21 May he received a grant of ten oaks from Kent; this and a grant on 17 December of twenty oaks from the royal woods in the Weald are the only pieces of evidence to suggest that he resided at times at his manor of Shelve, in Lenham.[2] His own roll for the foreign pleas business only of the last four eyres survives.[3] On 16 August Lexinton and he, with the household steward Ralph fitz Nicholas, held a short session at Westminster *coram rege* for a few cases adjourned thither from their eyre circuit of the preceding summer. The record of business done is in the same roll, headed simply 'Pleas at Westminster on the morrow of the Assumption in the 19th year',[4] but a final concord from this session, preserved among the main series of *coram rege* fines for Henry III,[5] shows the presence of the king and household steward. Some criminal business had been left outstanding when the justices had left Norfolk and Suffolk; for this and for recently brought possessory assizes from these counties Adam sat at Thetford on 9 September 1235 and a few subsequent days, with three local knights as colleagues.[6] His plea roll for this session survives;[7] the main hand in it is the main hand of his foreign pleas eyre roll and some of the subsidiary hands are also common to both rolls. On 30 September he was commissioned to sit at Stratford for an Essex assize with associates of his own choosing.[8] He rejoined Lexinton at Reading on 6 October for the opening of the Berks eyre; but the fines show him present only for the first week and a single foreign plea heard then concludes the business in his circuit roll.[9] During the rest of the year we have no certain evidence of his activity. It is possible that the duties of his escheatorship claimed him.

[1] *Cal. Pat. Rolls, 1232–47*, p. 87.

[2] *Close Rolls, 1234–7*, pp. 94, 217.

[3] Justices Itinerant etc. roll 80. It is the earliest example of a foreign pleas eyre roll, since such business was not regularly accorded a separate roll until the eyre visitation of 1247–9. It lacks one or more membranes at the beginning. Because of its contents it was included by Arthur Agarde among the Bench plea rolls. From about 1835 to 1888 it was included in the *coram rege* rolls, Hen. III. It was then mistakenly moved to its present class as a Cambridgeshire roll. It contains the foreign pleas of the eyres of: Herts, ms. 1–6d; Middlesex, ms. 6d–12; Cambridge, ms. 12–19; Huntingdon, ms. 19d–23.

[4] J.I. 1/80, m. 25.

[5] C.P. 25(1), 284/18, no. 52.

[6] Patent Roll 19 Hen. III, ms. 6d, 5d.

[7] Justices Itinerant roll 1173.

[8] Patent Roll 19 Hen. III, m. 4d.

[9] J.I. 1/80, m. 24.

The Bench resumed its sessions in Michaelmas term 1235 but because of the eyres its business was small and the senior justice, Thomas de Muleton, had as colleagues two newcomers in William de Culworth and John de Kirkby. The composition of the court in Hilary term 1236 is obscure. This is one of five terms under Henry III for which fewer than seven final concords survive and, unlike the four others, the evidence of the four surviving fines is confusing and contradictory. Of the two fines of the octave, a Kent fine has the three justices of Michaelmas term only while a Gloucestershire fine adds Adam to them, after Muleton. By themselves, these two fines suggest that the court at the opening of the term was composed of the three justices who had sat in the previous term and that Adam arrived after business had begun. But the Essex fine of the morrow of Candlemas (3–8 February) has Lexinton, York, Adam and Culworth, while the Norfolk fine of the octave of Candlemas (9–15 February) has Lexinton, York, Adam and William of St. Edmunds: York was on eyre in Hampshire up to the end of the period of the octave of Candlemas and Lexinton was on eyre in Wiltshire up to the Monday after Ash Wednesday (18 February); moreover, these justices were sitting at just these periods a year later, in Hilary term 1237. Clearly there is either a mistake or an element of fiction in the two last fines. One can suggest, tentatively, no more than that the justices of Hilary term 1236 were those who had sat in Michaelmas 1235, that Adam joined them after the beginning of the term and that William of St. Edmunds may have done so also. This failure to establish the composition of the court is particularly disappointing because of a well-known case which happened then.[1] The abbot of St. Augustine's, Bristol, was due to appear in the Bench on the octave of Hilary 1236 to defend an action of *quare impedit* brought by Thomas de Berkeley. He neither appeared nor sent an attorney. The court adjudged him to be in default; in so doing it erred, since the next stage of process in such an action was a writ for attachment, to be followed, if the defendant was still contumacious, by a reattachment and then a *habeas corpus*. The abbot therefore petitioned the king. The court *coram rege* heard his complaint, apparently in Easter week; it revoked the Bench judgment after it had heard the justices declare that they had acted according to the best of their knowledge. The action itself was eventually composed by an enrolled final concord. On 12 April 1236, the day before the opening of the Easter Bench term, two mandates issued.[2] One summoned Adam to sit in the Bench; the other, addressed to Muleton and his fellows, ordered them not to give judgment in any case where they were in doubt and the matter was not plain without first obtaining the king's assent. The abbot's case and these two mandates seem to go together. Raleigh, the senior justice *coram rege* and the king's chief adviser in legal matters, must have been mainly responsible for the decisions. An error of the Bench, weakened by the absence of its most outstanding experts

[1] *Bracton's Note Book*, iii, case 1166.

[2] *Close Rolls, 1234–7*, p. 348.

on eyre, is corrected; an order is issued to prevent future mistakes of the sort; a justice for whom Raleigh had a high regard is recalled to afforce the weakened court. It is clear from the order to Adam that he cannot have been present for part, perhaps the greater part, of Hilary term. Moreover, it is just at this time, in May 1236, that the flow of mandates addressed to Adam as an escheator ceases; at the same time Culworth relinquished his shrievalty of Essex and Herts: presumably these two were to hold no other office which might interfere with their work at Westminster, at least until such time as the end of the eyre visitation brought Lexinton, York and Norwich back to the Bench.

Adam, with Muleton as his senior and Culworth and Kirkby as his juniors, was present throughout Easter and Trinity terms 1236. The hands of the surviving roll for Easter term, by their correspondence with the hands in Adam's foreign pleas and Thetford rolls of 1235, indicate that this was his roll.[1] It includes a Surrey assize taken by Muleton and him at Lambeth on 27 April.[2] Probably because it was compiled by Adam's clerks, there are several references in this roll to the notes of final concords being held by Muleton's clerk, Reynold de Risinges.[3] Such references had been common in the previous decade but this is the latest roll in which they occur in any number. The final concords of Trinity term are unusual in that twelve out of the surviving forty-four have endorsements indicating that the money due for the making of the chirographs was to be answered for by one of two clerks: Roger de Whitchester, who was to become the keeper of the Bench writs and rolls in the next decade, and William of Holbeach, who was Culworth's clerk.[4]

Save that he is absent from one of the five fines of the quinzaine of St. Martin 1236, Adam is present throughout the terms from Michaelmas 1236 to Hilary 1238. From August 1236 practically all his assize and gaol delivery commissions were carried out with Culworth as his colleague. William de Culworth was one of several Northamptonshire men who became justices during the first half of Henry III's reign. His chief estates, of fees at Culworth and Sulgrave, co. Northants, and ½ fee at Ellington, in Maidenhead, co. Berks, were held of the Pinkeny barony.[5] He also had holdings in Northants at Weedon Lois and Wappenham which in 1241 he exchanged for ½ fee at Overthorpe.[6] His Essex interests are less certainly known but he presumably held lands there before acquiring, in 1237, rents in Great Waltham, near Chelmsford, held of the earl of Essex and Hereford.[7] In April 1226 he obtained the wardship of the daughters and heirs of Brian le Ewer, with their lands in Surrey, Essex, Suffolk and Yorkshire;[8] by 1235 the two girls appear with Essex

[1] K.B. 26/116A. [2] *Ibid.*, m. 10; cf. Patent Roll 20 Hen. III, m. 10d.
[3] K.B. 26/116A, ms. 4, 4d, 7, 12d, 14d.
[4] *Archaeologia Aeliana*, 4th ser., xxxv. 105.
[5] *Book of Fees*, i. 305, 579. [6] C.P. 25(1), 173/33, no. 457.
[7] *Essex Fines 1182–1272*, ed. R. E. G. Kirk, p. 117.
[8] *Rot. Litt. Claus.*, ii. 106; *Curia Regis Rolls*, xii. 2612.

husbands.[1] On the baronial side in the troubles,[2] William became sheriff of Essex and Herts in 1224, having previously served as under-sheriff; he continued in office up to the time of Peter de Rivaux's coup d'état in July 1232. As coroner and sheriff Adam and he must have been closely associated for many years. From 6 May 1233 to 2 May 1234 Culworth was sheriff of Berks. The changes brought about by the end of de Rivaux's regime sent him back to Essex and Herts, from 29 May 1234 to 3 May 1236. Meanwhile he was promoted to be a justice of the Bench in Michaelmas term 1235. He continued to serve as a justice of the Bench and on eyre, with a salary of £20,[3] until his sudden death about 8 July 1242, towards the end of that year's Trinity term.[4] From Michaelmas 1240 onwards he was again doubling this office with a shrievalty, that of Northamptonshire. He left a widow, Phillipa, and a son, William, who was of age at his father's death and rendered his father's last account as sheriff.[5]

On 1 June 1236, during Trinity term, Adam was commissioned with Hugh Giffard, constable of the Tower, to take Essex assizes at Stratford.[6] In August he and Culworth, with local knights, were commissioned for Essex assizes at Waltham.[7] During Michaelmas term they were commissioned to take Kent assizes at Greenwich on 12 November, to take an Essex assize at Colchester on 25 November and at some convenient date to deliver Colchester gaol at Chelmsford.[8] In Hilary term 1237 they were commissioned to take an Essex assize at Stratford on 20 January.[9] In Easter term they were commissioned to take Surrey assizes at Lambeth on 3 May.[10] In Trinity term they were commissioned for Essex assizes at Stratford on 21 and 28 June and 8 July.[11] In the Long vacation they were commissioned, with local knights, for gaol deliveries at Colchester and at Nayland, co. Suffolk, in August.[12] These are the last commissions recorded for Adam: in contrast to previous years he received none for the Christmas vacation of 1237–8 nor for the Lent vacation 1238 nor any for the home counties in term time. In the Long vacation of 1237 he was also the senior taxation commissioner in Herts for the collection of the

[1] *Close Rolls, 1234–7*, p. 87.

[2] *Rot. Litt. Claus.*, i. 323b.

[3] Although the letters patent for his salary are dated 14 Nov. 1237, *Cal. Pat. Rolls, 1232–47*, p. 204, his first *liberate* issued on 8 Feb. 1237 for the whole year 20 Hen. III (1235–6), *Cal. Lib. Rolls, 1226–1240*, p. 255. Others for yearly or half-yearly payments are *ibid.*, pp. 295, 376, 437, 460, 498, and *Cal. Lib. Rolls, 1240–5*, p. 50.

[4] He was present in all fines to the octave of St. John (1–7 July) and absent from all those later.

[5] *Book of Fees*, ii. 931, 938, 943, 945, 949, 954.

[6] Patent Roll 20 Hen. III, m. 12d.

[7] *Ibid.*, m. 4d.

[8] *Ibid.*, m. 2d; Patent Roll 21 Hen. III, m. 13d.

[9] Patent Roll 21 Hen. III, m. 13d.

[10] *Ibid.*, ms. 11d, 10d.

[11] *Ibid.*, ms. 9d, 8d, 7d.

[12] *Ibid.*, ms. 7d, 5d.

thirtieth.[1] Late in 1237 or early in 1238 he fined eighty marks for the wardship and marriage of the lands and heir of the Essex knight, Robert de Tilbury; as usual with royal servants who drew a regular salary, his annual salary was offset against the Crown debt, so that by Easter 1238 £20 of this debt had been discharged.[2] He was present in all the fines of Easter term 1238 up to Easter one month and in nine of the ten from the last period of the term, the morrow of the Ascension (14–20 May). Cornwall and Devon had been left out of the eyre visitation of 1234–6. Commissions and summons for their eyres, to open on 31 May at Launceston, issued on 8 April, with Adam as next senior to William of York; about 16 May an anticipatory *liberate* issued for Adam to receive an expense allowance of £10 for his work on eyre.[3] His death must have taken place between 16 and 19 May, for on 20 May, on his decease, the Tilbury wardship was granted to John Mansel, recently king's remembrancer in the exchequer and on the threshold of his enormously successful career.[4] On 24 May, William of St. Edmunds was commissioned in Adam's place for the eyres.[5] The vacancy left in the Bench by his death was filled by the promotion of Henry of Bath at the beginning of Trinity term. The exchequer, according to its normal conservative practice, retained in the pipe rolls the debit balance of fifty marks against him for the Tilbury wardship until on 12 February 1242 his son Simon fitz Adam obtained letters cancelling it because of the grant made to Mansel immediately on his father's death.[6]

The news of Adam's death must have been received with great satisfaction by Matthew Paris, whose lapidary phrases contrived to kill two birds with one stone by taking the opportunity to remark the fallibility of that enemy of monastic privilege, Robert Grosseteste:[7]

Adam fitz William, a man of the very shrewdest sort in worldly affairs and the riches which come from them, and of the very greatest foresight in conserving what he had acquired; who because of his wisdom had been appointed a Justice of the Bench: having schemed by every means to do harm to the church of St. Alban, went to bed one night, well dined, only to die suddenly before daybreak, intestate and with his wife hardly aware of what happened. William de Culworth, his colleague, friend and fellow justice, who was a very great friend of the bishop of Lincoln, lying out of loyalty affirmed before the bishop that Adam, while yet alive, had appointed him proctor and executor of his testament. So the goods, which abounded beyond measure, were allowed to be distributed among his kin and he was held to have been testate. Moreover Adam's wife, the agent and author of his hardness of heart, being pregnant by her husband, died miserably a few days later in childbirth, with her still-born son. Furthermore, both in his despatch box and in hers there were found writs of novel

[1] *Close Rolls, 1234–7*, p. 547.
[2] Pipe Roll 22 Hen. III, rot. 11d.
[3] *Close Rolls, 1237–42*, p. 125; *Cal. Lib. Rolls, 1226–40*, p. 331.
[4] *Cal. Pat. Rolls, 1232–47*, p. 220; *Close Rolls, 1237–42*, p. 54.
[5] *Cal. Pat. Rolls, 1232–47*, p. 221.
[6] *Close Rolls, 1237–42*, p. 391.
[7] *Gesta Abbatum*, i. 329–30.

disseisin, acquired only a little before for the great harm of the church of St. Alban.

Adam was indeed contemplating litigation against the abbey, for in the winter of 1237–8 a commission issued to William de Culworth and three local knights to take at Hertford on the quinzaine of Hilary 1238 an assize of nuisance brought by Adam against the abbot about a dyke raised in Radwell and Norton to the damage of his free tenement there.[1] Apparently he hesitated, for this assize was not taken; but another commission issued to the same justices for the same matter with the altered date of the octave of Trinity: by which time he was dead, so that the commission lapsed. Adam's wife, of whose christian name we remain ignorant, was not joined with him according to the commission but it is possible that she may have been joined in a separate writ. So Paris was able to close Adam's career to the complete edification of his fellow monks, leaving to the rough notes of the *Additamenta* the fact that Adam had made at least one benefaction to the abbey, of a silk cloth.[2] One can readily understand Paris's standpoint, that of an historiographer of a great and greatly privileged, therefore highly vulnerable, religious foundation; one can appreciate the impression which the successful career of a knightly neighbour would make on such a foundation, an impression which a really substantial benefaction might have cancelled. But neither with Adam fitz William nor with many of the other royal servants of Henry III's day can one allow the impression received from such a viewpoint to stand as if it were an objective estimate of the men whom with consummate artistry Paris characterized; never without the hint, acceptable to a celibate audience, that those who were married, like Adam, Geoffrey de Childwick and Henry of Bath, had wives worse than themselves.

[1]Patent Roll 22 Hen. III, m. 11d. The second commission was entered by amending the appointed date in the first.

[2]*Chronica Majora*, vi. 390.

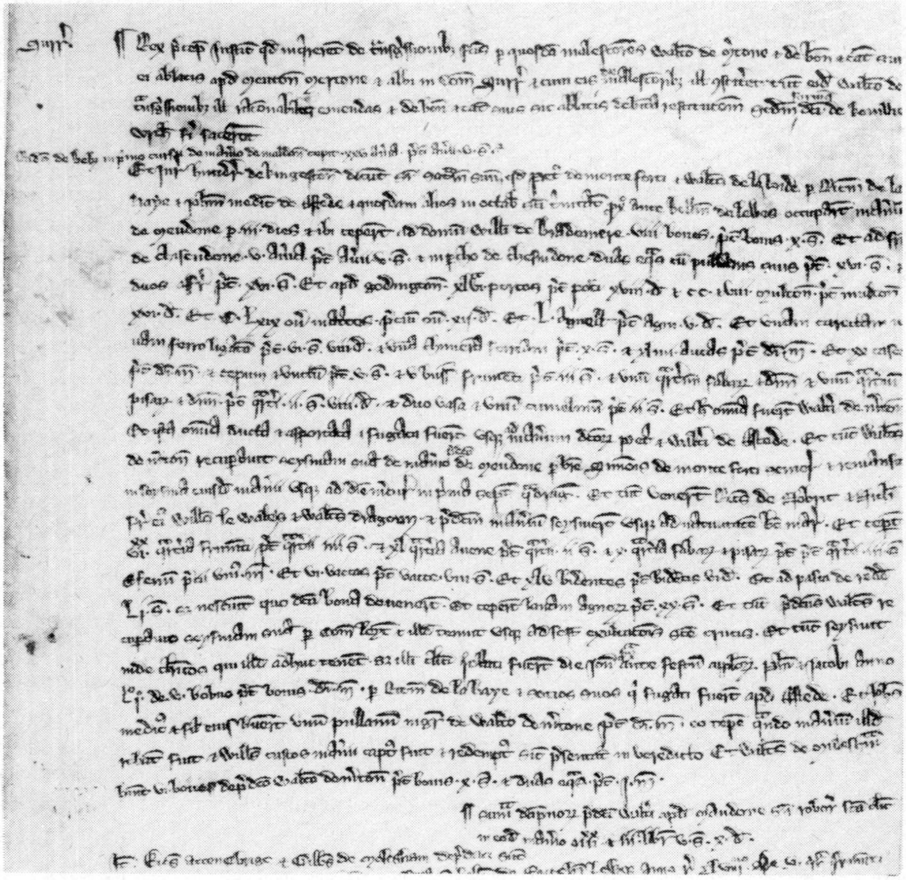

Details of the depredations suffered by Walter de Merton's manors in Kingston hundred, Surrey, in 1263, given by a jury of the hundred in 1268 before the justice appointed to inquire into trespasses committed during the Barons' War (Public Record Office, JUST 1/1207, m.5d: see pp. lxx-lxxi below).

IX

WALTER DE MERTON

Within a few years of, and probably before, 1210, a boy was born to William, a freeholder of the royal manor of Basingstoke, co. Hants, and his wife Christina. If not the only son, he was certainly the only son to survive infancy, along with his seven sisters: Agnes, Alice, Castania, Christina, Edith and two Mauds.[1] The boy was christened Walter. That he was baptized by the rector of Basing, of which Basingstoke was a chapelry, is only a possibility. Master Philip de Lucy, rector of Basing from 25 March 1204 until a date between 1231 and 1233, was a pluralist and a busy man in church and state: kinsman (perhaps nephew) of Godfrey de Lucy Bishop of Winchester, until the latter's death in September 1204; then a clerk of King John's chamber until July 1207; thereafter chiefly concerned in ecclesiastical affairs in Winchester diocese and secular affairs in Hampshire until his death in the winter of 1232-33.[2] But it is an intriguing possibility because, as we have already seen, master Philip's other livings included the church of Cuddington from a date between 1198 and 1206 until his death. It can hardly be mere coincidence that Walter, a Basingstoke boy and parishioner of a priest who held both Basing and Cuddington, should obtain Cuddington as his first living. Master Philip may have had some influence on Walter's early career. So may the members of the leading local family, the de Basings. Some of these had been among the many provincial families which sent one or more sons to establish themselves successfully in London. Basings occur in far too many of Walter's later deeds and business transactions for it not to be reasonable to infer that there were strong connexions, and perhaps kinship, between them and Walter's family. Moreover, Henry de Basing was a canon and subprior of Merton Priory and became its prior from November 1231 until December 1238. The priory held lands in the Basingstoke district and it seems that it was to the priory that Walter went for his education in the 1220s. This must have been largely completed before 1231 because 'Walter the clerk of Basingstoke' occurs as last witness (a position often filled by the writer of a deed) in a priory deed concerning Dorset lands in the closing years of the prelacy of Giles Prior (1222-31) of Merton.[3] In Easter term 1233, as we have already seen, prior Henry de Basing vindicated his title to the advowson of Cuddington against Laurence I de St. Michael. It seems that he then presented Walter to this living. In the Surrey eyre of October 1235 we find Walter, styled indifferently 'Walter de Basingstoke' and 'Walter the parson of Cuddington' bringing a novel disseisin against Laurence I de St. Michael.[4] In the Hampshire eyre of January and February 1236, Maud relict of Robert de Basing brought an action for dower against Peter de la Clythe, tenant of ½ virgate at Basingstoke, and another; the defendants vouched Walter de Basingstoke to warrant.[5] Walter, after an adjournment, warranted and then in turn vouched Christina daughter of Robert le Neuman to warrant. An adjourned date was given to Christina, by her attorney William son of Walter, and her sisters Basilia and Sehylda. But meanwhile Walter, with the style of 'Walter parson of Cuddington', composed the action by a deed in which he admitted owing Maud de Basing 30*s*. for her dower.[6] Sehylda granted a release of her interests in the estate to Walter, styled 'Walter de Basing clerk'.[7] Peter de la Clythe is known to have married Walter's sister Alice. This action suggests that the marriage had taken place in, or shortly before, 1235, and that Walter had given Peter, as Alice's marriage portion, the ½ virgate which he had recently bought from Christina. Since Walter was attending this eyre in his own interests it is not surprising to find that the Prior of Merton appointed him attorney, as 'Walter the clerk', in an action against William de Haniton about land in Basingstoke.[8] By a deed which was probably made about this time, William de Haniton granted twenty acres in Basingstoke to Richard Elfeit and his brother Nicholas Oliver. The witnesses of this deed are headed by 'Walter the parson of Cuddington and his father William'.[9] Walter's sister Castania is known to have married Richard Elfeit, probably about this time. In these years Walter, as 'Walter the clerk', witnesses deeds of Prior Henry de Basing.[10]

From all this it is reasonable to infer that Walter, as an alumnus and, when occasion arose, a legal agent of Merton Priory, had been presented to Cuddington in 1233, was soon afterwards beginning to arrange marriages for his many sisters, and until the spring of 1236 was known either simply by his christian name, or by the name of his birthplace or by the name of his living at Cuddington. He was, on occasion, to use the name of his living at least until 1239 (nos. 52, 54, 61); but by May 1238 he had assumed the surname which he was to make famous and, through his Oxford foundation, enduring. Thenceforward he was Walter de Merton.

His mother Christina died not long before May 1238. As she held some land and rents in her own right, these descended to Walter. He found that the bailiffs who had recently managed the royal manor had enhanced the rents due from the estate and obstructed the rents payable to it. He therefore secured an inquest into both these holdings and his own, which included the ½ virgate that had been the subject of litigation in 1236 and another estate, whose deed of acquisition survives.[11] As a result of the inquest his holdings were consolidated and were to be held in future at 15*s*. rent of the king in chief, that is free from the machinations of the manorial bailiffs. Walter saw to it that the inquest was enrolled on the close rolls and also obtained a royal charter confirming his tenure.[12] Young clerks unconnected with the royal court were not usually able to do such things. Walter was not styled 'king's clerk' in the inquest and there is nothing to suggest that as yet he had fee or robes in the royal household. But his career was to lie in the chancery; and owing to the peculiar circumstances of Henry III's minority, the chancery was not fully in the king's control until 28 August 1238. From 1218 it was managed by Ralph de Nevill (Bishop of Chichester, 1222-44), keeper of the seal and under chancellor from 1218, chancellor from 1226 and confirmed in office for life later. The leading men of Nevill's chancery naturally secured emoluments as royal clerks; the younger men had to serve for some years before such benefits came their way. There is, indeed, no direct evidence to show that Walter de Merton worked under Nevill. But without some such supposition it is difficult to see how Walter got his inquisition enrolled and a royal charter on favourable terms in 1238, or why men who are known to have been working under Nevill then, like Silvester de Everdon and Robert de Shottendon, should later have witnessed Walter's deeds.[13] Moreover, on 11 August 1238 Walter secured a grant from a Hampshire knight of a virgate in the fields of Basingstoke and nearby Eastrop; the first witness was 'Ralph Bishop of Chichester the king's chancellor'.[14] What is in many respects the central transaction in this cartulary helps to strengthen the belief that Walter entered the chancery under Nevill. That in marrying off his sisters Walter should choose a thriving freeholder who held lands in Cuddington and

Ewell is not surprising, nor that in buying lands for the chosen sister he should obtain one estate that was held of Merton Priory. But he bought a bigger estate which, apart from a quite shadowy connexion with Chertsey Abbey, was held of the Creon fee; and, as we have already seen, the Creon fee was held from 1227 until 1244 by Ralph de Nevill. Since one of the estates Walter bought was held of the priory with which he had such enduring connexions, it is not unreasonable to believe, in view of the evidence recounted, that the other was held of his former and still nominal departmental chief; still nominal, because although Nevill was removed from active control in 1238, he retained his right to the fees and title of chancellor, and even recovered office from May 1242 until his death early in February 1244.

The sister whom Walter was marrying off in 1239 was Agnes, who may have been the third or fourth child among the girls. We have seen that her sisters Alice and Castania seem to have been married by 1236; their husbands, Peter de la Clythe and Richard Elfeit, always in that order, witness most of Walter's Basingstoke deeds of the late 1230s. In some of Walter's deeds made within a year or two of 1240, including the main Surrey deed of his purchase of the manor of Malden, these two men are followed by Robert Edred, who is known to have married Walter's sister Edith.[15] It is therefore certain that two of the sisters were married before Agnes, and possible that a third was also; and it is probable that those who were married before her were older than she. Seven deeds in this cartulary concern Agnes's marriage to Gilbert fitz Osbert either directly (nos. 27, 56, 58, 60, 61) or indirectly (nos. 52, 54). It is true that in all these deeds she is named as Gilbert's wife, with nothing directly said about a recent marriage. But the purpose of the transactions is so obviously to provide her with a marriage portion that we can hardly err if we conclude that her marriage took place about Easter 1239. The deeds contain a number of turns of phrase, including one for introducing the witness list, that are so characteristic of Walter's early deeds that it seems likely that they were all drafted by him; they have therefore been translated in full.

The main transaction was the purchase by Walter from John Blanch of the whole of the latter's estate held from Chertsey Abbey and the Creon fee in Ewell: that is, both the land that John held in demesne and the rents and services due from tenants who held from him. Because it was a grant of all lands and tenements, neither the lands nor the rents are particularized. The final concords which were made to strengthen the conveyance (notes 58, 60) describe the demesne land as twenty acres; but, like the deed (no. 58) merely list the tenants, of whom there were ten, without giving either their rent or particulars of what they held. Later evidence shows that the tenants' holdings included a mill, houses in the village and rents due from undertenants, in addition to lands. Since Walter was buying the estates for the benefit of Agnes and her children, he arranged to take John Blanch's place in the tenurial chain above Gilbert and Agnes; if the couple were to die prematurely, leaving children, the wardship of these children, Walter's nephews or nieces, would thus pass to Walter and not to Chertsey Abbey or the holder of the Creon fee. He reserved to himself the usual nominal quit-rent of a pair of white gloves or 1*d*. at Michaelmas, while Gilbert and Agnes were to discharge the due rents and services to the superior lords. The amount of these rents is not expressed. In the early fourteenth century the rents due to Chertsey and the Creon fee were 20*s*. 8*d*. and 26*s*. 5*d*. respectively (nos. 190, 185); but these figures, especially for Chertsey, covered other later acquisitions.

The first deed in the series (no. 56) is a straightforward grant by John Blanch to Gilbert and Agnes of all his lands and their appurtenances in Ewell, for ten marks. This was witnessed by Walter and two of his friends and agents, Robert of Cirencester and Geoffrey de Basing, and four local freeholders. After it was made, the couple were presumably put in formal seisin of the land at a ceremony in Walter's rectory at Cuddington. The next deed (no. 61), which mentions this ceremony, is a covenant in which Walter is joined; by this, John promised to put the couple in full seisin of all the lands and tenants, to hand over the chief house of the estate, to emend the charter just made and to cause a final concord to be made in the king's court. Save for one Londoner, the witnesses are all local men. This deed appears to have been made between 10 April and 1 May 1239. The emended deed (no. 58) seems to have been made at the same time as the promised final concord (note 58), on 6 May or the six days following, since the deed is witnessed by three of the Bench justices as well as by Robert of Cirencester and five local men. Both deed and fine describe John's estate in greater detail, list the tenants, cover a dower portion held by John's mother and a possible future inheritance; both explain that the couple are to hold from Walter. The deed goes on to safeguard the interests of Agnes and her children by providing that, if Walter dies, these lands shall become part of their portion when Walter's estate is divided among his sisters. Subsidiary to this is John's transfer of the couple's services from himself to Walter (no. 60). This was witnessed by two of the Bench justices, along with Robert of Cirencester and two local men; it was reinforced by a final concord made on 8 July. Two other deeds about the Blanch estates appear to have been made immediately before the main conveyance (nos. 52, 54): in each case the grant is to Gilbert and Agnes, while Walter heads the list of otherwise local witnesses. The first concerns a purchase by the couple for five marks of four acres from John son of Peter Wulfin, these acres being half of an estate that had formerly been held by John's aunt, and which John had recently recovered after an action in the Wallington manor court against Reynold Young. Both John Wulfin and Reynold Young were tenants of the Blanch estate. The second deed was a confirmation to the couple by John Blanch both of this conveyance, by John Wulfin, and of the couple's possession of the ten acres that had come to Gilbert from his uncle (nos. 55, 57, 47) and for which, as we saw, Gilbert had secured a confirmation (no. 62) soon after his succession. By these deeds, John Blanch confirmed to the couple everything that Gilbert held from him before Walter bought the whole estate; taken together with the main transaction it meant that the interests of Agnes and her children in the whole of the Blanch estate had been fully safeguarded.

Since Ewell was a former demesne manor of the crown, litigation or conveyancing about lands in it by royal writ could normally only be conducted by the little writ of right close. It is true that when the Prior of Merton invoked this rule in defending an action brought by John de Horton in the 1263 Surrey eyre, he heard the jury declare that the rule had never been observed about lands in Ewell.[16] But things were different in 1239. Indeed, in the 1241 Surrey eyre the daughters of the late Osbert Cake won an action brought against them by invoking this rule, which the knights of the county court and the sheriff, as well as the jury, declared to be then observed in Ewell.[17] Walter de Merton, as a freeholder of the royal demesne manor of Basingstoke, knew all about this limiting rule. The two final concords made in the Bench in May and July do not mention the writ on which they were grounded, a fact which means that they were initiated by a writ of right patent. Both conclude by saying that a special writ had been obtained to enable the fines to be made, notwithstanding that Ewell was ancient demesne of the crown. Such writs were not easy to obtain; the fact that Walter obtained them to avoid a possible flaw in the conveyance is a further piece of evidence suggesting that he was then working in the chancery, where these writs were penned.

The lesser transaction was the purchase by Walter from William Ballard of all the latter's lands in Ewell; for this there was only one deed (no. 27). This contains the same safeguards for the inheritance of Agnes and her children should Walter die, and it describes how livery of seisin had been made to the couple in the prior's court, presumably at Ewell, by the priory cellarer, the usual monastic obedientiary to undertake such matters. The witnesses are headed by Mr. Philip de Hamme, who seems to have been the priory's Surrey steward, and include most of the priory's leading Surrey tenants, together with Walter himself and Robert of Cirencester. Here again, since the whole of Ballard's land was being conveyed, its quantity is not given. From a later rental (note 27) we know that it consisted of a yoke or virgate (thirty acres), to be held at a rent of 5*s*. 4*d*.

No consideration is given in Ballard's deed. In the first of the Blanch deeds (no. 56), Gilbert and Agnes are said to have paid John Blanch ten marks (£6 13*s*. 4*d*.) for his estate; it is likely that this comprised the sum of £3 10*s*. said to be still payable in the slightly later covenant (no. 61) and possible that it comprised the £5 said to be given in the relative final concord (note 58). In addition, Walter is said to have paid John Blanch one mark for the arrangement whereby he took John's place in the tenurial chain (note 61). Ballard's deed (no. 27) expressly says that the land was bought with Walter's money; the Blanch deeds contain no such direct statement but imply the same. Taken together with the two deeds made to tidy up the Blanch estate immediately before the hand-over (nos. 52, 54), it looks as if Walter had laid out some £15 at least over Agnes's marriage portion and its conveyancing expenses, or half as much as Gilbert had himself laid out in acquisitions since he received his uncle's lands: it may have been much more than this. If we are right in believing that Walter began work in the chancery between 1236 and 1238, these purchases, like most of his purchases in the later 1230s at Basingstoke, were made with the income he was receiving from the numerous small fees for his departmental work.

In 1240 these funds were applied to a larger, and eventually more momentous, purchase: the manor of Malden with Chessington, on the northern boundary of Cuddington and Ewell, and the manor of Farley, in the North Downs some eight miles to the south-east.[18] These manors constituted three knight's fees, part of the Watevill fee of the extensive Clare lands in eastern Surrey. In 1240 they seem to have been on the market at a bargain price because the mesne title was disputed, the manors themselves were heavily incumbered with dowers, portions and mortgages, while the tenant in chief, Richard de Clare, heir to the earldoms of Gloucester and Hertford, was (until September 1243) a minor in the king's ward and his estates were administered by Walter's colleagues in the king's service, the royal escheators. The chief mesne tenant was William de Watevill, head of the Essex branch of a family which had held in Surrey since the Conquest. He lived on his Essex manors, had leased at farm all the Surrey lands he held in demesne, was heavily indebted to the Jews and had conveyed a substantial interest in Malden to his father in law Richard fitz Simon, another prominent Essex knight, when he married Richard's daughter Gillian early in the 1230s. The title of the sitting mesne tenants was in dispute. Until the late twelfth century these tenants had been a knightly family that took its name from Malden and acquired extensive lands in several counties. On the death of Eudes de Malden the manors passed to his sister Gunnora and so to her husband Brian fitz Ralph, an Essex knight, who was on the baronial side in the troubles of 1215-17, seems to have died soon after 1218 and was succeeded in quick succession by his sons Brian and Eudes, each of whom left a widow entitled to dower in their lands. These widows were: Isabel, relict of Brian, who had by 1225 taken as a second husband the Kentish knight William de Whitfield, and had been allotted the whole of Farley as dower; and Cecily de Gravenel, relict of Eudes, who had been allotted one third of Malden with Chessington. Since the mid-1220s the title to the subordinate mesne tenancy had been in intermittent dispute among various persons claiming different degrees of kinship with Gunnora de Malden, of whom Richard de Vaubadon was successful; in 1240 this title, with the remaining two-thirds of Malden with Chessington and the services of the two dower tenants, was held by Sarah daughter of Richard de Vaubadon and her husband Roger de Bavent, a Kentish knight.[19] The contestant was Peter son of John de Cuddington. Seven others believed themselves to have some sort of potential interest. Except for the Whitfields, who resided sometimes at Farley, all those with established rights in the tenurial chain were rentiers to whom Malden was not a residence but merely a source of income. Malden's manorial economy was being run by that shrewd and ubiquitous business man Simon de Suwell, who held the manor at farm and whom we have already met with later in his career. The steps which Walter took to obtain these manors parallel, in a larger field, his shrewd conveyancing over his sister Agnes's marriage portion. As the story, which has never been clearly told, concerns the next parish to Cuddington and Ewell and many of the persons who figure in this cartulary, it may usefully be recounted here. We must also note that on 11 July 1240, at the time the major arrangements were in train, Walter was appointed along with Peter de Tany, a very distinguished Essex knight most active in affairs of his country, as commissioner to examine the state of the king's demesne lands in cos. Kent, Middlesex, Essex and Herts.[20]

Walter's initial move was to secure from William de Watevill an admission and confirmation that the manors were the right of Peter de Cuddington, to be held from William by the accustomed services, which seem to have been nominal quit-rents, and the obligation for scutage on the three fees when scutage or aids were levied. This Walter did by covenanting to pay off the £100 that William owed to the Jew Abraham son of Aaron of

London within ten years of St. Mark's day (25 April) 1240; and by agreeing to save William harmless in the suit which Sarah and Roger de Bavent were then litigating against him to establish their title.[21] Walter also agreed to pay Simon de Suwell half the expenses for the sowing he had done that spring in Malden; William and Peter were to pay the other half and Walter and Peter were to share the crops when harvested in the autumn.[22] Two deeds covered these matters. Peter de Tany heads the witnesses of the first; both were witnessed by Walter's closest friends and legal agents, Robert of Cirencester and Thomas of Windsor, whom he was later to present successively to the rectory of Malden. The second deed was made at the New Temple, that English headquarters of the great military order that provided banking and safe deposit services to princes, prelates and magnates; and which was linked with their old Holborn headquarters by the New Street, in which the lodgings established by Ralph de Nevill and many of his chancery staff were to be maintained and extended during the centuries by their successors until the Street became known as Chancery Lane. This deed is the first evidence that we have of Walter's connexions with the New Temple where, at his death in 1277, much of his vast store of personal cash and securities were in safe keeping. Walter had no difficulty in paying off the Jewish debt by instalments; on 25 April 1249 Walter and William issued their mutual acquittances to confirm the completion of the bargain.[23] On 2 October 1249 Walter celebrated this by obtaining a royal charter of freewarren in the three manors, now effectively his.[24]

The next step in 1240 was to buy out the interests of the Bavents. This Walter did by intervening in the suit in progress and composing it by a final concord made on 6 October 1240 in the Cambridgeshire eyre (the Bench was not in session in 1240-41),[25] whereby the couple admitted Peter de Cuddington's right to their own two thirds of Malden and to the reversions of the two dowers, in return for Peter's surrender of his interest in the former de Malden manor of Cocking, co. Sussex. In addition to the parties, Watevill, the Whitfields and Cecily were all present in court to sanction the agreement, while seven other persons, or their representatives, registered latent claims. Walter paid the Bavents £20 for all this, the payment, as so often with royal servants, being recorded in the *coram rege* roll, on 27 October.[26] The way was thus open for the purchase of Peter de Cuddington's now clear title. This was done by a final concord made in the Cambridgeshire eyre on 20 October,[27] and by a deed, probably made at Cuddington, a few weeks later.[28] The final concord described the consideration as £100; the deed translated this into real terms: Walter was to maintain Peter and his wife Juliana for ten years from November 1240. The deed also shows that, with characteristic shrewdness, Walter had not lost sight of Peter's abandoned title to Cocking, since it was agreed that Walter should receive this if ever Peter established his right to it. Robert of Cirencester, Thomas of Windsor and three of Walter's brothers-in-law witnessed this deed. The three brothers-in-law, with some Basingstoke men, also witnessed the release of interests in Malden and Farley to Walter that was made by Roger de Ridel', the only one of the seven other claimants whose title was sufficiently strong for Walter to bother about extinguishing it.[29]

But Peter's deed mentions that all the deeds that William de Watevill had held about the portion conveyed to his father in law Richard fitz Simon were being handed over to Walter's clerk sir R[obert of Cirencester].[30] Richard was dead, but the guardians of his infant son Simon fitz Richard proceeded to exploit his claim, which Robert of Cirencester defended as Walter's attorney between the spring of 1241 and summer of 1242.[31] Eventually the action was adjourned because of Simon's minority until the next Surrey eyre. But before then, and probably in the summer of 1246, Simon released his interests by two deeds, in return for which Walter paid off £50 of another Jewish bond, of £58, that William de Watevill had apparently contracted on the security of Simon's estate.[32] Robert of Cirencester was the only member of Walter's entourage to witness the deeds; most of the other witnesses were leading knights of Essex, but the first two were Silvester de Everdon, keeper of the seal 1244-46, and John de Gatesden. Gatesden, from small beginnings as sheriff's clerk in Surrey during 1221-6, had been a prominent king's clerk from 1231 to 1244 and had acted as keeper of Basingstoke manor in 1228-9. This release was strengthened by a final concord made on 2 June 1247.[33]

Although Walter's bargain with William de Watevill was not completed until April 1249 he was, so far as the world was concerned, the mesne lord of the manors from October 1240 onwards. With the drive to increase the number of knights from 1244 onwards he was, in June 1245, distrained as the holder of three fees or more than £20 of land in Surrey, but speedily secured exemption.[34] From about this time he was engaged in many conveyances with his tenants at Malden and Farley of the sort usual with manorial lords. He also expanded his interests into Tolworth, which divided Chessington from Malden.

About 1220 Eudes fitz Brian had alienated a considerable estate in Chessington to James de St. Clare, to hold at the usual nominal quit-rent; much of this had soon afterwards passed, apparently through the Jewry, to a Cambridgeshire clerk, Acer de la Dune.[35] Acer conveyed most of it to Isolda Russel of Chessington, with whom he had apparently lived; Walter secured control of this estate by agreement with Robert de St. Clare in a deed made 28 October 1245 or 1246.[36] This is the first of his local deeds to be witnessed by his brother-in-law Gilbert of Ewell and such local men as William Picot and William de Brademere, both of Tolworth, and Philip Young of Ewell, as well as by his friends Robert of Cirencester and Thomas of Windsor. But before Acer had conveyed the lands to Isolda he had, in the Surrey eyre of October 1235, secured a wood of six acres in Chessington in exchange for surrendering his appurtenant right to firewood and timber from the whole of the manorial woods.[37] Walter was not able to buy out Acer's right in this small wood until 1257, when he did so by a final concord dated 27 April, in which Dulcia de Malden, sister and heir of the deceased Peter de Cuddington, was joined.[38]

Walter's earliest Tolworth conveyances were made about 1248-50 with Elias de Grapelingham, who had daughters but no sons to succeed him. By these, Walter secured a house and lands, the rent from a small estate which Elias had granted to a married daughter Alice, and the reversion of a meadow which Elias had leased to Merton Priory for the term of his own life, with further rents receivable meanwhile until this reversion fell in.[39] Robert of Cirencester, now parson of Malden, heads the witnesses of all three deeds which, in addition to Walter's older associates, like Thomas of Windsor, Gilbert de Ewell and William de Brademere, include Ralph de Planaz, who had recently inherited from his brother John the former Tolworth manor, Adam Whitlock, otherwise Adam the miller, who held one of the mills in Ewell, and William Dudekin, a prosperous freeholder at Sanderstead who was to be closely associated with Walter over the next thirty years. When Elias de Grapelingham died early in 1252, Merton Priory duly surrendered its lease to Walter by a deed dated 19 May;[40] Elias's widow Alice surrendered her dower claims in the lands her late husband had granted to Walter;[41] and Ralph de Planaz, as superior lord, issued his confirmation.[42] Dudekin witnessed all three deeds and Gilbert de Ewell two. Soon afterwards, litigation in a local court was composed by a covenant between Walter on the one part and William de la Strode and his wife Maud and Odo de Tolworth and his wife Beatrice on the other. William (died about 1262) was for many years a leading burgess and often a bailiff of Kingston; Odo was the head of a cadet branch of the once knightly family; their wives were either Elias de Grapelingham's daughters or else the sisters of the husband of Elias's daughter Alice, now dead.[43] By the covenant Walter retained his possession of part of the deceased Alice's estate in return for his surrender to the four of the rest. This deed is among the latest to be witnessed by Mr. Philip de Hamme and, as it concerned Kingston burgesses, it is the first of Walter's deeds to include the leading Kingston burgesses such as John Aubyn (the borough's first coroner, 1255-63), Peter le Templer, John des Arches and Hugh del Eschaunge, all of whom served many times as borough bailiffs.

A year or so later Walter was engaged in Malden conveyances following the death, soon after June 1253, of the leading Leatherhead freeholder William de Appeldurleg, who had held rent in Malden. From William's son John, Walter secured the rent, while from William's widow Maud Walter secured a release of Maud's dower interest in the rent.[44] As usual, Dudekin, Gilbert of Ewell and John de Shawford are among the witnesses but the dower release includes two new members of Walter's entourage: Colin (otherwise Nicholas) de Thedden and William de Aketon. Nicholas is known to have married Walter's niece Alice, daughter of Walter's sister Christina and the Hampshire freeholder Thomas de Worting. William de Aketon was a Buckinghamshire man, closely associated with Thomas Tayllard who married Walter's sister Edith after the death of her first husband Robert Edred. The presence of both these men in this witness list makes it reasonably certain that these marriages had been contracted by 1255 at latest and also suggests that Alice de Worting was one of the eldest of Walter's many nephews and nieces who survived infancy.

Walter's Farley deeds, made between the late 1240s and early 1260s, were naturally witnessed chiefly by men of the Croydon and Wallington district, some of whom, like William de Pyrile and Eudes Pinget, figure in this cartulary.[45] Of Walter's entourage only Robert of Cirencester,[46] Thomas of Windsor,[47] and William Dudekin,[48] usually figure among the witnesses. The exception is a grant that Dudekin himself made to Walter of land he held in the manor, to which Gilbert de Ewell, John de Shawford and several Malden men were witnesses.[49] It is likely that this was because Dudekin took part in the management of Malden manor. Walter's relations with the Whitfields at Farley seem to have been amicable until their tenancy ended with Isabel's death not long after 1255. But his relations with Cecily de Gravenel were strained, probably because, like many dowagers, she exploited her lands ruthlessly with no regard for a future she and hers would not enjoy. Eventually Walter brought the usual action alleging waste of dower against her; this was composed by a final concord made in the court *coram rege* on 13 October 1255, whereby Walter bought Cecily's dower in return for a life pension of eight marks payable yearly at Bernesol' (unidentified) where she lived.[50] Having extinguished the last of the incumbrances that had helped to make Malden a bargain in 1240, Walter secured a confirmation from Richard de Clare, earl of Gloucester and Hertford.[51] This may also have been made in mid-October 1255 a time when, because of Henry III's devotion to St. Edward which made his feast perhaps the greatest social occasion of the year, most of the great men of the kingdom were gathered at Westminster. Walter's departmental chief, Henry de Wengham, headed the witnesses who included two of the royal household stewards, the king's secretary and one of the *coram rege* justices before whom the final concord had been made, followed by leading knights of the earl's household. In and about 1256 Walter secured an eight year lease of a meadow, and subsequently a release of it and other acres from Brian de Malden, one of his leading tenants who seems to have been the head of an illegitimate branch of the old family.[52] Most of the usual witnesses occur in the lists of these deeds including for the last time, as first witness, Mr. Philip de Hamme; and as last witness, and perhaps writer of both deeds, 'Thomas the clerk' who seems certainly to be the Thomas of Bath who emerges as Walter's principal agent in later years and succeeded his master in the archdeaconry of Bath.

This brief summary of Walter's Surrey conveyances has taken us far beyond 1240. That year also saw Walter secure a five year lease of his native manor of Basingstoke, to hold at a rental of £80, or £10 below the rent fixed before his grant.[53] It seems that it was while the manor was in his hands that he improved on a humble charitable foundation of his parents, especially of his mother, by founding, with the consent of his elderly father, a hospital there dedicated to St. John Baptist, for aged priests and poor wayfarers, on lands of his mother confirmed him in 1238.[54] Many additional grants which he secured for it seem to date from between 1240 and 1245, though in these years he also made further grants to his Hampshire kin. But for most of these years he was in the north. In 1241 Mr. Nicholas of Farnham, until 1229 a famous master in the University of Paris and thereafter a royal physician, a learned, pious and unselfseeking man, was reluctantly made bishop of Durham. Walter and Nicholas had presumably met in the king's household; but Nicholas had connexions with Merton Priory and our countryside, since he had held the priory living of Long Ditton.[55] Walter and his friend Thomas of Windsor went with Bishop Farnham to Durham, Walter to serve as the bishop's palatine chancellor and Thomas as one of the bishop's household clerks.[56] Rather more than a year before Farnham resigned his bishopric in February 1249, Walter seems to have resigned his chancellorship and returned south. But between 1247 and 1254 there is, at present, a gap in the evidences for his official career. The assumption must be that he returned to the royal chancery and served there in a senior position, because he is styled a king's clerk in his freewarren charter of 1249 and because Mr. William de Kilkenny, keeper of the seal and chancellor 1250-4, had been one of Walter's colleagues in Bishop Farnham's household. However, it is a peculiarity of surviving chancery records for most of Henry III's reign that they tell us much less about the chancery staff than do the records of the exchequer and law courts about their staffs.

From the promotion of Henry de Wengham to the chancellorship in January 1255 Walter's position as his principal lieutenant is plain, through his authorization of letters patent and close and his position in the witness lists of important royal acts. On 2 May 1255 he became a full member of the royal household with entitlement to robes;[57] from November 1255 he received those acceptable perquisites of royal service, grants of deer, firewood and building timber from royal forests, chiefly in Hampshire and Oxfordshire, but sometimes north of the Trent.[58] His more important private deeds were entered for safekeeping in the chancery rolls. One of these, entered in late October 1256, was witnessed by the *coram rege* justices Bracton and Nicholas de Turri, his old friends Thomas of Windsor and William Dudekin, John de Wyncflode, his chaplain, and several chancery clerks, including Walter de Odiham, perhaps a connexion, who was thenceforward often concerned in his transactions.[59] The deed was for a life lease of twenty acres meadow at Witford, in Mitcham, from Arnold de Wycford; and the arrangements supply a notion of Walter's then reasonable expectation of life, since they provided that if he died within thirteen years (that is, before 1269) his heirs should hold for the remainder of that term.

In 1258, at the momentous parliaments of Westminster and Oxford, the long mounting tension between king and magnates broke and the baronial reformers secured control. Wengham was continued in office at the first annual election of high officers of state in October 1258 and Walter, who had deputized for him in May, when he was ill between the two parliaments, again deputized for him in November 1258, and from July 1259 onwards when he became bishop of London. But Walter did not enjoy the same confidence among baronial leaders as Wengham had done. At the second annual elections in October 1259 he did not, as might have been expected, become chancellor; on 18 October Mr. Nicholas, archdeacon of Ely, was elected. But Mr. Nicholas accompanied Henry III on his visit to France between November 1259 and April 1260, when Henry III settled differences with Louis IX and manoeuvred against the baronial reformers. Walter, during this period, was at the head of the division of the chancery that remained in England. A well known dramatic incident shows him at Malden between Maundy Thursday and Easter 1260, just before the King's return, transacting speedily a mass of secret business.[60] When Henry III regained control in the summer of 1261, he appointed Walter as chancellor on 12 July, in another dramatic incident in which Mr. Nicholas handed the great seal to the king, who at once handed it to Walter, and Walter demonstrated his seisin of office by immediately sealing some letters with it.[61] Walter had reached the highest administrative post in the kingdom; but he had done so as the king's man in an England growing more bitterly divided. His official salary was £400, payable in half-yearly instalments, to support the costs of his department, whose staff at this time certainly included Walter de Odiham and the Suffolk clerk Thomas de Stagno (*cf.* no. 126) and possibly included the young Yorkshire clerk William de Hamelton.[62] The additional emoluments characteristic of king's clerks continued, ranging from a living in the king's gift and remission of the fine payable for a wardship to grants of timber for building at Basingstoke and one of his northern churches, bream from a royal fishpond and the right to import fifty casks of wine duty free.[63]

The kinsmen of most knights or clerks who prospered in state or church could expect to benefit from that prosperity in a rich variety of ways, depending on their age, sex, condition and the means available. Boys could enter their prosperous relation's household, or be placed by him, like girls if he were a clerk, in the household of a friend; girls who wished to enter religion could have their paths smoothed into a suitable nunnery; boys who were to become clerks could be supported at monastic schools or the university. It is likely that two of Walter's nephews were supported in this way before 1262, namely Oliver Elveit and William the eldest son of Gilbert and Agnes de Ewell. But by now Walter had many nephews growing up and he seems to have decided on a more regular arrangement for the support of those and others of his young connexions studying in the schools. On 7 May 1262 he secured from Earl Richard de Clare leave to assign his manors of Malden, Chessington and Farley to support clerks studying in the schools, according to an ordinance or provision he would make.[64] As befitted a deed concerning the chancellor and one of the greatest of the magnates, the deed was witnessed by three bishops in whose dioceses Walter held preferment, by the leading members of the courts *coram rege* and the Bench, and by the earl's household knights and clerks, including Sir Walter de Kinardesley, who was perhaps his most prominent tenant in Surrey. On 8 July Walter secured a charter transferring the hospital that he had founded at Basingstoke into the king's patronage and care.[65] Apparently, therefore, he was divesting himself of one responsibility in order to undertake another. That he made some arrangement with Merton Priory to ensure that the profits of the manors reached the priory and were applied to the support of the chosen clerks, and that there was supervision of them at the university, is probable. But the manors remained in his control as a series of events prevented any more formal arrangement. In July 1262 Earl Richard died; his son Gilbert, from whom a licence would be necessary, would not come of age until 2 September 1264. Moreover, the young Gilbert's wavering sympathies lay at this time with the baronial party.

Then, in the summer of 1263, came a sudden reversal of fortune. The return of Simon de Montfort to England revived the baronial party; the armed march of Simon and the marcher lords, young Gilbert de Clare among them, on London in the summer brought the baronial reformers to control once more. In the general displacement of the leading officers of the king's government, Walter was dismissed on 19 July and replaced by Nicholas of Ely. The armed march had been the signal for widespread attacks by baronial partisans on the property of royalists. All Walter's Surrey manors suffered heavily.[66] On 13 June men from Ashtead Manor occupied Malden and stayed there three days. They were acting under the orders of the two lords of that former de la Mare manor: Peter de Montfort the younger, who had married Henry de la Mare's daughter. and Walter de la Hyde, who had married Henry's widow. From Malden, Chessington and, especially Cuddington, they drove off or carried away to Ashtead goods valued at some £33. That most of this was taken from Cuddington suggests that perhaps Walter's agents at Malden had attempted to preserve his property by sending it thither in the hopes that, as belonging to the rector, it might escape; or it may be that much of it was out at pasture on the Sparfield, where Malden and Cuddington intercommoned. The chattels ranged from 427 sheep of various sorts, forty-six pigs, forty-four geese, eight draught oxen, two horses and foals, twenty cheeses, a quantity of wheat, beans and pease, down to kitchen and field equipment and the manorial stocks and chain. William de Brademere, who was then acting as keeper or warden of the manor, also suffered loss of personal goods. Farley was despoiled by the men of another baronial leader, Henry de Hastings, who held it from 15 July to 15 August and carried off an even larger quantity of goods, including empty wine casks and faggots of firewood, to the value of some £70. At some time between August and October, while the baronial government was in firm control, Walter recovered seisin of Malden by an order from Simon de Montfort, and of Farley by a similar order from Henry de Hastings. It is doubtful if he remained in a subordinate position at the chancery after July 1263; but from October onwards the king once more began to oust the baronial control. Walter must then have returned. In January the king went to France, for his cause and that of the barons to be arbitrated by Louis IX at Amiens. Walter went with him, to be his chief representative at the arbitration.[67] The Mise of Amiens was wholly in Henry III's favour: it must have been as a reward for his services that Walter, on 18 January 1264, secured the baronial privilege of taking a deer or two whenever he passed through the royal forests.[68] But the Mise made civil war inevitable. When the king returned in February it was to find London virtually held against him and the baronial forces concentrating in the midlands and west. What evidence there is suggests that Walter stayed in the king's train until it reached Oxford, which became the royal mobilization headquarters.[69] By March the country was in an uproar; on 12 March Malden and Farley were seized once again.[66] The occupation this time was different. Gilbert de Clare's part in 1263 had earned him control of his marcher lands, but he was still a minor, unknighted. Nevertheless he was, next to Earl Simon, the most powerful man in the kingdom: he was also Walter's overlord. Under Gilbert's orders, his Surrey steward Walter Dragoun and other officers seized both manors into their *de facto* lord's hands and remained in occupation, receiving the tenants' Easter rents and commandeering corn, hay and livestock, no doubt for provisioning the baronial forces; the lesser officers also commandeered corn and forage from Cuddington and from the parson of Farley. In all, some £42 of Walter's goods and rents were taken from Malden and Cuddington and about £9 worth from Farley. Gilbert's men held Farley until 15 August and Malden until 8 September.

Meanwhile, after their initial success at Northampton, the royalists had fought and lost Lewes. Gilbert de Clare, knighted by Earl Simon on the eve of Lewes, had assumed his earldom and was one of the two most powerful men in the kingdom. Malden and Farley had not been Walter's only estates to suffer in March 1264. The Finsbury prebendal property just outside the northern wall of London that belonged to his St. Paul's canonry had been ravaged and occupied by Londoners, especially bitter against royalists; attacks had been made on his property elsewhere within districts under baronial control.[70] But from Malden and Farley had, apparently, come funds since 1262 to support his nephews and other young connexions in the schools. The depredations since June 1263 can have left nothing available from this source. With the baronial government in victorious control Walter's career in the state seemed at an end; but there remained his career in the church, and on 6 July 1264 he availed himself of the government's order, designed to rusticate royal clerks, that ecclesiastical persons might reside and dwell safely at their benefices, by securing a protection on proposing to do this.[71] On 26 July he secured a simple protection valid until 29 September, the usual passport for travelling about the country.[72]

What he did in those weeks marked the effective beginning of England's oldest university college by the setting up of the 'House of the scholars of Merton' at Malden. Under a warden and two or three priests, the house at Malden would administer the manors of Malden and Farley to support twenty clerks studying at Oxford under the university authorities, all under the supervision of the Bishop of Winchester. The ordinance, approved by the king and Bishop of Winchester, was enrolled on the face of the charter rolls between charters dated 24 August and 12 September 1264.[73] His own deed of assignment is undated, but must have been made at the same time and probably at Cuddington.[74] It nominates for the twenty places eight of his nephews and such others up to the number as he thinks fit, and it reserves his own right to live at Malden and draw supplies from the manor when he wishes. The witnesses are local men, most of whom occur in this cartulary or have been mentioned for other reasons: William de Brademere, John de Horton, John des Arches, Philip Young, Hamo de Planaz, Brian de Malden and William de Gardino. The same men witness another deed at the same time, whereby Walter obtained leave to assign the manors from the last surviving heir of Peter de Cuddington, Maud, the daughter of Dulcia de Malden, and her husband Osbert le Blont, a prosperous freeholder of the Kingston district.[75] Save for his former patron, Nicholas de Farnham, the men for whose honour and salvation the foundation is said in the ordinance to be made are those of the tenurial chain above Walter as lord of the manors: the deceased Earl Richard de Clare, his young son Gilbert, the elderly William de Watevill and the deceased Peter of Cuddington. For, as we have seen, Earl Gilbert's men held Malden until 8 September. On 2 September the earl came of age and so *de jure* entitled to the lands and earldom he had gained *de facto* since the early spring and victory at Lewes. On 7 September he issued a charter confirming the manors to Walter; on 8 September his bailiffs handed over seisin of Malden to Walter; on 9 September the earl issued his licence for Walter to assign the manors; on 14 September, the feast of the Exaltation of the Cross, Walter put the clerks in possession of Malden.[76] The house of the scholars of Merton had been founded and among its members were three sons of Peter de la Clythe, Robert and Philip the sons of Gilbert de Ewell, a son of Richard Elfei and Walter de Portsmouth, who was to succeed his uncle as rector of Cuddington. Presumably these were the nephews whom Walter had been supporting from these manors since about 1262.

The ordinance had provided that yearly on the feast of the Exaltation of the Cross, the anniversary of the foundation, a deputation of scholars should visit Malden to examine the warden's administration. But before the 14 September 1265 came, Earl Gilbert's quarrel with Earl Simon, and his change of sides, had brought about the final and most overwhelming change of fortune at Evesham. Walter's career in secular affairs, which had seemed at an end, entered its most successful phase. Seven years, from 1265 to 1272, were divided between serving the king at his council, in his chancery and on various special commissions, and in promoting the House of Merton's scholars by buying property and building at Oxford, and acquiring property for it from friends and from luckless baronialists whose confiscated estates had been made redeemable on heavy terms that drove not a few into the Jewry. For two years, November 1272-September 1274, between the old king's death and the young king's return from crusade, he was back in office as chancellor. Three years as Bishop of Rochester followed, from his consecration in October 1274 until his death, by an accident, on 27 October 1277, when he must have been nearly seventy.

In the first flush of victory, at Winchester in October 1265, the leading royalists who had suffered in the war obtained grants of some £100 of what could now be called rebel's lands. Walter secured his grant on 28 October, to be made up from the lands of two Montfortian comrades in arms from the western outskirts of Oxford: Gilbert de Elsfield, who had been a household knight of the baronial justiciar Hugh le Despenser with whom he died at Evesham; and Robert fitz Neil, who held Iffley with many lands in cos. Bedford and Bucks.[77] As a result of this transaction the name of Fitznells became fastened, some fifty years later, to the lands of this cartulary. A prorogation of a lawsuit in which Robert fitz Neil was involved in May 1265 suggests that he may also have been in Despenser's household; certainly Robert and Gilbert together secured a year's protection on 1 June 1265.[78] Some of the inquests on rebel's lands in the autumn of 1265 speak of Robert being also killed at Evesham; in January 1266 a clerk began entering on the close rolls a covenant between Walter and Grace who was the wife of Robert fitz Neil, but he broke off after the opening lines.[79] This makes it possible that Robert still lived, perhaps wounded, in some baronial garrison or religious house. A day after his protection expired, on 2 June 1266, a safe conduct until 8 July was issued for Robert.[80] But by 15 September he had certainly died, since his widow Grace then secured a year's protection.[81] Hugh le Despenser had been Walter's colleague as justiciar in 1260-1; he was also the son-in-law of the royalist hero Philip Basset, who had been justiciar in the government of July 1261-July 1263. It is possible that Walter's acquisition of these men's lands may stem from these connexions.

Like many of the leading young men of Surrey, Lawrence II de St. Michael had been on the baronial side. One of Earl Warenne's leading knights, John de Walton, who was also Surrey commissioner for rebels' lands, crossed the downs to seize Cuddington soon after Evesham. Walter intervened to make Lawrence's peace with the king so that Cuddington was restored to him, seemingly without a stiff redemption.[82]

The first manor that Walter obtained for his foundation after the war was only an hour's ride from Malden. The manor of Thorncroft in Leatherhead had been held of the Clare honor by the baronial Montfichets since the early twelfth century.[83] Its tenancy was granted to the Wiltshire knight

John de Chereburgh soon after he came of age in 1198[84] Old John—he did not die until 1269—was now living in retirement, after being active in the affairs of his counties until the 1250s and in Copthorne hundred matters until the 1230s; and after being out with the barons against King John and, in 1233 out with the Bassets, as one of their household, against Henry III. Some time after 1258 he had conveyed Thorncroft to Philip Basset and his wife Ela Countess of Warwick, reserving a rent of £20 payable to his agent at Newark Priory.[85] By a deed dated 3 November 1266, fortified by a final concord on 27 January 1267, Philip and Ela granted Walter for life all they held of John de Chereburgh's gift at Leatherhead, subject to the £20 rent, with reversion to the House of Merton's Scholars at Malden.[86] Most of the witnesses were Basset household knights but the last three were members of Walter's household, including Roger Tayllard and, for the first time, Richard de Brademere, the son of William de Brademere who may have died that summer.

That spring a last alarm came to these parts when Earl Gilbert de Clare made his demonstration of force at London in order to get better terms for the defeated baronialists, who for half the war had been his companions. The manors now under the control of Merton's House came to no harm from his men. But the Ashtead men, no doubt rankling under the defeat of their lord and of Earl Warenne's seizure of the manor after Evesham, repeated on 28 April 1267 their foray of 1263. It was on a much lesser scale, for they only drove off from Malden to Ashtead some of the clerks' oxen and horses, along with the manorial serjeant whom they held to ransom.

Earl Gilbert's move was successful; the disinherited secured better terms and a special eyre was arranged to deal with all matters concerned with lands seized and trespasses committed during the troubles. On 20 January 1268 the Surrey sessions of this eyre opened at Bermondsey and there, from 3 February onwards, Walter's case against those who had despoiled his lands in 1263 and 1264 was heard, opening with the detailed statement of the damages from which we have already drawn.[87] Since the Earl of Gloucester and his men had earned a general pardon for their acts it was difficult to bring those concerned in the seizures of 1264 into court, though in October 1268 Dragoun reached a settlement whereby he was to pay Walter twenty marks.[88] Process continued against the many other defendants, in some cases taking the actions into the court *coram rege,* where on 6 July Walter appointed Mr. Peter de Abingdon, warden of Merton's House, as his attorney in these actions, while on 8 July he issued his second charter to his house.[89] By this he confirmed them in possession of Malden and Farley, notwithstanding that the original grant had been made in wartime, as well of the newly acquired Thorncroft and lands at Gamlingay, co. Cambridge. Richard de Brademere was among the witnesses; along with the brothers Roger and Thomas Tayllard, Nicholas de Thedden, William Dudekin and, to a lesser extent, William de Aketon, Richard figures in most of the many charters which Walter made to his house in the next few years.[90] The Tayllards and Thedden are specifically mentioned as valets, or lay members, of Walter's household in 1269; but Dudekin and Brademere are mentioned in another matter in 1272 which suggests that they held a similar position.[91]

Two of Walter's own deeds from these last years are in our cartulary (nos. 71, 120). The first, a spinster's release of a life corn rent, supposes an earlier deed whereby Walter acquired the rent; the other is Walter's last gift to his church of Cuddington. The only reason which can be suggested for their presence in the eventual Fitznells archives is that they came into the possession of Mr. William de Ewell among others of his uncle's muniments while he was acting as executor. It was in March 1275 while staying at Merton Priory that Walter drew up his last testament.[92] Mr. William was appointed senior executor; William Dudekin was the only layman among the six others, and he was left 100 marks, among the bequests to rank highest for payment. Bequests to friends and members of his household who occur in the present cartulary included 40*s*. to Richard de Brademere, £5 to John de Shawford and his wife, forty marks to Roger Tayllard, thirty marks to Nicholas de Thedden, his wife and boys, 40*s*. to William de Aketon, and a silver cup and dishes to Walter de Odiham. Though he retained many of his livings after his consecration as Bishop of Rochester, because of the rather small income from the episcopal revenues, he seems to have resigned Cuddington, for his nephew Walter de Portsmouth witnessed one of his deeds as rector in January 1277. To the poor of this parish he left twenty marks.

Walter was active until the end. In the autumn of 1277 he made a last visit to Durham; soon after his return, or perhaps while returning to the south, he was thrown from his horse in crossing a river. The shock and exposure seem to have brought on his last illness, but on 26 October he was still able to add a short codicil to his will, to which he added brief verbal instructions on the following day, when he died. He was buried in his cathedral church at Rochester.

Acknowledgements

The document reproduced on the dust cover is Public Record Office, Curia Regis Rolls (KB26) 104, m.8d. Both that and the plate accompanying article IX are crown copyright material and are reproduced by permission of the Controller of Her Majesty's Stationery Office.

Notes to Walter of Merton (IX lviii-lxxv)

1 E. Hobhouse, *A Sketch of the Life of Walter de Merton* (1859), app. iii (from Merton College Record 1827 A).

2 W. D. Macray, *Calendar of the Charters . . . relating to Selborne and its Priory . . . in . . . Magdalen College Oxford* (Hampshire Record Society, 1894), 2, 14; F. J. Baigent and J. E. Millard, *History of Basingstoke in the County of Southampton* (1889), 651-3; A. W. Goodman, *Chartulary of Winchester Cathedral*, 12, 73, 329; *Rotuli Litterarum Clausarum*, I, 21b-108b, *passim*; *Rotuli Litterarum Patentium*, 51-74b, *passim*; *Close Rolls, 1227-31*, 340.

3 Merton Cartulary, f. 117 (95).

4 *The 1235 Surrey Eyre*, nos. 61, 190 (J.I. 1/864, mm. 2, 7).

5 J.I. 1/775, m. 1d.

6 *Ibid.*, m. 10d.

7 Baigent and Millard, *Basingstoke*, 594 (no. 4), calendaring Merton College Record 1771.

8 J.I. 1/775, m. 6d.

9 Baigent and Millard, *Basingstoke*, 596 (no. 10), calendaring Merton College Record 1748.

10 Merton Cartulary, f. 119 (97).

11 Baigent and Millard, *Basingstoke*, 595(6) and *cf.* C.P. 25(1), 203/7, no. 10.

12 *Close Rolls, 1237-42*, 131-2, undated but soon after last previous entry of 21 May 1238; the latter part of the charter roll of 22 Henry III is now damaged and the charter is lost, but the Hampshire account in the pipe roll refers to it, E. 372/82, rot. 12d.

13 Baigent and Millard, *Basingstoke*, 595 (no. 6) and Merton College Records, 1097, 1099.

14 Baigent and Millard, *Basingstoke*, 595 (no. 8), calendaring Merton College Record 1754.

15 Baigent and Millard, *Basingstoke*, 594 et seq. (nos. 5, 6, 8-13, 16, 30, 31), all from Merton College Records.

16 J.I. 1/874, m. 1.

17 J.I. 1/867, m. 4.

Walter de Merton (contd.)

18 The most recent accounts of this transaction are in *V.C.H. Surrey*, III, 523-4 and IV, 282, and K. N. Ross, *History of Malden*, 8-12; they have many errors and omissions.

19 Some account of the family is given by L. F. Salzman in *Sussex Arch. Coll.*, 63-6; but his sketch pedigree errs over the last generation and was made in ignorance of Richard de Vabadun's successful claim, on which *cf. Curia Regis Rolls*, XII, 930, 1175, 1998; XIV, 1548; *Bracton's Note Book*, ed. F. W. Maitland, 1077; C.P. 25(1), 283/11, no. 156.

20 *Close Rolls, 1237-42*, 220.

21 Merton College Record 927 (and Liber Ruber, f. 1).

22 Merton College Record 928.

23 Merton College Record 1092.

24 *Cal. Charter Rolls, 1227-57*, 345.

25 C.P. 25(1), 283/11, no. 163 (and Liber Ruber, f. 1d), calendared in *Sussex Record Society*, II, no. 357.

26 K.B. 26/121, m. 6.

27 Merton College Record 899 (Liber Ruber, f. 5d).

28 Merton College Record 929 (Liber Ruber, f. 1d).

29 Merton College Record 1093 (Liber Ruber, f. 2, where there is also a letter, the original of which is now lost, showing that Walter had obtained the bond of a debt of 12*s*. due from Roger, which was cancelled by this conveyance). Roger seems to have been a tenant of the Colevills at Carshalton: *Curia Regis Rolls*, XIV, 1561, 1592; *The 1235 Surrey Eyre*, nos. 25, 226, 307.

30 Merton College Records, 920-6. If Gillian bore William no children, Richard was to enjoy a life tenancy, but if Gillian bore William children then Richard was to be only tenant at will; there was expressly no warranty, and Richard was to lease back the lands as Gillian's marriage portion. This arrangement was clearly designed to defeat creditors and ensure the lands to Gillian.

31 J.I. 1/867, ms. 1, 13d; K.B. 26/123, ms. 19, 22; K.B. 26/124, m. 27.

32 Merton College Records, 1097 and 1099 (Jewish starr attached and a translation of it made by Thomas Bodley, 30 Aug. 1574).

33 C.P. 25(1), 226/12, no. 34 and Merton College Record 1098 (Lib. Rub., f. 2).

34 *Close Rolls, 1242-7*, 355.

35 Merton College Records, 944, 940 (Liber Ruber, ff. 4, 4d).

36 Merton College Record 939 (Liber Ruber, f. 3d).

37 C.P. 25(1), 225/9, no. 21; *cf.* K.B. 26/114, m. 6.

38 C.P. 25(1), 226/16, no. 5 and Merton College Record 941 (Liber Ruber, f. 4); *cf.* J.I. 1/872, ms. 2d, 12d.

39 Merton College Records, 930-2 (Liber Ruber, ff. 2d-3).

40 Merton College Record 942 (Liber Ruber, f. 3).

41 Merton College Record 934 (Liber Ruber, f. 3); cf. K.B. 26/147B, m. 17d.

42 Merton College Records, 935, 936 (Liber Ruber, f. 3).

43 Merton College Record 937 (Liber Ruber, f. 4d).

44 Merton College Records, 1101, 1094, 1103 (Liber Ruber, ff. 2d, 2).

45 Merton College Records, 584-8, 591 (Liber Ruber, ff. 7, 7d).

46 In 591.

47 In 588, 591.

48 In 584-5, 588, 591.

49 Merton College Record 586.

50 J.I. 1/872, m. 11; C.P. 25(1), 284/19, no. 123.

51 Merton College Record 907 (Liber Ruber; f. 5).

52 Merton College Records, 1102, 1100 (Liber Ruber, f. 2d); abstracts in Ross, *Malden*, 10-11.

53 E. 371/7, m. 6, /8A, m. 4; E. 372/85, rot. 7d.

54 Baigent and Millard, *Basingstoke*, 42-5 and 602 (no. 4).

55 Merton Cartulary, f. 125 (103), in Heales, *Merton*, app. LXVI, at p. xl.

56 For Walter: D.L. 136/3/46; *Finchale Priory Deeds* (Surtees Society, VI), 108-9; Durham Priory Deeds, 2.1. Pont. nos. 13, 17; Durham Priory Register 1 (part 2), f. 8; Durham Almoner's Deeds, 6.5. Elemos. 2. For Thomas, deed 2.1. Pont. no. 17, register 1 (part 2), f. 8, and Cartuarium Vetus, ff. 166v, 175v. Except the

Walter de Merton (contd.)

first, at the Public Record Office, the documents are all at the Prior's Kitchen, Durham.

57 *Close Rolls, 1254-6*, 74.
58 *Ibid.*, 242, 277, 291-2; *Close Rolls, 1256-9*, 88, 259, 347; *Close Rolls, 1259-61*, 93, 301.
59 *Cal. Patent Rolls, 1247-58*, 527.
60 *Close Rolls, 1259-61*, 157-9.
61 *Cal. Patent Rolls, 1258-66*, 165.
62 *Cal. Patent Rolls, 1247-58*, 527; *Close Rolls, 1256-9*, 276; *1261-4*, 299, 329; *1264-8*, 13, 101, 301.
63 *Cal. Patent Rolls, 1258-66*, 194, 217; *Close Rolls, 1261-64*, 32, 40, 49, 50, 80.
64 Original now lost, but printed by J. Kilner, *Account of Pythagoras's School at Cambridge*, 51, and thence more accessibly in P.S. Allen and H. W. Garrod, *Merton Muniments*, 8.
65 *Cal. Charter Rolls, 1257-1300*, 44.
66 J.I. 1/1207, m. 5d.
67 *Cal. Patent Rolls, 1258-66*, 377.
68 *Ibid.*, 377.
69 *Ibid.*, 308, 383; *Close Rolls, 1261-4*, 342.
70 J.I. 1/1207, m. 9d; *Cal. Patent Rolls, 1258-66*, 461; *Close Rolls, 1261-4*, 402.
71 *Cal. Patent Rolls, 1258-66*, 331.
72 *Ibid.*, 328.
73 *Cal. Charter Rolls, 1257-1300*, 49.
74 Merton College Record 902 (Liber Ruber, f. 5), in Hobhouse, *Walter de Merton*, 14-15.
75 Merton College Record 1096 (Liber Ruber, f. 2).
76 Merton College Records, 597, 909 (Liber Ruber, f. 5); J.I. 1/1207, m. 5d.
77 *Cal. Charter Rolls, 1257-1300*, 58; C. 55/3, m. 2; *Cal. Patent Rolls, 1258-66*, 310, 352, 467; *Cal. Inquisitions Misc.*, I, no. 625.
78 *Cal. Patent Rolls, 1258-66*, 428.
79 *Cal. Inquisitions Misc.*, I, nos. 292, 633; no. 333 says merely 'killed in battle'. *Close Rolls, 1264-8*, 238.
80 *Cal. Patent Rolls, 1258-66*, 428.
81 *Ibid.*, 601.
82 J.I. 1/1207, m. 3d.
83 Merton College Records, 633, 634; *Book of Fees*, II, 684; *V.C.H. Wilts*, VII, 99.
84 Merton College Record 634; *V.C.H. Wilts*, VII, 99.
85 E. 40/4586.
86 Merton College Records, 646-8; C.P. 25(1), 283/16, no. 427.
87 J.I. 1/1207, m. 5d; *cf.* ms. 10, 11, 11d.
88 *Ibid.*, m. 11. But this £20 was still unpaid in 1271: E. 13/1F, m. 3d.
89 K.B. 26/185, m. 22.
90 E.g. Merton College Records, 186, 646, 1307.
91 *Close Rolls, 1268-72*, 166, 527.
92 J. Kilner *Pythagoras's School*, 82-6; J.R.L. Highfield, *Early Rolls of Merton College*, 79-84.

X

Robert of Nottingham, Justice of the Bench, 1244–6[1]

ROBERT OF NOTTINGHAM is perhaps the most obscure of all the men who served Henry III as justices of the Bench; certainly he is the most obscure of those who were senior justices of that court. Foss could only repeat on his official career what Dugdale had discovered two centuries before—that he was a justice in 1245—while he had to admit that he could find nothing at all about his personal history. The *Dictionary of National Biography* omits him. The outlines of his career are simple. Robert de Lexington, the eldest of five distinguished brothers from a knightly family in Nottinghamshire, was for a quarter of a century a Bench justice. For at least fifteen of these years Robert of Nottingham was Lexington's clerk. Immediately on his master's retirement, towards the end of Michaelmas term 1244, Robert of Nottingham was promoted to be a justice himself, and with seniority over several men who had become justices while he was still a clerk. In the following year, during the temporary absence of his two seniors on eyre, he was himself senior justice of the Bench for 1245 Easter and Trinity terms. At the end of 1246 Easter term he left the Bench: the evidence suggests that this was through retirement rather than death and that he may have lived until the twelve-fifties. To some extent the obscurity of his career is due to lack of sources. Fewer Bench and eyre rolls survive from the twelve-thirties than from any other decade under Henry III; there are no complete rolls from the fifteen eyres of Lexington's circuit of 1234–6 and no rolls at all from the seventeen eyres of Lexington's circuit of 1239–41. Thoroton's *History of Nottinghamshire* is very inadequate for the first half of the thirteenth century; few of the county's deeds are in print. The justification for assembling the meagre facts so far known about Robert's career, from the main published and readily workable unpublished records, is simply in order to furnish the salient details of his career for other workers on the thirteenth century who may come across references to him.

The earliest reference to Robert shows him at work in the Bench in Easter term 1229, when he was attorney to receive a fine.[2] A private deed of Robert de Lexington is enrolled in the surviving plea roll for Trinity term 1230; Robert of Nottingham is last but one of the witnesses, who included several of the Bench justices.[3] In the summer of 1231 Lexington was next senior to Stephen de Segrave among the justices who held the

[1] All documents referred to in the notes are in the Public Record Office and are cited by their class reference or call number.

[2] *Curia Regis Rolls*, xiii. 2166.

[3] *Ibid.*, xiv. 103.

Yorkshire eyre, about 8 June–20 July. In several places in the Crown pleas roll of the eyre Lexington appears as receiving the goods declared deodand or their moneysworth. On four occasions Robert of Nottingham also receives deodands, once on Lexington's behalf.[1] Roger de Thurkelby, his fellow clerk who is first found in the Bench in Michaelmas 1230, was also with the justices and is mentioned as receiving deodands also on four occasions, on two of which he handed them over to Lexington.[2] In the foreign pleas roll kept for the puisne justice Adam fitz William in Lexington's eyre circuit in the summer of 1235, in a case adjourned to the autumn from the Huntingdon eyre, held about 1–15 July, Robert of Nottingham was given custody of a chirograph.[3] In the deed of a conveyance effected by Stephen de Segrave in Lexington's Worcester eyre of 1241, held about 8–21 April, 'Robert de Notingham, Clerk to R[obert] de Lexinton' occurs seventh among ten witnesses, at whose head are the eyre justices.[4] Towards the end of Trinity term 1243 two cases were adjourned to be heard before Lexington in the long vacation, at Nottingham on Tuesday after St. James (28 July) and at Lincoln on Tuesday after St. Peter's Chains (4 August); in each case the writ was meanwhile entrusted to Robert of Nottingham.[5]

These references are, of course, very much fewer than those we possess for William de Raleigh and William of York during their careers as clerks but they are about the same as those which we possess for Robert's younger contemporaries Thurkelby and Roger de Whitchester and more than we possess for Bracton and Nicholas de Turri, four men who also became justices after service as clerks. They are enough for us to be reasonably certain that Robert of Nottingham began his work as a clerk in, or perhaps a little before, 1229; and that he was the personal clerk of Lexington (as Raleigh was the personal clerk of Martin de Pateshull) and not a clerk appointed by the chancellor for service in the Bench (like William of York or, in the later stages of his career, Roger de Whitchester).

The date of Lexington's retirement from the Bench can be fixed with precision. In Michaelmas term 1244 he was present as senior justice with Thurkelby, Jollan de Nevill, Gilbert de Preston and John de Cobham as his colleagues in all the fines up to those of the morrow of All Souls and in three of the four of the morrow of St. Martin, covering the period 12–17 November. In the other fine of this date and in all those of the octave of St. Martin, Robert of Nottingham appears instead, after Preston and before Cobham. This immediate promotion of a justice's clerk on his master's retirement had happened once before, when Raleigh similarly succeeded Pateshull in 1229.

Moreover, like Raleigh, Robert of Nottingham was rapidly given seniority.

[1] J[ustices] I[tinerant] etc. roll 1042, ms. 8, 8d.

[2] *Ibid.*, ms. 5, 13d.

[3] J. I. etc. roll 80, m. 22.

[4] *Descriptive Catalogue of the Charters in the possession of Lord Fitzhardinge at Berkeley Castle*, ed. I. H. Jeayes (Bristol, 1892), no. 271.

[5] K. B. 26/130, ms. 18d, 25.

For the remainder of Michaelmas term 1244 Thurkelby acted as senior justice but this was only a temporary measure. After nearly two decades of administrative service, as bailiff, deputy-sheriff and sheriff, Henry of Bath had in Trinity term 1238 been promoted to the vacancy left in the Bench by the sudden death of Adam fitz William. He served continuously at the Bench and on eyre until the summer of 1241, when he undertook a mission to Ireland. On his return he sat as a junior justice of the court *coram rege* during the winter of 1241–2. Among a number of key appointments made before Henry III left on his expedition to Poitou and Gascony in May 1242, Henry of Bath was made sheriff of Yorkshire. He retained this office until 1248 but from 1245 exercised it through deputies, for in Hilary term 1245 he was recalled to the Bench as senior justice. Thurkelby, whose effective promotion as a justice ranked from the Norfolk eyre of January 1240, was next in seniority to Bath; but in Hilary term 1244 Robert of Nottingham was accorded precedence over Nevill, Preston and Cobham whose promotions had been made respectively in April 1241 (the Worcester eyre), January 1240 (the Norfolk eyre) and April 1244 (Easter term).

In the summer of 1245 two interim eyre circuits were held and, as usual, the senior justices presided over these. Bath with Nevill and others held the Norfolk and Suffolk eyres between late April and late July.[1] Thurkelby and Preston held the Lincoln eyre (24 April–25 June and 23–29 July) and the eyre at Nottingham (30 June–20 July) which at this time served both Nottinghamshire and Derbyshire. Also assistant to Thurkelby in this circuit was Bracton. It was the only occasion on which Bracton served as an eyre justice. It gave him the opportunity to recover for his recently acquired church of Gosberton, co. Lincoln, some land which his predecessor, Gilbert de Treylly, had converted into a lay fee and alienated.[2] This episode he recalled when, in discussing changes in donor's intentions in the *De Legibus*, he cited, somewhat acidly, the case of 'a certain church in Holland' where the terms of a gift had been altered from 'to the parson and his successors' to 'to the parson and his heirs'.[3]

In the absence of Bath and Thurkelby, Robert of Nottingham became the senior Bench justice for Easter and Trinity terms 1245. Since Cobham was the only other justice left at Westminster, and the Bench usually needed three or four justices, two former justices were recalled. William of St. Edmunds, whom the chirographers treated as the senior of the two, had begun his career as a protégé of Stephen de Segrave, had served as a Bench and eyre justice for most of the time between September 1232 and November 1236, had been a justice of the Jews between 1240 and 1244, had served on diplomatic missions at other times and had undertaken a normal share of

[1] The files of the feet of fines of these eyres are lost. A single chirograph from a monastic archive has been included in the regular series of feet: C.P. 25 (1), 213/18, no. 38. A few copies of chirographs occur in monastic cartularies.

[2] J. I. etc. roll 482, ms. 14d, 34.

[3] Bracton, *De Legibus Angliae*, ed. G. E. Woodbine, i. 105 (fo. 32). Gosberton is in the Parts of Holland.

work as an assize and gaol delivery commissioner and commissioner for special matters. The other was master Robert de Shardelawe, who had begun brilliantly as a canonist representing the king at Rome and on returning to England had become a Bench justice in October 1229. He had served continuously as a Bench or eyre justice until he was disgraced in dramatic circumstances, in July 1232, for implication in the disturbances against Italian clerks. He had only returned, from the obscurity of his disgrace, to the royal service in 1244, when he was again acting as the king's proctor in Rome. Thus all three of Robert of Nottingham's junior colleagues in these two terms had been justices while he had been a clerk: one has to go back to the careers of Raleigh and William of York for a parallel to this.

With the return of Bath and Thurkelby to the Bench for Michaelmas term 1245, Robert of Nottingham resumed his place as third in seniority of the justices. He sat throughout Hilary and Easter terms 1246 but then concluded his brief career as a justice. Unlike all his other colleagues, during the period when he was sitting, he had not been commissioned for such vacation business as taking possessory assizes and delivering gaols. Apart from the feet of fines, some 247 of them, the only Bench record to survive from this period of office is an essoin roll for Michaelmas 1245 and Hilary 1246.

What little we know of his ecclesiastical preferment suggests that, like Lexington, he was well beneficed. In the Buckinghamshire eyre of (12–27 October) 1232, in which Lexington was next senior to William de Raleigh, Peter de Goldington recovered the church of Stoke Goldington against the prior of Huntingdon after a stubbornly contested action for right of advowson.[1] Peter thereupon presented 'Robert of Nottingham, subdeacon' to the living, which in the 1291 *Taxatio* was worth £13 6*s*. 8*d*.[2] Later in the century there was to be legislation about justices and clerks who obtained presentations to disputed benefices. It is possible that the benefice was promised to Robert if his good offices secured a favourable decision, but such presentations are common enough at this date: Pateshull himself was alleged to have secured Rampton, co. Nottingham, while the right of presentation was still being litigated. On 22 June 1235 Robert of Nottingham was instituted to Almondbury, near Huddersfield, co. York, on the presentation of John de Lacy earl of Lincoln, from whom Lexington held lands.[3] The living was worth £40 in the 1291 *Taxatio*. Robert still held it on 11 December 1242, when a commission issued for Henry of Bath to take an assize of common of pasture which Robert, as rector of Almondbury, was bringing against a neighbouring manorial lord, Baldwin le Tyes, about common in Woodhouse and Farnley Tyas pertaining to his freeholding in Almondbury.[4] In 1238 Hilary term the young Norfolk knight Bartholomew de Creake was defending litigation brought by a

[1] J. I. etc. roll 62, ms. 10d, 19d, 31d.
[2] *Rotuli Hugonis de Welles* (Lincoln Record Soc., iii, vi, ix), ii. 89.
[3] *Register of Walter Gray* (Surtees Soc., lvi), p. 69.
[4] Patent Roll 27 Henry III (C. 66/54), m. 4d.

group to whom he had leased some of his manors in order to liquidate his debts to Christians and Jews.[1] In the course of pleadings it was admitted that he had retained the right to choose a clerk for presentation to the church of Helmingham, co. Suffolk; and that he had chosen Robert of Nottingham: whereupon the Bench, over which Lexington then presided, issued letters for Robert's admission. This living was worth £20 in the Norwich valuation of 1254 and £18 in 1291. Another link with East Anglia comes in a recognisance entered in the Bench plea roll for Easter 1243, whereby Hamo Chevre, a Norfolk knight, bound himself to repay Robert de Nottingham twenty marks in four half-yearly payments from Michaelmas following.[2] On 16 August 1238 Robert, still in subdeacon's orders, was instituted to Sutterton, co. Lincoln, on the presentation of Croyland abbey.[3] This living was worth £36 13*s.* 4*d.* in 1291. In the Berkshire eyre of (6 October–3 November) 1241 Robert, as Robert of Nottingham parson of Blewbury, began litigation by assize *utrum* against Osbert Turpyn and his wife Joan, about the considerable estate of two hides at Blewbury.[4] After adjournments in the Bench,[5] the action was eventually concorded on the morrow of St. John (25–30 June) 1242, whereby, for the consideration of 100 marks, the defendants admitted Robert's right to hold the estate at a cummin rent.[6] The estate seems to be the same as that which, in the great survey of 1242–3, Robert was holding of the alien priory of Noyon or Charleval.[7] Blewbury was not a mere rectory but the prebend of a Salisbury canonry, worth forty marks in 1226 and £40 in 1291: the presentation at this time seems to have belonged to the Templars.[8] Robert is styled canon of Salisbury in papal letters of 23 January 1244 which permitted him to hold an additional benefice.[9] Lexington had been a canon of Salisbury since about 1228 and his influence may have secured the Blewbury prebend for his clerk at some time in the twelve-thirties.

The total of Robert's known preferment thus comes to some £150 at the values of the 1291 *Taxatio* and was probably worth rather less in his day. He may not have held all at the same time; but it is very probable that he held others of which we know nothing. By contrast, Pateshull, at the height of his career, had his preferment taxed at 1,600 marks for the clerical tenth; William of York, about the time he was promoted to be senior justice *coram rege* in October 1242, held preferment worth at least £800 gross according to the 1291 valuation. The value of Lexington's preferment has yet to be calculated, but it is unlikely to have been less than York's. There can be little doubt that Robert had prospered during his career,

[1] K.B. 26/119, m. 6d.
[2] K.B. 26/128, m. 14d.
[3] *Rotuli Roberti Grosseteste* (Lincoln Record Soc., xi), pp. 2, 23.
[4] J. I. etc. roll 37, m. 20d.
[5] K.B. 26/123, m. 21.
[6] C.P. 25(1), 7/14, no. 5.
[7] *Book of Fees*, ii. 865.
[8] *Fasti Ecclesiae Sarisberiensis*, ed. W. H. Jones (1879–81), pp. 367–8.
[9] *Calendar of Papal Registers*, i. 204.

without approaching the heights of his more distinguished contemporaries.

Much less is known about his lay interests, and that little all points to holdings in the Soar valley, on the boundaries of Nottinghamshire and Leicestershire. It is there, at Ratcliffe, that the de Nottingham family emerges in the career of sir Henry de Nottingham under Edward I.[1] No doubt Robert came from this family and held some lands there, but there is no evidence about this. An action which we first pick up in Trinity term 1243 against Roger de Altesteade or Alstede, for suit of mill at Kegworth, co. Leicester,[2] was composed by an enrolled final concord in Hilary 1244.[3] Roger agreed to give Robert 20*s.* on Ascension day (12 May) and to restore to his man Norman three bushels of flour and a sack which he had taken from him; in return Robert waived his claim to damages and reserved the right to move his mill. Kegworth was just across the Soar valley from Ratcliffe and was a Segrave holding; perhaps Robert had a lease there. By a final concord of the octave of Hilary (20 January) 1247, the prior of Repton granted Robert of Nottingham a life lease, at a nominal rental, of two carucates at Sutton and Bonnington, in the Soar valley just south of Ratcliffe and Kegworth.[4] This is one of the pieces of evidence which suggest that Robert left the Bench for retirement; a life lease would be a good investment on retirement and a reasonably good bargain for the priory. Unfortunately there is no Repton cartulary to show what the consideration for the conveyance may have been.

By October 1250 Robert had ceased to hold the Blewbury canonry, for in Michaelmas term that year a Bench action was being defended by master Nicholas, parson of Blewbury, who is to be identified with Nicholas de Teissun, who held this prebend.[5] The two hides which Robert had secured here in 1242 did not pass with the prebendal estate; they remained in the de Nottingham family until it ended with a female in the late fourteenth century, the manor being known as Nottingham's fee.[6] The only other of Robert's livings in which an immediate successor can be traced is Sutterton; but whereas Robert had held the rectory, charged with a pension to Croyland abbey, the new presentation, in 1245–6, was to an endowed vicarage.[7]

The second piece of evidence to suggest that Robert lived some years after 1246 is the appointment of 'Robert of Nottingham, clerk' as one of two attorneys by Henry of Bath in Michaelmas term 1251.[8] Earlier that year Henry had suffered a disastrous check to his career, resulting in his dismissal from the senior justiceship of the court *coram rege* and the loss of all his other offices for alleged corruption in judgments. The case in which

[1] *Knights of Edward I,* comp. C. Moor (Harleian Soc., 1929–32), iii. 278. *Thoroton's History of Nottinghamshire*, ed. J. Throsby (Nottingham, 1790), i. 183.

[2] K.B 26/130, m. 1.

[3] K.B. 26/132, m. 6.

[4] C.P. 25(1), 182/9, no. 344.

[5] K.B. 26/143, m. 12d. Cf. *Fasti Ecclesiae Sarisberiensis*, p. 368.

[6] *Victoria County History of Berks.*, iii. 366.

[7] *Rot. Rob. Grosseteste*, p. 80.

[8] K.B. 26/145, m. 12d.

Robert was engaged was one brought by Lincolnshire litigants immediately on Henry's disgrace, apparently in response to the proclamation that all those who had cause for complaint should bring their actions; it had passed to the Bench after preliminary investigation *coram rege*.[1] Henry of Bath, who during his disgrace seems to have been living chiefly in Lincolnshire on estates which his eldest son had acquired by marriage, might well have turned to a former colleague to represent him in this action and possibly others. Lexington lived for seven years after his retirement from the Bench; Robert may have lived as long or longer after his retirement, for in July 1258 a Robert of Nottingham, from cos. Derby and Nottingham, admitted owing the household steward Robert Walerand five marks, which were to be repaid at Westminster at Michaelmas 1259.[2] This brings us to within a few years of the beginning of the career of sir Henry of Nottingham, just after the Barons' War. However, it seems probable that between Robert and sir Henry there was another member of the family, no doubt a brother, nephew or cousin of Robert, some facts about whose career may be contained in the unpublished plea rolls of the twelve-fifties and early twelve-sixties.

Robert was not the only member of his family to be associated with Lexington. Henry of Nottingham, who by 1219 was rector of Bulwell, co. Nottingham, and a canon of Southwell, seems also to have held a prebend in the royal chapel of Pontefract and to have died not long before September 1241.[3] By a final concord in May 1245, Lexington, who had himself been a canon of Southwell since 1214, granted a bovate at Warsop and a wood which he had assarted at Saundby, co. Nottingham, to a local man, charged with a yearly payment of 20*s*. to the chapter of Southwell to support a chaplain 'at the altar of St. John the Evangelist, where the bones of sir Henry of Nottingham of pious memory lie'.[4]

[1] J. I. etc. roll 1178, m. 1.

[2] K.B. 26/158, m. 18d.

[3] *Book of Fees*, i. 287; *Close Rolls 1237–42*, p. 329; *Cal. Patent Rolls 1232–47*, p. 258.

[4] C.P. 25(1), 182/9, no. 305.

MARTIN PATESHULL AND WILLIAM RALEIGH [1]

THE speculations of Dr. Kantorowicz about Bracton and the composition of the *De Legibus* provoked rejoinders. Among the most trenchant is Mr. H. G. Richardson's *Azo, Drogheda and Bracton*,[2] a main purpose of which is to show the improbability of the suggestion that Bracton composed the *De Legibus* while serving as clerk to William Raleigh and before Raleigh ceased to be the senior Justice of the court *coram rege* in the summer of 1239. Kantorowicz derived his knowledge of Bracton's life and times from the discoveries and suggestions of others; perhaps for that reason his speculations might fail to be informed and disciplined by that understanding of ascertained fact and right feeling for the probable and possible in conjecture, which sometimes comes from a profound study of the written evidences of a period. Maitland, however, had made such a study of the times of Martin Pateshull, Raleigh and Bracton; but in one passage Mr. Richardson carries his attack beyond Kantorowicz to Kantorowicz's sources, and seeks to disprove Maitland's suggestion that Raleigh may have been Pateshull's clerk and so have inherited from him those plea rolls of the Bench and eyres which Bracton later used.[3] Mr. Richardson will allow Raleigh 'to have acted in 1221 and 1226 as clerk to justices itinerant, among whom Martin of Pattishall was the most prominent' but he at once qualifies this by adding 'he seems at that time to have been a royal clerk. Apparently, therefore, their relations were official rather than personal, and the fact that Raleigh had some of Pattishall's eyre rolls in his possession implies neither his employment in a personal capacity nor that he served Pattishall in the bench. We may go further and add that, certainly from 1225, when Raleigh begins to figure in the chancery rolls, his activities are quite incompatible with the discharge of the duties of a clerk to the judge of the bench, whether in a private or an official capacity.'

[1] The following class references have been used for original records in the Public Record Office: K.B. 26 for Curia Regis Rolls; J.I. 1 for Eyre etc. Rolls; E. 159 for Exchequer Memoranda Rolls (King's Remembrancer) and E. 368 for Exchequer Memoranda Rolls (Lord Treasurer's Remembrancer). Dates and details of eyres referred to are taken from an exhaustive list of them which I have prepared for the reign of Henry III, while biographical matter about William of York for which no authority is furnished is based on 'Six Letters concerning the Eyres of 1226–8', *Eng. Hist. Rev.*, lxv. (1950), 492–504.

[2] *Eng. Hist. Rev.*, lix. (1944), 22–47.

[3] *Op. cit.*, 28–9.

However, if we examine carefully the records of Raleigh's activity in the chancery rolls from 1225 until May 1229, when he became a justice of the Bench, we shall find nothing in them to support this assertion.[1] There is little to examine: a couple of taxation commissions, in 1225 and 1227, and a couple of judicial commissions, in 1226, in one of which, however, and in one other matter, the William of Raleigh concerned may not be the future justice. In the first, on 15 February 1225, Thomas de Muleton, then the justice of the Bench next in seniority to Pateshull, was appointed to head the panel of assessors for the fifteenth in Lincolnshire, to sit at Lincoln on 2 March; Raleigh was subsequently added to this panel.[2] This was Lent vacation business; indeed to enable the taxing to proceed rapidly throughout England the Bench had ended its Hilary sessions rather earlier than usual, with the period called the octave of Candlemas in the fines and Hilary one month in the plea rolls (roughly 9–15 February). Moreover, two other Bench justices and a large number of royal and other clerks were called on to serve in the various panels. Pateshull was not engaged, so if Raleigh was his clerk it need not have interfered with his service and would have fitted in well with a visit to his Northamptonshire living at Blatherwycke. Muleton, moreover, seems to have had a high opinion of Raleigh, for a few years later, in Trinity term 1231, when he had for some time past transferred his interests to his northern estates (where his eldest son Lambert succeeded him), he settled his estates at Whaplode and Holbeach on his younger son Thomas, received this son's homage in court before his fellow justices and committed him and his estates to Raleigh 'as to a steward'.[3] No doubt by arrangement, to help him keep an eye on the young man and his lands, the patrons of Whaplode, Croyland abbey, then presented Raleigh to the rectory, which he held until his episcopal consecration in 1239.[4] In the second matter, in the autumn and winter of 1226–7, Pateshull with two other justices, William de l'Isle and Richard Duket, was on eyre in the north; there are two pieces of evidence which show that Raleigh was with them as a senior clerk.[5] On 30 January 1227 Raleigh was appointed along with de l'Isle and Duket to tallage in Cumberland and Northumberland.[6] Under Richard I and John the commission to justices in eyre seems normally to have empowered them to tallage; under Henry III this was no longer so, but in the earlier years, when a general tallage was ordered, advantage was sometimes taken of their presence in the provinces

[1] Some of Mr. Richardson's citations are irrelevant, since they are appointments made after Raleigh became a justice.

[2] *Cal. Pat. Rolls, 1216–25*, pp. 561–2; *Rot. Lit. Claus.*, ii. 146b.

[3] K.B. 26/109, m. 17d. Muleton was then senior and Raleigh next him among the Bench justices.

[4] *Register of Hugh of Welles*, iii. 187; *Grosseteste's Register*, pp. 24, 36, 122. He was succeeded by Robert Lexington who held the living till his death.

[5] *Eng. Hist. Rev.*, lxv. 495–6.

[6] *Rot. Lit. Claus.*, ii. 208b.

to give them a special commission and so ease the burden on the other tallagers, as in this case. By the time the commission reached them the circuit would have been completed except for the Northumberland eyre; they tallaged in that county, but it is uncertain whether they did so in Cumberland, whose eyre had been postponed.[1] Here it is Raleigh's presence with Pateshull which explains his inclusion in this commission; the main judicial work of the circuit, in Lincolnshire, Yorkshire, Lancashire and Westmoreland, was over and he transacts this fiscal business, perhaps as Pateshull's deputy, with Pateshull's junior colleagues. It is possible that his fellow clerk, William of York, who was certainly with the justices in the Northumberland eyre, also acted as a tallager.[2] The two judicial commissions both concern Devonshire. On 4 January 1226 a William of Raleigh was appointed the senior of four assize justices, to take an assize at Exeter on 10 February; his colleagues included Warin fitz Joel, the junior justice of the Bench, and Hugh Peverel.[3] We shall see that it is possible that this Raleigh was not the future justice. On 8 January a William of Raleigh who seems certainly to be the future justice was appointed to sit with Peverel and the sheriff of Devon, on a date they were to arrange, to hear the Devon aspects of a dispute between that great baron of the west country, William Briwer, and his estate steward, Herbert le Pynu.[4] However, the Bench remained in session until early March, with Warin among the justices;[5] so it is quite likely that both these commissions were carried out later than the date appointed and in the vacation. Commissions to four justices were often carried out otherwise than appointed. For example, Ralph de Bray was appointed one of four justices to sit at Exeter on 30 June 1226[6]; they did not sit then and Bray did not sit at all, for by his own patent he appointed a William of Raleigh in his place and the assize was taken on 14 July.[7] Similarly, in the last session Pateshull held for Essex assizes, at Stratford in February 1229, he heard a case which had been put down for hearing by four justices a little earlier.[8] There remains the other matter. On 20 October 1225 the men of Devon agreed to pay 200 marks for the right to choose their own sheriff for three years from Michaelmas 1225, the sheriff to receive £30 yearly for expenses and to answer for all the issues of the

[1] The Northumberland tallage is recorded in Pipe Roll 10 Henry III but there is nothing under Cumberland in this or the next year.

[2] See below, p. 167.

[3] *Cal. Pat. Rolls, 1225–32*, p. 71.

[4] *Ibid.*, pp. 73–4. Other commissioners were appointed to deal with the Cornwall and Devon aspects of this affair. Mr. Richardson is mistaken in believing that this had any connexion with the accounts of William Briwer the younger, who in October 1225 retired from being sheriff of Devon; his deputy was Roger de Langeford.

[5] The latest fines are dated 'Candlemas one month' (2 March onwards); Warin appears in all of them.

[6] *Cal. Pat. Rolls, 1225–32*, pp. 72–3.

[7] *Devon Fines*, ed. Reichel, i. no. 141: a rare example of a fine made before justices *ad hoc assignati*.

[8] K.B. 26/105, m. 11; cf. *Cal. Pat. Rolls, 1225–32*, p. 282.

county.[1] On the same day 'William de Ralegh' was appointed to keep the county,[2] which he did for the stipulated three years. Next day, as sheriff, he was ordered to arrange for the election of a coroner, apparently in his place, though the wording of the writ is not quite straightforward.[3] Foss hesitated to identify the sheriff with the future justice [4]; Lady Stenton thought identification improbable.[5] Mr. Richardson thinks there is no doubt about the identification. Not a few sheriffs in the earlier years of Henry III's reign were responsible for, but did not themselves discharge, the routine of administration; Mr. Richardson, aware that Raleigh and the sheriff of Devon are distinguished as separate persons in the commission to deal with the Devon aspects of the Briwer-le Pynu affair, hints that Raleigh was such a sheriff. We shall return to this question of identity and show that there are some grounds for believing that the sheriff of Devon was a layman and knight whose landed interests lay in the country north and west of Barnstaple, on the fringe of Exmoor. For the moment it is only necessary to point out that Mr. Richardson's identification of the future justice with the sheriff of Devon adds no strength to his case. If Raleigh were the sheriff then on Mr. Richardson's own admission his duties did not prevent him, in 1226–7, from serving as a clerk on eyre, for several months, in counties most remote from Devon and over a time when he should have made his Michaelmas proffer. If his duties allowed him to do so much it is hard to see why they should not have allowed him at other times to work under Pateshull in the Bench at Westminster.

Mr. Richardson's case is thus open to some doubt. Having excepted against it we may now state our own. It is that generally, from 1219 (probably for some years earlier) to 1229, in eyre and in the Bench, Raleigh served Pateshull, though he may not have been present throughout the whole of every term of the Bench, in every eyre or in all the vacation assizes in which Pateshull sat; and that, whether or not Raleigh's standing grew with the years (towards the end of the period he seems to have been the equal, if not the superior, of several junior justices), his service was to the end personal rather than official, if such a distinction must be drawn: and Mr. Richardson himself seems to have doubts about the validity of the distinction in these years. For the main facts of our case we may do what medieval litigants sometimes did: put ourselves on the rolls of the court, but with the difference that we do not vouch the record of pleas but the ephemeral *trivia* of a decade of clerks. For during this period and a little beyond it there is an abundance of references in these rolls to men who

[1] *Cal. Pat. Rolls, 1216–25*, p. 544.

[2] *Ibid.*

[3] *Rot. Lit. Claus.*, ii. 67a: *Mandatum est Willelmo de Raleg' vicecomiti Devon' quod loco eius qui prius fuit coronator . . . eligi faciat alium coronatorem.*

[4] *Dictionary of the Judges*, p. 545.

[5] *Selden Society*, vol. 53, p. xviii.

seem to be acting in a clerical capacity about the court, in the Bench and on eyre. Many of these references occur when parties, having compromised an action, are given a day for taking their chirographs; we may be told who holds the note from which the final concord will be drafted or, less often, who has the chirographs themselves or the particulars of the lands concerned. Sometimes we are told that a man has been given custody of charters produced in a suit, or holds an original writ that has presumably not been filed. Sometimes money is paid through the agency of the court; we are told who is to receive it or who is to act as a pledge for the payment being made. Some of these references, mainly about notes and chirographs, appear at the end of the record of the relevant plea; others appear among those brief entries which commonly occupy a few inches at the top and rather more at the bottom of membranes. It was apparently the clerks' practice to use these places for entering the record of replevins, attornments, certain adjournments, obligations for payments, recognizances and so on, leaving the body of the membrane free for later recording pleas. It remained the practice to use the bottom of membranes for miscellaneous entries long after the development of separate rolls for attornies and plevins; but the fashion of referring to men who are acting in a clerical capacity about the court declines quite sharply about 1231, after giving us a glimpse of Roger de Thurkelby at his duties as a clerk in the Bench. Many men are mentioned in these capacities and of some we know that they so acted and little more: Miles the chirographer, for example who, as Lady Stenton has remarked, was unique in authenticating *per Milonem* many of the feet of fines made during Pateshull's western circuit of 1221–2.[1] Others achieved some distinction, like Nicholas de Neville.[2] But there are two men who appear throughout this period, men referred to so often that they can hardly have been other than senior clerks and who each became justices of the Bench, senior justices of the court *coram rege* and, Matthews converted from the seat of custom, bishops; William Raleigh and William of York. It is fortunate that Raleigh had such a colleague, for William of York was undoubtedly a king's clerk, so that his early career can usefully be contrasted with Raleigh's.[3]

There is one mention of Raleigh before the civil war, when in 1214 he held a chirograph.[4] Then, in the first surviving complete roll under Henry III, for

[1] *Curia Regis Rolls*, viii. 167; x. 106; *Selden Society*, vol. 59, pp. xvi–xvii.

[2] *Curia Regis Rolls*, viii, *passim*.

[3] My survey was first made from the original rolls; subsequently, the Deputy Keeper of the Records and Sir Cyril Flower have materially helped the survey to be exhaustive by permitting me to use the indexes prepared by Sir Cyril for the volumes now in the press: *Curia Regis Rolls*, volumes xi (Hilary 1223–Mich. 1224); xii (Hilary 1225–Easter 1226); xiii (Easter 1227–Hilary 1230). References are accordingly given to these volumes. They are by volume and case number not (as in references down to vol. x) by volume and page. For Raleigh, references to the original rolls have also been given, for these volumes in the press.

[4] *Curia Regis Rolls*, vii. 267.

Michaelmas 1219, we find him holding the notes of final concords and chirographs.[1] In Hilary 1220 he holds a chirograph and acts as an attorney to receive one [2]; in Easter 1220 he acts as an attorney to receive judgement and money for a concord is paid through him [3]; in Michaelmas 1220 he receives the first part of a payment on behalf of Thomas de Albo Monasterio and in Hilary 1221 receives the final instalment.[4] During these terms William of York holds notes and, in one case, note and chirographs successively.[5] In Easter 1221 we find Raleigh holding notes and learn that he has an aumbry or cupboard in which he has put a chirograph.[6] There is no Trinity term in 1221; Segrave is in the north with the justiciar, while Pateshull is beginning his western circuit of the eyre that lasts, with brief intervals, until the following January. As Lady Stenton has pointed out, Raleigh goes with Pateshull; he acts as an agent for a payment during the Salop eyre and authenticates the membranes of the amercements roll of the Warwick eyre.[7] The Bench resumes its sessions in Michaelmas term 1221 but Pateshull reaches it from the west only in late November. During this term we find William of York holding notes, acting as an attorney to receive a Neville fine and writing a Neville charter which is enrolled [8]; the only mention of his colleague occurs when, at the end of a case, the writer remarks 'we have not got the note because William of Raleigh has it.'[9] But in Trinity 1222—the rolls of the two intervening terms are wanting—Raleigh is back and holds a chirograph,[10] while William of York holds notes and has custody of a charter.[11] Rolls survive for only two of the next five terms in which the Bench sat: Hilary and Michaelmas 1223. In Hilary term William of York has notes and chirographs [12]; Raleigh has a writ.[13] In Michaelmas term William of York has notes and also has the note and extent of lands in a Wiltshire case in which Raleigh has custody of the charters[14] ; Raleigh also has a chirograph, has paid to the exchequer money received as an agent and is to receive money on another account, while a payment due from William le Bigod is to be made 'before the Justices of the Bench, into the hands of M. de Pateshull' or William de Raleg''.[15]

So far these references show Raleigh acting in a responsible position in the Bench, going on eyre with Pateshull and being treated as Pateshull's deputy.

[1] *Curia Regis Rolls*, viii. 40, 77; 23, 145.
[2] *Ibid.*, pp. 186, 206.
[3] *Ibid.*, pp. 294, 390.
[4] *Ibid.*, ix. 208; x. 10.
[5] *Ibid.*, viii. 137; ix. 218, 221, 235, 244, 323, 345; viii. 72, 254.
[6] *Ibid.*, x. 94, 111, 127; 78: *in almonera sua.*
[7] *Selden Society*, vol. 53, pp. 422, 429, 432.
[8] *Curia Regis Rolls*, x. 175, 177, 185; 250; 217.
[9] *Ibid.*, p. 181.
[10] *Ibid.*, p. 343.
[11] *Ibid.*, pp. 287, 308, 339; 322.
[12] *Ibid.*, xi. 145, 353, 402; 253, 482, 576.
[13] *Ibid.*, 597 (K.B. 26/82A, m. 19).
[14] *Ibid.*, 1162, 1241, 1346; 1201 (K.B. 26/83, m. 22).
[15] *Ibid.*, 741, 923, 1298, 1375 (K.B. 26/83, ms. 5d, 11d, 25, 28).

Sir Cyril Flower would go further and claim that the first five of Pateshull's extant rolls were substantially written by Raleigh.[1] The body of Pateshull's rolls for 1219 Mich., 1220 Hilary with Easter, 1220 Trinity and 1220 Mich. appear to be written by the same hand, which is large, flowing, with a slight backward tilt and with a distinctive preference for certain forms of letters. The fifth roll covers Pateshull's Bench activity for the whole of 1221 and much though not all of it is written in the same hand.[2] Pateshull had held the Hertford eyre in December 1220 and the pleas begin with some Essex and Herts. cases which had been adjourned into the Bench and were dealt with before Hilary term began.[3] The full proceedings for Hilary and Easter terms follow (the former cut short by the Bytham affair) but Pateshull did not return to Westminster from his western circuit until late November so that for Michaelmas there is matter only for the very end of term, with a membrane of memoranda on matters arising out of that circuit which he wished to discuss with the Council.[4] In Easter term, in a Berkshire suit in which the parties were given a day in November to take their chirographs, the writer adds 'we now have the note'; in the other surviving roll for that term, after a similar entry of this adjournment, the writer adds 'William of Ralegh' has the note.[5] The hand that wrote 'we now have the note' seems to be the hand that predominates in the first five of Pateshull's surviving rolls; the parallel passage suggests that it is the hand of Raleigh. A claim advanced by the editor of the *Curis Regis Rolls* is grounded in a profound knowledge of these records and commands our respect; nevertheless, in fairness to Mr. Richardson's opinion, we may see what can be advanced against it. It can be objected that it infers too much from a single passage. In Pateshull's four earlier rolls we sometimes find the impersonal 'we have the note'; but where there are other rolls for the same terms we find that the records of these cases also have 'we have the note'.[6] Again, in Pateshull's rolls we find Raleigh referred to along with Nicholas de Neville, William of York, Miles, Phillip, John and the rest; perhaps some of these references are not in the predominant hand of the rolls but entries made in the hands of other clerks, yet there are references to Raleigh which seem to be in the predominant hand.[7] Finally, to narrow matters to Easter term 1221 we find the holders of notes mentioned on ten occasions in Pateshull's roll. Four times the holder is William of York; the other roll, whose owner is unknown,

[1] *Curia Regis Rolls*, viii. p. vi, x. 1; *Introduction to the Curia Regis Rolls, 1199–1230* (Selden Society, vol. lxii), pp. 8–10, 32, 271.

[2] K.B. 26/71, 72, 74, 77 and 79.

[3] K.B. 26/79, ms. 3–4; according to the fines this was done at the Tower of London. The editorial note, *Curia Regis Rolls*, x. 3, is mistaken in suggesting that the Bench itself sat at Hertford.

[4] K.B. 26/79, ms. 31–3; the editorial note, *Curia Regis Rolls*, x. 167, does not notice the connexion of the memoranda with Pateshull's circuit.

[5] *Curia Regis Rolls*, x. 127 (K.B. 26/79, m. 21 and 80, m. 11).

[6] *Ibid.*, viii. 35, 38, 43, 58, 63, 234, 256.

[7] Compare originals of *Curia Regis Rolls*, viii. 40 and 77 with 145.

omits to mention who holds the note in these four cases.[1] Once the holder is 'William' and once he is Miles the chirographer; the other roll also gives these names.[2] Twice the holder is Raleigh; in one case the other roll also has Raleigh but the second case does not seem to occur in it.[3] In the two remaining cases the holder is 'we'; in the first case the other roll also has 'we'[4]; it is in the second case, as we have seen, that it has Raleigh. We are of course very much in the dark about the mechanical side of business in the Bench. The clerks had presumably to assist in arranging the hearing of cases from the writs, to assist in taking essoins, replevins, attornies and the like, to write judicial writs, draft the notes of final concords, keep documents produced in suits, file up the returned judicial and original writs, write the essoins and plea rolls and so on. Precisely how this was done we do not know. Presumably there were one or more senior clerks, with a small staff, who served the court impersonally and probably owed their appointment to the chancellor; in addition there were clerks employed by particular justices. But we do not know how many clerks there were, what seniority there was among them and how they divided their labour. An investigation into the way in which the plea rolls and the (unhappily neglected) essoin rolls of this period were prepared would lend itself to an interesting study, especially for the palaeographer, since some of the hands in the rolls are very distinctive; pending such a study we may feel that the claim that Raleigh wrote the major part of the first five of Pateshull's extant Bench rolls is not fully established. However, it cannot be denied that in this one crucial passage it seems to be Raleigh or the small staff under Raleigh—not William of York, Nicholas de Neville or any of the others or their staff—who is responsible for preparing Pateshull's rolls.

From Trinity 1224 to Hilary 1229 there is at least one roll for every term in which the Bench sat, except for Easter 1225. William of York has a note and chirographs in Trinity 1224 and is mentioned ten times as holding notes and once as being an agent for payment in Michaelmas 1224.[5] Raleigh is not mentioned in Trinity term but in Michaelmas term he acts as an agent for payment and also receives a charter for safe-custody.[6] In Hilary 1225 William of York holds notes on five occasions.[7] There is no routine entry about Raleigh but there is a record of a conveyance to him (or to a namesake) by Thomas de Weston of land

[1] *Curia Regis Rolls*, x. 42, 63, 80, 95; the corresponding cases occur in K.B. 26/80, ms. 2, 5, 4d and 8d but the omission is not noted in *Curia Regis Rolls*.

[2] *Ibid.*, x. 78, 106; compare K.B. 26/80, ms. 6d and 9.

[3] *Ibid.*, p. 94 (compare K.B. 26/80, m. 8d) and 111.

[4] *Ibid.*, p. 77 (compare K.B. 26/80, m. 6d).

[5] *Ibid.*, xi. 1636, 1665, 1676, Trinity; nos. 2071, 2120, 2370, 2390, 2508, 2690, 2779, 2781, 2836, 2855 and (agent) 2462, Mich.

[6] *Ibid.*, 2541, 2636 (K.B. 26/85, ms. 21, 25).

[7] *Ibid.*, xii. 16, 48, 283, 358, 381.

at Bray, in Devon (apparently that near South Molton).[1] It is the sort of enrolment that anyone closely connected with the court could have made on their own or another's behalf. It was in the Lent vacation following that Raleigh was commissioned as a tax assessor for Lincolnshire. In Trinity 1225 it is William of York's turn to be unmentioned; for Raleigh we have a note that the instalments of a composition which ended a Northamptonshire suit between litigants from Nassington and Yarwell are to be paid, during July and August, at Raleigh's house at Blatherwycke, a few miles west of these villages.[2] This house we may assume to be the rectory: Raleigh seems to be obliging neighbours by letting the payments be made there in vacation rather than in term at the distant Bench. Blatherwycke, on the Basset fee, was a home of the Engaynes. Viel Engayne had presented Raleigh to the living in 1220; he held it until his consecration as bishop of Norwich.[3] If we go forward a little we find that in November 1228 Raleigh received the wardship and marriage of the heir of William Engayne.[4] Mr. Richardson, who otherwise ignores Raleigh's connexion with the Engaynes and Northamptonshire, regards this as simply an emolument for a royal clerk; perhaps it was rather a piece of business which Raleigh undertook for the family. Blatherwycke lay close to Kingscliffe forest whence, in April 1231, Raleigh received a gift of ten oaks.[5] Gifts of venison, or licences for hunting, were made to him in November 1230 and July 1231 from Rockingham forest, farther away to the south-west;[6] under the de Rivaux regime, when many royal servants received some additional office, Raleigh was made life Keeper of Rockingham Castle.[7] It may be but a coincidence that Raleigh obtained a living in, and maintained a close connexion with, the county that is peculiarly associated with Pateshull; though curiously enough, in the year that Raleigh was presented to Blatherwycke, Pateshull and he occur together as witnesses to a deed of institution made at Northampton on 24 May 1220, in the short Whitsun recess.[8]

About the beginning of Michaelmas term 1225 we find that Raleigh still has his cupboard at Westminster and has put into it a writ of novel disseisin in a Northants suit that has been respited for want of recognitors and is to be taken by Pateshull at Northampton on 22 December.[9] Later in the term he is given the custody of charters and a chirograph and, about the end of November, he puts a chirograph into the cupboard.[10] It was in the course of this term, as we have seen,

1 *Curia Regis Rolls*, 111 (K.B. 26/89, m. 3d).

2 *Ibid.*, 553 (K.B. 26/90, m. 5d).

3 Bridges, *History of Northamptonshire*, i. 275, 278–9; *Register of Hugh of Welles*, ii. 99; *Register of Robert Grosseteste*, p. 193. *Cf.* also the action of darrein presentment, Viel Engayne v. Prior of Fineshed in Trinity 1239: (K.B. 26/120, m. 7).

4 *Cal. Close Rolls, 1227–31*, p. 131.

5 *Ibid.*, p. 491.

6 *Ibid.*, pp. 459, 514.

7 *Cal. Pat. Rolls, 1225–32*, p. 490.

8 *Welles Register*, ii. 185.

9 *Curia Regis Rolls*, xii. 908 (K.B. 26/88, m. 8).

10 *Ibid.*, 1121, 1574 (K.B. 26/88, ms. 16d, 33d).

that a 'William de Ralegh' became sheriff of Devon. William of York also had some work to do during the Christmas vacation, being appointed to join with the sheriff in hearing a case in the county court at Huntingdon on 20 December[1]; possibly he was going to spend Christmas at his nearby living of King's Ripton. In Hilary 1226 he appears in a private capacity, putting in a claim as the parson of Easington, an Aûmale living in Holderness.[2] The Aûmale connexion reappears when he acts as the earl's attorney, is indeed styled the earl's clerk, when receiving charters at the end of Easter term 1226.[3] In Hilary term Raleigh puts another chirograph into his cupboard and is the pledge for a payment in a Norfolk suit.[4] In Easter term he is not mentioned. Only one other person seems to be mentioned as holding notes and chirographs in these terms and he, irritatingly enough, is simply 'William'. [5] One is tempted to assume that he is William of York, although once at least he may be Raleigh.[6] For among the many clerks who were called on to serve in assesssing the fifteenth in 1225 there was a certain 'William of the Bench', who was in the panel for Cambs. and Hunts. and who was granted a *liberate* in the same authority as Nicholas de Neville, similarly employed elsewhere.[7] These facts suggest that the name is a soubriquet for William of York, for these are the counties in which one would expect to find him act and, because of his connexion with Ralph de Neville, one would expect to find him securing an allowance for his services; it so happens that, as William of York, he does not appear in any of the many panels of tax assessors although, like Nicholas de Neville and Raleigh, a great number of royal and other clerks were employed as tax commissioners. If William of York is identical with 'William of the Bench' then it is highly probable that he is identical with the 'William' of the Bench plea rolls; it is hardly rash to believe that he was an official so well known that his toponymic could sometimes be omitted or forgotten. Before assuming this for certain, however, we would need to know rather more of the career of William of London before he first sat as a justice, during the justiciar's tour of the west with the king in the late summer of 1226, for after this 'William' is no longer to be found constantly at work at Westminster.

[1] *Curia Regis Rolls*, 1282; compare 1554, 1944.

[2] *Ibid.*, 2283; the relative fine, made about 16 May following, is also endorsed with his claim: C.P. 25 (1), 284/18, no. 21. *Gray's Register* (Surtees Society, lvi) 33 does not record his presentation to this living until March 1230, but in 1228 a chancery messenger went to him at Easington, *Cal. Liberate Rolls, 1226–40*, p. 84.

[3] *Curia Regis Rolls*, xii. 2414.

[4] *Ibid.*, 1651, 1858 (K.B. 26/94, ms. 3, 10).

[5] *Ibid.*, 85, 178, 252, 378, Hilary 1225; 1157, 1162, 1207, 1367, 1444, 1448, 1480, Mich. 1225; 1754, 2003, 2115, Hilary 1226; 2231, 2263, 2337, 2394, Easter 1226.

[6] The Norfolk suit in which 'William' holds a note, *ibid.*, 1448, seems to be related to that in which Raleigh is pledge for a payment, 1858.

[7] *Cal. Pat. Rolls, 1216–25*, pp. 536, 565. Possibly, however, this *magister Willelmus de Banco* or *de Bancis* was a member of the de Bancis family, who were prominent in Cambridgeshire.

Between Easter 1226 and Easter 1227 there were no sessions of the Bench. It was in the autumn and winter of 1226–7, beginning at Lincoln on 15 September, that Pateshull went on circuit in the north, taking with him as clerks both Raleigh and William of York. The latter had personal reasons for going on a northern circuit, for in addition to his older Yorkshire interests he had very recently been presented to the living of Kirk Deighton, near Knaresborough, and with any luck he would have an opportunity of visiting this and the rest during the circuit. There can be little doubt that his friendship with Ralph de Neville helped him to secure this convenient appointment as a clerk on eyre and ensured that he received a *liberate* for his expenses.[1] No such allowance is recorded for Raleigh, nor had he any known personal interests in the north which might have prompted him to serve with justices who already had an experienced clerk with them rather than with the justices in Segrave's circuit in the midlands and west or with the circuit which opened later, in February 1227, under Muleton in the south-west. We shall find it hard to avoid concluding that Raleigh went with Pateshull simply because he was Pateshull's right hand man. All the rolls of this circuit are unfortunately lost. We know directly of Raleigh's presence only through a famous letter written by William of York and a deed which the two clerks and the justices witnessed during the York eyre. We have already seen that when judicial business was nearly over, about February 1227, Raleigh assisted the junior justices in tallaging in Northumberland and perhaps in Cumberland also. There was a fourth member of this tallage commission: 'William of the Bench'. We know not merely that William of York was present during the Northumberland eyre but also that he later brought back to the exchequer the estreats of the fiscal matter of that eyre, so the probability that this was his soubriquet is heightened; this tallage commission and the 1225 taxation commission provide the only known references in the close and patent rolls to 'William of the Bench'.

When the Bench reopened the king sat with his justiciar and justices, throughout Easter term and for part of Trinity term 1227; this was no doubt a public manifestation of his recently proclaimed assumption of royal power. Though Pateshull was at Westminster there are no routine references to Raleigh in either term. William of York holds a note and particulars of land in Easter term; in Trinity term he holds an original writ, is given custody of a suspect charter under Pateshull's seal and also holds particulars of lands.[2] There were no Michaelmas sessions of the Bench, for the visitation of the general eyre was resumed, with three circuits. These made heavy demands on the professional justices, yet someone had to be found to go up to Carlisle to hold the Cumberland eyre that had had to be omitted from Pateshull's programme in the preceding winter through lack of time. Choice fell on William of York as the legal expert

[1] *Eng. Hist. Rev.*, lxv. 495–6.

[2] *Curia Regis Rolls*, xiii. 63; 260, 361, 384.

for the Cumberland commission, though he did not want to go and tried, unavailingly, to be released.[1] Why was he chosen rather than Raleigh, who seems certainly to have had the longer service as a clerk in the Bench? We may conclude that it was because William of York was a king's clerk who could be commanded to serve as a clerk in the Bench or on eyre or as a justice, whereas Raleigh went with Pateshull. For Pateshull opened the Kent eyre at Canterbury on 15 September and continued the main sessions there until about 20 October. In the body of the civil pleas of this eyre a case concerning the advowson of Eythorne was adjourned to be heard at Rochester on the Monday after St. Luke (25 October 1227),[2] presumably on the way back to Westminster, where Pateshull was on 28 October.[3] The hearing and judgement in this adjourned plea was entered in a membrane that is filed up after the record of crown pleas and seems to be devoted to business held at this short session at Rochester on the way back; in the case next but one after it Raleigh is mentioned as holding a writ.[4] The only other clerks mentioned in the roll seem to be Richard and John[5]; there do not seem to be any references to clerks in the roll of Pateshull's next, Essex, eyre but if ever either of these rolls were edited and indexed more references might come to light. Meanwhile, William of York stayed in the north. He was there when the king came to keep Christmas at York, he held a special inquest at Grimsby in January, promoted Neville interests with the archbishop of York, came south after Easter to act as a justice under Segrave at Huntingdon in April 1228 and then went north again, to act as a justice in the Durham eyre, *sede vacante*. In June he was still in the north, holding an assize at York. But Pateshull reopened the Bench for Hilary term 1228 and Raleigh was there, holding a chirograph and a note and acting as the agent for a payment.[6] In Easter term he is not mentioned; there were no Trinity sessions. Pateshull was then holding the Norfolk eyre, but of his roll only a small fragment of crown pleas survives. In September and October he held his last eyre, for Suffolk; his roll seems to contain only one mention of a clerk, one Richard de Sancto Rumaldo, who had a note which he put among the unfinished writs.[7] During the Kent eyre a Richard also held a note and in both of these eyres one of Pateshull's colleagues was William de l'Isle; in Hilary 1230 we find Richard, clerk of William de l'Isle, holding a note[8]; so perhaps the three references concern the same clerk.

[1] *Eng. Hist. Rev.*, lxv. 497–500.

[2] J.I. 1/358, m. 15; the entry refers to a fuller record on the roll for Hilary 10 Henry III, which must be Pateshull's now lost roll for that term, for the entry in *Bracton's Notebook*, iii, no. 1699, has a *postea* not in the extant roll for that term, K.B. 26/89.

[3] A fine was made *coram rege* on that date: C.P. 25 (1), 284/18, no. 38.

[4] J.I. 1/358, m. 28.

[5] *Ibid.*, ms. 13, 15.

[6] *Curia Regis Rolls*, xiii. 413, 532, 553 (K.B. 26/96, ms. 3, 8, 8d).

[7] J.I. 1/819, m. 25.

[8] *Curia Regis Rolls*, xiii. 2771.

We come now to what is one of the most interesting of all these references. Michaelmas term 1228 opened later than usual, about 20 October, but little was done until Pateshull, Segrave and their colleagues reached Westminster from Suffolk, which they did about 3 November.[1] Pateshull's own roll for the term does not include the earlier proceedings, before he arrived, but there are two other rolls which do so, covering the whole term.[2] Under the period 'Michaelmas five weeks' (about 3–11 November), the rolls record an adjournment to the octave of Hilary (20–26 January 1229) to hear a jury in a Devon suit in which William Briwer is defendant against a prosecution that is nominally on the king's behalf. They continue the record with a note that the same day has been given to Henry the king's son (an illegitimate son of King John) concerning the Devon manor of Huntshaw 'as appears in the record in Easter three weeks' runs Pateshull's roll; [3] but the two other rolls run, instead: 'as appears in the roll in Easter three weeks in the roll of W. de Raleg''.[4] Pateshull's roll for the previous Easter term survives, filed up with his roll for Hilary and membranes of Lent vacation business at Norwich and Yarmouth and a Trinity gaol delivery at Northampton. In it the second membrane of the period 'Easter three weeks' (16–22 April) contains the record of separate suits in which Briwer and Warin of Bassingbourn are defendants against the king, whose prosecutors are claiming that each of them holds a Devon manor which ought to revert to the king.[5] Further proceedings in the same term in Briwer's suit have been added in a *postea* and the same hand has added a note that Henry the king's son is defendant in a third suit, of the same kind, concerning Huntshaw, and that for this the jury called in Briwer's suit is to serve. Briwer and Henry were then adjourned to Michaelmas one month (the period 27 October–2 November). When that period came the prosecutors did not proceed, possibly because the justiciar and his few colleagues then sitting in the Bench felt that it would be more prudent, in such suits of considerable importance, to await the return of Pateshull from Suffolk. Then, when Pateshull arrived, the further adjournment to the beginning of Hilary term was made. Three clerks make their entry of that further adjournment and in doing so have to refer to a roll of the previous Easter term in which there is an explanation that the same jury will serve for both suits. Pateshull's Easter term roll seems to be the roll to which they refer; the clerk writing Pateshull's roll

[1] See note at end of this article.

[2] K.B. 26/100 is Pateshull's roll; 99 is William of London's roll, from internal evidence, but the earlier part of it seems to be a copy from another roll now lost, and the statement on m. 2 that the pleas are of the quindene of Michaelmas before William of London may be an error of the copying clerk since (i) the Bench was not then in session and (ii) William of London was with Pateshull at Catteshull until the period Michaelmas one month; 98 is the roll of another justice, compiled independently of the other two.

[3] K.B. 26/100, m. 4d.

[4] K.B. 26/98, m. 6d (= *Curia Regis Rolls*, xiii. 994) and 99, m. 6.

[5] K.B. 26/96, m. 11 (= *Curia Regis Rolls*, xiii. 612–13).

for the current term calls that Easter roll simply 'the record'; the clerks of two other justices call it Raleigh's roll. These two clerks had perforce to refer to the Easter term roll of another justice, for the eyres had then been in progress, so that of the justices sitting at Michaelmas only Pateshull and William de l'Isle had been present in the Bench throughout the Easter term.[1] This reference suggests that to the clerks in the Bench in November 1228, while Pateshull was still a justice and Raleigh a clerk, Pateshull's rolls were Raleigh's rolls.

About the same time Pateshull and Raleigh seem also to have been closely associated in the minds of litigants. In William of York's Hampshire eyre of 1236 Ismenia, relict of Phillip le Ercevesque, brought an action of dower for a rent in Southampton against John de Lillebone.[2] She had begun a similar action in Lexington and Muleton's Hampshire eyre of 1228, when John had excepted that she had not been legally espoused since Phillip had married her while his lawful wife Denise was alive. This action seems to have been adjourned into the Bench, for near the end of Michaelmas term 1228 the bishop of Winchester was directed to investigate and certify the facts of Ismenia's marriage.[3] 'Afterwards she came, with the bishop of Winchester's letters, to London, before M. de Pateshill' and W. de Raleigh' '; another action, between herself and Denise, shows that her visit must have happened during Hilary term 1229, while Pateshull was a justice and Raleigh a clerk.[4]

Raleigh is not otherwise mentioned in Michaelmas term 1228, but William of York has once more returned to his clerical duties, holding a note and being the pledge for a payment in a Yorkshire suit.[5] In Hilary term 1229 he is mentioned six times as holding notes, while Raleigh is then given custody of a charter.[6] With the end of that term, which closed with the period called Hilary five weeks in the roll and the quindene of Candlemas in the fines (a period of a few days from 16 February), Pateshull brought to an end his distinguished career as the senior professional justice, a career whose beginning in the fines is marked, aptly enough, in one made at Northampton on 14 December 1217, in which he follows William Marshall *Rector Regis et Regni* and Hubert de Burgh, justiciar.[7] He had become dean of St. Pauls about the previous August but his retirement seems not to have been due to this promotion but to ill-health, for he had not many months to live and in August 1227 he had complained to the chancellor of being much handicapped by an obscure malady.[8]

[1] See note at end of article.
[2] J.I. 1/775, m. 11.
[3] K.B. 26/98, m. 13d (= *Curia Regis Rolls*, xiii. 1195).
[4] *Bracton's Note Book*, no. 324 (= *Curia Regis Rolls*, xiii. 1609).
[5] *Curia Regis Rolls*, xiii. 1023, 1003.
[6] *Ibid.*, 1426, 1428, 1486, 1488–9, 1496; 1631 (K.B. 26/105, m. 14).
[7] C.P. 25 (1), 282/8, no. 5.
[8] *quadam infirmitate occulta qua detentus ac gravatus fui quamplurium: Ancient Correspondence*, vol. vi, no. 128.

Easter term 1229 opened, as usual, in the period of the quindene of Easter (29 April–5 May) but the fines are not dated by this period; instead the very unusual dates of the Invention of the Cross (3 May) and the morrow of the Invention (4 May) are employed, possibly because the business done at an adjourned session of the Surrey eyre prevented the Bench from opening on the 29 April. Raleigh is not included among the justices in the fines of the first date; he is named in five out of the fifteen fines of the second date and in all of those of the subsequent periods of the term, running from Easter three weeks (6–12 May) onwards. The date of his promotion as a justice of the Bench can thus be narrowed to 5 or 6 May 1229; for practical purposes it follows immediately on Pateshull's retirement. William of London's plea roll for this term gives the names of the justices thus: Segrave, Raleigh, Lexington, William of London, Muleton and their colleagues.[1] This, however, is not the order in the fines, where the chirographers are undecided whether Raleigh or Lexington should come next after Muleton and Segrave but agree in placing them before Thomas de Kaunvill and William of London. By Michaelmas term they have resolved their doubts: Raleigh precedes Lexington, although Lexington had sat as a justice during the greater part of Raleigh's service as a clerk. When Henry III went to Poitou in 1230 the chancellor remained as the head of the administration in England with Segrave as his colleague; the two regents undertook a tour that summer through the midlands and north, doing a good deal of judicial business. Thereafter Segrave's only regular appearance in the Bench was for a part of Hilary term 1232, at a time when Muleton and Raleigh were away, holding the Kent eyre. After Henry III's return to England in the autumn of 1230 there are slight indications in the plea rolls and the chancery and exchequer records which suggest possibly that Segrave acted as a justice in the king's train and that something like a court *coram rege* was then formed; these indications deserve thorough investigation, and so does Segrave's judicial career during the next two years, apart from the few months, June–August 1231 and June–August 1232, when he was on eyre. Meanwhile, Muleton and Raleigh were the senior justices of the Bench until, in Michaelmas term 1233, the chirographers unanimously reverse the former precedence; throughout that term and Hilary 1234 Raleigh comes before Muleton and he is still the senior justice of the Bench up to the time he leaves that court, during the period Easter one month (21–27 May): he is named in only five out of the fifteen fines dated by that period. The council of Gloucester opened on 23 May; Raleigh was obviously summoned away from Westminster to Gloucester and he went, taking with him his Bench

[1] K.B. 26/102, m. 1; the ascription is on internal evidence, including the fact that London is the only justice who sat in all three of the assize sessions recorded on m. 19. He sat in the Bench only at the end of Easter term and for that term the roll has every appearance of being a copy of another justice's roll.

roll for the current term. For although that roll is lost the extracts which Bracton made from it show that, with Raleigh's move, it changed from being a Bench roll to being a *coram rege* roll, for on its membranes was recorded the reversal of the outlawries of Hubert de Burgh's rescuers, a judgement which Raleigh delivered at Gloucester in the name of their peers on 27 May.[1] So, in just over five years, the man who had worked under Pateshull as a clerk in the Bench had himself become the most senior of all the king's justices. For two of those years William of York continued to serve as a clerk in the Bench. He is mentioned in the usual capacities in Easter 1229 and Hilary 1230 [2]; in the following summer he seems to have accompanied the chancellor and Segrave in their tour of the midlands and north.[3] It is now increasingly common to find him referred to not simply as *Willelmus de Eboraco* but as *dominus Willelmus de Eboraco*. In Michaelmas 1230 he was back in the Bench; we learn that he has a clerk named Roger, while in another entry in which he himself holds the particulars of lands, Roger de Thurkelby holds the note.[4] Perhaps these two Rogers were the same: one Yorkshireman being the junior colleague of another. But in December 1231, when Thurkelby gets a gift of fish, he is said to be Raleigh's clerk; [5] so perhaps he was also serving Raleigh a year earlier and William of York's clerk Roger may have been Roger of Whitchester, concerning whom there are some indications, between 1230 and 1246, which suggest that he was serving about the Bench and then in the court *coram rege*. William's promotion to justice came with the opening of Easter term 1231. The chirographers soon accord him precedence over the junior justices who had been sitting while he was a clerk; but he always comes after Muleton, Raleigh and Lexington so long as the two former sat in the Bench. He was still next to Lexington in the last Bench term before he succeeded Segrave as the senior justice *coram rege* in 1242.

We may now return to the problem of the identification of Raleigh with the William de Ralegh who was sheriff of Devon, 1225–8; we shall not reach a clear-cut solution but it can be shown that the probability seems on the whole to be very much against the identification. The exchequer records are not very helpful. The retiring sheriff, William Briwer the younger, had already made the proffer of Michaelmas 1225 through a clerk, Nicholas de Tailur.[6] The sheriff Raleigh made his own first proffer at Easter 1226, through a clerk named Richard, but he appeared in person for the view of his account of 14 May following.[7] At the

[1] *Bracton's Note Book*, case no. 857.

[2] *Curia Regis Rolls*, xiii. 1824, 1831, 2014, 2108; 2297, 2299, 2355.

[3] Among the fines made during this tour was one at Coventry on 9 September concerning the advowson of Sandal: *Yorkshire Feet of Fines, 1218–31*, ed. Col. J. Parker, nos. 472, 472A. The relative deed, made there on the same day, has William of York among the witnesses: *Early Yorkshire Charters*, ed. C. T. Clay, vol. viii, no. 129.

[4] K.B. 26/107, ms. 1d, 17, 23d, 32.

[5] *Cal. Close Rolls, 1231–4*, p. 8.

[6] E. 159/8, m. 12.

[7] *Ibid.*, ms. 1, 3d.

Michaelmas proffer in 1226 his clerk Nicholas appeared, made no payment but said his master was coming with money, an excuse which the Exchequer accepted without comment.[1] His account for the first year was begun on 24 October 1226 when he appeared in person [2]: at a time when the future justice seems to have been with Pateshull on the northern circuit. There had been a slight overlap of functions with Briwer's deputy sheriff, Roger de Langeford (a leading Devon knight), who had collected some of the sheriff's aid and perquisites in the month that had elapsed between the beginning of the financial year and the new sheriff's appointment; but there is nothing at all to support Mr. Richardson's suggestion that Briwer's accounts were embroiled or that the elder Briwer's estate steward, Herbert le Pynu (another leading Devon knight), had had anything at all to do with the county administration while the younger Briwer was sheriff. There is no record on the Memoranda rolls of the subsequent proffers, of 1227-8. On 9 May 1227 the sheriff again made his view in person.[3] There is a reference to him in the Bench roll of the same term. In a Devon suit on a writ of right the tenant appeared but not the demandant 'and William de Ralegh', the sheriff, is present and admits that he received the king's writ putting the case at Westminster and . . . that. So he is in mercy'.[4] Plainly he had forgotten to execute a *pone*. Even so, the demandant was amerced for non-appearance and his amercement appears in the roll of Bench amercements, covering Easter 1227 to Hilary 1230, that is to be found filed up after Raleigh's roll of the latter term.[5] But the sheriff is not mentioned in that roll, nor is any amercement for a contempt or trespass debited against him in the pipe roll. Sufficient amercements rolls are preserved from the earlier part of Henry III's reign for it to be evident that many persons put in *misericordia* did not become liable to an *amerciamentum*, though the fact of the pardon or waiving is often not recorded on the plea rolls. If, as we believe, the clerk in the Bench was not the sheriff, he could no doubt have used his good offices to see that his kinsman was excused the amercement. On 30 September 1227 the sheriff was not present for the Michaelmas exchequer, so the county was ordered to be taken into the king's hand and he was commanded to come on 20 October to answer and account.[6] This seems to be mere routine process, for he did not account until 12 November; [7] there is no record of an interruption of his office or of his paying an amercement for the default. The Memoranda rolls for 13 Henry III are wanting, so we do not know when he made his last view or account or final proffer. There were the usual small amounts outstanding on several heads in his last account, which were later

[1] E. 368/10, m. 3.
[2] *Ibid.*, m. 15 and E. 368/9, m. 17d.
[3] E. 368/9, m. 10 and /10, m. 8d.
[4] *Curia Regis Rolls*, xiii. 52 (K.B. 26/97, m. 1); the right hand margin is defective.
[5] K.B. 26/104, m. 26.
[6] E. 158/9, ms. 18, 18d.
[7] *Ibid.*, m. 7.

gathered together and finally cleared in 1235–6.[1] There are many routine mandates to him during the two years for which we have the Memoranda rolls, but nothing out of the ordinary. During his last year of office Muleton and his colleagues held the Devon eyre, from about 26 May to 26 July 1228, at the time Pateshull was in Norfolk; unfortunately no roll of this eyre survives. The next Devon eyre was not held until 1238; the main roll survives and in it the name which heads the list of former sheriffs is: *Willelmus de Ralegh' miles*.[2] It is very doubtful if our Raleigh would ever have been so described. In 1238, in the Charter rolls and elsewhere, he is usually given his ecclesiastical dignity of *Thesaurarius Exoniensis*; before then, if qualified at all, he is *clericus*. From the final concords and pleas of this 1238 eyre we learn that there was a William of Raleigh knight, who is sometimes called William of Raleigh senior, to distinguish him from his own son William, who is usually called William of Raleigh junior. From these and other records we can discover a little about William of Raleigh, knight, who represented the senior of the several branches of the Raleigh family.[3] He held Raleigh (in Pilton, just outside Barnstaple) and Challacombe as a mesne tenant of the Tracy Honor of Barnstaple; he also held Arlington of Philip de Columbers and had land at nearby Coxleigh, in Shirwell. His interests in Braunton hundred are reflected in his acting as surety for several men of this hundred who made fines or were amerced in its crown pleas in 1238; and in his buying the year, day and waste of lands in Barnstaple belonging to a felon, who may have been his tenant. He also seems to be connected either tenurially, by kinship or by friendship with the former justice, Warin fitz Joel (long a leading man in Devon), with Thomas de Santon (of Braunton), with

[1] Pipe Roll, 20 Henry III, Devon account.

[2] J.I. 1/174, m. 24. In two deeds published in the county court while he was sheriff he is simply *W. de Ralegh vicecomes*: *Monasticon Dioecesis Exoniensis*, pp. 174, 186.

[3] *Book of Fees*, ii. 772, 782 and the following information from J.I. 1/174. W. of R. senior with his son W. of R. junior, Reynold and William Cole and Hugh of Raleigh and others are defendants in a novel disseisin against Richard Beaupel; W. of R. jnr. is dismissed from the suit and judgement is given against W. of R. senr. (representing the others), Warin fitz Joel and W. of R. jnr. being the sureties for his amercement: m. 2d (terms of settlement are in Reichel, *Devon Fines*, no. 270). W. of R. senr. and jnr. are sureties respectively for appellor and appellee in a compromised appeal and both are mainpernors for the appearance of an appellee in another suit, both appeals in Braunton hundred: m. 33. W. of R. senior is surety for a fine by the abbot of Cleeve, surety for an amercement by Warin fitz Joel, surety for an appellee in a compromised appeal from Braunton hundred, purchaser of the year, day and waste of a Barnstaple felon's house, and mainpernor for two associates of Thomas de Santon who are defendants in an action of trespass from Witheridge hundred: ms. 4, 6, 33, 33d, 34d. In addition, W. of R. jnr. is attorned by his wife in a plea against Ralph de Albemarle, which is compromised: ms. 2d, 6d (cf. *Devon Fines*, No. 276); he is recognitor for grand assizes: ms. 18d, 19d; he is surety in civil actions for amercements by Wymund of Raleigh, William de Wydeworth (a coroner) and Alan Bassett (in an action against Ralph of Dadescombe) and in crown pleas for a man in Crediton hundred: ms. 10d (*bis*), 14 (*bis*), 35d. In the civil pleas of the Devon eyre of 1218–19 William of Raleigh appears only along with other knights of the Honor as a surety for his lord, Henry de Tracy, in an important suit: J.I. 1/180, m. 4.

members of the Cole family, with the Beaupels and with Cleeve abbey, near Dunster (which had interests in Braunton). In 1238 he was an elderly man—his son William, a Devon taxation commissioner in 1237–8, had married Clarice, relict of Robert de Albemarle and had a daughter who by January 1247 had married into the Pomeroy family[1] —so that it is possible that as a young man he was the William de Raleghe who in 1198 was engaged in conveyances with William Briwer of lands in Chittlehampton, Radworthy, Brendon and Kentisbury, all within the same districts of Exmoor or the country around Barnstaple.[2] Though the senior representative of the family, he seems to have been a country gentleman who lived quietly at home, holding his lands as a mesne tenant or on lease and having little litigation in the royal courts. Many such men escape reference in the records of royal government for years at a time—the record of the 1238 eyre apart we find much less about him than about Wymund of Raleigh, of a cadet branch—and it is in deeds that we must hope to find further information. The elucidation of the thirteenth-century pedigree of the Raleighs is a task that awaits the historians of Devon; whatever conclusions they may reach, we have shown that the career of the future justice continued under Pateshull, on eyre and in the Bench, during the years 1225–8 that a William of Raleigh was sheriff of Devon. So it is probable that it was William of Raleigh knight who, perhaps after serving for some years as coroner, was chosen in 1225 by those leading men of Devon who had paid a very large sum for the right of nominating one of themselves as sheriff. If we accept this, then the apparent difficulty in the commission to deal with the Devon aspects of the Briwer–le Pynu affair, of a William of Raleigh being associated with a sheriff who is also William of Raleigh, will disappear; perhaps it was the knight and not the future justice who was commissioned about the same time for an assize, for sheriffs were often so commissioned in the days when four knights took assizes.

Having followed Raleigh and William of York to the end of their service as clerks it may be useful to compare and contrast their careers, since Mr. Richardson has suggested that Raleigh's service was necessarily official and impersonal, rather than personal to Martin Pateshull. During most of these years the royal power is largely in commission: a few great men manage the affairs of a very young king who acquires only gradually a household commensurate with his dignity, and full control over it. Most men who are king's clerks in those years seem to be either men who had served John or younger men who owe their position to one of the great men who are managing the young king's affairs. William of York is certainly a king's clerk. He holds the royal living of King's Ripton (presented by one of those great men, Pandulf); writs of *liberate* call him

[1] *Cal. Close Rolls, 1234–7*, p. 548; *Cal. Liberate Rolls, 1226–40*, p. 327; Reichel, *Devon Fines*, no. 454.

[2] Reichel, *Devon Fines*, nos. 21, 23.

'our trusty and well-beloved clerk'; many years later, when he is one of an episcopal deputation pleading for the liberties of the Church, his royal master has not forgotten that once he scribbled royal writs. He seems to be on very friendly terms with Segrave—they were neighbours in Huntingdonshire—but even so he does not seem to be personally connected with any of the justices. He sits in the Bench or goes on eyre as a clerk as the chancellor instructs him; he serves for a few eyres as a justice, then resumes work as a clerk for several years. So far as the courts are concerned his services appear to be impersonal and official. We can hardly say for certain what his functions were, for the plea roll references which we have cited, though numerous, are casual. Maitland thought that he might be the prothonotary or senior clerk of the court; but this was based on a reference to his activity in Michaelmas 1221, when Pateshull and Raleigh were away on eyre.[1] Possibly he was a forerunner of Roger of Whitchester, who in 1246 was the first Keeper of the Rolls and Writs of the Bench of whom we have the record of appointment. But a king's clerk under the minority could have personal ties: William of York's lay outside the Bench, with a man who was administrator and politician; for those letters in which, among other things, he begged or thanked the chancellor for writs of *liberate* show that he had very strong personal ties with Ralph Neville. In them and in some of the references which we have noted we see him writing Neville deeds, doing little services for Nevilles in the Bench, promoting Neville interests in the north, asking Ralph Neville's advice about his personal affairs, accompanying Neville on a judicial tour; once, when commissioned for the Cumberland eyre, he even implies that a royal mandate will not be obeyed unless he is assured that it is also Neville's will. Many years later when he becomes the senior justice *coram rege* Ralph Neville has the great seal restored to him for the last few years of his life. If this is but coincidence it is apt enough, for during his years as a clerk, allowing for all flattery, William regarded himself as Neville's man: *mihi vester penitus*. Even so, he is a Yorkshireman with ambitions and local interests; we have seen him

[1] Ranulph fitz Henry, tenant in a Yorkshire action on a writ of right heard during the octave of St. Martin 1221, put himself on a grand assize and the parties were adjourned to Hilary four weeks, according to the only extant roll for the whole of Michaelmas 1221 (K.B. 26/78, m. 16d = *Curia Regis Rolls*, x. 244). *Bracton's Note Book*, no. 149, gives the Hilary proceedings, showing that there had been an error in enrolling the adjourned date: 'William of York's roll' had one date, all the other rolls had another date. Bracton marginated the case as an important precedent for action when the date appointed in the main roll (apparently here that of William of York) differs from that in the other rolls of the clerks and justices. But although everything turns on the precise dates, his copyist abbreviated them to 'such a day' so we do not know whether or not the Bench upheld the date in William of York's roll; nor do Bracton's remarks under essoins in the *De Legibus*, f. 352b (ed. Woodbine, iv. 113) clarify the matter. The other rolls had the octave of such a day. If it was the octave of Candlemas then K.B. 26/78 may be one of them, since that period and Hilary four weeks seem to be equivalents. If it was the octave of Hilary then K.B. 26/78 would seem to be William of York's roll; this is possible, since it contains enrolments of three Neville charters (one of which William wrote) and has both essoins and pleas; we need not suppose it to be in his hand.

acting for the earl of Aûmale in a passage that might suggest he was only a parson from Holderness, did we not know from his own letters that he could hope to refresh himself by only an occasional visit to those parts.

During these years we do not find Raleigh receiving a royal living nor does he obtain a *liberate* when he goes on eyre as a clerk. A Devon man, he yet has a sustained connexion with Northamptonshire, which seems to have been Pateshull's native county and was certainly more often visited by Pateshull on vacation business than the many other counties in which he held livings. Herefordshire was one of the other counties; Pateshull sometimes held assizes there or delivered the gaol, for he held the livings of Dilwyn and Pencombe and while archdeacon of Norfolk (1226–8) he made a grant of land which he held at Pencombe of St. Peter's, Gloucester; the witnesses seem to be unconnected with the courts except for *Willelmus de Ralege clericus*.[1] If the plea rolls associate Raleigh with a justice it is with Pateshull; when he goes on eyre it is with Pateshull. He does not interrupt his clerical career to serve as a justice on eyre but is working in a clerical capacity up to the term in which Pateshull retires; then he is not merely promoted to be a justice himself but is promoted with seniority. If we accept Sir Cyril Flower's suggestion that the hand which predominates in Pateshull's earlier rolls is Raleigh's hand there may be further evidence for his activity. The same hand may have penned a note sent by Pateshull to Ralph Neville about the time of the siege of Bytham or Bedford as a testimonial for the bearer: 'since medical men are very necessary when besieging castles, Master Thomas is coming to the army on my advice: I know him to be an expert'.[2] Pateshull's other extant letters, one of which dates from August 1225 and the others from August and September 1227, are not in that hand nor are the later plea rolls, except possibly for a revision or addition here and there. But the hand does seem to appear in endorsements on some final concords of Pateshull's later years, both from the Bench and from his circuits of 1226–7, 1227 and 1228. In the concords of most terms and eyres in these years there are usually a few whose agreement, as written by the chirographers, required some modification before the chirographs were cut and delivered to the parties. This was effected by endorsing them with a clause or two; such endorsements seem never to be in the hands of the chirographers; there are a number of feet which, to all appearance, have endorsements in the hand which predominates in Pateshull's earlier rolls. William of York when a clerk had an assistant competent to carry on in his master's absence; Raleigh may well have had a small staff to help in his duties and, as the years passed, most of the routine writing may have been done by his assistants. If we cannot say for certain what those duties were, yet, whether or not he was a king's clerk, the accumulation of many pieces of evidence

[1] *Cartulary of St. Peter's Gloucester* (Rolls Series), ii. 121.
[2] Ancient Correspondence, vi, no. 75.

seems to point not towards the official and impersonal service of a William of York but towards a personal service and loyalty to Martin Pateshull, a service which may well have begun towards the end of John's reign when Martin was himself a senior clerk.

As to Pateshull's rolls, there seems to be no reason why Raleigh should not have retained them after 1229; many of them were needed for current business and it would have been natural for them to remain with the man who seems to have been responsible, under Pateshull, for their preparation and custody rather than for them to be given over to another clerk, since that man was now himself a justice. It would probably have been pointless to divide the accumulation into those still needed and those no longer needed for current business and to deposit the latter in the treasury of the receipt of the exchequer; nor, indeed, is there any evidence in these years to suggest that such deposit was regular or that the treasurers were actively interested in the custody of plea rolls no longer needed in the courts. There is some suggestion of continuity in the list of (possibly outstanding) Bench amercements which is filed up with Raleigh's own roll for Hilary 1230, for this list runs from Easter 1227 to Hilary 1230 and where a note is necessary to explain that there was no session because eyres were being held it refers only to Pateshull's eyres; whoever drew up the list appears to have had at his disposal Pateshull's eyre and Bench rolls for 1227–9 and Raleigh's rolls since then.[1] If Raleigh kept these rolls in 1229 there was every reason why he should have retained them when, in May 1234, he moved to the court *coram rege*. It is no more than a vague possibility that there had been a court *coram rege* under Segrave and the stewards from the autumn of 1230; if it existed, no evidence has yet been found to suggest that it regularly enrolled its proceedings. As Maitland suggested, it may have fallen to Raleigh to organize that court in 1234; a series of recent Bench rolls would then have been useful for reference, for the court was often away from Westminster. The justices whom Raleigh left behind in the Bench, and their clerks, would have had all the records needed for current business: plea and essoin rolls for the past decade or more, files of writs and so on. The probability seems to be that until Raleigh retired from the court *coram rege* in the early summer of 1239, after his election as bishop of Norwich, he or his clerks had in their custody Pateshull's rolls and his own. There may have been a few strays in the accumulation, for Bracton wrongly ascribed the Lincoln eyre of 1218–19 to Pateshull and a roll for Hilary 1223, demonstrably not Pateshull's, has a note (possibly in Bracton's hand) at the top of a dorse of a membrane to the effect that the proceedings below are ascribed to a different period of the term in the (now lost) roll of *W. de Raleg'*.[2]

We may claim, therefore, that Mr. Richardson's criticism of Maitland's suggestion fails. Indeed, it seems reasonable to regard that suggestion no longer

[1] K.B. 26/104, m. 26.

[2] K. B. 26/82, m. 6d.

as a probability but as an established fact: Raleigh served Pateshull for a decade or more and inherited his rolls, which Bracton later used.

Note. To show that Bracton was never one of the regular Bench justices, Maitland supplied a list of the justices who sat in the Bench under Henry III as *Table the First* to his Introduction to *Bracton's Note Book.* He was careful to explain that the list was compiled from a minority only of the fines of the reign and suggested that a more exhaustive examination would lead to modifications. The files which he examined (for Beds., Berks., Bucks., Devon, Derby, York and Divers Counties) contained about one-fifth of the extant Bench fines of the reign and the *Table* merely lists the justices term by term, distinguishing those who appear to have sat for only part of the term from those who appear to have sat throughout. The *Table* is eminently serviceable within its limits, but for any term in which there was a change or changes among the justices (and there are more such terms than the *Table* suggests) the only satisfactory way of discovering the composition of the court is to examine all the fines for the term. Where the changes are at all complicated the results are best shown by setting out against the fines of each date the number of appearances made by each justice; a less satisfactory way is to summarize the results for the term, indicating the approximate dates on which justices not present throughout arrived or left the court. The following is a briefer summary of the results of examining all the fines for Easter 1227 to Hilary 1229 and a full summary for Easter 1229; it should be compared with the *Table* in *Bracton's Note Book*, i. 140.

The members of the court are given in the order of precedence accorded them by the chirographers, which usually does not vary. The number after each justice is the total of the fines in which he appears. The dates are approximate, being normally the first date of a period; *e.g.* Hilary three weeks is translated as 3 February but fines so dated may have been made at any time between 3 and 9 February.

1227 Easter, 29 fines (quindene of Easter to Easter five weeks = 25 April to 16 May).

The king 29, Hubert de Burgh earl of Kent and justiciar of England 29, Martin de Pateshill' 29, Thomas de Muleton' 26 (comes after 25 April), Thomas de Hayden' 29, William de Insula 8 (leaves before 2 May).

1227 Trinity, 16 fines (octave of Trinity to St. John three weeks = 13 June to 15 July).

The king 6 (leaves after 20 June), H. de Burgh etc. 16, Pateshill' 16, Muleton' 15, Hayden' 16, Robert de Lexinton' 2 (comes 30 June), W. de Insula 1 (comes 30 June).

1228 Hilary, 13 fines (octave of Hilary to Hilary three weeks = 20 January to 3 February).

Martin de Pateshill' archdeacon of Norfolk 13, Thomas de Kaunvill' 13, W. de Insula 13, Richard Duket 13.

1228 Easter, 27 fines (quindene of Easter to morrow of Ascension = 9 April to 5 May).

H. de Burgh etc. 8 (regularly only from 2 May), Pateshill' etc. 27, Muleton' 1 (which may be a chirographer's error), John Marshal 7 (from 2 May), Stephen de Segrave 20 (leaves after 16 April), William fitz Warin 18 (leaves after 16 April), W. de Insula 27.

1228 Michaelmas, 28 fines (Michaelmas one month to morrow of St. Andrew = 27 October to 1 December).

H. de Burgh etc. 2 (leaves after 3 November), Martin de Pateshill' dean of St. Pauls 27 (comes 3 November), Muleton' 28, Segrave 26 (comes 3 November), Lexinton' 24 (away between 3–12 November), Kaunvill' 23 (away between 3–12 November and on

1 December) W. de Insula 4 (present between 3–12 November), William of London 26 (comes 3 November).

1229 Hilary, 3 fines (morrow and quindene of Candlemas = 3, 16 February).

Pateshill' etc. 3, Muleton' 3, Segrave 3, Lexinton' 3, Kaunvill' 3. The first session of the Surrey eyre was held at Lambeth at the beginning of February by Segrave, Insula, London and Richard Reinger, who later in the month adjourned to Westminster, where a number of fines from counties other than Surrey were made before them, as Justices itinerant.

1229 Easter, 43 fines (Invention of the Cross to Vigil of Ascension = 3 to 23 May).

Muleton' 43, Segrave 43, Lexinton' 43, William de Ralegh' 24, Kaunvill' 26, William of London 3. Ralegh' precedes Lexinton' in eight fines.

Date	Fines	M.	S.	Lex.	R.	K.	Lon.
Invention of Cross (3 May)	9	9	9	9	—	9	—
Morrow of Invention (4 May)	15	15	15	15	5	15	—
Easter three weeks (6 May)	10	10	10	10	10	1	1
Octave of Invention (10 May)	2	2	2	2	2	1	—
Easter five weeks (20 May)	2	2	2	2	2	—	—
Vigil of Ascension (23 May)	5	5	5	5	5	—	2

XII

'Martin de Pateshull of Good Memory my Sometime Lord'

A TRANSLATION is given below of a deed, made probably late in 1235 or in 1236, by William de Ralegh, rector of King's Somborne, Hampshire, in favour of his manorial lord Margery de la Ferté. Ralegh's career is well known: clerk to Martin de Pateshull, possibly from about 1214, certainly from 1219 until 1229; successively justice, 1229-33, and senior justice, 1233–4, of the Common Bench; senior justice *coram rege*, 1234–9; bishop of Norwich, 1239–43, and of Winchester, 1243–50. Margery requires a slight sketch. She was the youngest of the five daughters of William Briwer,[1] the west-country man who was probably the greatest expert of his day in financial matters and the acquisition of estates, who rose in the royal service in the closing years of Henry II, was a leading servant of Richard I and John, and an elder statesman under Henry III till his death in 1226. Margery's married life was not of the happiest. Her first husband was the Norman William de la Ferté, whom she apparently married within a few years of 1200; William died in 1216, when he can have been barely thirty; but their daughter Gundred was then already married to Pain de Chaworth (to use the Anglicized form of Chaurces) and had borne her eldest son Patrick.[2] After an uncertain interval Margery married Odo de Dammartin, last of the male line of quasi-honorial barons of the Clare earls; Odo became mentally deranged some time before his death, which happened shortly before 8 April 1225.[3] Margery then had some troublesome litigation about her Dammartin dower, heard before Martin de Pateshull both in the Bench and in his general assize and gaol delivery session for Surrey in June 1225.[4] By late October or early November 1225 Margery had married, as his second wife, the elderly baron Geoffrey de Say, of West Greenwich.[5] The marriage was still subsisting in the spring of 1228; but it had been dissolved, on unknown grounds, by divorce, before Geoffrey in August 1230

[1] I. J. Sanders, *English Baronies* (Oxford, 1960), p. 123, gives a succinct account of the Briwer daughters.

[2] *Early Yorkshire Charters*, vi, ed. C. T. Clay, pp. 53–4.

[3] *Curia Regis Rolls*, xii. 344, 2509, 2518, 2594.

[4] J. I. 1/863, m. 1 (the first, and only non-assize, cases heard in the session); *Curia Regis Rolls*, xii. 853, 897, 1475, 2518. Unpublished documents cited in this note are in the Public Record Office.

[5] *Curia Regis Rolls*, xii. 1475.

succumbed among many others to the epidemic which swept through Henry III's forces in Brittany.[1]

As, briefly, in 1225, Margery then resumed her first husband's name and was known as Margery de la Ferté until her death, shortly before 4 February 1237.[2] Following the death, on 25 February 1233,[3] of her brother, William Briwer the younger, all the great possessions assembled by her father which had not been used to found religious houses or as outright marriage gifts for daughters were divided into five parts for Margery, her one surviving sister and the heirs of her three deceased sisters. On 10 June 1233 Margery fined 100 marks for her share and on 15 June order issued for her seisin of this;[4] Somborne was the chief manor of her share. The first year in which Margery had her purparty in Somborne was thus, roughly, June 1233–June 1234.

The purparties had been given subject to minor adjustments, which were effected partly by deeds and partly by litigation. William de Percy, who had married the third Briwer daughter Joan, received the neighbouring manor of Ashley as the head of the share which came to him as guardian of their five daughters.[4] By a covenant made on 20 July 1233 William and Margery tidied up certain conflicting interests of the two manors.[5] The twelve witnesses to the deed, headed by Margery's son-in-law Pain de Chaworth, were drawn equally from Percy and Ferté tenants. The latter included Richard de Cardevill and Walter Powis. Richard, who witnessed prominently all Margery's deeds, may have been her steward, for he acted as her attorney *coram rege* in 1235 and in the 1236 Hampshire eyre; he was a leading Hampshire knight.[6] The Percy group included Wymund de Ralegh, who had become a household knight of William Briwer in the latter part of John's reign, had served the younger William Briwer and then, about 1230, had passed into the service of William de Percy, in which he continued until, and indeed after, the latter's death in 1245: for it was he who carried out William's arrangements for the commemoration of Joan Briwer's obit at Sandon hospital, Surrey, where she was buried and where William's heart was also interred.[7] These arrangements, in the form of an agreement between Wymund and the prior of Sandon, were ratified shortly after 1245 by the diocesan, who was then William de Ralegh.

Margery de la Ferté also effected agreements by covenant with the heads

[1] *Ibid.*, xiii. 495, 1244; xiv. 1555 (=*Bracton's Note Book*, ed. F. W. Maitland (1887), ii, no. 574).

[2] *Close Rolls 1234–7*, p. 414.

[3] *Close Rolls 1231–4*, p. 198, taken with *Monasticon*, ed. J. Caley and H. Ellis, vi. 481.

[4] *Excerpta é Rotulis Finium*, i. 242–3; *Close Rolls 1231–4*, p. 229.

[5] Duchy of Lancaster Great Cowcher, vol. ii (D.L. 42/2), Hants. no. 15.

[6] *Curia Regis Rolls*, xv. 1423B; J. I. 1/735, m. 3 and cf. mm. 1, 2, 3d. Richard also witnessed D.L. 42/2, Hants. no. 45 and Margery's charter in *Monasticon*, vi. 482.

[7] C. A. F. Meekings, 'The early history of Sandon hospital', *Surrey Archaeol. Collections*, lvii (1960), 78–80.

of two great Winchester monasteries, releasing her claims for suit to the court of her hundred of Somborne in respect of lands which they held in it. Both are undated but must have been made about 1233–5. The eleven witnesses of the covenant with Isabel abbess of St. Mary Winchester were headed by William de Raliche and Walter abbot of Hyde; they included Richard de Cardevill.[1] The twelve witnesses of the covenant with Walter abbot of Hyde were headed by William de Raleya, Stephen prior of Mottesfont and Robert de Raleya; they included Richard de Cardevill and Walter le Pois.[2]

A fourth covenant was effected by an enrolled deed in the Hampshire eyre of 7 January–9 February 1236, being an amicable conclusion to an action of novel disseisin defended by Margery against a niece.[3] By it there was, in effect, a confirmation of the covenant of July 1233 and a further tidying up of interests between Margery and her eldest Percy niece Joan, together with the latter's husband Henry de Ferlington, to whom William de Percy had by now made over Ashley.

Because many of the central court rolls of 1233–5 are wanting, only slight traces remain of the tidying up of the Briwer purparties that required litigation.[4] In Margery's case they had probably been concluded by about 18 May 1235, when, in pursuance of an order of the court *coram rege* presided over by William de Ralegh, one of the canons of Mottesfont arrived at Westminster from the priory with a portable desk full of Briwer deeds.[5] Mottesfont, across the wooded Test valley from Somborne, had been founded by William Briwer about 1200, with endowments that included the advowson of King's Somborne. Like so many religious houses, it acted as a safe-deposit for its patrons' deeds and valuables. Prior Stephen was in office there for many years, since it was he who presented Ralegh, probably in 1229, and among the Chaworth deeds which he witnessed after 1237 is one dated 11 March 1259.[6] Ralegh and his *coram rege* colleagues went through the contents of the desk, extracting six royal and seven other charters which concerned only Margery's share. These they delivered to Margery who was apparently personally present in court. There were a number which did not concern Margery at all, which they returned to the desk. But—the problem is familiar to the local archivist who today has to deal with family papers—there were a large number which concerned Margery indeed but concerned also the other Briwer coheirs, since they dealt generally with Briwer estates. These also were therefore returned to the desk, for the canon to take back to Mottesfont where they could be consulted if need arose. From the succinct description of Margery's deeds

[1] D.L. 42/2, Hants. no. 21.
[2] *Ibid.*, no. 31.
[3] J. I. 1/735, m. 13d.
[4] *Curia Regis Rolls*, xv. 526, 1423B.
[5] *Ibid.*, p. 1472.
[6] D. L. 42/2, Hants. no. 47. Prior Stephen also witnessed Hants. nos. 45 (Margery) and 39 (Patrick de Chaworth).

which Ralegh's clerk entered in the roll we can identify them as those which, through the merging of the Chaworth estates with the house of Lancaster in the fourteenth century, were copied to form the oldest core of the Duchy of Lancaster Great Cowcher's Hampshire section; the originals are scattered among the several artificial collections into which Duchy of Lancaster deeds have been methodized.

In an article which appeared years ago in these pages,[1] the present writer sought to vindicate Maitland's guess (made from the evidence of Bracton's *De Legibus* and a necessarily very incomplete study of the plea rolls of the twelve-twenties) that Ralegh had been Pateshull's clerk. From a fairly exhaustive study of the evidence it was possible to show that, certainly from 1219, perhaps from about 1214, until 1229, when the onset of his fatal illness compelled Pateshull's retirement, Ralegh worked under him as clerk, in the Bench, on eyre and on other judicial assignments; and more than once journeyed with him privately. All the evidence pointed 'towards a personal service and loyalty to Martin Pateshull': in contrast to the evidence about Ralegh's equally distinguished contemporary William of York, who looked to the chancellor as his patron and who served courts and justices impersonally. The present deed happily furnishes a description of Ralegh's relationship to Pateshull in Ralegh's own words.

From a fairly wide reading of deeds of Henry III's time it seems safe to say that the number of parsons or dignitaries who referred to their predecessors in deeds as 'of happy memory' is not large; and, aside from those instances where the predecessor is an Edmund Rich or a Richard de Wych, a man of renowned sanctity, the phrase usually suggests the relationship of benefactor, or colleague, or membership of a household. The term 'my lord', when not used of the king, or of a tenurial or an ecclesiastical superior is, of course, the normal one for a benefactor: often met with in deeds founding chantries or obits where the donor is remembering both his family and those who have helped him in his career. Nor is the word 'amor' the everyday currency of deeds. Whether as clerk in the twelve-twenties or later as a justice, Ralegh must often have had to deal with Margery's affairs; an elderly widow was no doubt grateful for his help.

It is not known when Pateshull became rector of Somborne. Since he was a leading member of the government during Briwer's later years, a word from the latter would no doubt have procured his presentation if a vacancy occurred there at any time between about 1218 and 1226. When Pateshull was taxed for the ecclesiastical sixteenth of 1226 he paid 100 marks, indicating preferment of a total value of about £1070.[2] So far, at the valuations of Pope Nicholas's taxation, barely half that amount can be accounted for by benefices he is known to have held about 1226–9. He presumably resigned the living some time between March 1229, when illness caused his retirement from the Bench, and his death in the autumn; and Prior Stephen then presented Ralegh. Ralegh resigned the living on his election to the

[1] *Ante*, xxvi. 157–80.

[2] *Calendar of Patent Rolls 1225–32*, p. 249.

bishopric of Norwich. A collusive action of darrein presentment was then brought in the Bench in June 1239 by Margery's grandson, Patrick de Chaworth, against Prior Stephen, in which Patrick defaulted so that the prior thereby secured judgment, which was in effect confirmation of his right to the advowson.[1] A similar action was heard at this time, again between lay lord and head of a religious house, about another of Ralegh's vacated livings, that of Blatherwick, co. Northampton. In the Somborne case both Prior Stephen and the jury said that Stephen himself had presented Ralegh to the church.

In the roll of the 1236 Hampshire eyre in two different cases there stands marginated against the names of Richard de Culeston and of Ralph the chaplain of Somborne the notes: 'memorandum quod est capellanus W. de Ral.'.[2] Such notes are extremely uncommon; the present writer can recall only one similar, against a defaulter in the 1255 Surrey eyre who was apparently a connection of the justice Alan de Wassand.[3] The eyre justices at Winchester in 1236 included William of York and two others of Ralegh's former colleagues. One of them presumably caused these notes to be penned to ensure favourable treatment of the chaplains. Ralph needed it, since failure to prosecute his action had put him at risk of an amercement. One or both of the chaplains were presumably the priests who ministered on Ralegh's behalf at Somborne.

The partition of the Briwer inheritance left the Briwer religious foundations without a single, certain, patron. Margery's death soon removed the last member of the founder's own family from the neighbourhood of Mottesfont. So it is not surprising that as soon as Ralegh had gained possession of Winchester, Prior Stephen turned to the former rector of Somborne. By a certificate dated 15 March 1245, on the grounds of the house's lack of a patron, Ralegh formally took Mottesfont priory into the protection of himself and his successors in the see of Winchester as patrons.[4]

Robert de Ralegh was a brother of William, probably a younger brother whose career was cut short by death. There are a few references to him as active in the Common Bench between 1220 and 1230, once as William's agent;[5] he follows William in witnessing other deeds between about 1229 and 1234, one of which, a grant to the dean and chapter of St. Paul's, specifically styles him as William's brother.[6] When the Norman abbey of Grestein recovered the advowson of Marsh Gibbon, Bucks., after litigation, Robert, in subdeacon's orders, was instituted to this living soon after 9 February 1230.[7] William himself had held this abbey's living of Norton sub Hamden,

[1] K. B. 26/120, m. 16 (forthcoming *Curia Regis Rolls*, xvi. 912).

[2] J.I. 1/735, m. 6.

[3] J. I. 1/872, m. 39d.

[4] Hist. MSS. Comm., *Various Collections*, iv. 144.

[5] *Curia Regis Rolls*, viii. 261; x. 254; xii, no. 2244; xiv, no. 485.

[6] St. Paul's Dean and Chapter Deeds, Box 26, Country Deed 38; *Cartulary of St. Bartholomew's Hospital*, ed. Nellie J. M. Kerling (1973), no. 1197; Northamptonshire Record Office, Photocopy 342.

[7] *Rotuli Hugonis de Welles*, ii (Canterbury & York Soc., iii, 1908), p. 78.

Somerset, since at least 1219 and by 1242–3 had for some time held interests in Marsh Gibbon and Bix Gibwin, Oxon. Robert was still living at Marsh Gibbon on 29 September 1234 but vacated the living between June 1235 and June 1236, probably dying during that year.[1]

Duchy of Lancaster Great Cowcher, vol. ii (*Public Record Office, D.L. 42/2*), *Hampshire no. 43.*[2]

To all Christ's faithful present and to come William de Ralegh parson of the church of Sumburn greeting in the lord. Be it known to you that there was a dispute between the lady Margery de Feritate and myself in the first year in which she had Sumburn manor for her purparty, about how many and what kinds of beasts my church of Sumburn and its parsons were used and ought to have pasturing in the manor with the demesne beasts of the lord of the town. Until at length, although formerly, in the time of Martin de Pateshull of good memory my sometime lord the parson of the same church, an inquest was fully made about this, yet again by many discreet and trustworthy men the inquest was made and found that the said church and its parson ought and used to have in pasture with the demesne beasts of the town's lord everywhere save in two parks: twelve bullocks, two cows with a free bull who may go where he will with herding; one hundred sheep and a ram; thirty pigs and a boar. So that the parson of the same church could not have more beasts in pasture in his church's name with the lord's beasts, saving however to him common of pasture in that town where others of the town have common if he wish to have more beasts there. It was found also that the parson had a right to husbote and heybote in the wood of the town's lord and wood for fuel by view of the lord's forester if being warned he comes though it shall not be stayed because he do not come. And lest, by the passing of time, any péril or damage might threaten lady Margery or her heirs if out of her love and for my service she do me the grace of permitting a larger number of beasts in her demesne pasture I have made this writing to which I have put my seal. Witness these: sir Stephen prior of Motesfunt, sir Richard de Cardovill, Robert de Ralegh, master William de Cerney, Walter Powis, Walter Wellebef, sir Robert the chaplain, Geoffrey Percevent and many others.

[1] *Bracton's Note Book*, iii, no. 1189; *Rotuli Roberti Grosseteste* (Canterbury & York Soc., x, 1913), p. 340.

[2] This transcript of crown copyright material appears by kind permission of the Controller of Her Majesty's Stationery Office.

XIII

ALAN DE WASSAND (✠1257)

Alan de Wassand was the least obtrusive of the several Yorkshiremen who served Henry III as judges. Foss's notice of him, in the *Dictionary of the Judges*, is very brief yet has several inaccuracies; the *Dictionary of National Biography* does not notice him at all. The present account of his career, composed largely from printed sources, is intended to do no more than provide a biography which will serve until more records are published and some unpublished records can be searched exhaustively.[1] The main facts of his career, as at present ascertained, are that something is known about him between 1231 and 1246, when he became a justice of the Bench; that he retired in 1255 and that he died in 1257.

In the first half of the thirteenth century the Wassand family, in addition to their holdings at Wassand, near Hornsea in Holderness, seem to have held also at Ilton, near Masham, possibly as tenants of Fountains abbey, and to have been tenants of Durham episcopal manors at South Otterington and Thornton le Street.[2] The Meaux chronicle refers to some members of the family who were Alan's contemporaries, but they do not mention him.[3] This suggests that he may have belonged to a branch of the family living outside Holderness. There are somewhat circumstantial grounds for believing that he was the brother of Adam de Wassand, who in the 1220s was the senior member of the family at South Otterington. The evidence is as follows. On 29 December 1226, Adam de Wassand presented Richard de Wassand to the Wassand moiety of South Otterington church.[4] In an undated Fountains charter which may come from the 1230s, Alan and Richard de Wassand are witnesses along with Alan de Staveley.[5] In another undated Fountains charter, Alan de Wassand and Adam his brother occur along with Alan de Staveley as witnesses to a grant made to the abbey by Adam de Staveley.[6] It may be added that on 22 July 1240 Alan released his interests in seven bovates of land at Elslack, in Broughton, to Alice de Staveley, who seems to have been the daughter and heiress of Adam de Staveley.[7]

1 Plea rolls of the Bench and of eyres cited in this article are referred to by their Public Record Office call numbers, respectively in the class Curia Regis Rolls (*K.B.* 26) and Rolls of the Justices Itinerant etc. (*J.I.* 1).

2 *Victoria County History, North Riding*, i, 327, 445; ii, 50.

3 *Chronica de Melsa* (*Rolls' Series*), i, 308, 368; ii, 97, 220.

4 *Gray's Register* (*Surtees Society*), 14 (no. 56).

5 *Fountains Chartulary*, ed. W. T. Lancaster, 702. The grantor and abbot is John, the prior is Ralph of Oxford. The grantee is John le Harpur of Swinton, who occurs in a conveyance of 1234 : *Yorkshire Fines*, 1232-46, ed. Col. John Parker, 25-6. In 1231, Richard de Watsant was Alan de Staveley's attorney : *J.I.* 1/1042, m. 1d.

6 *Fountains Chartulary*, 55.

7 *Yorks. Fines*, 1232-46, 77 (no. 917).

What is known of Alan's career before 1246 points to very close connexions with the Stuteville family and suggests that for a time he was a member of the archbishop of York's household.

As to the Stuteville connexion. In the Yorkshire eyre held in June—July 1231, Nicholas de Stuteville had to defend an action brought by Thomas de Aslakeby and his wife about common of pasture in Southwood pertaining to tenements in Fadmoor and Gillamoor. His case was conducted by *Alanus de Watsand ballivus ipsius Nicholai*, who won it.[1] Nicholas was also represented by Alan, this time described as his attorney, in a case brought by Thomas Fossard about the wardship of an estate at Sutton under Whitestone Cliffe.[2] Not long after 1 October 1231 Alan witnessed the confirmation by Nicholas of a seven year lease to the archbishop of lands at Boltby and Ravensthorpe.[3] In October 1233 Alan acted as Nicholas's attorney in two final concords made in the Bench at Westminster.[4] Then on 3 September and 10 November 1233 the archbishop confirmed two grants made to Alan by William, the rector of Bossall, who seems to have been William de Stuteville.[5] The first was of William's life interests in the corn and pulse tithes from Sand Hutton, a Bossall chapelry, which he granted at a rent of four shillings yearly until Alan obtained another benefice; the second was a grant of the same tithes from Flaxton, another chapelry. Then, not long before 8 March 1236, Osmund de Stuteville, rector of Cottingham, granted Alan for life the tithes from Skidby, a chapelry in his parish.[6] Next, on 29 July 1240, Eustace de Stuteville granted Alan a carucate of land and forty shillings rent at 'Holm'.[7] This place may have been Paull Holme, on the Humber; for in Hilary and Easter terms 1243 Alan was litigating in the Bench in a plea of covenant concerning half an acre of land and three acres of meadow at 'Holm' against Abraham de Pagula and Simon de Preston.[8] Alan also witnessed two undated charters of Eustace de Stuteville, one of which was concerned with lands at Middleton, near Pickering, where by 1247 at latest Alan was rector.[9] Finally, Alan witnessed an undated quitclaim by Robert de Bowforth which rounded off a grant made by Robert de Stuteville III to Keldholme priory.[10] A fellow witness is Nicholas the clerk of Buttercrambe, a township in Bossall that recalls Alan's interests at Sand Hutton and Flaxton.

The evidence for Alan's connexion with the archbishop of York is of two kinds. Between 1238 and 1243 he occurs as a

[1] *J.I.* 1/1042, m. 4. [2] *Ibid.*, m. 14.

[3] *Early Yorkshire Charters*, ed. C. T. Clay, ix, 129; *cf. Gray's Register*, 239, note.

[4] *Yorks. Fines*, 1232-46, 6-7 (nos. 614-5).

[5] *Gray's Register*, 63 (no. 268), 64 (no. 274); *cf. ibid.*, 5, 6, 20.

[6] *Ibid.*, 73 (no. 313); *cf. ibid.*, 5 (no. 19).

[7] *Yorks. Fines*, 1232-46, 83 (no. 950).

[8] *K.B.* 26/127, m. 18d. In the Yorkshire eyre of 1246 a Simon de Preston was acting as attorney for Henry de Stuteville : *J.I.* 1/1045, m. 45.

[9] *Early Yorkshire Charters*, ix, nos. 56, 57.

[10] *Ibid.*, 227.

witness, along with men known to have belonged to the archbishop's household, in at least five archiepiscopal instruments. The first, dated 13 May 1238, is William of York's charter of institution to the royal living of Kirkham.[1] The next, of 16 September 1241, is a confirmation of a grant made to the Ripon chapter.[2] The third is the archbishop's confirmation on 29 January 1242 of a grant made to the Southwell chapter by Robert de Lexington, then senior justice of the Bench and himself a canon of Southwell.[3] Next there is a deed of an institution to West Rounton which was made at Reading on 20 July 1243;[4] the archbishop was at this time senior regent during Henry III's absence in France and so was in the south of England. Finally Alan occurs in a deed concerning Gray family matters that is undated but whose witnesses enable it to be assigned to 1239-41.[5] In the other kind of evidence we find Alan acting as the archbishop's attorney in legal proceedings in royal courts. He so acts in a conveyance to the archbishop of houses at York that was made in January 1241, during the concluding session of a Yorkshire eyre.[6] He is then found so acting in a series of final concords concerning Gray family interests in Oxfordshire, mainly at Coggs, which were made in April and June 1241, during eyres in southern England, and in July 1242 and April 1246 in the Bench.[7] In Easter term 1244 he was so acting in another plea concerning the archbishop's Oxfordshire interests.[8]

A man who served in the household of so celebrated an elder statesman as archbishop Gray might pass easily into the royal service, but such a man would not be appointed a justice of the Bench unless he had had a solid experience of judicial administration. Many of the men appointed in the first half of Henry III's reign had acquired such experience as sheriffs or royal administrators. For example, Alan's senior colleague during his first four years as a justice was Henry of Bath, who had served for over a decade as sheriff in various counties before becoming a justice and who until 1248 was still nominally sheriff of Yorkshire. Some men rose to a judgeship from service as clerks in the courts. For example, William of York had served for some fourteen years as a clerk in the Bench before becoming a justice; in 1246 he was the senior justice of the court *coram rege*, provost of Beverley, canon of York and the holder of several Yorkshire benefices. The justice next in seniority to Henry of Bath in the Bench was Roger de Thurkelby, an East Riding man who had served nearly a decade as clerk in the Bench before becoming a justice and who had built up a considerable network of estates

[1] *Gray's Register*, 82 (no. 354).
[2] *Memorials of Ripon* (*Surtees Society*, vol. 115), iv, 48.
[3] *Gray's Register*, 196, note 6.
[4] *Ibid.*, 92, note.
[5] *Calendar of Charter Rolls*, 1226-57, 388.
[6] *Yorks. Fines*, 1232-46, 102 (no. 1035).
[7] *Oxfordshire Feet of Fines*, 1195-1291 (*Oxford Record Society*, vol. 12), 115, 121, 124, 126, 131.
[8] *K.B.* 26/134*A*, ms. 3, 4, 7.

in the wolds. Alan must have been doing something more than act for members of the Stuteville family or serve in the archbishop's household before his promotion. However, there is no evidence of his having acted in any judicial or administrative capacity in the royal service before 1246. The evidence already set out shows him acting as an attorney in the Bench or in eyres in 1233 and in 1241-6 and himself litigating in the Bench in 1243. It is therefore possible that he was at work as a clerk at Westminster or in eyres for some years before 1246, having secured this appointment through the archbishop and his fellow Yorkshiremen William of York and Roger de Thurkelby. In this connexion it may be noted that within a month of his own promotion, Roger de Whitchester, who is known to have been one of William of York's protegés, was appointed keeper of the writs and rolls of the Bench. Had the vacancy in this office been caused by Alan's promotion to be a justice?

The date of Alan's promotion can be fixed to within a few days after 29 April 1246, a little after the beginning of Easter term.[1] The Bench had been depleted because Roger de Thurkelby had begun an eyre circuit in the north, taking two others of the regular Bench justices with him. Alan was appointed as an additional justice at Westminster. He does not occur in any of the final concords made on the quinzaine of Easter, the first period in the term; he occurs in three of the seven made during the next period, Easter three weeks (covering business done between 29 April and 5 May) and in all thereafter. Of his three colleagues, one retired and one died in the summer so that by Michaelmas term 1246 Alan was Henry of Bath's only colleague. In September 1247 Bench sessions were suspended for two years while Henry and Alan began an eyre circuit, with colleagues, that lasted until July 1249. During this time they held eyres for the counties of Cambridge, Huntingdon, Essex, Hertford, Surrey, Kent, Sussex, Hampshire, Wiltshire and Middlesex. The Bench resumed sessions in Michaelmas term 1249; thenceforward Alan sat in all terms until Michaelmas 1255. He was, indeed, commissioned for another eyre circuit in the winter of 1252-3 but he did not serve.[2] He was only twice absent, for no more than a few days, about 13 October 1252 and 11 April 1255.[3] In all, he is named as a justice in some 1,644 final concords made in the Bench and in some 947 made in the eyre circuit of 1247-9. The chirographers never adopted a particular spelling of his name; their commonest forms were Wadsa(u)nd, Watsa(u)nd or Wassa(u)nd and occasionally we find oddities like Waughesand and Waxant.

[1] Details of his career as a justice in the Bench and eyre are based on a complete survey of the final concords of Henry III's reign.

[2] *Close Rolls*, 1251-3, 247; *Calendar of Patent Rolls*, 1247-58, 161.

[3] In 1252 he is present in only 5 of 8 fines made on the octave of Michaelmas and in 26 of 27 made on the quinzaine, but in all later fines of that term. In 1254 he is present in only 3 of 8 fines made on the quinzaine of Easter but in all later fines made in that term. Perhaps in each case his arrival was delayed after the vacation.

The plea rolls do not often mention the justices in their judicial capacity, but there are occasional references. For example, in Michaelmas term 1252 a writ of right in a Lincolnshire case was accidentally damaged and the clerk notes in the plea roll that the device or signet seal (*signum*) of sir Alan de Wassand was appended to the damaged writ, in case the writ should be challenged at some later time.[1] During the king's absence in France in 1253-4 there is a marked increase alike in the plea rolls and chancery rolls of notes of authorizations of this or that order by a particular official. So in Michaelmas term 1253, for example, we find Alan authorizing the adjournment of certain actions either alone or in company with a colleague, master Simon of Walton.[2]

In addition to his service as a judge in term time his vacations, like those of his colleagues, were partly occupied by taking possessory assizes in the provinces. Until about 1242 the great majority of such assizes had been taken by four local gentlemen of knightly status; a minority only were taken by two justices of the central courts in association or by one such justice with powers to choose his own colleagues from local knights or ecclesiastics. But from about 1242 this last sort of commission rapidly ousted the others, so that nearly all assizes were taken by justices of the central courts, stewards of the royal household or senior clerks in the chancery. The assize commissions are recorded on the dorses of the patent rolls, but they are omitted from the printed *Calendar of Patent Rolls*. In the regnal years 33 to 36 and 38 Henry III only, the dorses of the patent rolls were not sufficient for entering all the assize commissions. The overflow was entered on the close rolls and is included in the text of the printed *Close Rolls;* but it includes too few of Alan's commissions to give a proper picture of his activity.[3] No commissions are recorded for Alan in 1246-7; his first issued, undated, early in 1248.[4] Out of a total of some 470 commissions issued during the regnal years 32 and 33 Henry III (28 Oct. 1247—27 Oct. 1249), Alan received 52 individual commissions and four in association with fellow justices. The number of commissions for each of the twelve counties he had to visit were as follows: Northumberland, 4; Westmorland, 2; Cumberland and Lancashire, 1 each; Yorkshire, 34; Lincolnshire, 3; Nottinghamshire, 1; Cambridgeshire, 5; Huntingdonshire and Bedfordshire, 1 each; Essex, 2; Surrey, 1. His commissions for 1249-55 conform to the same pattern, which is readily explainable. His main sphere lay in Yorkshire and the four northern counties, where his benefices

[1] *K.B.* 26/147 *B*, m. 13d.

[2] *K.B.* 26/148, m. 14 (*bis*), m. 17 (*bis*), m. 23d.

[3] They occur in *Close Rolls*, 1247-51, 369 (34 Henry III), 536-7, 559, 561 (35 Henry III); *Close Rolls*, 1251-3, 233, 236, 250, 253 (36 Henry III); *Close Rolls*, 1253-4, 147-8, 150-2, 158-9, 164 (38 Henry III). They total: Yorks., 12; Kent, 4; Notts. 2; Lincs., Northants., Rutland and Cambs., 1 each. His Lancashire commissions are listed in *Calendar of Lancashire Assize Rolls*, part ii (*Lancs. and Cheshire Record Society*, vol. 49), 222-3.

[4] *Patent Roll* 32 *Henry III*, m. 10d.

and lay estates lay and where he spent most of his vacations. Then some six or eight times a year—certainly at the beginning and end of the Christmas, Lent and Long vacations, possibly also of the Whitsun vacation which lasted three weeks—he travelled to or from the north on his journeyings to Westminster; so he received commissions for counties traversed by one of the main roads to the north, or easily reached from them. Lastly he received commissions for the home counties. Sessions for these were commonly held by Bench justices in or just out of term time at places not far from Westminster : at Stratford Langthorne for Essex, at Greenwich for Kent, at Bermondsey or Lambeth for Surrey. In 1247-9 he was on eyre in southern England and received only three such commissions. In later years he received many more. In the regnal years 34—36 Henry III (October 1249—October 1252) he received some 94 commissions, alone or with colleagues, as follows : Northumberland, 3; Cumberland and Westmorland, 1 each; Yorkshire, 15; Derbyshire, 1; Notts., 9; Leics., Northants. and Rutland, 1 each; Lincs., 4; Beds. and Hunts., 1 each; Cambs., 7; Herts., 6; Essex, 6; Kent, 27; Middlesex, 2; Surrey, 4; Berks. and Sussex, 1 each. The comparative fewness of his northern commissions in this period was due to an eyre being held for Yorkshire in 1251-2, which attracted much northern business from outside the county as well as the county pleas. Unfortunately none of Alan's assize rolls survive, so we cannot trace his vacation work in detail.

The Bench plea rolls also provide some indications of his vacation activity, for in addition to taking possessory assizes the justices of the central courts also undertook stages of business in connexion with pleas being litigated in their courts. For example, in Trinity term 1253 the Nottinghamshire parties to a conveyance by final concord, who included a husband and wife, were adjourned to the octave of Michaelmas for receiving the chirographs of their fine, because the wife had not yet made her acknowledgment of the terms of the conveyance : "and meanwhile let her make acknowledgment before Alan de Wassand when he comes to those parts" as he would do when he went north at the end of term.[1] In Michaelmas term 1253 the parties in a Cumberland action reach a stage in the pleadings when they agree to the material point being settled by an inquest. The sheriff is given a date for summoning the jury "and then let it be enquired here, or else before A. de Wassand if before then he comes to those parts."[2] Alan seems to have found the jury originally summoned, no doubt in the Christmas vacation, to be insufficiently informed; he apparently held the inquest again in the Long vacation, for he returned the record of the inquest at the beginning of the next Michaelmas term. In June 1254 we find him being instructed to

[1] *K.B.* 26/149, m. 18d. Robert de Amundevill v. Richard son of William de Gray and wife Lucy.

[2] *K.B.* 26/148, m. 33d. Roald fitz Alan and wife Isabel v. William de Warthwyk.

receive the attornies of some members of the York chapter on his next journey through that city.[1]

Apart from the routine possessory assizes and business connected with litigation in the Bench, Alan seems to have undertaken only two special commissions. When the king left England for some time it was usual for an assize of Arms to be held; Alan took the assize for Northumberland and Yorkshire in the Long vacation of 1253.[2] In 1252-3 his colleague, William de Wilton, in the course of holding an enquiry into coinage offences, had prejudiced the liberties enjoyed by St. Albans; this led the abbey cellarer to conduct an expensive law suit that ended in judgment for the abbot in the Low tide parliament of 1254. As a result of this judgment the inquest into the coinage offences of the men in the abbey's franchises was to be reheard; Alan was commissioned for this in May 1254.[3]

Alan continued to take assizes for some time after his retirement from the Bench. During 40 Henry III (28 Oct. 1255—27 Oct. 1256) he received 10 commissions for Yorkshire, 2 for Lancashire and Nottinghamshire, and 1 each for Cumberland, Lincolnshire, Bedfordshire and Cambridgeshire. His last recorded commission issued about 9 September 1256.[4] He had not been alone in taking Yorkshire business. Roger de Thurkelby and, to a lesser extent, Henry of Bath, with their Yorkshire interests, took a fair amount of business in that county. In the four northern counties he shared business with John de Lexington, a steward of the household and member of the court *coram rege*, who came from a brilliant Nottinghamshire family and who had acquired more northern interests through marriage with Roger de Morlay's widow followed by appointment (1252-5) as justice of the northern forests and keeper of several northern castles. Lexington died about the same time as Alan. Northern litigants then came before others, most commissions issuing to Peter de Percy, who was never a member of a central court, with some assistance from others including Giles of Erdington, a retired Bench justice.

About the time Alan was promoted to the Bench it was becoming customary for the judges to receive an annual salary; the authorities for the payment of the half-yearly instalments of such salaries are entered in the *liberate* rolls. No half-yearly instalments are recorded for Alan. The only grants found concerning him so far are that on 21 May 1247 he was granted 40 marks, payable out of the revenue in Yorkshire (his two fellow justices in the Bench occur in the same authority), that in 1249, when on eyre, he received 20*li.* payable from the revenue of Kent, and that on 17 May 1252 he was granted 20 marks, payable out

[1] *Close Rolls*, 1253-4, 141.
[2] *Close Rolls*, 1251-3, 493.
[3] *Calendar of Patent Rolls*, 1247-58, 377; *cf. Gesta Abbatum . . . Sancti Albani* (*Rolls Series*), vol. i, 341-2.
[4] *Patent Roll* 40 *Henry III*, m. 5d.

of the revenue in Lincolnshire.[1] However, we cannot be sure that he did not receive an annual salary; it may have been paid other than by *liberate* on revenue accountable at the exchequer. Many of his colleagues received frequent marks of royal favour in the shape of timber or game from royal forests. The only such gift recorded for Alan seems to be one of three bucks from Galtres forest, in May 1255.[2] It was a common practice for the justices and other royal servants to enter details of casual loans on the rolls of the courts or of chancery. Two such recognizances entered on the Bench plea rolls show that Alan commanded considerable resources. In Michaelmas term 1252 the prominent Lincolnshire knight William de Kyme borrowed 42*li.* from Alan and Thomas de Dureme, repayable on 18 November 1252.[3] In Michaelmas term 1253 Alan himself borrowed 67½ marks from his fellow justice, master Simon of Walton. Of this sum, 60 marks were to be repayed at the New Temple in London by 2 February 1254 and 7½ marks were to be repayed at St. Ives' fair in Huntingdonshire, by 3 May following.[4]

Something has already been said about Alan's early ecclesiastical and lay interests. Apparently in 1247 he obtained a papal dispensation to hold Heversham along with Middleton (in Ryedale deanery, near Pickering) without cure of souls.[5] The terms of the dispensation suggest perhaps that he had held Middleton for some time but had only recently obtained Heversham. It is not clear who possessed the advowson of Middleton at this time, but it may have been a Stuteville living and so may have been one more example of the patronage he received from that family.[6] It was worth 53*li.* 6*s.* 8*d.* according to the 1291 *Taxatio*. Heversham, near Morcambe Bay in Westmorland, was in the patronage of St. Mary's York and valued at 100 marks in the *Taxatio*. Alan's Westmorland interests are reflected in pleas of debt which he brought in the Bench in Michaelmas term 1250 against Henry of Nottingham for 14 marks and against Hugh de Sokebred for 5 marks.[7] In Trinity and Michaelmas terms 1253 there are stages of another plea of debt against a Westmorland man, Roger son of William son of Ketel, against whom Alan claims 12*li.* 3*s.* 4*d.*[8] All royal justices and servants habitually made use of the royal courts for such matters. In 1245 Alan was litigating in the Cumberland county court against Thomas the parson of Brigham and paid a mark for the action to be transferred to the Bench at Westminster.[9] He must have had some kind of an estate in Cumberland, possibly in the Cockermouth district, since the

[1] *Calendar of Liberate Rolls*, 1245-51, 124; *Pipe Roll* 33 Henry III, Kent account; *Calendar of Liberate Rolls*, 1251-60, 48.

[2] *Close Rolls*, 1254-6, 127.

[3] *K.B.* 26/147 *B*, m. 11.

[4] *K.B.* 26/148, m. 43.

[5] *Gray's Register*, 98-9 (no. 448).

[6] *V.C.H., North Riding*, ii, 455, 460.

[7] *K.B.* 26/143, m. 10d.

[8] *K.B.* 26/149, m. 21; *K.B.* 26/148, m. 22.

[9] *Fine Roll*, 28 *Henry III*, m. 11.

payment was summoned in that county and cleared in the Cumberland account in the pipe roll.[1] This transfer of an action to the Bench supports the belief that he was at work in that court before his promotion.

On 11 May 1255 a papal dispensation issued for him to hold a canonry of Ripon without cure, beside his other benefices already dispensed.[2] On 30 May the chancery issued instructions pursuant to this dispensation.[3] This suggests that he had only recently obtained his canonry. He is mentioned as a canon of Ripon in a donation charter which has been ascribed to 1242;[4] but he is not styled canon of Ripon in his attestations to archbishop Gray's deeds. This was the highest dignity he obtained.

Matthew Paris, the great St. Albans historian, found a place in his *Chronica Majora* or *Gesta Abbatum* for royal justices who had tried St. Albans cases during his lifetime. To those whose misfortune it had been to give judgment against the abbey in a suit Matthew accorded Obituaries which hinted uncharitably at their subjects' eternal fate. But Alan's session for coinage offences in the protomartyr's franchises had been the mark of an abbey triumph in 1254. It is quite possible that on that occasion Alan had been entertained in the abbey and Matthew had met him. Moreover, Alan had been in the Bench in 1250 and 1252 when some matters had gone favourably for the abbey.[5] So when news of Alan's death reached Matthew he wrote a brief but kindly obituary to say that Alan had been a special king's clerk and judge, who had happily laid down the burden of judgeship before he died, about Epiphany tide 1257.[6] Matthew then went on to record the death of Alan's fellow assize commissioner in the north, John de Lexington.

[1] *Cumberland and Westmorland Pipe Rolls*, ed. F. H. M. Parker, 115, 119.

[2] *Calendar of Papal Registers*, 1198—1304, 316.

[3] *Calendar of Patent Rolls*, 1247-58, 230.

[4] *Memorials of Ripon*, iv, 73.

[5] *Chronica Majora*, vi, 175, 299.

[6] *Ibid.*, v, 610. In his paper *The Tournament in the Thirteenth Century* (*Studies Presented to F.M. Powicke*, 256), Mr. Denholm Young suggests that Alan died as a result of injuries received at a great tournament held at Blyth in June 1256. His citation of the *Chronica Majora* is inaccurate and he seems unaware that Alan was an elderly ecclesiastic. The suggestion is groundless.

XIV

ROGER OF WHITCHESTER (†1258).

Roger of Whitchester was a Northumbrian whose career was spent almost wholly in southern England, for he was one of many north countrymen who served Henry III in judicial administration. The *History of Northumberland*, Vol. XIII, gives a brief notice of him in his family's pedigree.[1] Foss's equally brief notice of him in the *Dictionary of the Judges* has several inaccuracies; the *Dictionary of National Biography* does not include him. The present account of his career, compiled from the main printed sources and some readily workable unpublished records, is intended to serve as a reasonably full biography until the time when more records of Henry III's reign (such as the plea rolls of eyres in which Roger served as a clerk or justice or of southern English counties in which he held estates) have been printed, or until someone attempts a more exhaustive search of unpublished records. The principal facts of his career are: that he was the eldest, or eldest surviving, son of sir Robert de Whitchester, whom he succeeded in 1244; that at some time before 1244, possibly as early as 1230, he entered the service of William of York, one of the most distinguished of Henry III's judges; that in 1246 he was appointed keeper of the rolls and writs of the Bench (later the court of Common Pleas), being the first such official known from the surviving chancery rolls; that in 1254 he was promoted to serve as a justice, in eyre and at

[1] P. 225. The name is spelt in a considerable variety of forms, e.g. Whicestre, Whycestre, Whytcestre, Wicestre, Witcestre, Wycestre, Wytcestre, Wythcestre; for simplicity the modern form has been employed throughout, including quotations.

the Bench; that he acquired by lease a number of estates in the south; and that he died about September 1258.

Roger's family is generally considered to have been the tenants at Whitchester of the Crauden family, who held the manor from the northern Bolbec barony. His father Robert is the first of the family of whom anything certain is known. He served as sheriff of Northumberland, very probably as the nominee of his lord Hugh de Bolbec III whom he immediately succeeded, from 14 January 1221 to 11 February 1223. Thereafter he was active in county affairs, serving in 1229, 1231, 1236 and 1238 as an assize commissioner and in 1230, 1234 and 1237 for gaol deliveries.[2] In the great survey of 1242-3 he is returned as holding from the Bolbec barony $\frac{1}{4}$ of the manor of Benwell by military service (as $\frac{1}{8}$ of a fee) and 40 acres at Heddon on the Wall by socage tenancy for 15d. rent.[3] In 1220 he was apparently holding 4 oxgangs at Eachwick in Heddon of the Delavals (who held of the Bolbecs) and at some time in the 1220's or 1230's he bought 60 acres of woodland at Benwell of William de Kimble (who held of the Bolbecs), which he proceeded to clear and cultivate.[4] His most considerable holding was also not held of the Bolbecs immediately. The manors of Whitchester, Houghton and part of Wallington had been held of the northern Bolbec barony since early in Henry II's reign by the Crauden family, who came from Croydon near Royston in Cambridgeshire.[5] A damaged final concord was made in the Bench at some time between November 1221 and October 1222 between John de Crauden and Robert de Whitchester and his wife Isabel concerning this estate.[6] By it, John admitted Robert's right and Robert granted it to

[2] For assizes: *Calendar of Patent Rolls 1225-32*, 351, 443, 447; Patent Rolls, 20 Henry III m. 9d and 22 Henry III m. 10d. For gaol deliveries: *CPR 1225-32*, 365; *C.P.R. 1232-47*, 76; Patent Roll Henry III, m. 9d, cf. *Close Rolls 1234-7*, 241.

[3] *Book of Fees*, ii, 1113, 1123.

[4] *History of Northumberland*, XIII, 87 (citing Hodgson's *History*, III, iii, col. 124) and Northumberland 1256 eyre roll in *Surtees Society*, vol. 88, 12-13.

[5] *History of Northumberland*, XIII, 101; Hodgson's *History*, II, i, 252-3; Farrer, *Feudal Cambridgeshire*, 14-16.

[6] *Northumberland Fines* (Newcastle on Tyne Record Series, vol. x), no. 61.

John for life at a nominal rent, with reversion to Robert and his heirs by Isabel to hold of John's heirs at a rent of £5 payable half yearly on 2 February and 1 August: the estate to revert to John and his heirs if Robert died without heirs by Isabel. The probable explanation of this conveyance would seem to be that Isabel was herself a Crauden, possibly a sister or daughter of John, who was thereby making provision for her children. The conveyance was to be the source of much litigation during the rest of the century. The first such action was probably begun in 1235, for before Easter term 1236 Isabel de Whitchester had essoined herself *de malo lecti* in it and appointed her attorneys.[7] It was brought by Robert de Beverley and his wife Sybil daughter of Hugh de Crauden against Robert de Whitchester and his wife Isabel and was compromised by a final concord made in the Bench on the morrow of St. John (25 June) 1236.[8] By it, Robert and Isabel admitted the right of Robert de Beverley and Sybil, in return for which admission the latter granted the estate to Robert and Isabel for their joint lives at a yearly rent of 10 marks, payable half yearly on St. Cuthbert's days (20 March and 4 September): the estate to revert after their deaths to Robert de Beverley and Sybil and their heirs. By 1242 Robert de Beverley and Isabel de Whitchester were dead and Sybil de Crauden had begun another action against Robert de Whitchester, who early in 1243 essoined himself *de malo lecti* and appointed attorneys.[9] This too was compromised by a final concord, made in the Bench on the quinzaine of Michaelmas (13 October) 1243.[10] By it, in return for Robert's admission of her right, Sybil granted it to him and his heirs by his late wife Isabel at the increased rent of £8, payable half yearly as before: a special clause was added whereby Robert promised not to sell, pledge or alienate the estate or any

[7] *Northumberland Pleas* (Newcastle on Tyne Record Series, vol. ii), nos. 363-4.

[8] *Northumberland Fines*, no. 131; where for "January" read "June".

[9] *Northumberland Pleas*, nos. 419, 423-4.

[10] *Northumberland Fines*, no. 178.

part of it. Although the fine conveyed the whole fee, in her writ Sybil had excepted 1½ carucates, 3 messuages, a toft and a mill from Whitchester manor and ½ carucate and a messuage from Houghton manor. From a later action we know that Robert remarried after Isabel's death; it is reasonable to conclude that his second marriage took place about the time of this action, whose object was to secure the inheritance of his children by his first wife. In Easter term 1244 we find Sybil de Crauden litigating against Roger de Whitchester in a plea of fine made, that is for the payment of the rent stipulated in the final concord just described, and before 8 June 1244 Roger was being distrained to take up knighthood.[11] We may therefore conclude that Robert de Whitchester died some time between October 1243 and April 1244 and was succeeded in his tenancy by Roger.

The earliest notice which we have found of Roger is of his institution by the archbishop of York (the see of Durham being vacant) on 4 September 1226 to the rectory of Elsdon, in Redesdale, on the presentation of Richard de Umfravill.[12] We do not know how long Roger held this living, but in 1245 the incumbent was Vincent Cornwalais.[13] The only other preferment Roger is known to have held is the Sussex rectory of Ovingdean, near Brighton. One Edmund had held this rectory since before 1219 until his death in 1248.[14] The right to the advowson was litigated in the Sussex eyre of 1248 (in which Roger was keeper of the writs and rolls) when judgment was given for three coheirs and their husbands.[15] Roger was probably presented soon afterwards by the coheirs, for there exist his letters testimonial as rector, dated 20 December 1252 and 31 January 1253, whereby he

[11] *Northumberland Pleas*, no. 433.

[12] Gray's Register (Surtees Society, vol. 56), 11.

[13] Inquisition on death of Gilbert de Umfravill, Inquisitions post mortem Henry III, file 3, no. 9. The value of the living there given is 80 marks, not 40 as in Hodgson's *History*, II, i, 88.

[14] P.R.O. Ancient Deeds, Treasury of Receipt (from Lewes priory archives) A 14198, 14221, 14227.

[15] J.I. 1/909A, m. 5.

confirmed the release to Lewes priory of the right to some tithes in his parish about which he had been litigating before judges delegate.[16] Dugdale thought Roger held a canonry of St. Paul's but was confusing him with Roger of Worcester of an earlier generation who held the Brondesbury prebend 1192-1230.[17] It is surprising that we find no evidence of his having held other benefices in Gray's register, in the rolls of the bishops of Lincoln that cover most of his career, in the chancery enrolments by royal presentation *sede vacante*, or in plea rolls and deeds. It is, however, possible that he obtained preferment in dioceses for which there are no registers, such as Canterbury, London or Rochester.

In an entry in the Bench in Michaelmas term 1230 there is reference to "a certain roll which Roger the clerk of William of York holds".[18] William had been a senior clerk of the Bench since the winter of 1218-19 if not earlier and we know from his own correspondence that he had other clerks working under him. It is not certain that this Roger was Roger de Whitchester, for another Roger was at work in the Bench about this time: Roger de Thurkelby, from William's native East Riding. But in another entry of the same term there is a memorandum that William of York has the particulars of certain lands while Roger de Thurkelby has the note of a final concord to be made about these lands.[19] Possibly, therefore, William's clerk Roger and Roger de Thurkelby were not identical; and in December 1231 Roger de Thurkelby is said to be the clerk of William's lifelong friend and colleague, William de Raleigh. But after the death of Robert de Whitchester we have certain evidence of Roger de Whitchester's association with William of York. As we have seen, in succeeding to the family estates Roger

[16] P.R.O. Ancient Deeds, Treasury of Receipt (also from priory archives) A. 14222, 14228 (of which a cartulary copy is in *Chartulary of Lewes Priory* (Sussex Record Society), II, 56-7).

[17] *Origines Juridiciales*, 21; cf. Newcourt's *Repertorium*, ed. Hennessy, 14.

[18] This and other Bench plea rolls cited are in an artificially made Public Record Office collection whose call reference is K.B. 26, by which they are cited: *K.B. 26/107*, m. 23d.

[19] *Ibid.*, m. 32.

became liable to take up knighthood or to be distrained to do so and just at this time, with a Welsh war imminent, there was considerable pressure from government on all those with this liability. William of York was now senior justice of the court *coram rege* and we may safely assume that it was he who secured the issue on 8 June 1244 of an order to the sheriff of Northumberland respiting until further notice distraint of knighthood on Roger de Whitchester: " because we desire that clerks occupied in our service should be in better condition than others and . . . Roger . . . has borne himself laudably in the service of William of York."[20] The little we know of Roger before 1246 is consistent with his having been in the courts since 1230, and it must be remembered that fewer plea rolls of the Bench and eyres have survived from the 1230's than from any other decade under Henry III. In Trinity term 1231 Roger was acting as attorney for William de Percy in a Sussex action in the Bench.[21] Certain evidence of his presence as a clerk in the Bench comes from the feet of fines for 1236 Trinity term, for 12 of the 44 fines surviving from this term bear endorsements indicating that the money due for the making of the chirographs is to be answered for by clerks, a thing unique in the fines of Henry III.[22] One has "W. de Holebech' is to answer", another "W. the clerk of sir W. de Culewrth' is to answer", whence we may deduce that William of Holbeach was clerk to William de Culworth, the junior justice. The others all refer to Roger: seven have "Upon R. de Whitchester"; two have "R. de Whitchester is to answer"; one has, more explicitly, "And R. the clerk is to answer for the money for this chirograph". In Trinity

[20] *Close Rolls 1242-7*, 247.
[21] *K.B. 26/109*, m. 7.
[22] Although most of these fines have been calendared by local societies, the endorsements have been noticed by only two editors. References, in the Feet of Fines Henry III (class call number *C.P.* 25(1)) are: 54/35, nos. 523-4, 54/36, no. 528 (Kirk, *Essex Fines 1182-1272*, 114-15); 84/16, no. 225; 92/7, no. 114; 129/26, nos. 14, 16 (Massingberd, *Lincs. Fines John—Henry III*, 293); 146/10, no. 139; 172/17, no. 350; 196/5, no. 12; 233/12, no. 52; 258/5, no. 1.

term 1243 Roger held the chirographs of the final concord of a very important family settlement between the midland baron Gilbert de Segrave and his step-mother Ida, which he must certainly have done in his capacity as William of York's assistant.[23] Finally, among the essoins of the octave of Hilary (20 January) 1246 we find William of York attorning Roger in his place in a Surrey action in the Bench.[24]

On 28 May 1246 Roger was granted by letters patent an annual salary of £10 as keeper of the writs and rolls of the Bench.[25] The warrants for the payment of the half yearly instalments of this salary from the Easter half year 30 Henry III (1246) to the Easter half year 39 Henry III (1255) were enrolled on the *liberate* rolls, the first being dated 27 May 1246 and the last dated 11 May 1255.[26] There are no earlier warrants to a previous keeper so that any predecessor Roger may have had was not an official with a salary chargeable to the royal revenue. Except in 1248-9 the warrants were all for payments in cash at the exchequer, which indicates the closeness of Roger's ties with Westminster; for if he had been spending any considerable part of his vacations in the north he would, like some of his colleagues in the courts, have occasionally secured a warrant payable locally out of the revenues of Northumberland or Yorkshire. Roger also received an annual robe as a member of the royal household. The warrants for such gifts seem only to be enrolled regularly after the baronial reformers of 1258 exerted a measure of control over the household. But early in 1251, when there was an economy drive, there is a batch of warrants in favour of some royal servants including one which issued on 5 January 1251 ordering the wardrobe officials to give Roger a robe "as he

[23] *K.B. 26/130*, m. 14d.
[24] *C.P. 21/1/2*, m. 10d.
[25] *C.P.R. 1232-47*, 480.
[26] *Calendar of Liberate Rolls 1245-51*, 55, 84, 117, 144, 178, 226, 258, 288, 305, 352, 386; *Calendar of Liberate Rolls 1251-60*, 39, 79, 127, 165, 179, 217. These include all instalments save that for 37 Mich. which was entered on a portion of a roll now lost.

has been accustomed to receive on previous occasions".[27]

Roger served at the Bench from Easter term 1246 until Trinity 1247 under the senior justice, Henry of Bath, and his colleagues, the next senior justice, Roger de Thurkelby, having been absent with other regular Bench justices on eyre since the beginning of 1246. In September 1247 Henry of Bath himself began a second eyre circuit which lasted until July 1249; during these two years sessions of the Bench were suspended. Henry and his colleagues held eyres for the counties of Cambridge, Huntingdon, Essex, Hertford, Surrey, Kent, Sussex, Hampshire, Wiltshire and Middlesex.[28] Roger accompanied them in his capacity of keeper of writs and rolls; the plea rolls supply occasional evidence of his presence, for example when he has temporary keeping of chirographs during the Wiltshire eyre.[29] To cover the extra expenses of travel Roger received warrants for additional allowances: on 12 January 1247 for £10 payable from the issues of the Essex eyre, then in progress, and on 20 October 1248 for 10 marks payable from the issues of the Kent eyre, just completed.[30] Moreover on 10 April 1249 the warrant for two instalments of his regular salary, Mich. 1248 and Easter 1249, were made payable from the issues of the Hampshire eyre, just completed.[31] During this visitation Roger, like most royal servants, took the opportunity to conduct some private business. In the Hampshire eyre we find William Bugge of Nottingham admitting that he owed Roger 6 marks for a horse which Roger had sold him and agreeing to pay this sum by Easter three weeks (25 April) 1249. In the Wiltshire eyre there is a stage of an action for a debt of 71s. 4d. which Roger had brought against Robert Splote of Sempringham, co. Lincoln; Robert did not appear so distraint of all his lands and chattels was ordered,

[27] *Close Rolls 1247-51*, 395.

[28] These and other details of eyres are taken from my *Eyre List Henry III*.

[29] Wilts. 1249 eyre, foreign pleas rolls: *J.I 1/997*, m. 3; *J.I. 1/777*, m. 13d.

[30] *C. Lib. R. 1245-51*, 161, 204; *cf.* Essex Account, Pipe Roll 32 Henry III, rot. 4d, and Kent account, Pipe Roll 33 Henry III, rot. 7d, where the payment is, however, 20 marks.

[31] *Ibid.*, 226; *cf.* Hants. account, Pipe Roll 33 Henry III, rot. 8d.

returnable on 1 July 1249 in the Middlesex eyre, of which the roll is lost.[32]

The Bench resumed sessions in Michaelmas 1249; thenceforward Roger acted as keeper until Trinity 1254 though he remained nominally keeper, drawing his salary, until Hilary 1255. He was succeeded by another, and eventually more distinguished, Northumbrian in Richard de Middleton, who rose to become chancellor.[33] None of the Bench or eyre writ files of Roger's term of office survive; nor are there any Bench plea rolls from 1246-7. From the 20 Bench terms, 1249 Michaelmas to 1254 Trinity, there are sixteen rolls from 12 terms; from the eyres of 1247-9 (Bath's circuit) there are civil and crown plea rolls from 5 and foreign plea rolls from 6.[34] There are several changes in methods of enrolment during this period. The most important was the creation of the foreign pleas rolls of eyres. Since the closing years of the twelfth century the work of the Bench and eyre had been closely integrated. When Bench sessions were suspended for an eyre visitation, as in 1247, the business hitherto conducted at Westminster was carried on in the circuits. Hence the justices heard civil pleas from many counties other than from that in which they were sitting. Down to the summer of 1247 it had been the practice to enrol all such pleas in a single roll. From the autumn of 1247, when Roger accompanied the justices in Bath's circuit, it became the practice for all the pleas from counties other than that in

[32] *J.I. 1/777*, ms. 10, 29.

[33] Richard was appointed at the lower salary of 10 marks, of which the first recorded *liberate*, for the Mich. half year 1256, is dated 28 October 1256: *C. Lib. R. 1251-60*, 368.

[34] The Bench rolls (*K.B. 26*) are: 1249 Mich., 136 main and 135 subsidiary; 1250 Hil., 137 main and 138 subs.; 1250 Easter, 140 main and 139 subs.; 1250 Trinity, 142 main and 141 subs.; 1250 Mich., 143 main; 1251 Hil., 216 (a fragment); 1251 Trinity, 144 main; 1251 Mich., 145 subs.; 1252 Mich., 147 B subs.; 1253 Trinity, 149 subs.; 1253 Mich., 148 subs; 1254 Trinity, 154 subs. The subsidiary rolls were probably those retained by Roger and the main rolls those kept by the clerk of the senior justice. The eyre rolls (*J.I. 1*) are: Essex, 232, Herts., 318, Sussex, 909 A and 909 B, Hants., 776 and Wilts., 996, all civil and crown pleas; Cambs., 81, Hunts., 343, Herts., 319, Surrey, 871, Hants. and Wilts., 777, Wilts. (a second copy), 997, all foreign pleas.

which the justices were sitting to be enrolled in a separate section called a "foreign pleas" or "pleas of divers counties" roll. These rolls were thus similar to the normal Bench roll. Indeed, after having been kept for many centuries among the eyre rolls they were removed about 1700 by Peter le Neve (who then had custody of them as a deputy-chamberlain of the exchequer) and placed with the Bench rolls, where they remained until about 1890 when they were once more separated. It must have been a distinct advantage for a keeper of rolls to have the eyre business arranged in a form strictly analogous to Bench business. During Bath's eyres we find another innovation, whereby the appointments of attorneys are entered in special sections instead of being entered promiscuously among the pleas;[35] but this innovation made only slow headway and did not become invariable practice until the 1260's. Although the Bench had been so known since Richard I's reign it is only with one of the rolls for 1249 Michaelmas term that the title *de Banco* is found in the formal headings and thenceforward it is generally employed. Moreover, until the 1240's the Bench rolls are still rather the rolls of particular Bench justices, whose vacation business they often contain, than the impersonal record of the court. Again, from 1249 Michaelmas onwards the rolls lose their former characteristic, except for some of those of chief justices. A mandate which issued to Roger on 24 June 1253 suggests that in his time only two rolls were kept, for he was then, at the beginning of Trinity term, commanded to let Roger de Thurkelby, the senior justice, have one roll while he was to retain the other and the writs.[36] While the part Roger may have had in these and other changes is uncertain it is certainly true that his term of office coincided with a period that saw an improvement in the arrangement of eyre business and a marked tendency for the Bench rolls to become the impersonal record of the court.

The plea rolls themselves, not unnaturally, have nothing

[35] There are attorneys sections in the Herts. and Wilts. rolls only.
[36] *C.R. 1251-3*, 374.

to say about Roger's routine activity in keeping writs and rolls, but they carry several incidental references to his work in other matters about the court. For example, in 1249 Michaelmas term and in 1250 Michaelmas term we find that money due as a result of litigation to a London citizen and to a Kentish lady has been temporarily entrusted to him.[37] In 1250 Trinity term he had temporary keeping of the record of an action in the Bath city court and of the writ which called it into the Bench; he also retained a deed of covenant in a Surrey case.[38] In 1251 Michaelmas term he had custody of the deeds in a Northamptonshire action until it was composed in the following Easter term; he was also commissioned to take locally the appointments of attorney of a Kentish widow who was litigating about lands in Sittingbourne.[39] In 1253 Trinity term he kept the chirographs of a final concord which concluded a Nottinghamshire action because their delivery had been adjourned until the justice Alan de Wassand took the wife's admission locally, as he would do when he travelled up to his Yorkshire estates in the long vacation.[40] In 1253 Michaelmas term Roger had keeping of a deed whose authenticity had been challenged in a Yorkshire action and he had temporary custody of the chirographs in a Wiltshire suit.[41] These references, if of no great importance, nevertheless give us a picture of an official of the court ever at hand to discharge various pieces of business on behalf of litigants; moreover these pieces of business were just those which Roger's own master William of York had been discharging when he was a senior clerk of the Bench in the years 1218-31.[42] We get a glimpse of the influence which Roger's position commanded when an untoward event occurred in his household about March 1252. His servant, Thomas Ernald, hanged himself in a noose which was

[37] *K.B. 26/135*, m. 30 and *K.B. 26/143*, m. 33.
[38] *K.B. 26/141*, ms. 30d, 13d.
[39] *K.B. 26/145*, ms. 48, 51.
[40] *K.B. 26/149*, m. 18d.
[41] *K.B. 26/148*, ms. 4d, 24d.
[42] *Bulletin of the Inst. of Hist. Res.*, vol. XXVI (1953), pp. 161-79.

apparently weighted with a sackful of Roger's clothes. The London coroner's jury seems to have brought in a verdict not of *felo de se* but of misadventure, so we must believe that it was an accident. On 21 March letters close addressed to the sheriffs and chamberlains commanded them not to confiscate the sack and its contents, worth the considerable sum of 20s. 10d. (as deodand), but to deliver them to Roger.[43] A little later a special commission was appointed to sit at the Tower on 14 April to hold the crown plea (reviewing the coroner's proceedings) concerning Thomas's death; for this purpose John de Wyvill, a justice of the Jews (replacing William de Breton, another justice of the Jews, who was sick), and the junior Bench justice, Giles de Erdington, were appointed.[44] The commission must have confirmed the coroner's verdict, since we hear no more of the affair.

After some years' service as keeper, Roger began to be commissioned to take possessory assizes. Until about 1242 the great majority of such assizes that were not taken in eyre had been taken by four local gentlemen of knightly rank, as Robert de Whitchester had served in commissions of four justices in Northumberland. A minority only were taken by two justices of the central courts in association or by one such justice with powers to choose his own colleagues from local knights or ecclesiastics. But from about 1242 this last type of commission rapidly ousted the others so that by 1248 nearly all special assizes were taken by justices of the central courts. The demand for such commissions steadily increased, making it necessary to issue them not only to the small number of justices of the Bench and court *coram rege* but also to the stewards of the royal household and a few other royal servants with considerable judicial experience. The assize commissions were recorded on the dorses of the patent rolls, but are unfortunately omitted from the published *Calendars of Patent Rolls*. In the regnal years 34, 35, 36 and 38 Henry III the dorses of the patent rolls

[43] *C.R. 1251-3*, 67.
[44] *C.P.R. 1247-58*, 156.

were not sufficient for all the commissions so the overflow was entered on the close rolls, and is included in the published *Close Rolls*. Commissions for which fines were payable were noted in the fine rolls; a very small number of these are included in the published *Excerpta e Rotulis Finium*.[45] Roger was first commissioned in the summer of 1251 for three Kent assizes, in each case as junior associate of the Bench justice Alan de Wassand.[46] In 1252 he received 11 commissions: 5 in Essex, in association with the local magnate and administrator Peter de Tany or the Bench justice Giles de Erdington; one in Surrey, with William le Breton; one in Kent in association with the exchequer baron and precious metals expert Edward of Westminster and 3 there alone and one in Suffolk alone.[47] Thenceforward he was usually commissioned alone. If we analyse under counties the total of some 126 commissions which Roger received in 1251-8 we see how remarkably his activity was confined to southern England and to two counties in particular.[48] The number of commissions, in rough geographical order, is as follows: Northumberland 5, Yorkshire 9, Nottinghamshire 1, Bedfordshire 1, Cambridgeshire 3, Norfolk 1, Suffolk 5, Essex 33, Hertfordshire 10, Middlesex 2, Kent 29, Surrey 6, Sussex 1, Hampshire 2, Berkshire 1, Wiltshire 3, Gloucestershire 1, Somerset 10, Dorset 3; the commissions for the last six counties nearly all issued when he was on eyre in those parts as a justice in 1255-6. For a north-countryman this pattern is exceptional. Roger's master William of York had taken assizes while still a clerk; but both then and as a justice he had taken assizes mostly in his

[45] In Roger's case only 13 are given, dated between October 1252 and August 1258: *Excerpta*, ii, 141, 154, 159, 174, 196, 206, 245, 248, 252, 265, 278-9, 286.

[46] P.R. 35 Henry III, ms. 9d, 8d, 7d.

[47] P.R. 36 Henry III, ms. 12d, 8d, 2d, 1d.

[48] Patent Roll 37 Henry III (18 commissions), ms. 23d, 21d, 18d-12d, 7d; Patent Roll 38 Henry III (6), ms. 4d, 2d, and overflow in *Close Rolls 1253-4* (3), 150, 158; Patent Roll 39 Henry III (10), ms. 17d-14d; Patent Roll 40 Henry III (18), ms. 17d, 14d, 11d, 8d, 6d-4d; Patent Roll 41 Henry III (21), ms. 17d-15d, 13d, 8d, 1d; Patent Roll 42 Henry III (36), ms. 17d, 15d, 13d-7d, 5d, 3d.

native county or in counties athwart the road there, apart from a few home county assizes which the Bench justices regularly took during term-time at Lambeth, Bermondsey, Greenwich or Stratford Langthorne. The pattern of most other commissioners was the same, for they took these assizes mainly in the lent and long vacations in the counties where their lay estates or ecclesiastical benefices lay or in counties on the road to them. If we had no other evidence than Roger's commissions to guide us it would be clear that he had acquired interests in southern England. Moreover his 14 north-country commissions were not spread throughout the period: he received 2 for Northumberland and one for Yorkshire in 1254, one for Yorkshire in 1255 and all the rest in 1258. Most of the commissions were routine matters, but in some cases it looks as if Roger's services have been obtained specially. There is no space to comment on these, but when, for example, in 1253 we find that Roger has been commissioned along with Philip Lovel to try an action between Simon Passelewe and the earl of Oxford concerning an estate at West Ham, it is interesting to remember that Lovel was the treasurer and senior justice of the Jews and that Passelewe was a great financial expert who soon afterwards also became a justice of the Jews. One commission must be examined in detail, however, for it seems to have been partly on account of it that Roger earned the animosity of Matthew Paris.[49] Early in 1253 he was commissioned to take a novel disseisin brought by John son of John le Laner and Alan fitz Richard against Alexander le Taillur concerning a tenement in St. Albans. John and Alexander were burgesses of St. Albans, being presumably a woolmonger and a tailor there. John obtained judgment in his favour and in order to prevent a reversal of the judgment by the procedure of attaint he thereupon procured a royal charter which for the future prohibited the holding of attaints of assize on tenements held in St. Albans, a pro-

[49] *Chronica Majora* (Rolls Series), VI, 268; *cf.* Patent Roll 37 Henry III, 21d, 13d.

hibition that was current in many boroughs whose municipal law differed from the common law of the country. John apparently had the support of some of his fellow burgesses but their initiative was derogatory to the abbot, whose borough St. Albans was, so with the support of the abbot and his legal advisers Alexander brought an attaint, for which Roger was again commissioned in the autumn. However, although there does not seem to be any record of the appointments of associates on the patent rolls, in fact two much more important justices were appointed to sit with him: Henry of Bath, now senior justice of the court *coram rege* and as such the chief judge of the kingdom, and the second most senior of the Bench justices, master Simon of Walton. They took the attaint at Barnet on 27 November 1253, but as so often happens the real issue never came to trial since the parties compromised the action before judgment. Roger's clerk presumably kept a record of his master's assize business but as with the majority of his fellow commissioners none of his assize rolls survive.

An eyre visitation began in 1252 but was soon adjourned on account of the king's visit to Gascony in 1253-4. After the king's return it was resumed in the autumn of 1254 with circuits under Gilbert de Preston and master Simon of Walton; but the Bench sessions were not suspended. There was therefore a need for some additional justices and this was the occasion of Roger's promotion. At the beginning of Michaelmas term 1254 Roger sat as a Bench justice for a few days only. He is not named in any of the final concords dated the octave of Michaelmas, but he is named in 13 out of the 34 dated the quinzaine of Michaelmas (covering business done 13-19 October).[50] He then accompanied Preston. The Essex eyre began on 19 October, under the nominal presidency of the abbot of Colchester but with Preston as senior justice and with Roger and William le Breton as his colleagues. During the winter they com-

[50] Even in these fines there are the following variants of his name: Whycestre 4, Wyc' or Wycestre 6, Witecestre, Wytescestre and Wycestres 1.

pleted the Essex (19 Oct.-2 Dec.) and Hertfordshire (14 Jan.-3 Feb.) eyres.[51] By *liberate* dated 18 November 1254 Roger was granted 25 marks for his service as a king's justice, payable from the issues of the Essex eyre.[52] The growing financial stringency caused by the king's Sicilian adventure led to a tallaging of the royal demesne boroughs and manors throughout England during the Lent vacation of 1255 in which the justices took part, mostly for districts outside their normal sphere; Roger with William Trussel conducted the assessments in the counties of Lincoln, Northampton, Rutland, Nottingham, Derby, Warwick and Leicester.[53] The assembly of the important parliament of Easter 1255 caused a suspension of the eyre visitation, so Roger returned to sit at the Bench for the whole of Easter term, the only complete term in which he sat there as a justice. In the summer the visitation was resumed, Preston with Roger and their colleagues holding the eyres for Surrey (24 May-20 June) and Kent (25 June-2 Aug.).[54] On 16 June Roger was granted an expense allowance of 20 marks, payable from the issue of the Surrey eyre.[55] One of the results of the Easter parliament was the holding of a special fiscal enquiry into royal rights during the long vacation; Preston and Roger took part by holding the circuit for Essex, Herts., Kent, Surrey and Sussex.[56] In the autumn the Kent eyre was completed (30 Sept.-20 Oct.) and the Sussex eyre was held (3-25 Nov.). During 1256 Roger was wholly on eyre with Preston, Hampshire (14 Jan.-23 Feb.), Wiltshire (24 April-26 May), Dorset (12-25 June), Somerset (8-29 July), Cornwall (30 Sept.-13 Oct.) and Devon (27 Oct.-2 Dec.) being visited.[57] On 21 April Roger was granted a regular salary

[51] *C.P.R. 1247-58*, 373. The rolls are: Essex, *J.I. 1/233-5*; Herts., *J.I. 1/320.*

[52] *C. Lib. R. 1251-60*, 185.

[53] *C.R. 1254-6*, 162.

[54] *C.P.R. 1247-58*, 436. The rolls are: Surrey, *J.I. 1/872*; Kent, *J.I. 1/361*, 1183.

[55] *C. Lib. R. 1251-60*, 226.

[56] *C.P.R. 1247-58*, 438.

[57] *C.P.R. 1247-58*, 511; *Close Rolls, 1254-6*, 399. The only roll is Hants., *J.I. 1/778.*

of 40 marks, payable half-yearly, for so long as he was on eyre, warrants for this issuing on 21 April (for 1256 Easter half year) and on 20 October (for Michaelmas half year).[58] Between August and December he also received a number of assize commissions for the western counties and during the first months of 1257 he was probably engaged in hearing these, for he had no special employment. After Easter, Preston and Roger with their colleagues went to East Anglia, which was then suffering from a severe famine that protracted the sessions and incidentally helped to bring about the political revolution of 1258. They held the Norfolk eyre (16 April-24 June and 13 Oct.-3 Nov.) and then the Suffolk eyre (18 Nov.-2 Dec. and 14 Jan.-3 Feb. 1258) in which some business still remained to be taken when famine caused its prorogation in April.[59] On 11 April and 23 October 1257 warrants issued for the half-yearly instalments of Roger's salary for Easter and Michaelmas 1257.[60] This was the end of Roger's career as an eyre and Bench justice.

Before dealing with the last months of Roger's life we may usefully consider his landed interests, beginning with those in the south which help to explain his spheres of activity as an assize justice. The first interest which he acquired in southern England seems to have been a lease of the manor of Goddington, in Oxfordshire, with lands appurtenant to it at Cowley and Twyford, just across the county boundary in Buckinghamshire, the places being in the upper Ouse valley between Bicester and Buckingham. These he obtained before 1235 from Thomas de Camville. Thomas held this estate of the Longspee earldom of Salisbury; among his other estates he also held in chief, of the escheated honor of Boulogne, two knights' fees at Fobbing and Shenfield in Essex and one at Westerham in Kent.[61] Of a direct connexion between Thomas and Roger nothing is known and it

[58] *C.R. 1254-6*, 411; *C. Lib. R. 1251-60*, 281, 378.
[59] *C.R. 1256-9*, 117, 134; *C.P.R. 1247-58*, 602. The rolls are: Norfolk, *J.I. 1/567-8;* Suffolk, *J.I. 1/820.*
[60] *C. Lib. R. 1251-60*, 364, 401.
[61] *Book of Fees*, ii, 1432, 1436.

is very probable that Roger obtained his lease through William of York's connexions with Thomas. For Thomas had been a colleague of Martin de Pateshull (senior justice of the Bench 1217-29) in the eyres of Kent, Essex and Herts. in the autumn of 1227 and had served as a Bench justice in Hilary and Michaelmas 1228 and for part of Hilary and Easter 1229 and must have been well acquainted with William, who was then a senior clerk of the Bench. Thomas died before 25 January 1235 and the wardship of his lands and heir passed to Hamo de Crevequer.[62] We first hear of Roger's interests from the roll of William of York's Bucks. eyre of 1241, when Roger attorned Mauger of Cowley and Alexander of Bedford in a novel disseisin against Ralph of Twyford, a leading man of the district who was senior elector and juror for Ploughley hundred in the Oxfordshire eyre which followed.[63] No plea in the action has been found. Then in the Bench in Hilary term 1245 we find Roger with his servant Stephen Turpin—who may have come from the family which emerges later in the century at Whitchester—bringing actions of trespass against John de Werlawe, sergeant of the earl marshal's manor of Twyford, and a very large number of local men for entering Roger's house at Twyford, maltreating his servants, carrying away his goods and so forth. None of the defendants appeared so process issued against them returnable at Easter three weeks, when at the prayer of the parties there was a further adjournment to Trinity one month.[64] The conclusion of the action has not been found. The action was probably based on a distraint of some sort carried out by the earl marshal's sergeant and manorial tenants for arrears of services due from Roger's lands at Twyford and Cowley to the earl's manor, services which Roger probably disputed. In the great survey of 1242-3 Roger is returned as holding $\frac{1}{4}$ of a knight's fee at Goddington of the Longspee Salisbury earldom.[65]

[62] *Excerpta e Rotulis Finium*, i, 272, 309; *cf. Close Rolls 1234-7*, 47, 294

[63] *J.I. 1/55*, m. 5d.

[64] *K.B. 26/127*, m. 2d; *K.B. 26/129*, m. 11.

[65] *Book of Fees*, ii, 825, 835.

Roger's local connexions are further shown in a recognizance on the Bench plea roll for 1243 Easter term whereby Lawrence del Brok, Roger de Wymbervill and others admit that they owe him 5 marks, which are to be repaid in moieties on 1 June and 1 August.[66] Lawrence was a lawyer who is found practising in the royal courts from about 1233 until 1247, when he was appointed king's attorney in which capacity he served until the close of the reign; both he and Roger de Wymbervill were also prominent Buckinghamshire knights. By Easter term 1244 Thomas de Camvill's son and heir Robert had come of age, whereupon by a recognizance entered in the Bench plea roll he renewed to Roger for two years from the quinzaine of Michaelmas next (13 Oct. 1244) the lease which his father Thomas had granted to Roger and his assigns of the manor of Goddington and the lands at Cowley and Twyford.[67] It is probable that Roger did not renew the lease in 1246, for he never took any assizes in Buckinghamshire. It is possible that Thomas granted the original lease to Roger as a trustworthy young clerk who would look after his infant son's interests.

The next interests Roger acquired were in Hertfordshire, for in the same plea roll of Easter 1244 there is a recognizance by Richard de Montfichet of Wallington whereby he granted to Roger a lease for 12 years of all his lands at Wallington, which lay at the foot of the chalk hills between Baldock and Royston.[68] Richard's namesake and overlord, Richard de Montfichet of Stanstead, was the famous baron who played a leading part in the opposition to king John and who lived until 1268, the last of the Magna Carta barons. One of his sisters and eventual co-heirs, Margery, was the wife of Roger's late lord, Hugh de Bolbec III, so it is not at all unlikely that Roger secured this lease through the family connexions. We have seen that the Camvilles held estates in Essex and Kent and in view of the later pre-

[66] *K.B. 26/129*, m. 2.
[67] *K.B. 26/133*, m. 6d.
[68] *Ibid.*, m. 2; *cf. V.C.H. Herts.*, iii, 120 and *Arch. Aeliana*, 3rd series, xxi, 142.

dominance of commissions for these counties when Roger took assizes it is possible that he obtained some interest in these estates, either directly or through Robert's guardian. However we have certain knowledge of one of Roger's Essex estates, for on 20 June 1253 a royal confirmation issued of a grant whereby Richard fitz Aucher leased to Roger for life all his lands at Epping, with the capital messuage, 18 acres of meadow at Waltham by the Lee and four acres in the common pastures of Nazeing, higher up the valley.[69] Richard came from a prominent Essex family which among other estates held the Waltham abbey manor of Epping. In thus acquiring an estate in the neighbourhood of the great forests of Waltham and Havering Roger was following the fashion set by some of his closest colleagues. His own master William of York had in November 1242 taken a long lease of the manor of Chingford, at the southern end of Epping forest, with a special clause to allow the recoupment of considerable building expenses.[70] In January 1248 Nicholas de Turri, a chancery and *coram rege* clerk who in 1251 became a justice of that court, began building up an estate at Aythrop Roding, in the upper Roding valley near Dunmow;[71] on several occasions he took Essex assizes with Roger. John de Lexington, a Nottinghamshire man who as household steward took part in the proceedings of the court *coram rege*, acted as keeper of the seal and eventually acquired Northumbrian interests through his marriage with Roger de Merlay's widow, bought in June 1248 the manor of Theydon Mount, on the Roding near Epping.[72]

Roger had other southern interests of which we hear from time to time. In the Bench roll for 1249 Michaelmas Humphrey de Bassingbourn, whose estates near Royston made him a neighbour and tenurial connexion of the Craudens at Croydon, confirmed the release of 40s. due from

[69] *Cal. Chart. Rolls 1226-57*, 435; *cf.* Morant's *Essex*, i, 48-9, 139.
[70] *Essex Fines 1182-1272*, ed. Kirk, 145.
[71] *Ibid.*, 170, 178, 184, 187, 197; *K.B. 26/143*, m. 14, *K.B. 26/144*, m. 9, *K.B. 26/145*, m. 17, *K.B. 26/162*, m. 30d.
[72] *Essex Fines*, 179.

Alice de Bruera for the wardship and marriage of Lawrence de Bruera which she had conveyed to Roger.[73] In the same roll we find that the sheriff of Norfolk had been ordered to distrain on the goods and chattels of Robert de Chardacre to the value of 8 marks 3s. 8d. due from him to Roger by a fine made in the Middlesex eyre of 1249; surety had been given but the money had not been paid so process issued returnable in Hilary term.[74] Possibly there is a connexion here which explains Roger's East Anglian assize commissions in 1252-3. Among the Bench recognizances of 1250 Trinity is one whereby Stephen de Titchmarsh admitted that he owed Roger 52 marks as a fine for redeeming his marriage and agreed to pay it by instalments over five years, from 1 November next; the first instalment was not paid however so process then issued returnable in Hilary 1251.[75] There is a possible connexion here with the Craudens, for although Stephen lived at Titchmarsh within the liberties of Peterborough abbey, he was a nephew and heir of Geoffrey de Caxton, who until his death about 1247 had been a prominent Cambridgeshire knight, a near neighbour and tenurial connexion of the Craudens. Moreover Geoffrey's kinsman Jeremy de Caxton, a *coram rege* justice who died about December 1249, had been for five years William of York's junior colleague in that court when Roger was his clerk. In Michaelmas term 1251 among the Bench recognizances there is one whereby sir Adam de Greynvill admitted that he owed Roger a rent of one mark payable yearly on 24 June;[76] Adam was a knight whose estates lay mostly in Somerset and Wiltshire and who became a prominent forest administrator, justice of the Jews and an assize and gaol delivery commissioner. Finally in 1254 Trinity term we find Roger bringing an action of debt with a Sussex venue against master Robert de Huntingdon, the vicars of Meeching (Newhaven), Iford and Southease, the porter of Lewes castle and

[73] *K.B. 26/135*, m. 1.
[74] *Ibid.*, m. 34.
[75] *K.B. 26/141*, m. 13d; *K.B. 26/143*, m. 31d.
[76] *K.B. 26/145*, m. 25.

several others, for the sum of 13 marks, which suggests that Roger was still rector of Ovingdean.[77] The conclusion of this action, in which the latest process was returnable by the bishop of Chichester (the defendants being clerks) on 3 November following is wanting owing to the loss of rolls. It is evident that Roger commanded considerable resources, which enabled him to purchase wardships, marriages and rents and to lease estates in many parts of southern England. The origin of these resources must have been the small fees which he probably collected from litigants for each writ filed and for the various other pieces of business which he transacted in the courts; for his salary as keeper of the writs and rolls can have done no more than enable him to maintain the necessary small staff of clerks to assist him. Similar pieces of evidence to those which have been assembled were no doubt on rolls now lost or may come to light from unpublished eyre rolls; the only important gap which has so far defied research is any certain knowledge of his interests in Kent, which he must have had because of the large number of assizes for which he was commissioned in that county.

His southern interests were the measure of his success in the royal service, but they did not prevent him from strengthening his family interests in Northumberland and it was from these that he made pious benefactions in the closing years of his life. In the great survey of 1242-3, just before his father's death, Roger was holding 40 acres at Heddon on the Wall in socage tenure of the Bolbec barony at 40d. rent.[78] In the Hunts. eyre of 1247, in which Roger was keeper of the rolls, Guy de Upton granted Roger his life interest in 40s. rent which he held of Tynemouth priory, Roger to pay him 20s. yearly on 8 November at St. Andrew's priory, Northampton.[79] Since Tynemouth was a St. Albans cell this conveyance may have been another reason for

[77] *K.B. 26/154*, ms. 4, 26.
[78] *Book of Fees*, ii, 1123.
[79] *Northumberland Pleas*, no. 459.

Matthew Paris being interested in Roger. On 27 August 1251, for a fine of 40s., Roger secured a grant of freewarren in his demesne lands at Whitchester, Haughton and Benwell.[80] When we consider this and his estate in the Essex forest country it is evident that Roger, like most of the secularly occupied clerks and prelates, enjoyed some hunting in vacations. The grant involved him in litigation with his overlord Hugh de Bolbec IV, against whom he brought an action for trespass of warren in the court *coram rege* of which inconclusive stages are found in 1252 Easter and 1253 Michaelmas terms, the last adjournment being to Easter three weeks 1254.[81] In 1253 Michaelmas he was also litigating against Hugh in a plea of covenant concerning his estate at Heddon and Haughton.[82] In a fine made in 7 May 1256, during the Northumberland eyre, concerning common pasture at Weetslade pertaining to the Bertram's manor of Mason, Roger was one of several non-parties who formally registered their claims.[83] An action concerning the lands which his father had bought at Benwell from William de Kimble was also heard in this eyre and shows that Roger had succeeded to this estate after his father's death and had granted it in dower to his step-mother Emma, who had subsequently married Richard de Rybef and was still living.[84] Finally, in the Bench in Hilary term 1258, Sybil de Crauden revived her litigation against the Whitchesters by bringing an action *de fine facto* against Roger, the fine being that already described which composed her action in October 1243. Roger, being then absent on eyre in Suffolk, was represented by attorney. Two final concords dated Hilary three weeks (3 Feb.) 1258 composed this action.[85] By one, Sybil

[80] *Cal. Charter Rolls, 1226-57*, 365; Hodgson's *History*, III, iii, col. 225.

[81] *Northumberland Pleas*, nos. 525, 544.

[82] *Ibid.*, no. 536.

[83] *Northumberland Fines*, no. 228.

[84] Surtees Society, vol. 88, 12-13.

[85] *Northumberland Fines*, nos. 183-4, where for "1248" read "1258"; the regnal year is lost but the only Hilary term in which the justices named in the fine sat together was Hilary 1258, which was also the first term in which the junior justice, Nicholas de Hadlow, ever sat.

granted a carucate, 2 tofts and a windmill at Whitchester to Roger and his heirs; possibly this was a small estate which his family had held since the twelfth century. The other concerned the main fee: Whitchester (except the foregoing) and Haughton manors and $\frac{2}{3}$ of Wallington; by it Roger admitted Sybil's right and she granted it to him and the heirs of his body at £8 rent, payable as before, and pardoned all existing arrears: the reversion being to Sybil and her heirs. The terms of this grant are surprising. For although it is probable that Roger, like the rest of the secularly occupied clerks in the royal service, had never been ordained priest, he must have had the four minor orders and may have proceeded to sub-deacon or deacon. Moreover during his wholly secular career he had refused the step taken by some of his colleagues who renounced their clergy and took up knighthood. We have seen that in 1244, as soon as he succeeded his father, he had obtained a respite from knighthood. On 9 June 1253 he secured a comprehensive life exemption from all the local duties to which knights and substantial freeholders were liable: service on jury panels in civil and criminal actions and as sheriff, coroner, escheator, verderer and regarder along with exemption from the liability to take up knighthood.[86] This aversion to knighthood is also reflected in the mentions of him in his capacity about the court in the plea rolls of 1249-54. William of York in the last years of his service as a clerk was often mentioned as *dominus Willelmus*: sir William. Roger was never so styled except when in 1251 Michaelmas it was noted that the deeds in a Northants. suit had been given temporarily to the keeping of *dominĩ R. de Whycestr'*: and *domini* has been subsequently struck through, very possibly by Roger himself, anxious to avoid any implication of knighthood.[87] The terms of the final concord would seem to suggest either that Roger was at last contemplating renouncing his clergy or else that he was deliberately barring

[86] *C.P.R. 1247-58*, 195.
[87] *K.B. 26/145*, m. 48.

the succession of his only surviving sister Joan de Ryal, wife of Walter de Wassington. He would seem to have had at least two brothers: in the litigation of 1242-3 Robert son of Robert de Whitchester had appeared as attorney for his father while in a conveyance of 1256 Roger was himself represented by his brother master Nicholas who, as we shall see, had died by September 1257. Roger was thus in 1258 the only surviving male representative of his family.

Thoughts of his family and of his own soul must have occupied him in his last years, for it is then that he made a number of benefactions to the Benedictine nuns of St. Bartholomew's priory at Newcastle. The earliest of which we have knowledge was made at Newcastle on the Thursday after Mid-Lent (3 April) 1253, Roger no doubt being at home for the Lent vacation.[88] By it he gave the nuns the 15 shillingsworth of rent, payable at Whitsun and Martinmas, which Richard Tote held of him at Shotton, for a light to be kept burning nightly before the tomb of his mother Isabel in the cloister and for a mass on the anniversary of his own death. The witnesses, which include men from whom he held land and his tenants, were: Eustace Delaval, William Heyrun then sheriff, Henry de Laval, Adam Baret, Robert de Faudon, Nicholas de Byker, John de Neweham, Henry of Carlisle than mayor of Newcastle, Stephen de Lyndeseye, Thomas de Merchingleye, Nicholas Scot, Gilbert de Mora, John de Byker and Stephen de Hadham. Some of these we shall meet as witnesses again but we may note that a Stephen de Hadham had represented his father as attorney in 1242-3. On 11 November 1253 he granted to sir Roger de Toggesdon a 20 years lease of half a carucate at Shotton, namely the land formerly of the demesne of Richard de Plessey which he had by gift of Adam Baret

[88] P.R.O. Ancient Deeds, Augmentation Office, B. 3082, an indenture with small fragment of seal. Brief abstracts of this and B. 3081, 3084-5 were given in *Proceedings*, 3rd Series, VIII, 155. They are from the convent's archives and all bear the monastic reference number *clv*. B. 3085 is a late thirteenth-century deed poll of *inspeximus* and confirmation of this made by Robert de Faudon, who styles himself Roger's kinsman.

together with the capital messuage lying to the east of the chapel of that town, the messuage to be maintained in as good or better condition: to be held at a rent of a mark payable at Whitsun and Martinmas, with reversion to Roger and his heirs.[89] Sir Roger paid 2 marks as consideration. The witnesses were: Eustace and Henry Delaval, William de Meynilhermer, John de Plesset, Adam Baret, Robert Faudon, John Son of Simon and Thomas de Esse. On 26 March 1254 by a deed made at Newcastle in full county court, no doubt when he was again at home for the Lent vacation, he granted his freehold of this estate to the nuns at a rent of ½ mark, payable half yearly at Whitsun and Martinmas to Adam Baret, for a mass on the anniversary of his death.[90] The witnesses were: Roger de Merleg', Eustace de Laval, William Heyrun then sheriff, Henry Delaval, Roger de Toggesdon, Adam Baret, John de Plesset, Robert de Faudon, John de Neweham, Nicholas de Byker, Gilbert de Mora, John de Byker and Stephen de Hadham. The next grant was made about 16 April 1256 during the Northumberland eyre; as Roger was then himself on eyre in Wiltshire he was represented by his brother, master Nicholas de Whitchester.[91] By it he gave the nuns the reversion of his 2 oxgangs at Fenham held by Richard de Rybef and his wife Emma as dower of Emma, who was Roger's stepmother, for a share in the prayers and benefits of the priory. The next grant was made at Whitchester on 28 September 1257, when Roger was at home for the long vacation.[92] The deeds for the first two grants to the nuns had expressed the gifts in the normal form as being made for his own soul and those of his father, mother, ancestors, heirs and parents, but to these were now added the souls of his brother Nicholas and of his sister Mabel, both of whom had presumably died recently. By it he granted five oxgangs at Dinnington, in Ponteland, to provide a chaplain to cele-

[89] B. 3084, indenture, seal lost.
[90] B. 3081, indenture, seal fragmentated.
[91] *Northumberland Fines*, no. 220.
[92] Text in Brand *History of Newcastle*, I, 212, note (1).

brate divine office for their souls. The witnesses included Hugh de Bolbec IV and these who had witnessed the earlier deeds: Eustace Delaval, John son of Simon, Adam Baret, John de Plesseye and Stephen de Hadham; from litigation in 1271 we know that another witness, Nicholas de Skiringham, was one of Roger's tenants.[93] The witnesses also include a Richard de Middilton, but there is nothing to show whether he was the future keeper of the rolls and chancellor. The last grant was made at Cateshull (a suburb of Bury St. Edmunds) where Roger was holding his last, Suffolk, eyre.[94] It is dated the octave of Martinmas (18 Nov.) 1257, though from the plea roll we know that the parties did not take their chirographs until 9 December. It was in effect a confirmation of the previous grants of land at Fenham and Dinnington, for by it Roger conveyed to the nuns 2½ oxgangs at Dinnington together with the reversion of the 2 oxgangs at Fenham and the 2½ oxgangs at Dinnington held by Richard de Rybef and his wife Emma in dower. It thus provided a further security that these estates should revert to the priory on Emma's death. This succession of benefactions in the comparatively short space of four years, beginning with the establishment of a simple light and obit rent and ending with the establishment of a chantry priest, suggests that Roger was feeling that his own death was not far distant.

The end of the Suffolk eyre was soon followed by the great crisis in the kingdom's affairs that led to the Oxford parliament and its provisions. During this time Roger had no special employment. He did not return to the Bench but between April and the end of August he received some 28 assize commissions, more than in any comparable period before. In addition to the usual home counties commissions (6 for Essex, 5 for Kent, 2 for Suffolk and Surrey, one for Hants. and Herts.) there were 6 for Yorkshire and 3 for Northumberland, which indicate that he intended to visit his family estates in the late summer, and one each for Beds.,

[93] *Northumberland Pleas*, no. 866, 879.
[94] *Northumberland Fines*, no. 239; *cf. Northumberland Pleas*, no. 585.

Cambs., and Notts. which he may have intended to take on his way to the north. The *liberate* roll is defective from May onwards, so that we do not know if his salary was continued with an instalment for 1258 Easter half year but it is probable that it was continued, for on 3 May the keeper of the wardrobe was commanded to provide Roger with such a fitting robe against the coming feast of Whitson as he was accustomed to have.[95] At the Oxford parliament the baronial reformers re-established the office of justiciar of England, appointing Hugh le Bigod. The assize commissioners seem thenceforward to have forwarded to the justiciar their estreats of the fines and amercements imposed by them in their sessions, for an estreat from Roger was handed over by Bigod to the treasurer, Philip Lovel, on 3 August.[96] It shows that he had heard several of the assizes for which he had been commissioned between April and late July. Bigod attempted a personal administration of justice that was far beyond the capacity of one man and which had soon to be abandoned. The difficulty of the attempt is shown by a mandate which issued about 2-4 August to Roger and Nicholas de Hadlow, the junior Bench justice, informing him that Bigod could not take the Essex assizes which he had appointed to come before him at Stratford on the Wednesday following and ordering them to take them along with his clerk.[97] The record of this Stratford session on the Wednesday before St. Lawrence (7 Aug.) is the only one which survives of Roger's assize proceedings, for it was entered in Bigod's own roll.[98] There are grounds for believing that the justiciar's clerk was Elias de Bekingham who was certainly present for he acted as surety for a baronial essoin cast on behalf of William de Beauchamp of Eton.[99] If Elias were Bigod's clerk the con-

[95] *Close Rolls 1256-9*, 220.

[96] Exchequer, Lord Treasurer's Remembrancer's Miscellaneous Roll [E. 370], 1/6, m. 3.

[97] Patent Roll 42 Henry III, m. 4d.

[98] *J.I. 1/1187*, m. 1d, 4d. 5, 5d, 30.

[99] *Ibid.*, m. 30.

junction is interesting, for on 10 August 1278 Elias himself succeeded to the office of keeper of the writs and rolls of the Bench and eventually became a Bench justice and one of the few who survived the wholesale dismissal of judges in 1290. The Stratford sessions were among the last pieces of work which Roger undertook. He may not have completed all his commissions, though only one, for Hampshire, is noted on the patent roll as not taken because of his death.[100] Matthew Paris, after mentioning the arrest of a sheriff about 8 September, says that about the same time Roger de Whitchester died.[101] Unfortunately no calendar or obit list of Newcastle priory survives which might enable us to know the date of his death more precisely, nor do we know how long the Whitchester chantry priests said masses for his soul. Matthew described him as a king's clerk and special counsellor who in bearing the burden of judicial office strove wholly to please the royal will. This characterization was penned not in praise but in condemnation. Anyone who has studied the *Gesta Abbatum* and *Chronica Majora* at all closely will know that no royal justice whose decision caused offence at St. Albans was spared an uncharitable obituary, just as those whose decisions found favour were praised. Matthew Paris probably remembered the St. Albans assize case of 1253 and may even have remembered that Roger had been William of York's clerk, for William of York's obituary occupies a high place in Matthew's more malicious characterizations. Matthew would, one feels, have written very differently had Roger's pious benefactions been made to the St. Albans cell at Tynemouth instead of to Newcastle. Nevertheless, though intended uncharitably, Matthew's characterization is not unfitting to an able man who spent many years in the royal service; and we have seen that Roger honoured the memory of his mother, his brother and his sister as much as Matthew did that of the protomartyr.

[100] Patent Roll 42 Henry III, m. 10d.
[101] *Chronica Majora* (Rolls Series), V, 716.

Notes on the de Abernon Family before 1236

'Some account of the family of Abernon, of Albury and Stoke d'Abernon', by Charles Spencer Perceval, appeared in these *Collections* in 1871[2] and remains the only serious study of a family that was prominent in county affairs until the failure of the male line in 1359. Spencer Perceval covered very thoroughly the printed sources then available but made little use of manuscript sources except for Symmes' Surrey Collections in the British Museum, now the British Library.[3] Not surprisingly, therefore, the descent does not emerge clearly until the death of Ingram de Abernon about December 1234. The general lack of printed sources then available for the 12th century is reflected in an extreme vagueness in Spencer Perceval's account. For the early 13th century there was much matter in the numerous publications of the Record Commission, but an unfortunate error by the official custodians of the records led him into considerable confusion. By a mistake which seems to have originated in the great Stapledon array of records in 1320–2 (when most of the older plea rolls were given labelled covers), and which was perpetuated by John Bradshaw when in 1624 he made the abstracts that were in 1811 printed in *Placitorum Abbreviatio*, a plea roll of 2 John was misdated 11 John. As a result the preliminary stages of an important action concerning the de Abernon family, which took place in 1200–1, seemed to occur about 1210, some years after the action had in fact been concluded. The various writers in the *Victoria County History of Surrey* who had to deal with the family were mostly content with Spencer Perceval's conclusions, leaving the 12th century still vague and the early 13th century very confused. Over twenty years ago it became desirable to place in the pedigree Gilbert de Abernon, the uncle and successor of the Ingram who died in 1234. As it was not possible to do this satisfactorily from Spencer Perceval's article it became necessary to cover such of the public records as have been published since 1871, together with a few of the obvious printed sources for the 12th century and some readily available unpublished sources. Attention was necessarily concentrated on the early years of the 13th century; it was impossible to rival Spencer Perceval's thoroughness by exhausting all the 12th century matter now in print or accessible in cartularies and deeds. Though much vagueness and confusion still remain, some gaps can be filled and some errors can be corrected.

Nothing further has been found of the Roger de Abernon who in 1086 under Richard fitz Gilbert held Albury and Molesey in Surrey and Freston in Suffolk. The cartulary of the priory of Stoke by Clare, virtually refounded in 1090 as a cell of Bec by earl Gilbert fitz Richard, contains confirmation charters issued by Archbishop Theobald while Roger de Pont l'Evèque was Archdeacon of Canterbury (1148–54)[4]. Two of the charters rehearsed briefly in the confirmation were tested by a Walter de Abernon; one was a grant by Earl Gilbert fitz

Richard himself (1090– between 1114 and 1117) and the other was a grant by Canevaz, that is Canevaz Makerel, one of the earl's knights. Their place among the other charters suggests that they were made not long after 1090; so Walter must have succeeded Roger, at least at Freston, by about 1100.

Also included in Archbishop Theobald's confirmation is a grant of the church of Freston (Frisentune), of tithes at 'Berue' (?Barrow, west of Bury St Edmunds) and 'la Bysse' and of the church of 'Wochinges' (which, from a papal confirmation dated 30 June 1174 describing it as the church of 'Wokinges' in Winchester diocese, must be identified with Woking) by an Ingram de Abernon, witnessed by his brothers Jordan and Walter and by his cousin William, who associate themselves with him in making the grant, and by Baldwin the priest.[5] Following Spencer Perceval we call him Ingram I. On 2 March 1112 or 1113 he witnessed a charter of Henry I in favour of Savigny Abbey, and some time between 1114 and 1120 another to Nostell Priory.[6] Between 1129 and 1135 he granted his lands at Molesey to Merton Priory, for the redemption of his soul and those of his father and mother, his brother Jordan and his lord Gilbert fitz Richard (died between 1114 and 1117), and for the salvation of King Henry, *qui me nutrivit*, and his lord Gilbert fitz Richard (died 15 April 1136).[7] Between Waverley's foundation in 1128 and the earlier of its confirmation charters in 1140 (in which this gift comes last in the list) he granted a hide at Oxshott, in Stoke d'Abernon, to the abbey.[8] In the levy of Danegeld in 1130 he was pardoned 56s in Surrey, 3s 4d in Essex and 7s 6d in Suffolk,[9] having no doubt a general charter of quittance from murder fines, Danegeld and the like on his lands. After these early glimpses of light there is a period of darkness. No de Abernon attested any surviving royal or Angevin charter during Stephen's reign.

Ingram I may have been succeeded by his brother Jordan; he was certainly succeeded by the latter's son Ingram, whom we may call Ingram II. This is shown by two charters in the Merton register which immediately follow Ingram I's grant of Molesey, and which must have been made either late in the time of Prior Robert I (1115–50) or early in that of Robert II (1150–67).[10] By the first, Ingram son of Jordan de Abernon for the salvation of his soul and the soul of his father Jordan confirms the grant made by his uncle (*patruus*)[11] Ingram, of the land of Molesey, to be held at a yearly rent of a mark payable at his manor of Stoke within the octave of Michaelmas. For this confirmation, Robert the prior and his canons give 10 marks from the money that Roger fitz Humphrey had given them. In the second charter Gilbert, earl of Clare (1138–52) confirms the grant made by Ingram son of Jordan of the land at Molesey of his, the earl's, fee, which the priory had by gift of Ingram's uncle (*avunculus*) Ingram. That the gift which is being confirmed is that made by Ingram I about 1129–35 there can be no doubt, since the three charters are together in the register, but unfortunately these copies give no witnesses. The most likely date for such a confirmation is shortly after Ingram II gained his inheritance, but that of course remains to be established. Ingram also appears, the seventh of 13 witnesses, in a general confirmation to Stoke by Clare by Gilbert, earl of Clare, the second witness of which was the Roger fitz Humphrey mentioned in the first charter.[12] Its date seems nearer to 1152 than 1138 but it has yet to be firmly dated.

There follows a period of considerable obscurity. In the last levy of the Danegeld in 1156, Walter de Abernon was pardoned 18d in Surrey.[13] He was probably the surviving younger brother of Ingram I and Jordan, holding one of the family manors by subenfeoffment. At some time about the middle of Henry II's reign (Round thought about 1166–74) a William de Abernon attested the grant by William earl of Gloucester to Richard de Lucy of Greenstead, in Essex.[14] Heales assigned to the time of Prior Robert III of Merton (1178–86) the grant of a presentation to a canonry witnessed by a Roger de Abernon.[15] The other references are all to an Ingram de Abernon: the earlier of these might concern Ingram II who, even supposing that he succeeded early in Stephen's reign and was then of age, might have lived well into Henry II's reign; the later ones cannot refer to Ingram II. Until it is possible to assign them more correctly they may for convenience all be treated as concerning an Ingram III.

In 1166, when the tenants in chief were called upon to certify the tenants and fees held of them, Ingram de Abernon held four fees in Surrey of the honor of Clare and half a fee in Devon of Robert the king's son.[16] The half fee in Devon consisted apparently of estates at Bradford d'Abernon, regarded as a quarter of half a fee, and at Drewsteignton, regarded as three quarters of half a fee;[17] the Drewsteignton estates seem thenceforth to have descended with those in Surrey. In the forest eyre held for Surrey in 1176 or towards the close of 1175, when most persons prominent in the county suffered some fine or amercement, the heaviest penalty of all, of 100 marks, fell on Ingram de Abernon; it was cleared by the next year.[18] In 1176 the eyre to administer the assize of Northampton was held in most English counties; Ingram de Abernon was amerced 20 marks for default in either Bedfordshire or Buckinghamshire, the debt being pardoned.[19] We cannot tell whether this default was in a plea or simply under the common summons of the eyre, but it probably indicates that already the family had acquired the manor at Pavenham, Bedfordshire, which they later held. Between 1173 and 1185 Ingram witnessed Richard earl of Hertford's confirmation to Stoke by Clare of Carbrooke (Kerebroc) church in Norfolk.[20] In 1189 after the coronation of Richard I, William Marshal spent his honeymoon at Ingram de Abernon's manor of Stoke.[21] In the same year, one Ernulf son of Aldwine was fined a mark for an assize against Ingram concerning a hide of land in Essex or Hertfordshire, a debt that was paid off by about 1194.[22] About 1193 we have the last piece of evidence yet known which shows that Ingram III was still alive, when he went security for 55 marks of a much larger sum whereby Ralph de Arden, who had supported John against Richard I, bought himself back into royal favour, Ralph's debt being also entered in the pipe rolls under Essex and Hertfordshire.[23]

With the return of Richard I from captivity there began a rapid and very large increase in the number of persons paying for writs, charters, licences and the like from chancery, and fining or being amerced in the course of judicial proceedings. This is reflected in a marked increase in the number of persons mentioned year by year in the pipe rolls. The fact that we hear no more for certain of Ingram III after 1193 suggests that he died about that time; we shall find some evidence which seems to indicate that by about 1194 he had been succeeded by a Roger de Abernon.

Before considering this evidence we must turn to the key action, mentioned at the beginning of this article, of Ralph de Clere versus Walter, William and Richard de Abernon. The background to the action may be briefly indicated. Roger de Clere (who died about 1183–4) married, as her second husband, Hawise de Gurnay and dowered her, among other estates, with the Hampshire manor of Lasham.[24] After Roger's death Hawise conveyed this estate to Ingram de Abernon. Roger was succeeded by his brother Ralph, who died about 1200, leaving a son Ralph II de Clere who was under age and became the ward of the greatest administrator of the age, Hubert Walter, archbishop of Canterbury. It was the archbishop who brought the action against the de Abernon brothers, the conduct of the action being under one of his household, Ranulf, the treasurer of Salisbury. The point at issue was the nature of the estate which Hawise could or did grant to Ingram de Abernon. The first known stage of the action took place in Trinity term 1200, when the parties were adjourned to the octave of St John (1 July) with licence to concord meanwhile; thence, at their own request, they were adjourned to the quinzaine of Michaelmas (13 October).[25] By then the de Abernon brothers had procured a writ ordering the action to be respited until Ralph de Clere came of age, to which the archbishop pleaded that it was not contrary to established practice for the action to proceed during the plaintiff's minority. No decision was made, the action being adjourned to the morrow of St Edmund (21 November) *coram rege* if the king were in England, otherwise to Westminster.[26] On that day Walter and William essoined *coram rege*, the latter's essoiner being one Richard 'de Audeberi', who may have come from the de Abernon manor of Albury; they were adjourned to the octave of Hilary (20 January) 1201, again *coram rege*.[27] The issue was now joined.[28] Ranulf pleaded that Hawise de Gurnay had been dowered with Lasham and had leased it to Ingram de Abernon at 100s rent for the term of her life by a charter, which he produced; and that since she was now dead the estate should revert to the lawful heir, Ralph de Clere. William and Walter pleaded that their deceased brother Ingram had granted to each of them one third of Lasham to hold in fee of him, by charters which they produced; the remaining third, from what follows, was granted to the fourth brother Richard. They renewed their earlier plea that the action should not proceed during Ralph de Clere's minority and vouched Roger the heir of Ingram to warrant their estates. The action was adjourned to Mid Lent (4 March) for the warrantor to appear; Ranulf the treasurer had also offered a palfrey for having a jury to give a verdict on the special point whether or not the brothers had intruded after the end of Ingram's life tenancy, and it was then to be decided whether or not a jury could be summoned to answer this. At Mid Lent, however, Walter and William essoined while Richard neither came nor essoined; they were then adjourned to Easter three weeks (15 April) but then it was simply noted that Walter had failed to produce his warrantor (Roger, the heir of Ingram III) and Ranulf was adjourned to the Sunday before Whitsun (6 May).[29] At some time during this Easter term Walter attorned William in his place.[30] On the Sunday before Whitsun Walter and William again essoined and were adjourned to the Wednesday before Whitsun one month (6 June);[31] it is at this point in 1201 that for the present we lose the first part of this action over Lasham, the part in which all three brothers are defendants. Before considering the second part, which is between Ralph de Clere and Walter de Abernon alone, we may consider the implications of what we have noticed and set out some further facts about Roger and Walter.

We have seen that Ingram III seems to disappear about 1193. In the lists of the scutage collected in 1194, the first scutage of Richard I, Roger de Abernon appeared for the first time in the pipe rolls, paying 20s, through the sheriff, for a fee in Hampshire as one of the knights with fees there whose chief honors lay elsewhere.[32] It looks as if the fee was Lasham, and, if so, this means that Roger had inherited it. Roger was also charged on one fee in Hampshire for the second and third scutages of Richard I, both put in charge for the first time in the pipe roll of 8 Richard I; for the first scutage of John, put in charge in 2 John; and for the second and third scutages of John, put in charge in 4 John. But in all these five scutages Roger's debt remains unpaid, so that in the roll for 4 John he is debited with five unpaid debts.[33] In that year there was a general clearance of the pipe roll: in the roll for 5 John (audit of the accounts in which began at Michaelmas 1203) Roger's debts no longer appear. It would seem that since 1194 he had successfully denied his liability for the Hampshire fee. On 25 May 1200 Roger de Abernon received royal licence to surrender his family estate at Abenon (Abernuin) near Lisieux in the Calvados district of Normandy to William Marshal, in exchange for an estate at Duxford and rent at Chesterford, Cambridgeshire, to be held as half a fee of the earl.[34] Two related deeds from the Waverley Abbey muniments show Roger interesting himself in affairs at Stoke d'Abernon.[35] The first is a grant in free alms to God, St Mary and the monks of Waverley by Gilbert Prudumme of half a virgate in Oxshott (Occasate) lying between the wood of Stokes and the monks' house, next to a way called 'Suthstrete'. It is tested by Sir Roger de Abernon, Robert de Watevill, Ralph de Imworth and his son Richard, William Fergant, Jordan the chaplain, Peter de Wotton and Henry de Hambledon. The second is the confirmation of this grant by Roger de Abernon, tested by Richard son of Everard, Gilbert Prudumme, Peter de Wotton, William Fergant, Jordan the chaplain and Henry de Hambledon.[36] Spencer Perceval gave a woodcut of Roger's seal, but he wrongly ascribed these and other de Abernon charters from the Waverley muniments to the reign of Henry II.[37] Roger, then, was the son and heir of Ingram III, whom he seems to have succeeded about 1193–4; since we hear nothing of a minority he must have been born by 1172 at latest. Their relationship is confirmed by a pedigree pleaded in the bench at Hilary 3 weeks (3 February) 1267 which is in another respect impossible to reconcile with the earlier evidence.[38] The case was one of right in a knight's fee, minus 6s rent and 3 acres, in 'Barwe' (?Barrow, in East Wakering), Barling and Thundersley, Essex, brought by John de Abernon against Cristiana, widow of Humphrey son of Walter. John gave a detailed account of the descent of this property from an Ingram de Abernon of the time of Henry II, who must be our Ingram III. Cristiana vouched Walter son of Humphrey (?her son) to warrant her the property. This he did, denied John's pleaded descent and then placed himself on the grand assize. Lack of surviving plea rolls from the succeeding terms prevent us from discovering the outcome. For purposes of comparison the pedigree pleaded in this case is given below p 166; it will be observed that it makes the three de Abernon brothers involved in the Lasham action sons of Ingram III, while the legal records of the period of that action make it clear that he was their brother. The evidence of the latter is obviously to be preferred.

The earliest notice which we have of the contemporary Walter de Abernon is in Trinity term 1194, from the earliest surviving plea roll, when we find him litigating against Ellis son of Walter concerning land at Lasham, the parties being adjourned to the octave of St Andrew (7 December) for a concord which does not survive.[39] We next hear of him in the main Lasham action in 1200–1. Then in 1204 William de Abernon agreed to pay half a mark for an assize of mort d'ancestor about one mark of rent at Molesey against Walter de Abernon, the action to be tried in the bench; the debt was cleared in the following year but the action has not been found in the plea rolls.[40] The rent was that due from Merton under the original grant. In Easter term 1205, Walter was defending an action of novel disseisin against William de Brademere concerning an estate at Leatherhead and Fetcham. Walter denied the disseisin by alleging that William's seisin of the estate was a mere intrusion effected while Walter was so dangerously ill that it was believed he would die. William pleaded legitimate enfeoffment by Walter, who fined 20s for a jury, the action being adjourned to the quinzaine of Trinity (19 June) for the jury to come.[41] However, at the adjourned date William withdrew his action, which had presumably been settled out of court.[42]

In the course of 1205 Ralph II de Clere came of age. Richard de Abernon was now dead but Walter and William renewed their action against Ralph and from the way in which they proceeded we learn that the previous action must have resulted in a judgment for the archbishop of Canterbury on behalf of his ward Ralph II de Clere. Towards the close of 1205 William de Abernon fined half a mark for a writ of entry against Ralph de Clere concerning one third of a knight's fee at Lasham and Walter de Abernon fined 40s for a writ of mort d'ancestor against Ralph also for a third of a knight's fee, the deceased Richard's share, at Lasham.[43] The latter action, though appointed to be taken in Hilary term 1206, was in fact heard at Easter one month (30 April) when the assize gave a verdict, for Walter and against Ralph, that Richard had died seised of the third of a fee.[44] Richard must have died before judgment in the earlier action had been given in favour of the archbishop and his ward, otherwise he could not have died seised. Walter had thus secured a possessory judgment giving him a footing at Lasham once more; although his brother William had apparently sued out the writ of entry that action was also prosecuted by Walter. In Hilary term 1206 Walter and Ralph were adjourned to the quinzaine of Easter (16 April), when Ralph claimed a view of the estate, for which the action was adjourned to Trinity three weeks (18 June).[45] We next pick it up in Michaelmas term 1206, when Walter and Ralph have made a compromise, each fining 10s for licence to concord the action.[46] They were adjourned to Hilary three weeks (3 February) 1207 to take the chirographs of the fine; one of the persons whom Walter attorned in his place to take the chirograph was Walter Prudumme, probably a kinsman of Roger de Abernon's tenant Gilbert Prudumme. In Hilary term the chirographs were not yet ready, so the parties were adjourned to the quinzaine of Easter (6 May) to take them; William de Abernon registered his claim to part of the lands in dispute.[47] The fine was in fact dated Easter three weeks (13 May).[48] By it Ralph and Walter partitioned Lasham, the former retaining the manor house and advowson in exchange for grants of various tenements, pasture rights etc, which are fully detailed. For us the interest lies in the clauses of warranty. Ralph II de Clere warranted Walter's share against all men *except* against those who might claim as of the stock of Ingram de Abernon, to whom that town was given, but warranted Ralph's share against those who could claim as of Ingram de Abernon's stock. As shown by the 1267 pedigree, in the spring of 1207 there were yet alive children or grandchildren of Ingram III who might eventually be entitled to claim an estate in Lasham. William de Abernon's claim is not endorsed on the foot of the fine as one might have expected; possibly in the weeks since Hilary term his brother Walter had bought out William's interests. From this point we lose sight of William de Abernon though we hear something of his son.

When next we hear of Walter it is in circumstances which suggest that he has succeeded Roger as head of the family. In 1210, as we have mentioned, somewhat obscure sessions, more political than legal, were held in most counties, being conducted in Surrey by Gilbert de Abinger and Gilbert Prudumme. Later a visitation was held by anonymous 'harvest time' justices by whom in many cases those who had conducted the previous visitation and some other leading men in the county were amerced very large sums indeed. In Surrey, Gilbert de Abinger was amerced 100 marks, Gilbert Prudumme 50 marks, Walter de Abernon 100 marks and Robert de Watevill 60 marks.[49] The offence is laconically described as a trespass; Walter and Robert had both paid off their debt by the following year.

Shortly after the outbreak of war between King John and the barons in the autumn of 1215 mandates were issued which seem to show that Walter de Abernon was on the baronial side, as might be expected from a tenant of Richard lord of Clare and earl of Hertford. The earliest mandates, dated 8 November 1215, were to three of the king's local governors, John son of Hugh, Herbert son of Matthew and the constable of Guildford, ordering them to give seisin to Colin de Molis of the lands in their bailiwicks lately belonging to Walter de Abernon.[50] There is a note that the lands were worth £40. John son of Hugh, a former sheriff of Surrey, was at this time in command at Windsor and Odiham castles and perhaps elsewhere; Herbert was sheriff of Sussex but is presumably addressed in a special capacity. Lasham was in Odiham hundred and perhaps was the estate lying within John son of Hugh's bailiwick; some of the other estates must have lain within Surrey for them to be within the constable of Guildford's bailiwick. On 15 November the sheriff of Hampshire was ordered to give Roger de Merlay seisin of land worth 50s at Hayling (Hallinges) which lately belonged to Roger de Abernon.[51] At first sight this would suggest that Roger was still alive and like Walter was on the baronial side. But it is doubtful if this was so. In the first place Roger, like Ingram III before him, was a friend and indeed a tenant of William Marshal, the most faithful of John's servants; one would not expect a man with such connections to be on the baronial side at the outset of the war. In the second place, on 16 March 1216, at a time when the barons' fortunes were at a low ebb, the sheriff of Hampshire was ordered to give Colin de Molis seisin of the lands in 'Helingéé' lately belonging to Walter de Abernon, the king having already made a grant to Colin of Walter's lands.[52] This seems to suggest that Walter had succeeded Roger at Hayling, perhaps before the mandate of October 1215 was issued. Thirdly, on a schedule in the close roll of 17 John there is a brief list of those in arms against the king.[53] Ralph de Clere and Walter de Abernon occur next to each other in this list; but there is no mention there or elsewhere to indicate that there was a Roger de Abernon on the baronial side. Also in this list is the name of Maud de Camoys, whom we shall meet with later as a sometime de Abernon dowager. On the whole the balance of probability seems to suggest that by 1215–16, possibly by 1210, Walter de Abernon, the eldest surviving brother of Ingram III, had succeeded Ingram's immediate heir Roger as the head of the family.

We can, however, be quite sure that Walter eventually succeeded Roger, for in Easter term 1220 Nicola, the widow of Walter de Abernon, was litigating by writ of dower against William Marshal the younger.[54] The action was adjourned to Trinity term and then settled.[55] Nicola was assigned dower at Duxford and Drewsteignton, where the estates were to be assessed and the surplus to a reasonable dowry (one third) was to remain with the earl. Duxford is a correction in the roll for Albury. For this settlement Nicola agreed to pay 30 marks and found seven securities each of whom pledged himself to the full amount: William Hansard, Gilbert de Abernon, Peter de Berghes, Walter Prudumme, Ralph the clerk of Chertsey, Adam Drew and John de Bures. These must have been tenants of Nicola's late husband; all were or became prominent in Surrey affairs. Nicola was to pay her money in three instalments; the first was paid in Michaelmas 1220, the second on Thursday after the Invention of the Cross (6 May) 1221.[56] Nothing is said in the pleas about Walter's heir or to indicate whether the heir was a minor or not. Dower was a reasonably speedy action. The royal court of the bench had reopened in the winter of 1217–18 after being in abeyance since Hilary 1215; in 1218–19 there was a Surrey eyre. Had Walter died during the troubles or soon after the establishment of peace it is perhaps likely that his widow would have obtained her settlement in the bench in 1218 or in the Surrey eyre. From what we know of the action it seems probable that Walter died in 1219 or even in the early months of 1220. Since he must have been of age when litigating over Lasham in 1194 he was born before 1173; but the probability is that he was well over 50 at his death. There are five charters tested by a Walter de Abernon among the Waverley Abbey deeds; three of the attestations are certainly by another Walter and it is likely that the other two are also, so we will return to them later.

Spencer Perceval pointed out that Walter was succeeded by his son Ingram, whom for convenience we will refer to as Ingram IV. Ingram IV played comparatively little part in county affairs. He does not appear in any Surrey grand assize panels. Not until 1233 did he receive his only assize commission when he was nominated second of the usual panel of four to sit at Leatherhead, the other members being William de la Mare of Ashtead, an ex-sheriff of vast experience, Richard de Dol, a Surrey knight, steward of Westminster Abbey and an exchequer expert who had been active since John's reign, and William de Wyke, a knight who held in Worplesdon and was long active in county affairs.[57] Some rather obscure entries in Michaelmas term 1221 and Trinity term 1222 suggest that he was then litigating in the bench about an estate at Freston, in Suffolk, one of the family's Domesday holdings.[58] What else is at present known about him comes from deeds in the same private collection as the Waverley Abbey deeds acquired by the British Museum in 1841 which were used by Spencer Perceval.

Only one of these comes from Ingram IV's lifetime.[59] By it Ingram granted to Peter the parson of Fetcham a virgate and a meadow which Richard son of Everard had held of his father Walter de Abernon in the town of Stoke, to hold at a yearly rent of 2s. saving foreign service. The witnesses were: Sir Richard de Stoke, knight; Sir Gilbert de Abernon, knight; Walter de Abernon; Master Andrew of Winchester, James Hansard, Simon de Muntut and William le Moyne of Loseley. We have already met Richard son of Everard as the first witness to Roger de Abernon's confirmation of the Prudumme grant to Waverley Abbey; clearly he was a de Abernon tenant at Stoke under both Roger and

Walter, a further piece of evidence that the latter succeeded the former at Stoke d'Abernon. What is known of the witnesses does not help to date the charter precisely.

Ingram IV died in November or early December 1234, for on 17 December the escheators were ordered to take his lands into the king's hand until his heir was known,[60] the Clare lands being in the royal ward during the minority of Earl Richard. Ingram's executors were the Dominican friars and others. In the court *coram rege* in Hilary term 1235 Gilbert bound himself to pay them £36 18s 4d, for which his sureties were Robert de Watevill, John de Cherburgh, William de Brademere and Adam Drew.[61] On 30 January 1235 Gilbert de Abernon did homage for his nephew Ingram's lands, which had been released to him by Ingram's cousin and nearer heir Jordan de Abernon.[62] The deed whereby Jordan released his interests fortunately survives.[63] By it, Jordan, son and heir of William de Abernon, released to his uncle Gilbert de Abernon all his interest in the inheritance of Ingram son of Walter de Abernon; and for this Gilbert granted Jordan all his lands at Duxford to be held at the service of half a fee. The witnesses were: William Hansard, Robert de Watevill, Walter de Abernon, Peter de Pirbright, Peter the parson of Fetcham, John Hansard and Adam Drew. These are de Abernon tenants, some of whom we have already met or shall meet again. There survives also an indenture of the dower settled by Gilbert on Ingram's widow Joan.[64] He granted her: the manor of Albury; the service of half a fee, with escheats, at Apps, in Walton on Thames, that had formerly belonged to Gilbert Prudumme; and all the lands at Drewsteignton in Devon. Joan was to hold these lands by such services as the lady Maud de Camoys used to do for them. The witnesses were: Sirs Ralph de Camoys, Hugh de Windsor, Walter de Utworth, William Hansard, John de Cherburgh, Robert de Watevill and Walter de Abernon, knights, Sir Hilary de Sira (the rector of Shere), Walter de Holdhurst, Reynold de Henton and Walter Marshal of Guildford. We may assume that all these were de Abernon tenants; the first seven were prominent at one time or other in Surrey affairs and mostly held estates in Surrey and other counties as extensive as the main de Abernon holdings, Ralph de Camoys, indeed, ranking as a minor baron.[65] Joan's dower was very similar to that which her mother in law Nicola had obtained in 1220. Both received Drewsteignton. Joan received Albury and Nicola probably did so, for although the name was deleted from the bench roll of 1220 Trinity and Duxford substituted that might have been because Albury was a Clare and not a Marshal manor and it was the dower from Marshal lands that was at issue. Nicola had received Duxford, valued in the original exchange of 1200 and in the exchange between Jordan and Gilbert in 1235 at half a fee; Joan could not be dowered there, since Gilbert had surrendered that estate, but she was granted an estate at Apps also valued at half a fee. She seems later to have brought her dower lands to a new husband, David de Jarpenvill.[66] Maud de Camoys had lost her husband Ralph I de Camoys some time before 1205, about which time she had married Hubert de Anesti; her son Ralph II de Camoys, the first witness to this charter, being then already of age.[67] It looks as if she was the widow of Ingram III who had been dowered with de Abernon manors from about 1195 to after 1220.

Since Gilbert was the uncle of both Ingram IV and Jordan, and they were the sons of Walter and William, the brothers of Ingram III, it follows that Gilbert must also have been a brother of Ingram III. It seems, therefore, that the main relationship and succession from about 1193–4 can be expressed as in Table 1, the names of those who were at some time head of the family being put in capitals.

TABLE 1

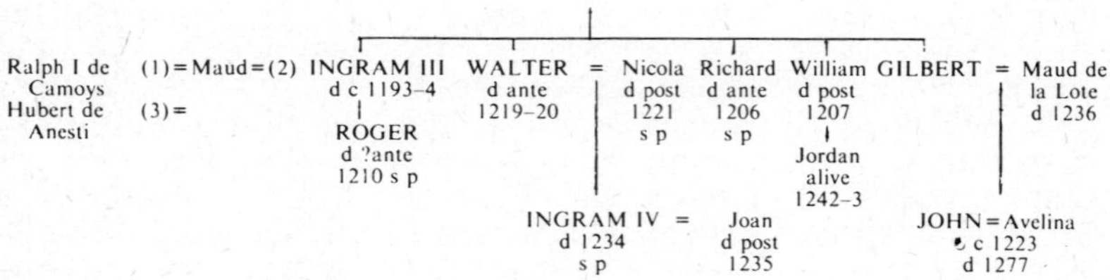

The information provided by the 1267 pedigree is given as Table 2; it will be noted that it includes a number of persons not otherwise known.

TABLE 2

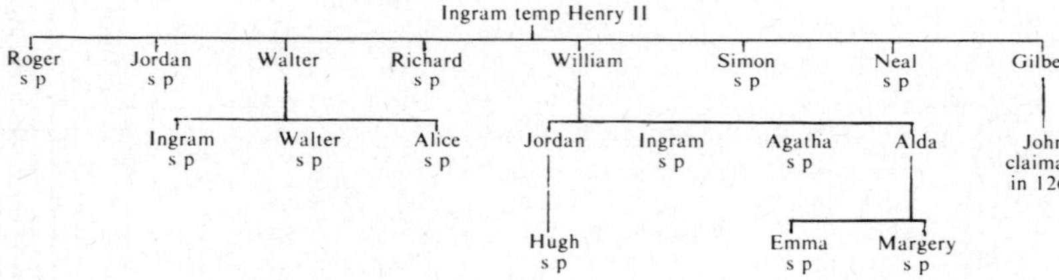

Table 1 will account satisfactorily for the most important members of the family about this time with two exceptions: Jordan de Abernon, who seems to have died in the reign of John, and Walter de Abernon who flourished during the first part of Henry III's reign. Before saying something of these two it will be useful to summarize what is at present known about Gilbert, whom we first met with in Trinity term 1220 as one of the sureties for the payment of Nicola's composition with William Marshal. It is in the same term that we first find him in the panels of Surrey grand assize jurors and he was active in this capacity to the end of his life, for in the Surrey eyre of 1235 we find him as elector of one grand assize panel and juror in nine more.[68] In 1228 he was the third of four commissioners appointed to take an assize at Guildford at Trinity three weeks.[69] His only other assize commission came shortly before his death, when he was the second of four justices, the first being Ralph de Camoys, appointed to take an assize at Guildford on the octave of Trinity (1 June) 1236; but he died before the assize was heard, his place being taken by Gilbert de Basevill.[70] He does not seem to have acted as a taxation commissioner nor is he to be found acting as an assize commissioner or on grand juries outside Surrey. We have seen him witnessing the grant made by his nephew Ingram IV to Peter the parson of Fetcham. There are two of his charters among the Waverley abbey deeds, both concerning the same grant.[71] By them Gilbert granted to Waverley all land held by Siward Puttoch in the town of Oxshott (Oggeset) with all its appurtenances, so that the monks should have in his foreign pasture of Stoke 6 beasts and 60 sheep; also a grove and a certain small meadow that Osbert Baril held lying to the west of that (ie Puttoch's) land; and to the east of a purpresture which in breadth went as far as the road (going from south to north) in the wood and in length went by that road up to the lands of Robert de Watevill. Furthermore Gilbert granted and confirmed to the monks all the tenements which they had of his or his predecessors' gift in Stoke and Oxshott by his or their grant and so that they have 120 sheep in the foreign pasture of Stoke as Ingram de Abernon and his predecessors granted.[72] There can be little doubt that this charter, with its confirmation of Ingram's gift, was made in 1236 soon after Gilbert had done homage for his estates. The witnesses include some names new to de Abernon charters. They were: William Hansard, Walter de Abernon, Robert de Watevill, knights; James Hansard, William Burel, William Page, Hugh Bacun, Jordan de Walton, John de Clere and Simon de Farnham. Appended to both charters is Gilbert's seal, showing a fleur de lys, in green wax. Gilbert as a young man can have had no hope of succeeding to the headship of the family for there were several elder brothers, seven according to the 1267 pedigree, and two of these had children. However the family found him a very minor heiress for a wife in Maud, who with her sister Eve was the daughter and coheir of Gilbert de la Lote (or Loce) of Headley. We learn this from a final concord made in the bench and dated Easter one month (13 May) 1218, which composed an action of *nuper obiit* (the normal action between coparceners) between Eve and her husband Martin de Cobham as plaintiffs and Gilbert and Eve as defendants.[73] The effect of the composition is that Eve leased to Gilbert and Maud for their lives her reasonable portion of the estate left by Gilbert de la Lote. This estate, the moiety of the deceased Gilbert's lands, consisted of 12 acres called 'Potterescroft', with a grove there and in the great field of 'la Lote' (or Loce); 19 acres to the south and seven acres in Drew's field to the north; and a moiety of 10 acres of wood called 'Inname' to the west. Gilbert and Maud were to rent this for 4s payable yearly for their lives, with reversion to Maud and Eve and Eve's heirs. So it was by Gilbert's marriage with Maud that the Headley estates came into the de Abernon family. Their son John, famous for his brass in Stoke d'Abernon church, must have been born about 1223. Gilbert, as we noticed from his last assize commission, died in May 1236. The Clare estates were still in ward to the king during the minority of Earl Richard and as Gilbert's son John was under age the wardship of the de Abernon estates was at the king's disposal: on 14 June 1236 John de Gatesden, that great Surrey and Sussex figure, then in the early stages of his career, fined 120 marks for the wardship and marriage.[74] In 1242–3 Gatesden was still holding the Surrey de Abernon fees; Pavenham, which was held of the Marshal honor of Pembroke, was in ward to the Knights Templar.[75] By 27 October 1245 John de Abernon had come of age, for he then granted to his brother William a messuage and 37 acres of land held by Richard de Stokes and 12 acres held by Adam Drew at Fetcham, to hold at 6d or a giltspur rent, paying scutage at 1s for £2.[76]

Before May 1248 he had married. The evidence for this comes from the earliest surviving assize roll, which happens to belong to the Surrey knight Henry de la Mare, who was a judge *coram rege* 1247–51 and 1251–6 and also a close neighbour of the de Abernons since his main seat was at Ashtead. On 2 May 1248 de la Mare sat at Brockham near Reigate to hear an action over common of pasture at Fetcham between John de Abernon and the master of the Hospital of St Cross at Reigate.[77] Towards the end of May de la Mare was in Nottinghamshire and he sat there at Blyth on 26 May to take novel disseisins brought by John de Abernon and his wife Avelina against Thomas de Chaworth concerning lands at Alfreton and Norton, Derbyshire, and Osberton, Nottinghamshire.[78] In each action judgment was given against Thomas. A wife would not normally appear as plaintiff in such actions unless her inheritance or interests were concerned. So we may reasonably conclude that John had come of age since 1243 and had married Avelina, who probably came from a Nottinghamshire–Derbyshire family; and that the pair were vindicating their claim to some of the estates which Avelina had brought with her. Thomas de Chaworth was about John's age, since he had himself been a minor in 1242–3, coming of age in 1246–7; his mother was Alice daughter of Robert de Alfreton of Norton.[79] The probability is that Avelina was connected with this family. The marriage may well have been arranged by John de Gatesden, for he had purchased the marriage as well as the guardianship of the de Abernon heir and his vast interests had ramified about 1241–3 into Nottinghamshire, where he acquired Averham and other estates near Newark.[80] The later career of John de Abernon lies beyond the limits of this article, but it will be recalled that it was he who brought the action concerning the Essex lands in 1267 and who produced the pedigree of the family with which, in common with his opponent on that occasion, we have had reason to disagree.

The little that is known of the Jordan de Abernon who is not placed in our pedigree arises from his father's marriage into the family of de Secchevill or, to use the modernized form, de Sackville. We do not know the christian names of Jordan's mother and father; but we know that his father married a sister of Henry de Sackville and that when Henry died without direct heir Jordan de Abernon became one of several coheirs to whom descended interests in an estate at Foston, Leicestershire, and lands in Devon.[81] These interests were bought out by a very distinguished royal servant, William Brewer, who was perhaps the most powerful and influential man in the western counties during the first quarter of the 13th century. In 1198 Easter term Brewer obtained a judgment by default against the Sackville coheirs concerning a knight's fee at Goodleigh, in Devon.[82] Later that year Jordan and another coheir fined 40 marks for an assize of mort d'ancestor against Brewer to be taken at Westminster on the morrow of Low Sunday (6 April) concerning their Sackville inheritance at Foston, Leicestershire, and Lyncombe, Devon.[83] This debt is first entered in the pipe roll for 10 Richard I under Warwickshire and Leicestershire, whence in the same year it was transferred to the Devon account. Jordan's share of the debt was not cleared until 1223, in the pipe roll for 7 Henry III. Meanwhile the action had been compromised. By a fine dated 7 December 1200 Jordan released his interests in a third of Foston, Lyncombe and Goodleigh in return for Brewer's recognition of his right to one third of Goodleigh excluding the manor house and advowson.[84] Jordan also issued a charter in the same terms, copies of which (but without the witnesses) are given in the Percy cartulary.[85] The course of Jordan's debt in the pipe rolls is as follows. The first payment on it was credited in 6 John (1204), being partly by the hand of Jordan de Abernon; in 7 John there was a further payment credited but this time by the hand of the heir of Jordan de Abernon, it being noted that the land was in ward to Ralph de Mora, at that time sheriff of Devon. Payment of the share originally owed by Jordan was attermed at one mark a year and from 8 John to 14 John (1206–12) this amount was yearly credited in the pipe rolls as paid in by Ralph de Mora.[86] This seems to suggest that Jordan de Abernon the nephew and heir of Henry de Sackville died about 1204 leaving an heir who was under age. In the first pipe roll after the end of the war between John and his barons, that for 2 Henry III, the debt is charged to Jordan de Abernon, who paid the usual yearly instalment of a mark and who continued payments until, after a blank in 6 Henry III, the debt was finally cleared with a payment of 23s 6d in 7 Henry III (1223).[87] This Jordan would therefore seem to have come of age between 1213 and 1218. Seemingly he was dead by 1235. The 1267 pedigree has a Jordan as the second son of Ingram III de Abernon, between Roger who succeeded Ingram and the three brothers involved in the Lasham action, but this Jordan is said to have died without an heir. In 1235 William Brewer's son died without direct heir and the documents concerning the parcelling out of the vast Brewer estates among coheirs show that the third share of Goodleigh was then held by William de Abernon.[88] By about 1242 he too was dead, for in the great feudal returns of 1242–3 the heir of William de Abernon is returned as holding a third of a fee in Goodleigh, of the honor of Plympton, as well as half a fee in Stockleigh and an eighth of a fee in Bradford d'Abernon, both of the Courtney honor of Okehampton.[89] Spencer Perceval gave a somewhat imperfect account of the descent of these Devon estates to this point and concluded rightly that they did not descend with the Surrey estates. But his other suggestion that the William who held in Goodleigh in 1235 was the William who was concerned in the Lasham action as the brother of Ingram, Richard and Walter is obviously incorrect, for by 1235 that William was dead and had been succeeded by his son Jordan, who made the composition with Gilbert and who in 1242–3 was still holding Duxford. On the whole it seems reasonable to conclude that the de Abernons of Stockleigh, Goodleigh and Bradford d'Abernon belonged to a branch whose nearest common ancestor with the Surrey branch is likely to have been the grandfather of the five brothers of our pedigree. But the connection may have been more distant than this since, as we noticed at the beginning of these notes, Ingram I, about 1130, seemed to have two brothers and a cousin; if, as seems likely, it was the elder of these brothers, Jordan, who was the ancestor of Ingram II, Ingram III and the rest of the brothers, then it is possible that the younger brother Walter or the cousin William may have been the ancestor of the Devon line.

The Walter de Abernon whom we have been unable to fit into the pedigree presents a different problem, for we know a fair amount about him but nothing at all from contemporary sources of his parents or possible descendants. The 1267 pedigree, however, makes him the younger brother of Ingram IV and says that he died without heirs, and this would not be inconsistent with the first mention which we seem to have of him; in 1220 Nicola de Abernon, who if the pedigree is right was his mother, attorned him in her place in her suit with the

Earl Marshal.[90] He does not appear in Surrey grand assize panels down to 1224 but we cannot be sure that the one in which we find him chosen in Michaelmas term 1232 was the first on which he was called to serve. There is no surviving roll for the 1229 Surrey eyre; in the 1235 Surrey eyre he was chosen in eight panels.[91] That he was knighted some time between 1224 and 1232 is certain for in Ingram IV's grant to the parson of Fetcham some of the witnesses are designated knights but Walter is not among them; on the other hand he is described as a knight in two of Gilbert's charters while in the third none is so designated but his name is among those of men known to be knights.[92] He probably held some of the family lands in Fetcham, since he was presented as a defaulter in Copthorne hundred in the 1235 eyre, made a grant at Fetcham to Henry le Moyne and acted as first witness in three other grants to Henry of lands there.[93] In that eyre he also went surety for a Blechingley man; two grants by him of lands there are known.[94] Walter was still alive in May 1241, for in the Surrey eyre held then he and his wife Maud withdrew an action of entry which they had brought against Robert de Manxey concerning 5s worth of rent in Lingfield.[95] One of their sureties for prosecuting this action had been Deudi le Noble, who is among the witnesses to one of the charters just mentioned and who was presumably a tenant. However, Walter de Abernon does not appear in any of the grand assize panels of this eyre and I have not carried my search for him systematically beyond this point. Spencer Perceval noticed that a Maud who was the widow of Walter de Abernon was litigating in 1268;[96] there seems no doubt that she was this Walter's wife. Among the Waverley Abbey deeds there is one witnessed by a Walter de Abernon who might be this Walter but who perhaps is more likely to have been the head of the family who died before 1220.[97] By it, Richard le Romer with the consent of his brother Adam granted to the monks half a virgate in Oxshott (Oggesahte) lying in the fields east of Oxshott and held of Henry Faber, with a messuage, meadow, grove and appurtenances, to hold at a rent of 6d yearly payable to Henry for all except foreign service. The witnesses were: Walter de Abernon, Gilbert Prudumme, Ralph de Imworth, Walter Prudumme and Richard Pincun. We may recall that when Walter de Abernon and Ralph de Clere compromised their action in 1206 and were given a day for taking their chirographs, Walter attorned Walter Prudumme in his place; and that both Gilbert Prudumme and Ralph de Imworth were concerned in the confirmation made by Walter's predecessor Roger de Abernon. Moreover Henry Faber himself granted land at Oxshott to Waverley Abbey by a final concord made in November 1202 and by a deed which may be about that date.[98]

NOTES

1 This article, originally written about 25 years ago, was found among Mr Meekings' papers following his death in 1977. It has been prepared for publication by Dr David Crook, an Assistant Keeper of Public Records, who has also rewritten it as necessary to take account of a pedigree of the family pleaded in a lawsuit in 1267. This was discovered by Mr Meekings after the article was written but was not incorporated into it by him. A few other recent discoveries have also been added. Some of the material appears in *The 1235 Surrey Eyre* (SyRS **31** (1979), 162–4) as biographies

of Walter and Gilbert de Abernon; the version given here supplements and occasionally corrects these. Unless otherwise stated, references to unpublished documents are to records in the Public Record Office (Chancery Lane).

2 *SyAC* **5,** 53–74 (hereafter S.P.)

3 British Library (BL) Addit MS 6167

4 BL Cotton App xxi, nos 136–7, printed in *Monasticon* **6,** 1659–60

5 BL Cotton App xxi, nos 143, 137; *Monasticon* **6,** 1660–1

6 Johnson, C. and Cronne, H.A., eds, *Regesta Regum Anglo-Normannorum* **2,** 1956, nos 1015, 1207; Farrer, W., ed, *Early Yorkshire Charters* **3,** 1916, no 1433

7 BL Cotton Cleopatra C vii, f 172v. The text is given in Heales, A. *Records of Merton Priory*, 1898, as appendix 2, and translated on pp 13–14

8 *Calendar of Charter Rolls 1300–26*, 372; Cronne, H.A. and Davis, R.H.C., eds, *Regesta Regum Anglo-Normannorum* **3,** 1968, no 921

9 *Pipe Roll (PR) 31 Henry I*, 51, 60, 99; cf S.P., note 10

10 BL Cotton Cleopatra C vii, ff 172v–173r. The texts are given in Heales as appendices 21 and 22 and are translated on p 14 and again on p 35. The numbers 510 and 511 assigned to them are Heales' own. At the head of f 172v is a note which seems to mean that they were also entered in the cartulary at f 67 of the original numeration, but ff 1–80 of that numeration are now wanting

11 This word is correctly transcribed by Heales at appendix 21, but he seems to have misread it as *proavus* for on p 35 he translates it as 'great-grandfather'. The translation contains various other small mistakes, eg the charter is not dated 7 October, nor was the rent to be paid 13s 4d

12 BL Cotton App xxi, no 23

13 *PR 2–4 Henry II*, 12; cf S.P., note 11, which wrongly gives the sum as 17d and the roll as 22 Henry II

14 *Essex Archaeol Soc Trans*, new series **7** (1900), 148

15 Heales, op cit, 32 (date assigned 1177–86) and text (from the cartulary, f 72) as appendix 18 (date assigned 1174–86)

16 Hall, H., ed, *Red Book of the Exchequer*, 1896, 405, 252

17 Reichel, O.J. 'Early descents of the manors in Wonsford Hundred.' *Trans Devonshire Assoc* **44** (1912), 324

18 *PR 22 Henry II*, 215; *23 Henry II*, 194

19 *PR 22 Henry II*, 20

20 BL Cotton App xxi, no 46

21 Meyer, P., ed, *Histoire de Guillaume le Marechal*, 1891–1901, lines 9545–50

22 *PR 1 Richard I*, 29, to *5 Richard I*, 4, the debt is repeated without action; in *6 Richard I*, 32, it is marked + and in *7 Richard I* it does not appear, being paid off by the sheriff among many others marked + in the previous roll. For Ingram's lands in Essex, see p 161

23 *PR 5 Richard I*, 9

24 On the de Clere family see Farrer, W. *Early Yorkshire Charters* **2,** 1914, 480–1 and *Honors and Knights Fees* **3,** 1925, 356–7 (with errors of dating due to the misdating of the Lasham action); cf *The 1235 Surrey Eyre* **1,** 182–4

25 *Curia Regis Rolls (CRR)* **1,** 184, 236

26 Ibid 279, 284

27 Selden Soc **67** (1948), no 3242

28 *CRR* **1,** 378

29 Selden Soc **67,** nos 3350, 3420

30 *CRR* **1,** 424

31 Selden Soc **67,** no 3457

32 *PR 6 Richard I*, 220

33 The basic details of these scutages were later collected from the pipe rolls by a 13th century exchequer baron, and for Roger can be seen in the *Red Book*, 91, 99, 148.

For the originals see *Chancellor's Roll 8 Richard I*, 67–8; *PR 9 Richard I*, 22; *10 Richard I*, 23; *2 John*, 100, 194; *3 John*, 105; *4 John*, 71, 80. S.P., note 18, knew only of the Record Commission edition of the Chancellor's Roll for 3 John

34 *Rotuli Chartarum*, 1837, 65; cf S.P., 54, 56 and note 3

35 BL Addit Charters 5528–9, which are endorsed with the old Abbey references 'D vii' and 'D viii'

36 Gilbert Prudumme was a knight who served on Surrey grand assizes between 1203 and 1220 and who in 1210 held the extraordinary judicial session for the county with Gilbert de Abinger. Plainly he was Roger's tenant; Roger heads the list of witnesses to his tenant's grant and then issues his own confirmation. On Ralph de Imworth and Robert de Watevill see *The 1235 Surrey Eyre* **1,** 210, 252

37 S.P., note 11, referring to BL Addit Charters 5530–1 and 5537. From the memoranda he gives it looks as if someone with little knowledge of hands looked at them on his behalf. Nos 5531 and 5537 are discussed below; 5530 is a charter of John I de Abernon (born between 1222 and 1227, died 1277), from its witnesses probably to be dated c 1248

38 KB 26/180, m 19; below, p 00

39 *Rotuli Curiae Regis* **1,** 1835, 53

40 *PR 6 John*, 105; *Rotuli de Oblatis et Finibus*, 1835, 198; *PR 7 John*, 154

41 *CRR* **3,** 308–9; *PR 7 John*, 155

42 *CRR* **4,** 15

43 *Rot de Ob et Fin*, 334, 336 (S.P., note 13), the debts being charged and paid in *PR 8 John*, 156

44 *CRR* **4,** 142

45 Ibid 64, 110

46 Ibid 293; cf *PR 9 John*, 146, 150

47 *CRR* **5,** 19

48 CP 25(1)/203/3, no 14

49 *PR 12 John*, 39; *13 John*, 250

50 *Rotuli Litterarum Clausarum* **1,** 1833, 235

51 Ibid 236b; S.P., note 15 mistakenly gives 3s

52 Ibid 251b

53 Ibid 270b

54 *CRR* **8,** 325

55 Ibid **9,** 88, 89–90

56 Ibid 209; ibid **10,** 84

57 C 66/43, m 7d. For brief biographies of Henry de la Mare and William de Wyke see *The 1235 Surrey Eyre* **1,** 220, 259

58 *CRR* **10,** 212, 312

59 BL Addit Charter 5540; woodcuts of Ingram's seal are given in S.P. p 59

60 *Excerpta e Rotulis Finium* **1,** 1835, 270

61 *CRR* **15,** no 1371

62 Ibid 272

63 BL Addit Charter 5541. S.P., note 23 is not a transcript of this but a rather poorly executed Latin abstract, which includes several errors

64 BL Addit Charter 5562. S.P. gives an incomplete abstract in note 20

65 For biographies of Camoys, Cherburgh, Drew, William Hansard, Holdhurst, Pirbright, Utworth and Windsor see *The 1235 Surrey Eyre* **1,** 176–7, 180, 191, 205–6, 207, 227–9, 249–50, 255–7

66 *The 1235 Surrey Eyre* **1,** 163, 213

67 *CRR* **4,** 47, 62; CP 25(1)/225/3, no 18

68 *CRR* **9,** 45, 88–90, 220; **10,** 32, 309–10; *The 1235 Surrey Eyre* **2** (Surrey Record Soc forthcoming), nos 53, 58, 70–1, 75–6, 78, 80, 87, 105

69 *Patent Rolls 1225–32*, 216

70 C 66/46, m 8d
71 BL Addit Charters 5532, 5531. Both bear the abbey endorsement 'D vj ij', but the latter carries the note 'we have another in which the metes are better and more distinctly given', so that 5532 is plainly the operative grant
72 The variants in 5531 are: (i) that Gilbert reserves to himself and his heirs the right to make purprestures at will in the woods granted; (ii) the bounds of the purprestures are given as in breadth the same as a purpresture of Alan Forester and in length running from Alan's purpresture to the lands of Robert de Watevill to the north
73 CP 25(1)/225/4, no 6. This is cited in the *Victoria County History of Surrey* **3,** 1911, 291, as supporting facts which are not to be found in it, and it is clear that the writer of the Headley article did not look at it. The 'Giles' de Abernon mentioned there is a blunder for 'Gilbert'
74 *Excerpta e Rotulis Finium* **1,** 305
75 *Book of Fees*, 1920–31, 685–6, 867
76 CP 25(1)/226/12, no 31
77 JUST 1/870, m ld, the commission for this action issuing on 13 April 1248: C 66/59, m 8d. The matter was settled by an enrolled final concord whereby the master and his men of West Humble were to have common for 40 sheep in Fetcham up to 'Grimesditch' from the arable towards Fetcham as Patrick's road runs from Polesden to the arable near Fetcham church
78 JUST 1/870, m ld, the commission issuing sometime in April: C 66/59, m 8d
79 *Complete Peerage*, sub Chaurces or Chaworth; Thoroton, R. *History of Nottinghamshire* **3,** 1797 ed, 402
80 Cf CP 25(1)/182/8, nos 284, 295, 298
81 More fully discussed in Farrer *Honors and Knights Fees* **1,** 1923, 231–2
82 *Rotuli Curiae Regis* **1,** 146–7; S.P., note 60
83 *PR 10 Richard I*, 160, 181; *Rot de Ob et Fin*, 50; S.P., note 61
84 Reichel, O.J., ed, *Devon Feet of Fines* **1** (Devon and Cornwall Record Soc **5,** 1912), no 67
85 Martin, M.T., ed, *Percy Chartulary* (Surtees Soc **117,** 1911), nos 445, 949
86 No action from *PR 1 John*, 191, to *5 John*, 73; *6 John*, 82; *7 John*, 20; *8 John*, 139; *14 John*, 72
87 *PR 2 Henry III*, 86; E 372/67, r 2
88 *Book of Fees*, 401; S.P. p 68; *Calendar of Close Rolls 1234–7*, 361
89 *Book of Fees*, 787, 785, 784; S.P. cites from the *Testa de Nevill* edition
90 *CRR* **8,** 325; cf *The 1235 Surrey Eyre* **1,** 163–4
91 *CRR* **14,** no 2256; *The 1235 Surrey Eyre* **2,** nos 56, 58, 70–1, 75–6, 80, 87
92 BL Addit Charters 5540, 5532, 5562, 5541
93 *The 1235 Surrey Eyre* **2** SyRS forthcoming, no 499; SyRO 65/1/1–4
94 Ibid no 368; Lambert, U. *Blechingley* **1,** 1921, 152–3 and plate
95 JUST 1/867, m15
96 *Excerpta e Rotulis Finium* **2,** 1836, 465; JUST 1/1200, m 16d; S.P. note 19 and p 58, where his conclusions are erroneous
97 BL Addit Charter 5537
98 CP 25(1)/225/2, no 39; BL Addit Charter 5536

XVI

TWO DAMMARTIN DEEDS

The Deed Collection at the Minet Library, Camberwell, includes a small accumulation concerning the Dammartin family and the former Augustinian hospital or priory of St. James at Tandridge, Surrey, which was founded by that family. This accumulation seems to have come from the estate records of a Tandridge property in the nineteenth century. The deeds range from the twelfth to the fourteenth centuries and concern Suffolk, Surrey and Sussex. With one exception[1] they have not been noticed by local historians, so it may be useful to give abstracts and notes on the two Sussex deeds.

ST. IVES or SENTIE, in HARTFIELD. At the Dissolution the manor of Sentie in Hartfield was held by Tandridge priory; the last conventual lease of the manor had been granted on 27 Feb. 1521 to John Hayward, for a term of 61 years at £4 rent,[2] subject also to a rent charge of 23s. 1d. to Withyham manor.[3] After the Dissolution the manor passed with all the other former possessions of the priory to John Rede by grant of 2 Jan. 1538.[4] The lease of 1521 was the earliest evidence for the place name Sentie that the editors of *Sussex Place Names* could find (Vol. ii, 368). *Minet Deed 3607*, which seems to represent the original grant of this estate to the priory, enables us to take the name back to the early thirteenth century. It is as follows:—

I, Alice de Danmartin daughter of Odo de Danmartin, grant to God and the hospital of St. James at Tanregge and the brothers of the same hospital there serving God for my soul and the souls of my father and mother and my ancestors and successors, in pure and perpetual alms all my land of Seintetie with all its appurtenances, to hold of me and my heirs quit of all service exaction and secular demands, in waters, meadows, mills, pastures, woods, groves, roads, ways and in all liberties, saving service due to the chief lords of that land; and I warrant that land to the hospital against all men and women. Witnesses: Odo de Danmartin, Adam Pincerna, William de Danmartin, Ralph de Pimpe, Robert Bernard, Robert the chaplain, William de St. John, Peter and Adam de Talewrth,' William de Warlingeham, Eustace de Wlkested,' Graland and Baldric de la Wdecot' and many others.

The monastic archivist has endorsed the deed: *Carta Alicie de terra de Sentetie;* the seal is lost. The first witness is the donor's brother; the rest are knights or prominent freeholders who were the Dammartin's tenants in eastern Surrey or western Kent, [all of whom witness other deeds of the family. Adam of Talworth (in Long Ditton, Surrey) was a knight active in county affairs who appears to have died in 1209 since in 1210 Hilary term his widow Mary began the first of several actions for dower in her late husband's lands.[5] Luke de la Woodcote (of Woodcote in Beddington, Surrey) was also a knight active in his county's affairs up to 1208; Graland and Baldric were his sons,[6] who join with him in witnessing an earlier Dammartin grant to Tandridge.[7] In 1204 Luke was acting as an attorney for Odo de Dammartin.[8] It seems likely that he would have witnessed Alice's grant had he been alive when she made her gift.] The deed may be dated as certainly before 1210 and possibly after 1208. [Nothing is at present known about the lives of the other witnesses to enable a more precise date to be suggested.]

Alice's father Odo was the head of the main English line of the Dammartins but the succession of this line in the late twelfth and early thirteenth century is very obscure. Alice's description of herself suggests that she was unmarried when making the grant. Her first husband was John de Wauton, a prominent knightly tenant of the earls of Warenne in Surrey and Yorkshire whom she must have married by 1222 at latest since their son and heir John received seisin of his estates on 28 May 1244 after coming of age.[9] Her brother Odo had been head of the family for some years when, after a period of insanity, he died between Feb. and April 1225, leaving Alice as his heir. In the years following, John and Alice were engaged in much litigation about estates alienated by Odo in his insanity and about the dower of Odo's widow. John de Wauton was one of the many who went on Henry III's expedition to Brittany in the summer of 1230; he died then, apparently in the epidemic of sickness which affected the army.[10] By May 1231 Alice had married Roger de Clare, whose elder brother Gilbert, earl of Gloucester and Hereford, had also died in the expedition of 1230.[11] Roger took part in the crusade of 1240-1, presumably in the English contingent led by Richard of Cornwall; he was believed to be on his way home in May 1241 but by August 1241 was known to be dead.[12] Thereafter, Alice seems to have leased or alienated her lands in southern England and to have retired to her East Anglian estates. She was living in 1249; litigation about conflicting grants of two of her Surrey manors suggests that she died about 1255.[13] There is evidence to suggest that after 1249 she married a third time. When the debts owing to the important Jewish banker Elias le Evesk were taken over by the King and charged in the pipe roll of 1259, the distinguished Sussex knight Nicholas de Wauncy and his wife Alice de Danmartin were entered in the Sussex account as owing £130.[14] This debt, like the rest of those owed to Elias, had of course been contracted some years before 1259, perhaps about 1252 when Nicholas left office after his second term as sheriff of Surrey and Sussex, heavily indebted to the King. Nicholas had certainly married Alice de Danmartin by 1251, when the couple were distraining a tenant for customs and services due in the manor of Mickleham, Surrey, which was one of the ancestral manors of the main line of the Dammartins.[15] An element of doubt about this Alice's identity remains, however, because William de Danmartin, the third witness in the deed, also had a daughter named Alice.[16] With Alice's death about 1255 the main English line of the Dammartins came to an end.

1 *Surrey Archaeological Collections* hereafter Sy. Arch. Coll. vol. 54 (1955), 88-9.
2 A. Heales, *The history of Tandridge Priory, Surrey* (1885), 45, 58, 137.
3 *Ibid.*, 52-3.
4 *Ibid*, 49.
5 *Curia Regis Rolls*, vi. 2-3.
6 *Chartulary of the Hospital of St. Thomas the Martyr, Southwark*, (privately, 1932), no. 827; *cf*, British Museum, *Add. Charter* 23544.
7 Heales, *Tandridge*, app. i.
8 *Curia Regis Rolls*, iii. 237, 246.
9 *Close Rolls 1242-7*, 191.
10 *Cal. Patent Rolls 1225-32*, 357; *Excerpta e Rotulis Finium*, i, 202.
11 *Curia Regis Rolls*, xiv, 1526 (also in *Bracton's Note Book*, ed. F. W. Maitland, I, no. 574); *Rotuli Litterarum Clausarum*, ii, 98.
12 *Excerpta e Rotulis Finium*, i, 334, 350; *Justices Itinerant Roll*, no. 867, m. l.
13 Norfolk Feet of Fines, Henry III, no. 1082; *Justices Itinerant Roll*, no. 1193, m. 4.
14 *Pipe Roll 44 Hen. III*, rot. 15d.
15 *C. P. 25(1), 226/14*, no. 36.
16 *Merton College, Oxford*, deed 917.

SOUTHWICK. Southwick was a Braose fee which in the thirteenth century emerges with the le Counte family as mesne tenants. The best account of the place does not notice the Dammartin connexion[1] but it seems certain that the Dammartins held a manor there for at least a century. About 1130 Odo de Dammartin, head of the English line, died, leaving a widow Basilia and a son Odo who succeeded him;[2] the younger Odo survived until after 1154 but was dead by 1166 when he had in turn been succeeded by a son Odo.[3] In a deed of William de Braose, ascribed by Salzman to about 1145, the second witness is ' Odo de Danmartin, my nephew.'[4] Since William de Braose had succeeded to his estates by about 1130[5] it is possible that it was the first of these Odos who married William's sister (in which case she may have been the Basilia widowed in 1130) and the second who was William's nephew. But since William de Braose survived until the 1180s and the deed may be later than 1145 it is also possible that it was the second Odo who married William's sister. In either case there was a marriage connexion between the Braose and Danmartin families in the first half of the twelfth century and it is reasonable to suppose that a gift of land at Southwick accompanied this marriage. Southwick appears among the 14 manors for which Odo de Danmartin obtained a royal charter of freewarren on 1 Dec. 1202.[6] Among the bequests made by Odo son of William de Dammartin to Tandridge hospital, apparently between 1218 and 1222, were oxen and pigs at Southwick.[7] We have seen that Alice de Dammartin's brother Odo became deranged towards the end of his life. In 1225 Hilary term Peter de Watevill was one of two principals who, with others unnamed, complained that they were being disseised of estates which Odo had granted to them; the justices ordered them to be restored to seisin but at Odo's request, and confession that he was incapable of looking after his affairs, they committed Odo and his seal to the guardianship of his brother in law, John de Wauton, and another Surrey knight, Gilbert de Pudingen.[8] Immediately Odo died, John and his wife Alice began litigation against those who had profited by Odo's insanity; [Thomas de la Graye was one of their attorneys in this.[9]] The action brought against Peter de Watevill was for a carucate at Southwick and after Peter had claimed a view of the estate the action was pleaded in the Bench at Easter one month 1226, Martin de Pateshull being then the senior justice [of that court.][10] John and Alice pleaded Odo's insanity in voidance of Peter's grant. Peter rebutting this, said that Odo, after being present at the seige of Bedford (June-August 1224) had gone to Norfolk, where he had knighted him, and had then held a great feast and gathering in Sussex where, in a good state of health, he had given him this estate. The justices reserved judgment, which they ordered to be given in the next Sussex eyre. A visitation of the eyre throughout the whole of England was planned to begin in the summer of 1226 and it was presumably thought that Sussex would be visited in the course of the next year or two. In fact, Sussex and Surrey were left out of the main eyre visitation of 1226-8 and did not receive special eyres on their own until 1229. But before these took place the dispute had been settled out of court by *Minet Deed 3611*, which is as follows:—

I, Peter de Watevile, for me and my heirs release to John de Wauton and his wife Alice and her Heirs Suwike with all its appurtenances, which I admit to be their right and which I had of the gift of Odo de Domartin and about which there was a plea between us in the King's court at Wemust ' before Martin de Pateshille then justice. For this release and admission of right John and Alice have given me 20 marks silver. Witnesses; sir Roland de Hacstede, sir Manser de Pecham, sir Nicholas Malem,' sir John de Burstowe, sir William de Domartin, Nicholas Hereman, Thomas de la Grave, Samson de Muleseye and many others.

The seal is lost; there is no endorsement.

We have seen that the action was pleaded on or about 17 May 1226. By Sep. 1227 Manser de Pecham was dead, for his widow was then litigating for dower.[11] The deed must therefore have been made between these dates and probably in 1226. A generation later it was produced in litigation. We have seen that Alice de Dammartin, after the loss of her second husband in 1241, alienated many of her estates. In May 1248 she conveyed three Surrey manors to Thomas de Warblington, who by 1251 had also obtained some kind of tenancy in Alice's dower manor in Norfolk.[12] It seems that he similarly obtained a grant of Southwick, for in the Sussex eyre of November 1248 John de Wauton the younger began an action of mort d'ancestor, grounded on the death of his father John (in 1230), against Beatrice relict of John de Warblington for 100 acres at Southwick.[13] Beatrice vouched Thomas de Warblington to warrant; Thomas warranted and in turn vouched the widowed Alice Dammartin to warrant. The central court of the Bench was at this time not in session because of the eyre visitation. The action was therefore adjourned to the 1249 Hampshire eyre, where Alice was essoined, and thence to the Wiltshire eyre at Easter one month, where she defaulted.[14] A further adjournment was then made to the Middlesex eyre at the Strand on 25 June for Alice to appear and warrant; the sheriff was also commanded to produce then the assize jurors of 1248 ' and William Daunmartin and Nicholas Hereman, witnesses in a charter which Thomas de Warblington has proferred in the name of Peter de Wauteville.' These were the only two survivors of the witnesses; of the others, Roland of Oxted is known to have died about January 1240, Nicholas Malesmeins between 1229 and 1234, John of Burstow between 1235 and 1239 and Samson of Molesey about March 1235. No roll survives from the 1249 Middlesex eyre but the action must have been determined then because there is no trace of it in the Bench plea rolls when that court resumed [sessions] in Michaelmas term 1249. John de Wauton was presumably unsuccessful because his father had only held the manor in his wife Alice's right and she had herself later alienated it.

1 E. F. Salmon, 'Southwick,' *Sussex. Arch. Coll.* vol. 63 (1922), 87-91.
2 *Pipe Roll 31 Hen. I*, 94, 98.
3 *Red Book of the Exchequer*, ed. H. Hall, i, 402.
4 *The Chartulary of Sele*, ed. L. F. Salzman, no. 9.
5 *Ibid.*, no. 10.
6 *Sy. Arch. Coll. vol. 54* (1955). 88-9, translating *Minet Deed 3606*.
7 Heales, *Tandridge*, p. 7 and app. ii.
8 *Curia Regis Rolls*, xii, 344.
9 *Ibid.*, 1396.
10 *Ibid.*, 1487, 2509.
11 *Justices Itinerant Roll*, no. 358, m. 28.
12 Surrey Feet of Fines, Henry III, 13, no. 50; *Justices Itinerant Roll*, no. 565, m. 20d.
13 *Justices Itinerant Roll*, no. 909A, m. 9.
14 *Justices Itinerant Roll*, no. 997, m. 11; there is an inferior record on a parallel roll, no. 777, m. 27.

XVII

The Early Years of Netley Abbey

by the late C. A. F. MEEKINGS, edited by R. F. HUNNISETT

It was in broken health that Peter des Roches, bishop of Winchester (1205–38), returned for the last time to England, about Michaelmas 1236.[1] On 31 October 1236, at Rochester, he made his last testament; this was given royal acceptance and confirmation at Windsor on 4 November, in the presence of some of the executors: Ralph de Nevill, bishop of Chichester (1222–44) and chancellor (1226–44), P. archdeacon of Winchester, Luke des Roches, archdeacon (by 1228–44) of Surrey, and the versatile architect and administrator Mr. Elias de Derham (c. 1167–d. 1245).[2] Bishop Peter rallied, to take some part in national affairs, as well as in his diocese, during the next two years. He died at his episcopal castle of Farnham on 9 June 1238 and his body was buried in his cathedral;[3] but his heart was buried at the Cistercian abbey of Waverley, a few miles south-west of Farnham.[4] In 1237 he had petitioned the Cistercian chapter general for leave to have a Cistercian monk and two lay brothers living with him.[5] This, the heart burial, and the notices accorded him by Waverley's annalist, reflect the private preoccupations of his last years: the founding of Cistercian houses in his native country and in his English diocese. The arrangements, unfinished at his death, were left to be completed by his executors, who notified the Order's chapter general at its usual mid-September meeting in 1238, when the investigating commissioners for the new foundations were appointed.[6]

[1] Matthew Paris, *Chronica Majora*, ed. H. R. Luard, London, Rolls Series, 1872–83, iii. 378. The Tewkesbury and Winchester annalists give the date of his reaching Winchester, in November: *Annales Monastici*, ed. H. R. Luard, London, Rolls Series, 1864–9, i. 102; ii. 87.

[2] *Calendar of Patent Rolls* (hereafter *C.P.R.*) *1232–47*, 166. This is the only known reference to 'P' archdeacon of Winchester, and may be an error. All printed texts and calendars cited without full bibliographical details are Public Record Office volumes published by Her Majesty's Stationery Office and listed in *British National Archives*, Government Publications Sectional List No. 24, revised annually.

[3] *Chronica Majora*, iii. 489. So also the Tewkesbury and Osney annalists: *Annales Monastici*, i. 108; iv. 86. Winchester gives wrongly 11 July (5 id. July instead of 5 id. June): ibid., ii. 88.

[4] *Annales Monastici*, ii. 319.

[5] *Statuta Capitulorum Generalium Ordinis Cisterciencis 1116–1786*, Louvain, 1933– , ii (1221–61), ed. D. J.-M. Canivez, (1237), 10.

[6] *Annales Monastici*, ii. 322–3; *Stat. Cap. Cist.*, ii. (1238), 27, 28.

For the French foundation, bishop Peter had bequeathed money to William, abbot (1238–44) of Cîteaux, who decided to supply the convent from his own house. The commissioners were William, abbot of Oratorio (Le Loroux, Angers), and John, abbot of the newly founded house of Pietas Dei (L'Epau, Le Mans). The latter was charged with the negotiations for its site, which was purchased for 600 *livres Turnoises* from William de Beaumont, and was in Touraine, near St. Paterne, between the Loir and the Loire. There, on 22 July 1240, it began its organised existence under abbot Reynold, with twelve monks and three lay brothers from Cîteaux, as the house of Claritas Dei, La Clarté Dieu.[7]

The English foundation was to be a daughter house of Beaulieu, the abbots of Waverley and Quarr being the founding commissioners. According to Waverley's annalist, it began its corporate existence on 25 July 1239, as the abbey of *Locus Sancti Edwardi* or Edwardstowe. A few years later, building commenced at what was then known indifferently as Letley or Netley, on the well-wooded northern shores of Southampton Water. The patronage was eventually assumed by bishop Peter's former pupil, Henry III. There have been numerous accounts of Netley abbey, of which the most important are those in Caley's edition of Dugdale's *Monasticon*, in the Hampshire volumes of the *Victoria County History*, and in Hamilton Thompson's *Netley Abbey*.[8] Valuable as these are, they are no longer sufficient, whether one is concerned with the early history of the abbey and its buildings or with the early growth of its possessions. Apart from evidence published since they were written, all the writers seem at times to be unaware of problems posed by the evidence on which their accounts are based. By a re-examination of familar evidence and an examination of the most recently published evidence and of some readily searchable unpublished sources, it is possible to supplement and correct these accounts.

The problems concerning the abbey's estates involve in some cases, surprisingly after so much has been written, accurate topographical identification and an understanding of the ways in which they were acquired. The major problems about the early history of the abbey itself are: the date when it was established at Netley; the date when Henry III assumed the role of founder; and the extent to which he, rather than bishop Peter's executors, can be found to be responsible for the foundation.

Apart from the usual published and unpublished sources, including the records of chancery, exchequer and courts of law, a small number of the abbey's deeds survive among exchequer collections, chiefly in those of the

[7] *Gallia Christiana*, Paris, 1715–1865, xiv. 327.

[8] W. Dugdale, *Monasticon Anglicanum*, ed. J. Caley, H. Ellis and B. Bandinel, London, 1846, v. 695–7; *Victoria County History of Hampshire*, ii. 146–9 (history of house, by J. C. Cox); iii. 472–6 (history of building, by Miss A. R. Grundy, with plan by Harold Breakspear); A. Hamilton Thompson, *Netley Abbey, Hampshire*, London, H.M.S.O., 1952.

King's Remembrancer's Office.[9] Because of nineteenth-century methodisation, the reason for their presence in this amorphous collection cannot be clearly established; though it was probably due to an event soon after the Dissolution, when the abbey's lands were still compact. Three features make it certain that they came from the abbey's general archives and had remained together for some time after the surrender of 1536 and were long stored as a separate group. First, they relate to several estates in Hampshire and also in Oxfordshire, Surrey and Wiltshire. Secondly, they have all suffered a common misfortune of careless storage that has left them damaged by damp and mutilation; indeed, some until recently existed in two halves under widely separated references. Lastly, though now apart from the deeds, there are the series of court rolls and ministers' accounts for all the abbey's estates, and these obviously came as a whole from the abbey's archives.

No cartularly survives, so along with royal confirmation charters and final concords, these deeds provide most of the evidence about the abbey's estates in the first decade or so of its history. Ten royal charters were issued in favour of the abbot and convent between 28 February 1240 and 12 April 1256. For various reasons, not all of these are to be found calendared in the volumes where they might be expected; the uneven method of this series of Calendars has led to their being calendared with varying fullness where they do appear. As a preliminary, it will be useful to list these charters, with references to the original enrolments and to the published abstracts or texts of them, to other copies of major importance, and with a note of the number of later confirmations.

I.	28 February 1240	Tun of wine yearly from Southampton prisage wines. C 53/33, m. 3. Calendared: *Calendar of Charter Rolls* (hereafter *C.Ch.R.*) *1227–57*, 250–1. Five later confirmations.
II.	15 March 1240	Confirmation of lands and rents. C 53/33, m. 2. Calendared: *C.Ch.R. 1227–57*, 251.
III.	4 June 1241	Confirmation of Letley manor. C 53/34, m. 3. Calendared: *C.Ch.R. 1227–57*, 259–60.
IV.	18 October 1242	Confirmation of lands and rents (acquired between March 1240 and October 1242). C 66/32, m. 2. Calendared: *Calendar of Patent Rolls* (hereafter *C.P.R.*) *1232–47*, 333.
V.	18 October 1242	Quittance of suits of shires and hundreds, etc. C 66/32, m. 2. Calendared: *C.P.R. 1232–47*, 333.

[9] In *Catalogue of Ancient Deeds* (hereafter *C.A.D.*), iii, brief abstracts of the following are given: Exchequer, King's Remembrancer, Ancient Deeds, Series D [E 210] 93, 131, 132, 153, 200 (+83), 230, 302, 323, 327 (+120), 630, 1216. Unless otherwise stated, all manuscripts cited are in the Public Record Office.

VI.	7 March 1251	Confirmation of all lands, rents and churches and grant of extensive liberties. C 53/43, m. 10. Brief note: *C.Ch.R. 1227–57*, 354. Text (errors and truncated): *Monasticon*, v, 696, no. i. Full text (taken from enrolment in Cartae Antiquae Roll (C52) 11, no. 26): Pipe Roll Society, New Series, xxxiii, no. 353 (31–32). Late thirteenth-century copies, possibly produced for this enrolment or the confirmation of 1285: E 40/3239(1) and 3240, noticed in *C.A.D.*, ii, 170. Six later confirmations.
VII.	20 March 1251	Free warren in demesnes, Hound market and Wellow fair. C 53/43, m. 10. Calendared: *C.Ch.R. 1227–57*, 354. Late thirteenth-century copy: E 40/3239(2), noticed in *C.A.D.*, ii, 170. One later confirmation.
VIII.	11 December 1251	Wellow market: C 53/44, m. 26. Calendared: *C.Ch.R. 1227–57*, 371.
IX.	4 July 1253	Three carucates in the New Forest (Roydon). Original charter roll defective; confirmation copy: C 53/117, m. 33. Calendared: *C.Ch.R. 1327–41*, 229. Two later confirmations.
X.	12 April 1256	Licence to enclose the three carucates (Roydon). Original charter roll mostly lost; confirmation copy: C 66/497, mm. 26–25. Calendared: *C.P.R. 1461–67*, 158. One later confirmation.

The later charters or patents of *inspeximus* and confirmation, and the royal charters which were thereby inspected and confirmed, were as follows:

1 September 1285	VI—*C.Ch.R. 1257–1300*, 322.
20 March 1330	I and 1 September 1285—*C.Ch.R. 1327–41*, 169.
13 July 1331	IX—*C.Ch.R. 1327–41*, 229.
20 February 1378	20 March 1330—*C.P.R. 1377–81*, 135.
25 July 1400	20 February 1378—*C.P.R. 1399–1401*, 329.
26 October 1414	25 July 1400—*C.P.R. 1413–16*, 267.
7 December 1461	VII, IX, X and 20 February 1378—*C.P.R. 1461–67*, 158.

The story of the estates will be taken first. Since the emergence and use of the place name are of some importance, the forms Letley and Netley have been used when one or other of the many variants of these basic forms appears. Edwardstowe has been used as the translation of *Locus Sancti Edwardi*.

The first check that can be made on the estates acquired for the abbey is through the confirmation charter of 15 March 1240, made to the abbot and convent of Edwardstowe and confirming six purchased estates, described simply by the name of the vendor and a place name, usually in a freakish form. Four of these are said to have been bought by bishop Peter (two, we shall find, certainly before 1236); the other two had presumably been bought by the executors, between June 1238 and March 1240. Three of the four estates bought by bishop Peter had been acquired from French ecclesiastical corporations; the probability must be that all three purchases were negotiated during his last visit to France and Rome in 1235–36. The purpose of the confirmation seems to have been in order to perfect title, before alienating three of the estates in an exchange. From the final concord made in 1241, in connexion with this exchange, we can obtain specifications for these three estates.

From William (William II de Beaumont, 23 September 1203–31 August 1240)[10] bishop and the dean and chapter of Angers, bishop Peter had bought lands at 'Hanseta' and 'Tedrigia'. These places, though not identified in the *Calendar of Charter Rolls* and elsewhere, are readily identifiable as Henset, a lost settlement in Little Bedwyn, and Totteridge, in Milton Lilborne, both in Wiltshire, some eight miles apart, south of Marlborough and on the edge of the Vale of Pewsey; Angers apparently held them by grant of Henry II.[11] The final concord of 1241 describes them as a virgate and 12 marks rent in the two places.

From Alan (de Cestreham, 1235–44)[12] abbot and the convent of St. Mary des Pres, Leicester, bishop Peter had bought land, tenements, moor, meadows, the site of a mill, rents and services in [East] Wellow, Hampshire, with the homage and service there of Richard de Bosco, that is the mesne lordship of Richard's freeholding or subordinate manor. Since the whole manor of Wellow was obtained in 1240–42, this earlier purchase became merged in what was to be one of the most important of the abbey's estates.

From Geoffrey (Geoffrey II de Losdune, 1234–shortly before August 1255),[13] bishop and the dean and chapter of Le Mans, bishop Peter had bought land in 'Wrelquinsten', that is Kingston Deverel, near Mere, Wiltshire. As this was not alienated in 1241, we have no contemporary specification. But we know that bishop Peter bought it for £40 to give to some religious foundation, through the agency of Mr. Stephen de Arenis, canon of Le Mans, before 13 April 1236; for on that date a papal confirmation of the sale issued, to be followed by mandates of 26 April to ensure that the purchase money was spent in buying possessions for Le

[10] *Gallia Christiana*, xiv. 572–3.

[11] *The Red Book of the Exchequer*, ed. H. Hall, London, Rolls Series, 1896, ii. 484, 489.

[12] A. Hamilton Thompson, *The Abbey of St. Mary of the Meadows, Leicester*, Leicester, 1949, 15.

[13] *Gallia Christiana*, xiv. 399.

Mans.[14] In the papal letter, the estate is called 'Dewrelquinston'. This seems to be the model for the odd form in the charter, perhaps trimmed by a clerk who thought the 'De' was a preposition, and who so converted it to 'Wrelquinsten'. Since, as already remarked, the forms for bishop Peter's other estates in this charter are also freakish, by comparison with those found in thirteenth-century plea rolls and final concords, this tempts one to believe that similar papal confirmations may have issued with the odd forms 'Henseta', 'Tedrigia', 'Asser' and 'Wolewe', and that the drafter of the charter was working from these papal documents.

Lastly, from William (William II Rachine, c. 1231–31 December 1241),[15] abbot and the convent of Croix St. Leuffroy, bishop Peter had bought the manor of Esher, Surrey, with an appurtenant rent of 100 shillings in Dorset. He probably bought it in 1235. Croix St. Leuffroy had been granted this estate, reckoned conventionally as a carucate and 72 shillings rent, by William the Conqueror in free alms; but in the Surrey eyre which opened on 6 October 1235 the Elmbridge hundred jurors were able to report that the abbey had sold it to the bishop of Winchester.[16] There is no Esher account in the episcopal manorial accounts for the year ending Michaelmas 1232. Those for the next two years are wanting. Esher figures for the first time in the accounts for the year ending Michaelmas 1236; until Christmas 1235 it was administered by the Farnham manor serjeant, obviously only a makeshift arrangement, and thenceforward, until 1238, by a serjeant of its own.[17]

The appurtenant rent in Dorset presents a little difficulty. The source of this rent is not named here or in the charter of 1245, whereby abbot Robert released Esher back to bishop Peter's successor, while reserving this rent. We do not know when or how Croix St. Leuffroy obtained the rent and made it appurtenant to the distant Surrey manor. But in 1219–20 the abbot of Cerne, Dorset, was claiming Esher manor against Croix St. Leuffroy, alleging that his predecessor, William de Luscel, had held it at some time in Henry II's reign.[18] There was, therefore, a link between the two abbeys in the twelfth century; so it was probably then that the Norman abbey obtained this Dorset rent. About its whereabouts there can be no doubt. The only rents outside towns to be mentioned in the great confirmation charter of 7 March 1251 were at 'Charlton'; the 1291 *Taxatio* shows the abbey with a possession valued at £5 at Charlton in Whitchurch deanery, Dorset archdeaconry, that is at Charlton Marshall, in

[14] *Les Registres de Grégoire IX (1227–1241)*, ed. L. Auvray, Bibliothèque des Ecoles françaises d'Athènes et de Rome, 2ème série, Paris, 1890–1955, no. 3109; also *Entries in the Papal Registers relating to Great Britain and Ireland* (hereafter *C.Pap.Reg.*), i. 152–3.

[15] *Gallia Christiana*, xii. 637–8.

[16] Justices Itinerant, Eyre Rolls etc. (JUST. 1) 864, m. 16d (in *The Book of Fees*, ii. 1363).

[17] Hampshire Record Office, Winchester Pipe Rolls 159284, m. 16; 159285, m. 11d.

[18] *Curia Regis Rolls*, viii. 20; and cf. 105, 192, 204.

Spettisbury, near Blandford.[19] The abbey was one of five religious houses drawing income from this manor. Cerne was not one of them; but it held the manor of Radipole, near Melcombe Regis, and there, in 1291, Netley held a small rent of ½ mark.[20] This heightens the belief in a twelfth-century link between Cerne and Croix St. Leuffroy, through which the latter acquired the Dorset rent.

The two estates bought since bishop Peter's death are described simply as lands sold by Robert, son of Luke de Mercinton, and by Henry Juete. Both were alienated in 1241, when the former was specified as 5½ virgates and 4 acres of land in Mildenhall, in Wiltshire near Marlborough, and the latter as 4 virgates at Farley, that is Farley Chamberlayne, near Romsey, Hampshire.

These six estates were all held in fee. It is likely that in 1240 the abbey also held several short-term leaseholds, since these provided a convenient investment for cash not needed immediately, but likely to be required some years ahead. We know certainly only about one such estate, namely two carucates at East Knoyle, near Mere in Wiltshire and not far from Kingston Deverel. This the abbot had secured in 1238–39 on a nine-years lease from the abbess of Wilton for, on 27 January 1244, when defending a claim in the Common Bench for dower, he pleaded this lease, of which three years were yet unexpired.[21] It is also possible that by March 1240 the abbey had taken longer leases, or perpetual leases at fee-farm rents, of some of the estates which it was to acquire in fee in the 1240s; but the earliest known transaction of this sort comes from June 1240, a little later than this first confirmation charter.

Thus of the six estates shown in the first check, three lay in Wiltshire, two in Hampshire and one in Surrey, with appurtenant rents in Dorset. With the possible exception of Wellow, in a well-wooded district on the northern outskirts of the New Forest, none of these provided a site suitable for a Cistercian monastery. They were primarily income-yielding estates, designed to support, not to provide the home for, a religious community. Since July 1239 the abbey had lived a communal existence; it is doubtful if it had yet acquired a permanent home.

The northern shore of Southampton Water then, and until much later, was densely wooded. Indeed, until well into the nineteenth century, the villages along it were more readily reached from Southampton by water than by land. Azo de Gisors, abbot of Beaulieu, and Robert, the Beaulieu monk who was Netley's first abbot, must have known the district well. Six years later, when the foundation of a new Cistercian house in Devonshire was under discussion, Azo visited three sites there before making his

[19] *Taxatio Ecclesiastica Angliae et Walliae auctoritate P. Nicholai, circa A.D. 1291*, London, Record Commission, 1802, 1846; cf. J. Hutchins, *The History and Antiquities of the county of Dorset*, 3rd ed., Westminister 1861–70, iii. 516, 524.

[20] *Taxatio*, 183b.

[21] King's Bench, Curia Regis Rolls (hereafter KB 26) 124, m. 22d; 130, m. 10; 132, m. 10.

final choice of Newenham.[22] It is likely that he, with the assistance of some of bishop Peter's former household who knew the county well, made a similar inspection in Hampshire and perhaps Surrey's wilder parts. The chosen site provided admirably for Cistercian solitude, while its access to the sea made the conveyance of building stone and materials easy. Negotiations to obtain the site must have been in train in March 1240 since, as remarked, the obvious purpose of the confirmation charter of 15 March 1240 was to perfect title preparatory to an exchange. It is even possible that a perpetual lease of the site had been obtained; but it is certain that, as yet, the site was not held in fee. The conveyancing was concluded by a final concord made in the week beginning 14 January 1241, in the Hampshire eyre held at Winchester by Henry of Bath and his colleagues.[23] Grounded on a writ of warranty of charter and framed in the then still novel form of an admission of right as of precedent gift, Geoffrey le Chamberleng granted Robert abbot of Edwardstowe and his convent the manor of Letley, to hold of him and his heirs in free alms, in exchange for the estates at Mildenhall, Henset, Farley and Totteridge (here called 'La Rugge'), which he was to hold of Edwardstowe for an annual payment of 2 lbs. of wax on the feast of the Assumption. Royal confirmation of the exchange was secured by the charter of 4 June 1241, for which the seal fees payable to Ralph de Nevill were 18s. 4d.[24] Henry III made his confirmation 'to God and the Blessed Mary and the house of Edwardstowe, *wherever that house may be founded*, and to the abbot and convent of the same place and their successors'. The phrase here italicised seems to confirm what has already been suggested about the convent's lack, as yet, of a permanent home; it has other implications which will be considered later.

The next check-point for the abbey's estates is the confirmation charter of 18 October 1242, made to the abbot and convent of Edwardstowe. This seems to cover all those estates which the abbey had obtained in fee between March 1240 and October 1242. The conveyancing to secure some of them may have begun before March 1240, just as we shall see that the conveyancing about others must have begun before October 1242 but, being then uncompleted, they are not covered by this charter. The five estates confirmed now were those, including Letley, in which the abbey had concluded its conveyancing in these two years and a half. On the same day another charter issued, similarly made, granting the simpler privileges: quittance for themselves and their men, lands and possessions, whether gifts or purchases, from suit of shire and hundred courts and payment of sheriff's aid and, where within the forest, quittance from the view of foresters, regarders, verderers and other officials. This charter was sent for information and publication to the chief justice of the forests and

[22] J. Davidson, *The History of Newenham Abbey*, London, 1843, 6, citing Bodleian Library MS. Top. Devon d. 5, fol. 19b.

[23] Common Pleas, Feet of Fines (hereafter cited as CP 25), (1)/203/7, no. 57.

[24] *Close Rolls* (hereafter *Cl.R.*) *1242–47*, 235.

to the sheriffs of the counties of Dorset, Wilts., Hants., Surrey, Berks. and Oxford. The address to Berks. and Oxford was in respect of the abbey's farm of North Leigh, but as this was not obtained in fee until 1247, it will be discussed later. In addition to Letley, the four estates were all manors or subordinate manors, some with distant appurtenances. Two were in Hampshire, and each rounded off possessions already acquired; the other two, in Dorset and Surrey, continued the pattern of bishop Peter's acquisitions.

Wellow, that is East Wellow, manor, with the patronage of the church and appurtenant estates in Totton and Testwood, in Eling parish on the banks of the Test at the head of Southampton Water, had been obtained from William de Hampton. The charter does not survive, but three other transactions soon after are documented. By a final concord, made in the Common Bench in the week beginning 1 July 1243, for which each party paid one mark,[25] Robert abbot of Letley bought out the dower interests in this estate of Denise relict of William's father, Stephen de Hampton, for a payment of 10 marks and a life rent of 15s. payable yearly on Easter Tuesday at Mottisfont. On 27 October 1243 the abbot of Edwardstowe for 8 marks secured a charter from Lawrence de Goldecot, husband of William de Hampton's daughter Mabel, which, with Mabel's assent, barred all her rights in the estate that William had granted the abbey.[26] This charter adds that Mabel had issued her own confirmation of her father's charter, and had handed over this charter and her own to the abbey. So the two principal subordinate interests in Wellow were barred. It was only then that the estate was further assured by a final concord, made in the Common Bench in the week beginning 21 May 1245, whereby William de Hampton, for £100, granted Robert abbot of Edwardstowe the manor and advowson of Wellow, to hold of him without any reserved quit-rent, discharging liability to the king for military service, that is paying scutages or aids.[27] When William de Hampton died, not long before November 1249, his widow Alice brought actions against the abbot for dower in both the estates at Wellow. The abbot successfully vouched to warrant him the abbot of Leicester (in respect of bishop Peter's acquisition), who had to supply Alice with lands worth 11s. 8d. in Leicestershire, and William's son and heir Stephen de Hampton (in respect of the manor); as Stephen now had insufficient lands left in Hampshire, he had to supply Alice with 9s. 0½d. worth of his lands in Oxfordshire.[28] On these valuations of dower thirds, the estate purchased from Leicester abbey was worth 35s. yearly and the rest of the manor purchased from William de Hampton was worth 27s. 1½d. The combined total, 62s. 1½d., is close enough to the valuation of Wellow grange at £3 in the 1291 *Taxatio*.

[25] CP 25(1)/203/7, no. 68; KB 26/130, mm. 13, 13d.
[26] E 210/132, in *C.A.D.*, iii. 419.
[27] CP 25(1)/203/7, no. 83.
[28] KB 26/135, mm. 32, 42d.

The abbey deeds include some characteristic thirteenth-century purchases of subtenancies to be added to the Wellow demesne, including one from Alexander de Cridiho, a man of sufficient standing to serve as a New Forest regarder in 1257, whose purchase price consisted of the paying off of his Jewry debts.[29] The appurtenant estates at Totton and Testwood were further assured by a grant from Agnes Peverel, relict of Richard de Wokesie, for which the abbot of Edwardstowe paid her 70 marks.[30] At the conventional twenty-years purchase, then normal, this suggests a value of 46s. 8d. for these estates, described as all she held in these two places, which were to be held at the symbolic quit-rent of 1 lb. of cummin yearly at Michaelmas. Among earlier deeds that came to the abbey with this conveyance there was a grant by William de Hampton, son and heir of Stephen de Hampton, to Richard de Terstewud, whereby, for 40s., he converted a rent of 2s., for a mill at Totton and a meadow at Gretenhaisse, to 1 lb. of cummin or 2d., at Michaelmas.[31] This seems to explain a stage in the acquirement of these estates and their sub-infeudation by the de Hampton family, and the need for the abbey to obtain further assurances to round off its grant from William de Hampton.

From Robert de St. John the abbot obtained his tenement in Hound, the mother parish of Netley, along with appurtenant salt rents. No charter or final concord appears to survive in connexion with this purchase, which made the abbey lords of the nearest considerable settlement to their house.

In Dorset the abbot obtained the manor of Waddon, in Portesham, or Broad Waddon as it was then called, on the hills between Dorchester and Bridport. It was bought from Margaret (Margaret I de Guerres, 1237–55),[32] abbess, and the convent of Montivilliers: another purchase of English lands from a French house. It is the first possession in which we can see the monks exercising their privileges under the second charter of 18 October 1242, for in the Dorset eyre of 1244 the Uggescombe hundred jurors presented that hitherto Broad Waddon had always done suit to this hundred, but that this suit had been withheld since the monks of Letley had obtained it.[33] When, in January 1247, the convent of the newest Cistercian house left Beaulieu to journey to their temporary buildings at Newenham, their nightly resting places were Christchurch priory, Bindon abbey, Waddon (4 January) and Ford abbey.[34] Because of the abbey's ownership, the manor lost its former name and became instead Waddon Fratrum or Friars' Waddon.

[29] E 210/7487, 5695 (cf. Exchequer, Treasury of the Receipt, Forest Proceedings (E 32) 156, m.6).

[30] E 210/7188.

[31] E 210/5351.

[32] *Gallia Christiana*, xi. 283.

[33] JUST. 1/201, mm. 3d, 4.

[34] Davidson, *Newenham Abbey*, 8, citing Bodleian Library MS. Top. Devon d. 5, fol. 24b.

Gomshall's acquisition is well documented, by three deeds, all made to or by the abbot and convent of Edwardstowe. The grantor, Matthias or Macy Bezilles, was among those Poitevins and Frenchmen who came to England when bishop Peter des Roches returned there in 1231. His abilities, alike as a courtier, diplomat and soldier, enabled him to serve Henry III, and also queen Eleanor, with devotion until his death about 1270. His manor at Gomshall, held as a quarter fee, had been the first substantial mark of royal favour conferred on him, by grant of 3 January 1233.[35] The first deed is a covenant, whose first four witnesses are Azo abbot of Beaulieu and three former members of bishop Peter's household: his ex-steward Mr. Humphrey de Mylliers, Hugh des Roches, archdeacon of Winchester, and Emery de Chanceaux.[36] By this, Macy agreed to grant the manor at a rent of £10 yearly payable at Midsummer. By the second deed, also a covenant, with the same first four witnesses, the abbot and convent agreed to pay Macy £200 and also to acquit him against the late bishop's executors of 20 marks, which he had owed bishop Peter; in return, they were to hold the manor quit of the £10 rent.[37] Both parties bound themselves to seek royal confirmation of this alienation of a tenancy in chief. By the third deed, without witnesses, Macy made an outright and unconditional grant of all he held in Gomshall by grant of Henry III.[38] The deed is dated on the eve of Ash Wednesday in a regnal year of which, even under ultraviolet light, only *vicesimo* is legible. The three deeds form a sophisticatedly interlocking piece of conveyancing: grant in fee farm, remission of the fee-farm rent, grant in fee. It is possible that there was little interval between them. The grant in fee had clearly not been made at the time of the royal confirmation charter of 15 March 1240, and since Mr. Humphrey de Mylliers died shortly before 20 April 1241,[39] it seems likely that the defaced year was 25 Henry III and so the date of the grant was 12 February 1241.

Among the abbey deeds are several that seem to come from the third quarter of the thirteenth century, concerning lands in both Gomshall[40] and in Ewhurst, to the south, into which the abbey's interests ramified:[41] the estates there naturally being made appurtenant to Gomshall Netley, as the main manor became called. Two of these concern Robert de Loseners;[42] there also survives a grant to him by Netley's second abbot, Richard (succeeded 1260), of all the land of Losenersh, to be held at a

[35] *C.Ch.R. 1226–57*, 174.

[36] E 210/327 (lower half formerly E 210/120), in *C.A.D.*, iii. 444, 417.

[37] E 210/200 (lower half formerly E 210/83), in *C.A.D.*, iii. 428, 413.

[38] E 210/131, in *C.A.D.*, iii. 419.

[39] *C.P.R. 1232–47*, 250.

[40] E 210/5406; Exchequer, Auditors of Land Revenue, Ancient Deeds, Series E (LR 14), 851.

[41] E 210/1504, 11253.

[42] E 210/5331, 7208.

rent of 17s. 6d. from Gomshall manor.[43] Gomshall was one of the most valuable of the abbey's possessions, being reckoned at £10 in the 1291 *Taxatio*, which corresponds exactly with the fee-farm rent first arranged by Macy Bezilles and, at twenty-years purchase, with the cash paid for it.

Macy was only an occasional witness to royal charters in these years, but he occurs as last of the nine witnesses to the royal confirmation of Letley manor on 4 June 1241. The two charters of 18 October 1242 passed at Bordeaux, while he was on detached duty. This was during Henry III's French expedition of May 1242–September 1243; and when he was there, the government of his regents in England undertook a great survey of fees in connexion with scutages being levied to support the expedition. Pursuant to writs issued in October and December 1242, the returns were largely made during the early months of 1243. In this, the abbey appears for the first time with a territorial appellation, in all three instances Netley. The abbey fees recorded in the extant returns were: Hound, held as one fee from Robert de St. John, through Richard de Hound; [East] Wellow, held as ½ fee; and Totton with Testwood, held as ⅙ fee; all of William de Hampton.[44]

The third and last check on the abbey's estates during its early years is provided by the royal confirmation charter of 7 March 1251. Unlike the charter of 1242 which, as we have seen, covered only estates acquired since the first confirmation of 1240, this lists all the places in which the abbey had lands and rents in fee. So, in addition to Letley, Hound, Wellow, Gomshall, Kingston Deverel, Waddon and the rent in Charlton, all of which we have discussed, it lists lands at Ashley, North Leigh, 'Latton' (not identified in any published version) and rents in Southampton and Southwark, as well as, more particularly, 100 acres at Shere with the advowson of that church. The new acquisitions may be taken in the order in which they seem to have been acquired in fee.

Esher, it will be noticed, was no longer in the abbey's possession. It was a very convenient staging post between the bishop's palace in Southwark or the royal court at Westminster and Farnham castle. Bishop Peter's successor, William de Ralegh, shortly after obtaining possession of his diocese, persuaded the abbot to sell it back for 100 marks and (a Cistercian touch) 200 sheep. The deed of surrender by R[obert], abbot of Letley, dated 1 April 1245, excepted the hundred shillingsworth of land in Dorset.[45] The witnesses were headed by A[zo], abbot of Beaulieu, and included Peter Russinol, a former member of bishop Peter's household. The consideration was, however, still unpaid at Ralegh's death in September 1250, and on 4 February 1251 a royal mandate issued to his executors, to pay the consideration to the abbot.[46] The order was

[43] Guildford Muniment Room, MS. 334/26.

[44] *Book of Fees*, ii. 694, 697, 698.

[45] *Chartulary of Winchester Cathedral*, ed. A. W. Goodman, Winchester, 1927, no. 453(1), p. 195.

[46] *Cl.R. 1247–51*, 410.

authorised by Peter de Rivaux, bishop Peter's kinsman and associate in government in 1232–34, now back in the royal administration after a long period of disgrace.

Shere, described variously as a *cultura*, a carucate, 120 or 100 acres of land, to which appertained the advowson of Shere church, was obtained by a grant dated 22 August 1243 from Roger de Clere to the abbot and convent of Edwardstowe, witnessed by Surrey knights and freeholders only.[47] The consideration was 300 marks. The carucate lay immediately west of the abbey's Gomshall demesne, north of the Guildford–Dorking highway, and was a compact tract of land, not a bundle of field strips. But much must lie behind the formal deed. Roger de Clere (c. 1205, succeeded to estates c. 1234, d. 1247), an honorial baron of the earls of Warenne, had inherited heavy Jewry debts, which caused him to sell or mortgage most of his lands.[48] Already he had granted the royal administrator, John de Gatesden, a rent of 100s. in his Surrey lands. In October 1244, after conveyancing in the court *coram rege*, he sold the rest of Shere, along with appurtenances and estates elsewhere, to another distinguished royal administrator, John fitz Geoffrey, for 285 marks and a life pension, secured on the lives of himself and his wife Maud.[49] But the plea roll shows that the whole of this purchase price was paid by John to the London Jewry, to liquidate Roger's debts there.[50] Even so, John fitz Geoffrey found that he had to buy out John de Gatesden's competing interests in March 1246.[51] This suggests that the sale to Netley may also have been in order to liquidate Jewry debts. Moreover, there was a tenurial connexion between the de Cleres and Beaulieu abbey, which held Soberton, Hampshire, from them.[52]

On Roger's death, his widow Maud de Fay began litigation for dower in October 1247; because of her late husband's sale of his estates, most of her numerous actions took many months to settle. The only one settled immediately, by surrender of dower about 13 October 1247, was that against the abbot of Edwardstowe for her dower third in 120 acres and the advowson of Shere.[53] This dower interest was soon extinguished, for Maud died shortly before 20 December 1249. Maud's own family had had a devotion to the Cistercians, for her brother John (d. 1241) had been accorded the privilege of a mass after his death from all priests of the Order.[54] The interest in what was left of the Clere estates and Maud's own Fay inheritance passed to a baby granddaughter whose father, a leading

[47] *Monasticon*, v. 696.

[48] Summarised from a biography to appear in *Surrey Eyre, 1235*, ed. C. A. F. Meekings, a volume shortly to be published by the Surrey Record Society.

[49] CP 25(1)/283/11, no. 199.

[50] KB 26/131, m. 17.

[51] CP 25(1)/283/18, no. 62.

[52] *V. C. H. Hampshire*, iii. 258.

[53] JUST. 1/81, m. 12d.

[54] *Calendar of Inquisitions Post Mortem*, i, no. 198; *Stat. Cap. Cist.*, ii, 1233 – 19.

Norfolk knight, attempted to recover what he could from his own wrecked marriage settlement of 1243. It was probably because of the threat of litigation in the years immediately after 1249 that the abbot, for 20 marks, secured a confirmation of Roger de Clere's charter from John earl of Surrey and Warenne, on 6 January 1252(–53).[55]

About the same time that Shere was acquired, the abbey obtained 'Latton', that is Laughton en le Morthen, in the West Riding of Yorkshire. It must have been obtained, at first on lease, by April 1244 at latest; but more probably in or before 1243, because on 10 and 28 May 1244 mandates issued to Henry of Bath, respectively as sheriff of Yorkshire and as keeper of the honor of Tickhill, to restore the abbot of Edwardstowe to seisin of all the lands and issues which he held of the abbot of Foucardmont.[56]

Foucardmont, founded as a Benedictine daughter house of Savigny in 1130 by the counts of Eu, for long lords of Tickhill, had become a Cistercian house in 1147.[57] Its many benefactions from the counts of Eu included the tithes from all their English demesnes. In or about 1238, Alice countess of Eu (d. 1247), in exchange for the abbey's surrender of its right to these tithes, granted it villein tenants at Carr and Hutton and freeholders in Laughton. This was the estate which Netley had acquired by 1244. An undated inquisition, to determine how the abbot of Foucardmont had held his lands in Carr, Laughton and Hutton, before he demised them in fee to the abbot of Edwardstowe, which from its hand and jurors seems to date from the 1240s, returned that Foucardmont had held the lands by grant of the countess of Eu in exchange for the tithes from her English manors.[58] The then rateable value was £19, made up of 28s. 4d. of the fixed rents of freeholders and £17 11s. 4d. of villeins' rents. Netley appears to have established its grange at Hutton, later Slade Hutton, not at Laughton; for it is under this head that its Yorkshire interests figure in the 1291 *Taxatio*, valued at £17. This far-distant estate was alienated in 1319, being sold for 380 marks to Roche abbey; in the deed, the abbot of Edwardstowe adds that he is also handing over the charter of countess Alice or Adelicia, which established the estate for Foucardmont.[59] The completion of this conveyance may have taken some time, for there also survive letters of attorney for livery of seisin to Henry Darcy and his brother Hugh de Totehill (apparently attorneys for Roche

[55] *Monasticon*, v. 696, no. ii; calendared in *C.Ch.R. 1327–41*, 169 and in the later confirmations of 1400, 1414 and 1461.

[56] *Cl.R. 1242–47*, 183, 190.

[57] *Répertoire Numérique des Archives Départmentales, Seine-Inférieure, Série H*, i, Rouen, 1921, 101; *Monasticon*, vi, part 2, 1086; E. C. Waters, 'The Counts of Eu, sometime Lords of the Honour of Tickhill', *Yorkshire Archaeological Journal*, ix (1886), 292–3.

[58] Chancery, Miscellaneous Inquisitions (C 145) 18, no. 4, calendared without jurors in *Calendar of Inquisitions Miscellaneous*, i. no. 414.

[59] 'Roche Abbey Charters', transcripts by S. O. Addy, ed. T. W. Hall, *Hunter Archaeological Society Transactions*, iv. part 3, 1935, 239 (charter viii).

abbey), which were made in chapter at Letley on 4 October 1329, under the abbey's common seal, with the seal of the then abbot William on the reverse.[60] At the time of Netley's acquisition, the abbot of Foucardmont was Robert II d'Envermeu (c. 1238–c. 1252).[61]

Ashley, in Litton Cheney, Dorset, a few miles west of Broad Waddon, was obtained in 1246 from the terre tenant of Litton, William de Liddington. It was assured by a final concord, made in the Common Bench in the week beginning 25 June 1246, and cast in a stereotyped form, whereby William admitted the right of Robert, abbot of Edwardstowe, to hold a carucate at Ashley as of his gift, in return for a share in the abbey's prayers.[62] This form effectively conceals any monetary consideration and no clues have yet been found to the circumstances of this conveyance.

North Leigh, near Witney in Oxfordshire, carried with it two interests in Berkshire: at Chaddleworth, north of the Lamburn valley, and a pension from the church of Hinton Waldrist, on the Thames south of Witney. By letters patent dated 30 June 1240, Robert abbot of Edwardstowe announced that, with the consent and assent of A[zo] abbot of Beaulieu, he had taken a perpetual lease from the abbot and convent of Locus Dei, in the diocese of Amiens, of their whole manor of North Leigh, with 10½ marks rent from the tenement of Robert de Chadelworthe and a *beneficium* of 5 marks from Hinton church: all to be held at a rent of 30 marks payable yearly at Longvillers at the feast of the Nativity of the Blessed Mary (8 September).[63] There was the usual clause for resumption if the rent were unpaid. The letters, engrossed in a noble charter format, were endorsed '*A De Lega in Anglia*', presumably during their short stay in Lieu Dieu's treasury, since they must have been surrendered when Netley bought the estate in fee. This was by a charter dated August 1247, whereby John (dates of prelacy uncertain) abbot and the convent of Lieu Dieu granted the estate to the abbot and convent of Edwardstowe for 600 marks, a sum representing the usual twenty-years purchase.[64] The estate is described in much the terms of the lease, except that rents in Oxford are added and the rent for Chaddleworth is not specified.

Lieu Dieu, in Ponthieu, had received all these interests from their local lords, the St. Valery family, in their English fees. In 1237 Simon de Pateshull, a midland tenant of the St. Valerys, had granted Ashford mill in North Leigh to the Benedictine priory of Snelleshall, near Whaddon in Buckinghamshire.[65] By an undated charter John prior (occurs 1231–47)

[60] British Library, Harleian Charter 44 F. 22.

[61] *Gallia Christiana*, x. 304.

[62] *Full Abstracts of the Feet of Fines relating to the county of Dorset . . . from their commencement in the reign of Richard I*, ed. E. A. and G. S. Fry, Dorset Records, v, 1896, no. 197, mistakenly attributed by the editors to Shaftesbury abbey.

[63] British Library, Additional Charter 20234.

[64] E 210/153, in *C.A.D.*, iii. 422.

[65] *The Cartulary of Snelshall Priory*, ed. J. G. Jenkins, Buckinghamshire Record Society, ix, 1952, nos. 207–8.

of Snelleshall, for 40 marks, granted his right in this mill to the abbot and convent of Edwardstowe, to be held at a rent of 4d. payable to Thomas de St. Valery and his heirs.[66] The abbey had thus rounded off its interests in North Leigh. It is interesting to note that Lieu Dieu was a daughter house of Foucardmont, a connexion which may help to explain why Foucardmont was influenced to convey Laughton en le Morthen to Netley, rather than to one of the numerous Yorkshire Cistercian houses. The fact that Netley leased North Leigh for some seven years before obtaining it in fee parallels the evidence of the Gomshall conveyance, and suggests that there may have been the same sequence at Laughton, if not for other of the acquisitions after 1242.

Nothing is known about the rents in Southwark, which were probably acquired from tenants of the Winchester episcopal manor or soke there. Something is known about the Southampton rents, most, if not all, of which were acquired from Agnes Peverel, relict of Richard de Wokesie, whom we have already met as the tenant at Totton and Testwood, nearby the borough. By a deed, probably made in the 1270s, the abbot and convent of Edwardstowe of Letley granted to Nicholas bishop (1268–80) of Winchester 58s. annual rent in Southampton which Agnes had given them.[67] This is itemised as: 30s. rent in East Street ward, formerly of Philip de Hampton; 20s. rent also there, which Agnes had acquired from Denise de Hampton, relict of William de Heriz (and perhaps identical with the widow of Stephen de Hampton, whose dower interests in Wellow had been extinguished in 1243); 8s. rent from a house in St. Lawrence's parish. The abbot and convent, with the mature style as 'of Edwardstowe of Letley, Ord. Cist., Winchester diocese', also executed a release of these rents, probably in the Southampton borough court, since the witnesses are confined to burgesses; in this they are not particularised but described as 'all we have in lands and rents in the town of Southampton, namely all we have in free alms of the gift of Agnes Peverel, relict of Richard de Wocksey'.[68] This alienation can have left the abbey with little in Southampton, for in the 1291 *Taxatio* the taxable value of its rents in both Winchester and Southampton was only 19s.

The only interest outside the holdings already discussed, of which the deeds give evidence, is the acquisition, for 10 marks, of a messuage in Wilton, Wiltshire, to hold at 3d. rent, this messuage being in the Wilton abbey fee.[69] The charter is mutilated and undated; the grantor's name is lost and what remains of the witnesses suggests the third quarter of the thirteenth century, rather than the 1240s or early 1250s.

The great confirmation charter of 7 March 1251 was followed on 20 March by a grant of free warren in nine demesnes. Six were in places

[66] E 210/93, in *C.A.D.*, iii. 414.

[67] British Library, Additional Charter 15697.

[68] Exchequer. Augmentation Office, Ancient Deeds, Series B (E 326) 3283.

[69] E 210/2072.

already discussed: Letley, Hound, Waddon, Ashley, Gomshall and Shere. The other three were all in Hampshire: Satchell, Sholing and Westbrook. Sholing and Satchell were both in Hound: Sholing north of the abbey, on the Bitterne side; Satchell, from which a subsidiary deed survives,[70] in the extreme south of the parish. Westbrook remains to be identified.

So far we have been concerned with temporalities. The spiritualities were limited to the parish church of Hound, with the chapelry of Netley, and to the two advowsons acquired with manors: Wellow and Shere. Papal licence issued for the appropriation of these two churches on 5 January 1245.[71] The Wellow appropriation was probably completed in 1251, since, by an instrument of arbitration made at Southampton on the eve of Palm Sunday (8 April) 1251, the taxation of the vicarage was promulgated by the official of the bishop-elect and by Hugh des Roches, archdeacon of Winchester.[72] The Shere appropriation was much more difficult and was not effected under Henry III. Hilary is well attested as rector there between the 1190s and late 1230s.[73] He may well have been there still in 1243, so that it was on his death that the abbot presented a clerk whose name has yet to be discovered. On 22 April 1253 the abbot received a papal faculty to appropriate on the death of this rector.[74] But when this happened, John fitz John (son of John fitz Geoffrey), the future baronial leader, challenged the right of abbot Robert by an action of darrein presentment. There must have been some weakness in the abbot's title, for, instead of letting the issue go to a jury, the abbot made a compromise in November 1258.[75] He released the rights of his house for £10, payable by 9 February 1259; in return, John presented the abbot's clerk, Walter de Chikehull or Chikewell, to the church. When Walter died, early in 1277, the then abbot attempted to present; but John's brother Richard, who had now succeeded to the lordship of the greater part of Shere, successfully pleaded the settlement of 1258–59.[76] The value of the advowsons was presumably reckoned in with the other appurtenances when Netley acquired Hound, Shere and Wellow; so the much higher values of the impropriated churches in the 1291 *Taxatio* may be ignored in arriving at a rough figure for the value of the possessions obtained by the abbey down to 1251, and for the cost of these purchases.

From what is known about some annual values in the 1240s and the

[70] E 210/3065.

[71] *Les Registres d'Innocent IV, 1243–1254*, ed. E. Berger, Bibliothèque des Ecoles françaises d'Athènes et de Rome, 2ème série, Paris, 1884–1919, i. 906; also *C.Pap.Reg.*, i. 211.

[72] E 210/230, in *C.A.D.*, iii. 432.

[73] *The Chartulary of the Priory of St. Pancras of Lewes*, ed. L. F. Salzman, ii, Sussex Record Society, xl, 1934, 51; *Chertsey Cartularies*, i, Surrey Record Society, xii, 1933, no. 87; Hyde Cartulary, British Library, Egerton MS. 2104A, fol. 106; British Library, Additional Charter 5562.

[74] *C.Pap.Reg.*, i. 358.

[75] JUST. 1/873, m. 10d.

[76] Common Pleas, De Banco Rolls (CP 40) 19, m. 61.

costs of some of the purchases, together with the valuations in the *Taxatio*, it is possible to make a rough estimate of both these figures. The value of all the estates bought, as conventionally assessed for taxation or conveyancing, comes to about £85 yearly, which has to be reduced to £69 for those held in 1251: that is, allowing for the sale of Esher and for the fact that Netley itself was acquired by an exchange. At twenty-years purchase which, from an examination of many hundreds of deeds, enrolled conveyances and final concords, seems to have been the contemporary norm, this would have cost just under £1,400 to buy in normal circumstances: somewhat under £400 for the six estates confirmed in 1240; rather over £1,000 for all those bought in fee in the 1240s. This disregards any discount which may have been available because the seller urgently needed cash to liquidate debts or was anxious to part with a distant property whose administration was difficult.

We do not know how much money bishop Peter bequeathed. The Waverley annalist says merely that 'before his death he assigned no small quantity of money, which might reasonably suffice for the foundation of the two houses and other necessaries. After his death, namely in this year [1239] they were founded by procurement of his executors'.[77] Matthew Paris, hitherto (like his predecessor, Roger Wendover) far from charitable in his notices of bishop Peter's career, was much impressed by his 'noble testament'. Mentioning the bequests which bishop Peter had made to his own foundations of Halesowen, Titchfield, Selbourne and God's House at Portsmouth, and to St. Thomas of Acre and the Pilgrims' Hospice at Joppa, both of which he had refounded in the Holy Land, Paris says that the least of the bequests was 500 marks to St. Thomas of Acre.[78] All we can legitimately infer is that the bequests for each of the two unestablished houses are likely to have been very much larger than the least (£333 13s. 4d.) to an existing foundation. Of course, the money would have only become available gradually, as the executors realised it from different sources: coin, plate, jewels and ornaments; crops and stock from private estates or from episcopal manors; debts, some of which, like Macy Bezille's, might have taken years to gather in. On the whole, there is no reason to doubt that bishop Peter's provision could have covered the purchases of the 1240s, with the stocking of the demesnes, and gone some way towards the cost of building and equipping the monastery and its church. It would not have been intended to cover the whole cost of the abbey, since for that benefactions could be expected from his friends and associates.

Two further points may be made. The first is the consistency of the endowment policy. The failure of Henry III's French expedition of 1230 made it plain—as events in 1242–43 underlined—that the English Channel would never again be an Anglo-Norman lake. French mon-

[77] *Annales Monastici*, ii. 322–3.
[78] *Chronica Majora*, iii. 489–90.

asteries and cathedrals must have found their more isolated English possessions increasingly uncertain assets. Scattered over the country, estates were potentially on the market, probably at prices below those which an unembarrassed English owner could have demanded. Bishop Peter, with his French connexions and the administrative shrewdness to which the accounts of his episcopal manors are eloquent witnesses, picked up some of them. But the pattern of his acquisitions from Angers, Croix St. Leuffroy and Le Mans was continued after his death by the purchases from Foucardmont, Lieu Dieu and Montivilliers. These, with those of bishop Peter's acquisitions which were exchanged for Netley, made up four-fifths of the temporalities as assessed in 1291 and, as already noticed, these assessments were identical with, or very close to, such assessed values as are known from the 1240s. Such a continuity in the pattern of purchases suggests a continuity in the persons of the purchasers.

One of those taking a large part in the purchasing must have been the abbot of the mother house. Azo de Gisors was responsible for completing the main buildings at Beaulieu; from it he sent the convents for Newenham and Hailes as well as Netley. He seems to have served at least once as a royal envoy to France and was certainly a friend and agent for the king's brother, earl Richard.[79] Bishop Peter, who had seen Beaulieu's growth in his diocese from its foundation, may well have sought advice from the house and its abbot when he began to contemplate founding Cistercian houses. But Azo's influence must have been mainly, if not entirely, exercised after bishop Peter's death. The continuity is stronger with former members of bishop Peter's household. Luke des Roches, sometime archdeacon of Surrey and one of the executors, continued an active interest in both Edwardstowe and La Clarté Dieu up to his death, about 1250. In his will he desired to be buried at Edwardstowe and he made its abbot his residuary legatee; though there is a doubt whether he died in England or at La Clarté Dieu, whither he had papal leave to retire.[80] Hugh des Roches, archdeacon of Winchester (c. 1237–1253), and Peter de Rivaux (d. before 10 January 1263) occur several times in connexion with Netley in these early years. They may have been among the executors not included in the select four named in the royal confirmation of 4 November 1236. Both were men of affairs, Peter especially of financial affairs, who may be expected to have been active in the interests of the patron with whom they had long been associated. They and several others of the former episcopal household, like Peter Russinol, remained active into the 1250s. Apart from the obligations of Luke and any of the others who were executors in that capacity, they were in a position to advise and assist in the acquirement of temporalities for the new foundation before and after bishop Peter's death, before the

[79] *C.P.R. 1232–47*, 94, 99, 248; *Chronica Majora*, iv. 138.

[80] Details taken from a study of Luke and his will which it is hoped to publish elsewhere.

house was founded and during its early years. The continuity in the pattern of purchases suggests that they did so.

The more scattered estates of French ecclesiastical institutions were not the only bargains on the land market. Embarrassed English knights and leading freeholders who had already mortgaged estates to the hilt with the Jewry or other lenders provided another source. We know that Macy Bezille was in the bishop's debt, that Roger de Clere and Alexander de Cridiho were in debt in the Jewry. We know, as yet, nothing of the circumstances of Henry son of Luke, Henry Juete, Geoffrey le Chamberleng, William de Hampton, Robert de St. John and William de Litton, though the terms of the last's final concord are those which often cloak a consideration that is a foreclosed mortgage or the liquidation of a debt. This is not to question that a religious devotion could still inspire grantors in the 1240s, even when they were granting for the consideration of full market value and not making free gifts. But such devotion is most likely to have inspired the smaller grants, of a few pennies-worth of rent in Southampton, Southwark or Winchester, or of the same or an acre or two in a freeholding within or adjacent to a demesne manor. The larger estates had to be acquired by the founders as economically as possible. Provided clear title could be obtained, the best bargains would naturally be those whose owners most urgently needed to sell. When we know more about the former English lay owners we may well find in this smaller proportion of the abbey's temporalities a similar continuity of pattern in the acquisitions, which will point in the same direction as the pattern of acquisitions from French ecclesiastical institutions.

The second point can be made much more briefly. It is that Henry III, though taking a very active interest in the foundation and benefiting it in many ways since 1239, had down to 1251 not given the house a single acre of land or a pennyworth of rent. This defect he seems to have decided to remedy in 1252. It is with a brief account of his gift that we end the narrative story of the abbey's estates.

The decision was to grant an uncultivated area of three carucates in the New Forest, at one hundred acres to the carucate, subject to an inquisition *ad quod damnum* to decide the best place. When the inquisition had been returned, orders issued on 22 March 1253 to the treasurer and to the chief justice of the forests to assign the three carucates at Dilton near Brockenhurst, a few miles west of Beaulieu; this order gave only general indications.[81] A fully detailed perambulation was included in the charter which Henry III issued on 4 July 1253, while he was waiting at Portsmouth to embark on his French expedition.[82] This shows that the land lay north of the village of Boldre, on either side of what was then called the Boldre water and is now the Lymington river, running up from the valley to the surrounding hills. The charter granted the usual rights to till, hedge and ditch the land, provided that the king's deer retained

[81] *Cl.R. 1251–53*, 332–3.
[82] *C.Ch.R. 1327–41*, 229.

access. Within two years the development of the land had proceeded sufficiently for this limitation to be irksome, so on 14 February 1255 permission was given for the land to be hedged and ditched sufficiently to prevent entry by the beasts of the forest.[83] This enclosure licence was confirmed by the last of the ten royal charters, on 8 April 1256.[84] This nameless tract of heath and scrub was developed as a grange and given the name Roydon—*le don le Roy*—which still preserves the memory of this royal gift.[85]

It may be useful to conclude this section on the estates by tabulating the values in the 1291 *Taxatio*, since these have not hitherto all been identified with Netley. In this the abbey occurs with the various forms of Letley (Letelegh, Lethelay, Letteley, Litteley, Lytteley), except in Lincoln diocese where it is Netley (Natele). There are no entries under Chaddleworth and Hinton Waldrist (192, 187); since these were appurtenant to North Leigh they must be included in its value. No rents are shown in Southwark (207).

Page references to the edition, and the approximate dates of acquisition, as already recounted, are given within brackets:

Temporalities

Winchester diocese (all at 214)	
Letley grange (in 1240–1)	3. 2. 0
Wellow (part by 1238, part by 1242)	3. 0. 0
Roydon (in 1253)	1. 0. 0
Gomshall (about 1241)	10. 0. 0
Southampton and Winchester rents	19. 0
Salisbury diocese	
Waddon and Ashley[86] (183—by 1242 and in 1246)	8. 13. 4
Radipole (183b)	6. 8
Charlton (184b—about 1235)	5. 0. 0
Kingston Deverel (186—about 1236)	10. 0. 0
Lincoln diocese	
North Leigh[87] (44b—leased 1240, in fee 1247)	10. 4. 8
Rents in Oxford deanery (43b)	3. 4
York diocese	
Slade Hutton[88] (305, 325—by 1244)	17. 0. 0
Total	68. 9. 0

[83] *Cl.R. 1254–56*, 39.

[84] *C.P.R. 1461–67*, 158.

[85] *V. C. H. Hampshire*, iv. 628 says astonishingly that there is 'no evidence of date of grant' because the writer ignored the evidence of the place name and the correspondence of the bounds in the 1253 charter with features in Roydon's surviving court rolls and ministers' accounts, as well as those still available on the ground.

[86] 'Wodetone et Wydetone'; the latter an obvious error for 'Lydeton', the normal thirteenth-century spelling of Litton [Cheney], in which parish Ashley lay.

[87] 'Forthley'!

[88] Identical with Laughton en le Morthen.

Spiritualities

Winchester diocese	
Hound rectory and Netley chapel (210)	6. 13. 4
Shere church (210b)	23. 6. 8
Wellow church (210b)	10. 0. 0
Total	40. 0. 0

Having completed the study of the abbey's temporalities, we may now consider the development of the house itself and of Henry III's interest in it. Throughout these years the house was probably under the rule of its first abbot, Robert. The majority of references to the abbot are, as usual, impersonal; but Robert is named in the final concords, already discussed, of 14 January 1241, 1 July 1243, 21 May 1245, 25 June 1246 and 20 June 1249;[89] he occurs in the deeds of 30 June 1240, 1 April 1245 and 8 April 1251;[90] he occurs in the litigation about the Shere advowson in the autumn of 1258.[91] He probably held office from July 1239 until December 1259; for on 11 January 1260 the escheator south of Trent was ordered to deliver the abbey of Edwardstowe Letley, taken into the king's hand on the death of abbot Robert, to brother Richard, who had been elected according to the Cistercian customs and statutes.[92]

Three members of the house are mentioned as representing their abbot in these documents: brother Abel in the final concord of 1241; brother Philip in the litigation against Mabel de Derneford in 1242; brother Richard of London (who could be the abbot elected in 1260) in the final concord of 1246.

In tracing the early development of the house we must often wish for the existence of a register, such as survives for the contemporary foundation of Newenham, to give us lists of the original monks and lay brothers, to tell us who gave stone and timber for the buildings or made other benefactions toward equipping the monastery and church; and to recount the stages of progress, from the dedication of the site to the saying of the first mass.[93] However, the Newenham register can be used as a standard against which to refer the less full and precise details recoverable about Netley. Newenham also was a southern English house,

[89] CP 25(1)/203/7, nos. 57, 68, 83; 47/11, no. 157; 251/16, no. 66. The two last have been calendared in *A Calendar of the Feet of Fines relating to the county of Wiltshire . . . from 1195 to . . . 1272*, ed. E. A. Fry, Devizes, 1930, 41 and *Dorset Fines*, 80, with Robert each time wrongly made abbot (of the Benedictine nunnery) of Shaftesbury.

[90] British Library, Additional Charter 20234; *Chartulary of Winchester Cathedral*, 195 and also in *C.P.R. 1313–17*, 676; E 210/230.

[91] JUST. 1/873, m. 10d; CP 40/19, m. 61.

[92] *Cl.R. 1259–61*, 24.

[93] Bodleian Library, MS. Top. Devon d. 5. Davidson, *Newenham Abbey* 4–36, draws on this largely for events 1245–57.

colonised from Beaulieu. The abbot of Edwardstowe was one of the two examining commissioners whom the Cistercian chapter general appointed in 1245, upon the proposal of Reynold de Moyun to found a new house.[94] The evidence we have of Netley's early benefactions—as distinct from the acquisition of estates—is unbalanced: almost all of it is also evidence of Henry III's interest, since it comes almost all from the records of his government.

In considering these benefactions it must be remembered that there is a distinction between Henry III as a benefactor and Henry III claiming to be a founder or refounder and then *the* founder, as he was to do. It must also be remembered that, entirely because of his own policy over the Winchester succession after 1238, the temporalities of this see were under his control from 11 June 1238 to 11 September 1244.[95] As an indication of the additional means which this placed at his disposal, the gross revenue of these temporalities, excluding the Somerset estates, from 11 June 1238 to 29 September 1241 was £13,247 4s. 11½d. About a quarter of this had to be spent on the manorial economies, the salaries and wages of permanent officials and on some customary alms and payments. Over a quarter was diverted into building operations at Winchester and elsewhere and to various royal gifts, fees and expense allowances, that would normally have fallen on a local branch of the ordinary revenue or have been paid in cash out of the exchequer or wardrobe. These included charitable donations, some of which might have continued bishop Peter's intentions, like 10 marks for the fabric of the Franciscan church at Winchester or £5 for the buildings of the Dominicans there. But after all these disbursements there was still a very large cash balance of which, as characteristic in these years, £4,448 0s. 5½d. went to the wardrobe and £1,003 6s. 8d. to the exchequer. For the Somerset manors, during the slightly longer period 11 June 1238–25 December 1241, the outgoings were naturally much less against a gross revenue of £2,111 15s. 6½d., enabling £1,488 3s. 2d. to reach the wardrobe and £430 6s. 8d. the exchequer. During the latter half of the vacancy, the total cash surplus was lower, because much of the revenue in 1242–43 was diverted to support the Gascon expedition which started from Portsmouth and was largely supplied through there. Even so, the long vacancy as a whole saw over ten thousand pounds reach wardrobe and exchequer as unfettered additional cash revenue.

Henry III's benefactions began as soon as the convent had commenced its corporate life in July 1239. His first took the practical form of grants

[94] *Stat. Cap. Cist.*, ii. 1245–33.

[95] The main accounts are in Exchequer, Pipe Office, Pipe Rolls [E 372] 85, m. 3 (14 June 1238–15 April 1240), m. 2 (15 April 1240–29 September 1241); 87, m. 3d (29 September 1241–29 September 1243); 88, m. 12 (29 September 1243–11 September 1244). The Somerset accounts are in E 372/85, m. 3 (11 June 1238–25 December 1241) and 86, m. 7 (25 December 1241–25 December 1242).

of altar wine and chalices. The order for the grant of a tun of wine issued on 13 August 1239.[96] The wine was to be supplied by the keeper of the king's wines at Southampton, from the prisage wines of the customs there; it was to be paid for by the Southampton borough bailiffs, as an allowable deduction from their farm. On 28 February 1240 this grant was made perpetual, by the first of the royal charters; the tun was to be supplied yearly at Mid-Lent.[97] This charter served as a standing order. Each year exchequer warrants grounded on it ordered the keepers of the Southampton wine customs to supply the tun and the borough bailiffs to pay for it. The warrants were minuted in the Liberate Rolls; the payments figure on the discharge side of the Southampton bailiffs' account, which is entered in, or just after, the Hampshire sheriff's account in the Pipe Rolls.[98] In normal times the warrants issued at varying dates between mid-December and mid-March. In 1240 the fees for charters were still payable to Ralph de Nevill; Edwardstowe was charged 12 marks for this charter but the sum was still unpaid in January 1244.[99] One would like to know whether Nevill, as a friend and executor of bishop Peter, eventually waived this debt in his will and whether he made any benefactions or bequests to Netley.

The order for chalices issued on 11 September 1239, directing the keepers of the Winchester temporalities to buy six silver chalices at 50s. each, for delivery to the abbot of Edwardstowe.[100] By 7 January 1240 the chalices had been provided and cost an additional 40s. 8d. to complete.[101] From this it seems that the original community included only six priest-monks. There may have been other monks, not yet ordained; Newenham's original convent comprised the abbot, twelve monks and four lay brothers.

On 27 February 1240 the keepers of the temporalities of Winchester were ordered to have two bells made, of 40 and 20 pounds weight, delivering them when finished to the abbot of Beaulieu, to keep for the abbot of Edwardstowe until that house was built.[102] These bells and their gear cost £31 6s. 8d.; they had been delivered by 4 November 1240.[103] Presumably the convent's temporary buildings, wherever they were, did not yet include an erection of sufficient strength in which the bells could be hung.

96 *Calendar of Liberate Rolls* (hereafter *C.Lib.R.*) *1226–40*, 407.

97 *C.Ch.R. 1226–57*, 250–1.

98 *C.Lib.R. 1226–40*, 455; *1240–45*, 27, 108, 164, 205, 284; *1245–51*, 16, 109, 175, 274, 337; *1251–60*, 26, 98, 160, 196, 277, 359, 429, 450, 493; *1260–67*, 17, 83, 118, 134, 141, 197, 251; *1267–72*, nos. 52, 522, 987, 1349, 1581, 1780. E 372/83, m. 1d; 84, m. 6d; 85, m. 7d; 86, m. 13d; 87, m. 9d; 88, m. 10d; 89, m. 12d; 90, m. 12d; etc.

99 *Cl.R. 1242–47*, 235.

100 *C.Lib.R. 1226–40*, 415; cf. E 372/85, m. 3.

101 *C.Lib.R. 1226–40*, 438.

102 Ibid., 457.

103 *C.Lib.R. 1240–45*, 2.

Meanwhile Henry III made what, at first glance, appears to be his largest benefaction. On 5 February 1240 the exchequer was ordered to deliver 800 marks (£533 6s. 8d.) to the abbot of Beaulieu, for the use of Edwardstowe abbey.[104] As a yardstick of the value of the cash involved, we may recall that when Reynold de Moyun founded Newenham in 1245 he bound himself to provide a hundred marks yearly for building expenses during his life.[105] The Issue Rolls are far too patchily preserved at this period for it to be possible to check the fulfilment of orders for the exchequer cash; the assumption is, that unless an order was reissued because of non-payment or partial payment, the original order was fulfilled, with reasonable promptness. The plain interpretation of the grant is that Henry III was making a gift from his own cash resources of a sum, additional to what the house had received from bishop Peter and his executors and other benefactors, that would have sufficed for some eight-years building expenses or the purchase of estates of an annual value of about £26 13s. 4d. Such an interpretation may be true, but there are some facts which raise doubts about it. In his five charters to the house between February 1240 and October 1242, Henry III grants or confirms simply as sovereign, without the least hint of a personal interest in the foundation, even when he is dealing with the abbey's site itself. That site was obtained in fee shortly after this grant: not for cash, but by surrendering three estates of the original foundation in exchange, as already described. None of the other royal gifts of 1239–44 was made out of exchequer, or wardrobe cash; that is, out of the net uncommitted revenue. They were made out of the resources casually available through the Winchester vacancy, by a charge on the farm of Southampton or by the assignment of a crown debt. Henry III made them at the minimum cost to himself. It is, therefore, possible that these 800 marks from the exchequer came ultimately not from the uncommitted royal revenue but from bishop Peter. They can have represented cash owed by the crown to the executors and payable, under the bishop's testament, to the benefit of Edwardstowe. The loss of both Patent and Close Rolls for October 1238–October 1239 has deprived us of the full knowledge of the arrangements made to acquit the crown against the executors, both in respect of the Winchester temporalities and the bishop's lay estates, after the initial grants of administration in June–September 1238.[106] Such a sum would certainly be commensurate as an adjustment on estates with a gross yield of over six thousands pounds. Another possibility is that bishop Peter had bequeathed such a sum, or more, to his former pupil, with a recommendation for its bestowal on pious objects. Without further evidence, this grant of February 1240 can hardly be taken unambiguously to be a gift by Henry III from his own resources.

[104] *C.Lib.R. 1226–40*, 446.
[105] Davidson, *Newenham Abbey*, 4–5, citing Cartulary, fol. 19b.
[106] *Cl.R. 1237–41*, 62, 79, 105.

Buildings, both temporary and permanent, must have been started at Netley by 1241. Despite the nearness of the New Forest, there were no recorded grants of royal timber until 1250. It looks as if any temporary wooden buildings, and much of the timber for the domestic range of the convent, were supplied by the arrangement of the executors, by the abbot of Beaulieu or by local benefactors, as was done a few years later at Newenham. Archeologists have yet to determine precisely the sources used for the stone of the convent and church. Beaulieu, by licence of bishop Peter, renewed *sede vacante* on 20 June 1241, took stone from Binstead quarries in the Isle of Wight.[107] This stone could have been shipped as easily to Netley as to Beaulieu.

By the summer of 1242 the abbey had become known by its toponymic. The first extant use of this seems to come from 3 November 1242, when Mabel, relict of William de Derneford, appeared in the Common Bench to prosecute her action of dower in Wiltshire lands against the abbot of Letley and others.[108] The writ on which this action was grounded would probably have been sued out in the preceding August or September. The form Letley (Letele, Latteleg) was used throughout the stages of this action which, so far as the abbot was concerned, ended with his surrendering dower in the two carucates at East Knoyle, already discussed, and in recompense having his lease of them prolonged. As already noticed, the form Netley was used througout the survey of fees in the winter of 1242–43; but in the next two years—in the conveyancing about Wellow and Shere in 1243, in the Dorset eyre of 1244 and in the Esher surrender of 1245—it is Letley again.

When Henry III left England in May 1242, the heavy expenses of assembling the expedition at Portsmouth were, understandably, largely met from the most convenient local source of revenue, the Winchester temporalities. For some time afterwards, cash was in short supply. The abbot of Edwardstowe must now have taken over control of his treasury from Beaulieu, since on 28 August 1242 at Winchester he advanced £100 towards the expenses of a rear party of knights.[109] The loan was repaid, from the Winchester revenue, sometime before the end of the financial year 1242–43.[110]

In April 1243 Henry III made his first unambiguous cash gift to the abbey, of 50 marks towards the fabric of the church.[111] Yet even this was ultimately at bishop Peter's expense, since it formed part of a crown debt of £100 (the remaining 100 marks of which were earmarked for the London House of Converted Jews) that had curious origins. In the spring of 1234 the baronial opponents of the regime of bishop Peter and Peter de Rivaux organised clever guerilla attacks against the property of the

[107] *Cl.R. 1242–47*, 107.

[108] KB 26/124, m. 22d; cf. 130, m. 10 and 133, m. 10.

[109] *C.Lib.R. 1240–45*, 145.

[110] E 372/87, m. 3d.

[111] *Cl.R. 1242–47*, 22.

regime's leaders. Bishop Peter began proceedings in trespass in the court *coram rege* against some of those who had attacked his Somerset estates. But by the time due for the defendants to appear, bishop Peter had been disgraced and was almost besieged in his palace at Winchester; Stephen de Segrave, the justiciar, who would have presided over the court and who survived the bishop's fall by a month, had himself just lost office. Bishop Peter not surprisingly failed to appear to prosecute and so was non-suited and put in mercy. Baronial amercements were normally remitted to the exchequer for taxing, where, at ordinary times, such a technicality would have led to the imposition of a sum between 40s. and 100s. Instead, it was taxed in a council now dominated by the triumphant opposition at the swingeing sum of £100.[112] Bishop Peter never paid it, either by cash or distraint. In fact, at his death it was his only significant crown debt. Eventually all of it seems to have gone to Netley, for by 19 April 1244 the executors had produced the £100 in cash; the abbot of Beaulieu and, somewhat ironically, Peter de Rivaux, were to deliver it to Netley.[113] The executors were thereby acquitted finally of all accounts for crown debts.[114]

On 29 October 1243, shortly after his return from France, Henry III directed the keepers of the Winchester temporalities to supply a hundred quarters of corn from Bishop's Waltham manor (not far to the north) to Edwardstowe.[115] This may mark a stage in the completion of the domestic range of the outbuildings. On 20 January 1244, following the decisive break with France, general orders issued for the seizure of all lands belonging to those of French allegiance. Numerous individual relaxations followed, including an order of 18 March 1244 to the sheriff of Hampshire to reseise the abbot of Edwardstowe of all his lands.[116] The mandates of May 1244 about the abbey's Yorkshire possessions, already mentioned in discussing the acquisition of Laughton en le Morthen, stemmed from the same cause and so probably did the issue of a general protection for the abbey on 6 March 1244.[117]

It is in March 1244 also that we first find Henry III claiming to be a founder of the abbey. On 5 March he issued an urgent order to the keepers of the Winchester temporalities to supply £100, from the first money coming in, to the abbot of Edwardstowe 'for the foundation of his church, whereof the king wishes to lay the first stone as founder'.[118] This payment is recorded in the discharge of the last keepers' account for the

[112] *Curia Regis Rolls*, xv. no. 1023; and cf. ibid., p. xxv.

[113] *C.P.R. 1232–47*, 423.

[114] E 372/87, m. 6d (Somerset and Dorset account for 1242–3); Exchequer, Lord Treasurer's Remembrancer, Memoranda Rolls [E 368] 15, m. 9 (note made 21/25 April 1244 in the Treasurer's Remembrancer's Memoranda).

[115] *Cl.R. 1242–47*, 131.

[116] Ibid., 170.

[117] Ibid., 183, 190; *C.P.R. 1232–47*, 421.

[118] *C.Lib.R. 1240–45*, 221.

part-year ending 11 September 1244.[119] Henry III's foundation stone is at the base of the north-east pier of the (four piers of the) crossing; it is set in the south-east face of this diamond-shaped pier, so that it faces towards the presbytery and altar, and is inscribed: *H. DI. GRA. REX ANGL'.*[120] Between *GRA.* and *REX* is a heart-shaped shield, surmounted by a cross *patée*.

If Henry III did lay this cross in person, the exact date is a matter for conjecture. Preoccupation with Welsh and Scottish affairs caused Henry III's visits to Hampshire to be much less frequent than usual betweeen March 1244 and June 1246. He was at Winchester only about 30 January–6 February 1245 and about 17–28 February 1246, before staying there from 8 to 15 June 1246 on the way to Beaulieu, where he stayed from 16 to 18 June for the dedication of his father's foundation on 17 June 1246.[121] Among the orders issuing from chancery while at Beaulieu was one on 18 June for two tuns of wine for Edwardstowe, one tun for mass and the other in repayment of a tun which the king had had while he was there.[122] These two tuns were additional to the routine annual tun under the charter of 1240. Clearly, therefore, the king had visited Netley some time not too long before 18 June 1246. His itinerary, established from all the chancery enrolments, published and unpublished, indicates only the overnight or major stopping places; there are no household accounts to indicate minor staging places or visits. Netley does not figure in the itinerary, neither does the nearby episcopal manor of Bitterne.

The dedication of Beaulieu was a great royal and ecclesiastical occasion which impressed all the chroniclers.[123] It was also a great Cistercian occasion. There, on the eve, 16 June, Richard of Cornwall secured a charter barring all future claims by Normans in the manor he had assigned for his new foundation at Hailes; the charter's witness list gives us the names of a number of prelates and magnates who were there for the occasion.[124] It was then, also, that Richard selected the convent for his new abbey.[125] Reynold de Moyun's charter for Newenham was certainly made in 1246; its witness list, including Richard of Cornwall and stewards of the royal household, makes it possible that it was also made during the Beaulieu celebrations.[126] Certainly these would already have drawn to court or to this neighbourhood all those who were also concerned with Netley. Henry III could have been there and back in a day, by horse and boat, on any of the three occasions he was at Winchester

[119] E 372/88, m. 12.

[120] Hamilton Thompson, *Netley Abbey*, 7. The opposite faces of this base are shown in the foreground of the plate, ibid., opposite p. 11.

[121] *Itinerary of Henry III*, compiled by E. W. Safford, with revisions by the present writer (Public Record Office Typescript).

[122] *C.Lib.R. 1245–51*, 60.

[123] *Chronica Majora*, iv. 562; v. 86; *Annales Monastici*, ii. 337.

[124] *C.Ch.R. 1226–57*, 294.

[125] *Chronica Majora*, iv. 562; v. 86, 124.

[126] Davidson, *Newenham Abbey*, 225–7; *Monasticon*, v. 691.

between March 1244 and June 1246. February, however, seems hardly the best month for laying foundation stones. It may, therefore, be that the visit before 16 June 1246 had been made only very shortly before: either in a day's outing from Winchester or by a slight diversion on the way from Winchester to Beaulieu, with an entourage sufficient for the occasion and a collation after the ceremony with food supplied by the royal household but with wine from the abbey's cellar. So, if the foundation stones were not laid by proxy in 1244, they may have been laid in June 1246. This would mean that the abbey's eastern range of domestic buildings, with the central cloister, and the refectory, kitchen and warming house to the south, would have been nearing completion in 1244 and completed by 1246, when work on the lower stages of the presbytery and the crossing of the church itself would be beginning.

That Henry III was considering himself a founder of the abbey is next apparent in Innocent IV's licence for the appropriation of Shere and Wellow churches, on 5 January 1245.[127] This was said to be granted in consideration of the fact that the convent had been founded anew by the king of England. But in the summer of 1244 Henry III's control of the Winchester temporalities came to an end and with this, except for the tun of wine in 1246, his recorded benefactions cease for nearly seven years, so far as chancery and exchequer records enable these to be traced. Of course, there may have been minor gifts from household resources, but none are traceable in the extant wardrobe accounts.

These were the years when, as we have seen, the endowments were being completed through the conveyances over Wellow, Ashley and North Leigh and the sale of Esher. In January 1246, on the eve of a great forest eyre visitation, the abbot of Netley secured letters confirming assarts of 12½ acres and ½ perch which previous owners had made at Wellow and of one perch which he had himself made at North Leigh.[128] On 12 February 1248 the more formal confirmation of a patent was secured for these.[129] Also in January 1246, arrangements were made for a perambulation to delimit the bounds between the abbey's lands at Hound and Netley and those of the Winchester episcopal manor of Bitterne, to the north-west.[130] At the same time as negotiations were conducted in the papal court at Lyons for the appropriation licence, a confirmation, dated 31 January 1245, was secured of the abbey's exemption from attendance at synods, with the annulment of sentences promulgated against them on this account: a privilege said already to have been infringed during the house's short existence.[131] The only other ecclesiastical activity outside his house by abbot Robert which may be inferred in 1245–46 is his duties as an inspecting commissioner for Newenham.

[127] *Reg. d'Innocent IV*, i. no. 906; *C.Pap.Reg.*, i. 211.

[128] *Cl.R. 1242–47*, 387.

[129] *C.P.R. 1247–58*, 8.

[130] *Cl.R. 1242–47*, 473.

[131] *C. Pap.Reg.*, i. 212; *Reg. d'Innocent IV*, i. no. 994.

The main landmarks in Newenham's early years were: the entry of the convent into their temporary buildings on 6 January 1247; the laying of the first foundation stone of the church on 6 July 1250; the laying of ceremonial foundation stones by the founder and others (in a similar position to those in the crossing at Netley) on 13 September 1254; the saying of the first mass on 25 March 1257, in the sacristy, that is at the extreme northern end of the domestic range, abutting on the south transept of the church and the corner where the northern and eastern walks of the cloister met. Newenham was a baronial foundation, with support from the founder's kin, knights and free tenants and from associates, lay and ecclesiastical, but with no significant royal support. Similar progress at Netley, assuming that work began in 1241, would be consistent with the laying of ceremonial foundation stones in 1246 and with the saying of the first mass in 1251, in the relatively confined space of the sacristy, where there was certainly provision for an altar, with adjacent piscina and aumbry that still survive. This would mark the fruition of communal life in the permanent buildings. The earliest part of the church to be completed was the south transept; it is possible that the chapels in its east wall were provided so that masses could be said there, instead of in the sacristy, in the years before the presbytery and choir were completed.

The saying of the first mass in the permanent buildings was regarded as a great event at Newenham. If at Netley this happened in 1251, it is not surprising that this year should be marked by the issue of three royal charters, including that of 7 March which came to be regarded as the main charter of the foundation, and should also see the renewal of royal benefactions. The benefactions were renewed when the king was taking advantage of another vacancy at Winchester by spending Christmas 1250 at Wolvesey palace. He had just visited Beaulieu and (17–18 December) Bitterne, whence he could easily have ridden to inspect progress at Netley, a few miles south-east. On 24 December the constable of Wolvesey was ordered to supply four marks to the abbot, to buy himself a censer with.[132] On 27 April 1251 the bailiff of High Peak was ordered to buy thirty cartloads of lead from the Derbyshire mines for the fabric of the abbey church.[133] Subsidiary orders issued to the sheriff of Derbyshire to convey this as far as Coventry, where the sheriff of Warwickshire would take over as far as Oxford, and thence the sheriff of Oxfordshire would conduct the waggon train to Southampton. In fact, however, the lead seems to have come down partly through eastern England, under the sheriff of Lincolnshire; by 14 August 1251 it had reached Southampton, where the bailiffs were ordered to deliver it to the abbot of Edwardstowe by the same weights as those by which they had received it.[134] Meanwhile, on 3 June 1250, the king had granted £100 towards the fabric of the

[132] *C.Lib.R. 1245–51*, 324.
[133] Ibid., 347.
[134] *Cl.R. 1247–51*, 490.

church.[135] But once more this grant was more apparent than real, since it represented simply a pardon of the fine of £100 agreed for the charters of 7 and 20 March 1250. This kind of giving was something of a scandal in monastic circles; Matthew Paris several times remarks on it, notably over Henry III's gift of 200 marks to the dedication expenses of Beaulieu, which consisted in fact of pardoning a swingeing amercement of this amount for a forest trespass which had been taxed not long before by justices who knew all about the impending dedication feast.[136]

More positive gifts followed on 15 September 1251, with orders for fifteen oaks apiece from Bere forest and the New Forest for the fabric of the church.[137] On 14 February 1252 came an order, authorised by Peter de Rivaux, for 50 marks from the farm of Southampton, to be paid by the bailiffs to the work of Edwardstowe church.[138] On 21 June 1252 there was a further order to the keeper of the New Forest, for five oaks for building at Edwardstowe.[139] These benefactions of lead and timber in 1251–52 certainly suggest roofing on a considerable scale. Henry III had another opportunity of inspecting progress before he again kept Christmas at Winchester in 1252, since he stayed at Bitterne on 18–19 December. On 12 January 1253 the exchequer was ordered to supply ten marks to the abbot of Edwardstowe for a silver-gilt processional cross.[140] Apart from Roydon, the last royal benefaction during abbot Robert's prelacy—indeed the last almost to the end of the reign—was an order on 20 April 1254 to the chief justice of the forests to supply twenty oaks for the fabric of Edwardstowe church.[141]

Taken together, these benefactions seem to suggest that by the beginning of 1253 the east end of the church—presbytery, north and south transepts—the choir—under the central crossing—and the first bay of the nave, which buttressed the tower over the central crossing and is of much earlier date than the rest of the nave (except, of course, the lower stage of the south wall which the nave shared with the north cloister walk) were substantially completed, roofed and leaded: so that it would be possible to hold the customary Cistercian Saturday procession. It was in 1253 that the abbot secured the chapter general's permission to hold a special feast of twelve lessons on 13 October, the feast of the translation of St. Edward the Confessor, at the same time as two Welsh abbeys received similar permission to celebrate the feast of St. Winifred.[142] At Henry III's petition the chapter general had, indeed, in 1253 permitted the special celebration of 13 October in all the English houses; but,

[135] Ibid., 452.
[136] *Chronica Majora*, v. 86.
[137] *Cl.R. 1247–51*, 500.
[138] *C.Lib.R. 1251–60*, 268.
[139] *Cl.R. 1251–53*, 110.
[140] *C.Lib.R. 1251–60*, 98.
[141] *Cl.R. 1253–54*, 235.
[142] *Stat.Cap.Cist.*, ii. 1253–24.

perhaps, this permission applied only to houses then existing. Like the gift of the processional cross, this licence suggests that during 1253 the monks' part of the church was sufficiently complete for the normal choir services and processions to take place in it.

In contrast to the stream of Henry III's benefactions is the testament made by Luke des Roches, sometime archdeacon of Surrey and rector of Epsom, seemingly about 1250.[143] It is the only closely personal record which we have from one of bishop Peter's circle. By this testament, Luke desired to be buried at Letley and appointed the abbot as one of his executors. Although, in the same year, Luke had papal permission to lease all his English preferment, in order to retire to La Clarté Dieu, it seems that he must have died in England: it is otherwise impossible to account for the presence of this testament, and an allied bond, in the same collection as the Netley deeds. Luke left the abbot his palfrey, and also a silver-gilt cup with a base and two silver cups without bases, in exchange for a bible which he had promised to the abbey but had, in fact, left at La Clarté Dieu. He confirmed a gift of books which he had already made to the abbey and he left all the debts owing to him towards the fabric fund of the abbey church. Aside from a few personal bequests, the other religious foundations remembered in his testament were all either foundations of the late bishop Peter or of his diocese.

The confirmation of lands, rents and churches in the charter of 7 March 1251 has already been discussed. The same charter's grant of privileges began with a recital of those usual in twelfth-century grants, concluding with those more modern and characteristic of the thirteenth century: the immunity of the corn of the monks and their men from the munitioning of castles; disafforestation of all their lands and acquittance from liability for the expeditation of their dogs; quittances of tolls in all fairs and markets, and over all roads and bridges, where these were levied throughout the realm, with free transit for their ships at sea; the right to the chattels of their men if forfeited either by flight on suspicion or by conviction of felony; the right to the amercements of their men incurred in any royal court; the right not to be impleaded except *coram rege*. The charter of 20 March 1251 was really appendant to this, granting free warren in their demesnes, as already discussed, a Monday market at Hound and a fair at Wellow on the eve and feast of St. Margaret. Mandates ordering the publication of the main charter were, on 23 April, directed to the authorities at Winchester and York.[144] On 3 June the exchequer was formally notified of the pardon of the fine for the pair of charters, and was ordered to enrol an abstract of the main charter.[145] On 4 June an order, authorised by Peter de Rivaux, who had witnessed both

[143] E 210/11204.
[144] *Cl.R. 1247–51*, 433.
[145] Ibid., 452.

charters, ordered publication in the exchequer and by the chief justice of the forests.[146] The abbot's exercise of these privileges can be traced in the rolls of common pleas and forest eyres, of the central courts and of assize commissioners, during the 1250s and 1260s.

The forest privileges made the most immediate impression in the chancery records. On 5 November 1250 and 21 February 1251, orders had issued to the keeper of Selwood forest (in respect of Kingston Deverel and its tenants) and to the chief justice of the forests, to respite process arising from the forest eyres and courts of the late 1240s, against the abbot and his men for the lawing of their dogs.[147] This, no doubt, was because the great charter was already in preparation. Even after the publication of the charter, a further order was thought necessary, on 4 August 1251, to stay all process on these matters.[148] When a new chief justice took office—Reynold de Moyun, the founder of Newenham—letters close of 20 December 1253 reminded him of the clauses in the abbey's great charter about both disafforestation and the lawing of dogs.[149] Henry III had been at Bitterne, just north of Netley, on 18 and 19 December, so these letters may have been the result of personal representation by the abbot. Privileges of this sort took time to become known among the foresters and verderers, who administered forest law at the covert side, and who themselves became liable to penalties if they allowed privileges to the unauthorised.

We have seen that Henry III pardoned the abbot's £100 fine for the two charters of March 1251. He could hardly have done otherwise, because in the great charter of 7 March, for the first time in his charters to the house, he was proclaiming himself to be its founder. In the five charters of 1240–42 he had granted or confirmed as king, as for any religious house with which he had no personal or even family connexion. He had done so, even though the charter of 4 June 1241, confirming the acquisition of Letley itself, provided an obvious opportunity for advancing any personal claim. But the unusual phrase of the confirmation is: *ubicumque domus illa fundata fuerit*, and not *ubicumque nos domum illam fundiverimus*. In 1251 the opportunity was taken, with the formula: 'We, for the salvation of our soul and the souls of our ancestors and successors, have granted, and by this our charter have confirmed, to God and the church of the Blessed Mary of Edwardstowe, which we have founded in Suthamptesir' and to the abbot and monks there serving and to serve God, the place in which their abbey is sited . . .'. With its complete confirmation of all lands, rents and churches, and the grant of extensive privileges, this was indeed a foundation charter: prized as such, as its enrolment in the exchequer Cartae Antiquae rolls and its frequent inspections and confirmations amply testify.

146 Ibid., 543; E 368/24, m. 10d.
147 *Cl.R. 1247–51*, 373, 416.
148 Ibid., 484–5.
149 *Cl.R. 1251–53*, 296.

Since the charters of 20 March and 11 December 1251 were virtually appendages to that of 7 March, it is not surprising that in them the language becomes once more the stereotyped language of any royal grant. But Henry III's own New Forest (Roydon) grants of 1253 and 1256 provided admirable opportunities to perpetuate the claim. The grant of 4 July 1253 is made 'inspired by God and the Blessed Edward King, our predecessor, and for the salvation of our soul and the souls of our ancestors and heirs': a classic founder's formula. The final form of his claim which Henry III committed to posterity in the charter of 8 April 1256 is the most elaborate, but it is also apologetic: 'the abbey of Edwardstowe, which Peter bishop of Winchester, of happy memory, proposed to found, but which would have been destroyed (*exilis esset*) had we not taken over its foundation and promotion; and, assuming that foundation in honour of God and the glorious Virgin Mary His Mother and of the Blessed Edward King, our predecessor . . .'. So, at the last, for this was to be his last charter to the house, Henry III found room to mention bishop Peter as co-founder, as least in intention. It is, it may fairly be claimed, a belated, grudging mention: made, not in the great charter, where surely it might fittingly have been placed, nor in his own only grant of land but in the mere licence to enclose this land from the forest, a charter only once to be later confirmed.

That bishop Peter had commended his proposed English foundation to the charity of his former royal pupil is self-evident from the Waverley annalist's notice of the foundation in 1239 of *Locus Sancti Eadwardi*. Cistercian listeners would have needed no reminder about Henry III's devotion to his sainted predecessor, whose office, since 1235, had been celebrated with special privileges in all English houses of the order. Yet this Cistercian annalist, writing about 1240, apparently knew nothing of any special part which the king had played in the foundation. In the surviving acts of the Cistercian chapters general, which seem reasonably complete for these years, there is no hint of an intervention by Henry III, although the troubled early history of some houses is reflected in these acts: for example, John de Monmouth's foundation of Grace Dieu, with five mentions between 1221 and 1236. Even Newenham received a second notice; though this, in the year after the appointment of the foundation commission, was merely an instruction to the abbot of Beaulieu to send a convent without awaiting a further licence. La Clarté Dieu received a four-years exemption from hospitality to monks and lay brothers of the order, to protect it, apparently, until 1243. As late as October 1242, despite his benefactions, real or apparent, which we have discussed, Henry III was not even hinting at any claim to be the founder in the charters, patents and writs issuing from his chancery. But by March 1244, at latest, he was considering himself as a founder or refounder.

Yet, as we have already seen, the story of the growth of the abbey's possessions in these years does not suggest any crisis but a continuous and consistent pattern of development from beginnings in bishop Peter's last years. If there was any crisis in the abbey's early history, it is likely to have been about the time of the foundation itself, in 1239, when the protracted Winchester vacancy may have put difficulties in the executors' way in realising bishop Peter's assets. For the length of that vacancy, the responsibility was almost entirely Henry III's. In 1241 the abbey had acquired the site for its permanent home, not by gift from Henry III but by exchanging three estates which it had been given by bishop Peter's executors from his acquisitions for the foundation. In August 1242 the abbot could make a short-term loan of £100 for the royal service.

If we seek a reason for Henry III's apparent change of attitude between 1242 and 1244 there is one which suggests itself. Returning early from Bordeaux after a quarrel with his brother about the conduct of the Gascon expedition, Richard earl of Cornwall narrowly escaped shipwreck in the gales of October 1242 and vowed to found a religious house in thanksgiving for his deliverance.[150] In 1235, earl Richard had been promised a general anniversary by the Cistercian chapter general.[151] In 1239 his first wife had been buried before the high altar at Beaulieu;[152] in March 1241, when he left on his visit to the Holy Land, the abbot of Beaulieu was made one of his three proctors for his ecclesiastical patronage.[153] So it is not surprising that his choice of foundation was Cistercian. His proposal to the Cistercian chapter general was in September 1243 committed to the abbots of Beaulieu and Byland, and he was allowed to choose the convent from whatever house he desired.[154]

The story of earl Richard's acquisition of the Norman escheats in Hailes is well known. His brother's formal acts in this connexion followed in successive years: 17 October 1244, confirmation of the acquisition of the manor; 15 July 1245, permission for a religious house there, accompanied by a grant for it of forty oaks from the Forest of Dean; 16 June 1246, while at Beaulieu for the consecration, a charter barring any latent rights of Normans in the manor.[155] It was also at Beaulieu's consecration that earl Richard chose the convent of thirteen monks for Hailes.[156]

Earl Richard's main decision, to found a Cistercian house in fulfilment of his vow, must have been taken between October 1242 and the summer following, when the application to the chapter general in September 1243 would have been prepared. Henry III was probably not in the closest touch with his brother in these months, since he was then still at

[150] *Chronica Majora*, iv. 229; v. 292.
[151] *Stat.Cap.Cist.*, 1235 – 6.
[152] *Annales Monastici*, i. 113; *Chronica Majora*, iv. 2.
[153] *C.P.R. 1232–47*, 248, 262.
[154] *Stat.Cap.Cist.*, 1243 – 20.
[155] *C.Ch.R. 1226–57*, 280, 288, 294; *Cl.R. 1242–47*, 329.
[156] *Annales Monastici*, ii. 337; *Chronica Majora*, iv. 562.

Bordeaux, immersed in his Gascon expedition. Moreover, he had seen his brother leave with ill humour and his own relations with the Cistercians were rather strained at this time.[157] Possibly it was not until he himself returned to England in October 1243 that he learnt the full details of the way in which his brother intended to fulfil his vow. If he was spurred to emulate his brother, he could not dispose of the same unfettered resources of wealth. But the founding of the House of Convertites, his preoccupation of the 1230s, was virtually complete; the great works at Westminister were only just beginning. The opportunity to emulate his brother in an economical way was readily at hand. By March 1244 he is calling himself Netley's founder, or at least one of the founders. In the great charter of 7 March 1251 he claims sole foundership, only eight months before that great gathering, dwarfing even the Beaulieu assembly of June 1246, which saw the dedication of Hailes abbey. In 1253 he repeats the claim when, for the first and only time, he grants Netley land. Only in the final charter of 1256 is there an apologetic reference to bishop Peter, under whose tutelage he and earl Richard had spent impressionable boyhood years at the start of his reign.

To conclude. The pattern of acquisition of Netley's temporalities suggests strongly that the main source of funds and skill in purchase was bishop Peter and his bequest and the continuing activity of members of his former household, some of whom were also his executors. We have no source, such as we have for Newenham, for gauging the scale of other benefactions except those from Henry III, who made many between 1239 and 1244 and again between 1250 and 1254, but, especially in the earlier period, made them at little or no cost to himself. Until 1242 certainly, perhaps until 1243, there is no sign that Henry III considered himself to be a founder or that anyone else so considered him. In 1242–43 his younger brother, Richard of Cornwall, decided to found a Cistercian house in fulfilment of a vow. From March 1244, at latest, Henry III put himself forward as a founder and by 1251 as *the* founder of Netley. In 1256 he committed the final version of his claim to his contemporaries and to posterity: he rescued and established what otherwise would have been the ruined or destroyed foundation of bishop Peter. No doubt he believed this to be the true version of the story. No doubt it was a version acceptable to the monks, to whom the certainty of the royal house as patron may well have been more attractive than the uncertainty of the bishop's lay kin or diocesan successors. How far other contemporaries accepted the version is uncertain. Many of the leaders in Church and Court of the late 1230s had passed away by the 1250s, but there were still some who had been in high office then and remained in high office, to whom the story of Netley's foundation and early years must have been

[157] *Chronica Majora*, iv. 228–9, 234–5, 257; *Cl.R. 1242–47*, 69.

known: men, that is, like Ralph fitz Nicholas, John fitz Geoffrey, Bertram de Cryoll and Peter de Rivaux, to confine ourselves to witnesses of the abbey's charters. Earl Richard, the friend of abbot Azo of Beaulieu, must also have known the story. The facts suggest that Henry III's version is not a completely true version of the story of Netley abbey's early years.

XVIII

THE EARLY HISTORY OF SANDON HOSPITAL

THE surviving records of major judicial visitations held in Surrey in the thirteenth century have been generally neglected by the county's historians: despite the fact that in the 1650s Edward Fauconberge, then keeper of the record office in which they were preserved, abstracted many cases from them and supplied complete place and rough subject indexes to his abstracts. This neglect seems to be the only reason why such authorities as Dugdale's *Monasticon*, Manning and Bray, and the *Victoria County History*[1] agree in saying, without evidence, that the Augustinian hospital or priory of Sandon, in Esher, was founded at the beginning of Henry II's reign. In the plea roll of the special eyre held by the newly appointed justiciar of England, Hugh le Bigod, at Bermondsey in November 1258 there is a case, duly abstracted by Fauconberge, which gives an outline history of Sandon hospital since its foundation.[2] This special eyre was designed by the recent reforming provisions of Oxford and Westminster to redress grievances for which there was no ready remedy by the ordinary processes of common law.[3] To this end a very informal procedure was introduced. Although many real grievances were redressed, the informality of the procedure and the disturbed state of the country led also to many cases being brought with doubtful justification. We have no hesitation in reckoning our case among the latter sort. It was a complaint brought by Robert de Watevill, grandson of the founder of the hospital, against master Geoffrey de Feringes, official of the bishop-elect of Winchester, and brother Thomas of London, canon of Newark and master of the hospital of St. Mary Magdalene, Sandon, about the mastership of the hospital. Master Geoffrey closed a distinguished ecclesiastical career as dean of St. Paul's, 1263–1267.[4] In 1240 we find him in one of the most famous ecclesias-

[1] *Monasticon*, VI, 675–677; *M. & B.*, II, 749–751; *V.C.H.*, Surrey, II, 118–119.

[2] Eyre, Assize, Trailbaston etc. Rolls: P.R.O. ref. J.I. 1/873, m. 10; *Index* 17103, f. 19d.

[3] *Cf.* E. F. Jacobs, *Studies in the Period 1258–1267* (Oxford Studies in Social and Legal History, VIII), chapter III, The Legislation of 1258–1259 and the Eyre of 1259–1260.

[4] *Newcourt's Repertorium*, ed. Hennessy, note a 134. His other known preferment was: the rectory of Denham, Bucks, in 1246, *Cal. Papal Registers 1198–1304*, 221; the moiety of the rectory of Elham, Kent, in 1246, *Cal. Patent Rolls 1232–47*, 484, *Close Rolls 1242–7*, 476; the mastership of St. Cross

tical households of the age, that of archbishop Edmund Rich, along with the archbishop's chancellor, master Richard de Wych, who later became bishop of Chichester and perhaps conferred on master Geoffrey the precentorship of Chichester which he later held.[1] He had been the official in the bishopric of Winchester since March 1244 or earlier, and continued in this capacity until the summer of 1260 or later.[2] He thus served two very different men: William de Raleigh, who after some 25 years' service as clerk, justice and chief justice in the royal courts became a bishop in the best tradition of the age and endured a bitter quarrel with his former master Henry III; and Aymer de Lusignan, the King's young Poitevin kinsman who had been jobbed into the see without any sort of qualification and who remained unconsecrated. As their principal agent in the administration of the diocese, master Geoffrey himself appears as a man governed by the best principles of the time: in this case being concerned for the proper conduct of the smaller religious houses in the diocese. There can be little doubt that if the bishop-elect had not been among the most obnoxious of the Poitevins, whom the reformers exiled and wished to have deposed, it is unlikely that Robert de Watevill would have brought his complaint.

Master Geoffrey had claimed and exercised a right to interfere in the presentation of the master of the hospital; Robert disputed this. In the course of his case, Robert pleaded the succession of masters since the foundation. The jury substantially confirmed his narrative, and judgement was given for him. What follows is, therefore, largely the facts as stated by Robert or the jury, with a little additional matter from other sources. The story concerns three members of the de Watevill family, grandfather, father and son, and all named Robert. A biography of the second of these will appear in a forthcoming volume of the Surrey Record Society; from it we summarize the main points about their careers. Robert the grandfather, whom we call Robert I, was a knight prominent in county affairs in John's reign who may have been hanged by prince Louis of France during the civil war of 1215–7. His son, whom we call Robert II, was also prominent in county affairs; he married Alina (de Sandford) and died a little before April 1243. His son and heir, whom we call Robert III, was then a minor, in ward to the abbot of Chertsey from whom the family held its manors of Esher and Coulsdon. He had come of age by 1253—probably several years earlier—and was the plaintiff in our case.

The hospital was founded in John's reign by Robert I de Watevill,

---

hospital, Winchester, before 1250, *Close Rolls 1247–51*, 326,380; the precentorship of Chichester cathedral, in 1256, *Cal. Patent Rolls 1247–58*, 515, and 1262, Eyre, Assize, Trailbaston etc. Rolls: P.R.O. ref. J.I. 1/912A, m. 12.

[1] *Cartulary of St. Gregory, Canterbury* (Camden 3rd Series, vol. 88), ed. A. M. Woodcock, no. 217.

[2] He has been found mentioned as the official of the bishop or bishop-elect in March 1244 (*Close Rolls 1242–7*, 238), September 1246 (*Chartulary of Winchester Cathedral*, ed. Goodman, 395), February 1250 (*Ibid.*, 215a), 1260 (*Close Rolls 1259–61*, 254, 279, 282).

who conveyed lands in his manor of Esher to RICHARD DE RIPPELE, whose name makes it possible that he was a canon of Newark. Richard built the hospital and was so successful in acquiring lands, rents and alms for the foundation that the hospital soon had eight chaplains as well as brothers and poor. Richard survived Robert I and must have died in Henry III's reign, for on his death the new master was presented by Robert II de Watevill, with the assent of the brothers of the hospital but without any need to obtain the assent of the bishop. The new master was RICHARD DE BLECHINGLEY. While the date of his predecessor's death is not known there can be little doubt that it was the second Richard who was the party to final concords made on behalf of his house in the Surrey eyres of October 1235 and June 1241.[1] From the dower litigation of Robert II's widow Alina in the Bench plea rolls of Easter and Trinity terms 1243[2] we learn that Robert had leased his manor of Esher at farm to John de Wilehal or Wylehal, a prominent merchant and former sheriff of London. We do not know when the lease was granted but it was probably in the late 1230s, when Robert was indebted to the Jew Abraham of Berkhampstead, and would have been obliged to get the maximum financial profit from his lands.[3] The dower litigation shows the master of the hospital holding 20 acres of land and 3 acres of woodland at Esher of the Watevills, which may be lands that Robert II granted after marriage. The next two masters were both presented by John de Wilehal, as farmer of the manor of Esher. The first of them was GILES, a canon of Newark. He appears on behalf of his house in granting a canon's corrody by a final concord made in the Bench on the octave of Hilary (20 Jan.) 1250[4] but, as discussed below, was probably in office by 1245. On his death IVES was appointed; from what follows he probably died in 1256.

On Ives's death, master Geoffrey de Feringes, in the name of the bishop-elect of Winchester, appointed brother THOMAS OF LONDON, a canon of Newark. Robert III de Watevill claimed that this was done without the assent of the brethren or of himself, and that as soon as the appointment came to his notice he ejected Thomas. But after negotiations with master Geoffrey he permitted Thomas to return and act as master for about a year. Then he again ejected him, whereupon master Geoffrey brought ecclesiastical pressure to bear, excommunicating Robert, and once again inducted Thomas as master: *constituit ipsum . . . rectorem*. Thus compelled, Robert allowed Thomas to remain; this was the state of affairs which Robert sought to remedy by his complaint under the provisions of Oxford and Westminster. He alleged that as a result of the

[1] Feet of Fines before 1509: P.R.O. ref. C.P. 25(1), 225/9, no. 9 and 226/11, no. 29.
[2] Rolls of the Bench and Court *Coram Rege*, Richard I—Henry III: P.R.O. ref. K.B. 26/128, m. 5; K.B. 26/130, ms. 8, 9d, 20d.
[3] *Close Rolls, 1237–42*, 111.
[4] Feet of Fines before 1509: P.R.O. ref. C.P. 25(1), 226/14, no. 11.

disturbances the hospital's goods had been so wasted that it now supported only two chaplains, whereas in Ives's mastership it had still supported seven or eight; the rest had been ejected by Thomas. There was a minor difference between Robert and the jury about the beginning of the chain of events started by Ives's death: Robert said one year ago, the jury said two years ago. Bigod gave judgment for Robert. Master Thomas was ordered to go away and cease to act as master; Robert was to appoint a fit successor, *talem custodem ydoneum eligat et in eodem hospitali constituat quem ad hoc competere viderit.* It is possible that he appointed RICHARD LE FRANK, who as master of Sandon hospital granted to John de la Rude a six year lease of lands at Burningfold, Farncombe and Thorncombe, to run from the morrow of St. Martin 47 Henry III (12 Nov. 1262).[1]

With the early history of the foundation thus set out it is possible to see rather more clearly the way in which the benefactions of William de Percy fit into it. As is well known, William succeeded to part of his father's barony between 1212 and 1214; he died about July 1245.[2] His first wife was Joan Briwer, fifth daughter of William Briwer who had been his guardian, and whose successful career in the royal service between the end of Henry II's reign and the early years of Henry III had enabled him to acquire vast estates and to grant appropriate marriage-portions to his daughters. The date of Joan's death is uncertain. It was before June 1233, but may have been a few months or even a year or so earlier. She was buried in front of the altar of the Blessed Virgin in the hospital church at Sandon. Now her husband held the Sussex Honor of Petworth, but so far as is known neither she nor her husband had any Surrey interests. It is, therefore, remarkable that she should have been buried in the church of a small religious house with which neither her own nor her husband's family had any connexion. The most probable explanation for this would seem to be that she had been taken ill while travelling in the neighbourhood of Esher, and that the hospital furnished the nearest suitable accommodation for a baron's lady. Esher was on the way from Westminster to Guildford, which the family may have taken in journeying to or from Petworth. Certainly it was from the accident of Joan's death that the early prosperity of the house flowed. Three of the relative deeds are in the Percy Cartulary; one is in the Sallay Cartulary.[3] William de Percy agreed to settle on the hospital an income of £23 6s. 8d., which was to support six chaplains to say masses for her soul. Since the greatest number of chaplains mentioned in 1258 was eight, this represents a very large augmentation of the hospital's revenues. It is just possible that the amount indicates Joan's age at her death, for in marks it is exactly 35, and there is no reason to believe that she was much older than that. By the most important of the deeds, William

[1] Guildford Muniment Room, deed 60/8.
[2] G.E.C., *Complete Peerage*, x, 452–455.
[3] *Percy Chartulary* (Surtees Society, vol. CXVII); *Sallay Chartulary* (Records Branch, Yorks. Arch. Soc., vol. LXXXVII).

granted the hospital the revenue from the lands which he held as Joan's marriage-portion at Foston, Leicestershire, and 20 marks due to himself in respect of a recent grant which he had made of his manor of Gisburn, Yorkshire, to the West Riding abbey of Sallay or Sawley, a Percy foundation.[1] The names of the witnesses to this deed, none of whom were Surrey men, suggest that it was made in Sussex rather than Yorkshire. The grant of Gisburn to Sallay, at 20 marks rent payable yearly by 1 July to William at Sandon, had been made to enable that abbey to support six chaplains praying for the souls of William and his second wife, Helen de Balliol (who lived until 1281).[2] A royal confirmation of this grant issued on 30 January 1242.[3] Several writers have concluded from this that the grant itself was made in 1242, and therefore that the later grant to Sandon must have been made between then and 1245. This conclusion assumes a delay of about ten years between Joan's death and the provision for chaplains; it also assumes that the grant to Sallay was made about the same time as the royal confirmation. Both suppositions are possible but unlikely. William's son and heir by Helen came of age between February 1257 and February 1258.[4] Helen must therefore have become his wife by 1236 at latest, and the grant to Sallay may have been made at any time between then and 1242, followed soon afterwards by the grant to Sandon. The fact that the rent for the grant to Sallay was to be payable to William at Sandon makes it plain that he was then interesting himself in the affairs of the house and needing cash to be available there. The transfer of the rent to the hospital and the conveyance of the lands at Foston were conditional on a final settlement of the promised £23 6s. 8d. being made from his estates. Such a settlement was never made; so Sallay continued to pay the rent until 1377, when it was remitted because of economic difficulties.[5]

The second deed is between Richard, master and keeper of the hospital of Sandon, and William de Percy, whereby Richard acknowledges the grant of a rent of 10 marks.[6] For this the hospital was to give £3 yearly from its chamber to John de Chuvilli and Richard de Chuvilli for clothes and shoes, and to provide them with the same food and drink as chaplains; after their deaths the 60s. was to go to support the charity of the house. This transaction seems to mean that William was purchasing two corrodies in the hospital on behalf of members of his household. It is not clear whether the 10 marks rent is in addition to the main conveyance, just discussed, or whether it might be in substitution for the lands at Foston. The transaction must be later than the main conveyance because the master went on to bind himself to secure, when William de Percy so

1 *Percy Chartulary*, no. 952, also in *Monasticon*, VI, 676, no. i; *Sallay Chartulary*, no. 34.
2 *Percy Chartulary*, no. 450; *Sallay Chartulary*, no. 33.
3 *Cal. Charter Rolls, 1226–1257*, 265.
4 G.E.C., *Complete Peerage*, x, 455.
5 *Sallay Chartulary*, p. 22.
6 *Percy Chartulary*, no. 947.

desired, that all the deeds between the hospital and him should be enchirographed in a royal court and that confirmation of them should be obtained from the bishop of Winchester. It is not clear whether the word enchirograph means that a final concord would be levied or that the deeds would be enrolled on the plea rolls of the Bench, court *coram rege* or eyre, which was a common practice. There are no such enrolments in the surviving rolls of any of these courts between 1234 and 1245 nor does such a final concord survive. In November 1239 William purchased the advowson of the Augustinian priory of Lynchmere or Shulbred, Sussex, and agreed to settle on it an income of £10 yearly; pending this settlement, as with Sandon, he made various grants to it which were the subject of a final concord in July 1240.[1] It is therefore likely that it was intended to make the Sandon grants the subject of a similar final concord.

It is possible that an episcopal confirmation was also never obtained. Between the death of Peter des Roches on 9 June 1238 and the return of William de Raleigh to England in the summer of 1244 no confirmation could have been secured. The last of the deeds seems to be a substitute for it, being bishop William's *inspeximus* of an agreement between prior Giles and Sir Wymund de Raleigh.[2] This must have been made between William de Percy's death in July 1245 and bishop William's final retirement to France in November 1249. Wymund de Raleigh was probably an executor of William de Percy's will, for he was a prominent Sussex tenant of the Percys and had witnessed three of the deeds already mentioned;[3] he was also a kinsman of the bishop.[4] William de Percy had been buried at Sallay, but from the deed we learn that his heart had been interred by Joan's body in the church at Sandon.[5] By the agreement the prior bound himself to have a lamp and 2 lb. wax candle burning before the altar of the Blessed Virgin during all masses celebrated in the church, at whatever altar they were said; in default the bishop could compel, and the Percy heirs could distrain, the master and his successors to discharge this obligation. There is no reason why the prior and Sir Wymund should have delayed in securing the bishop's *inspeximus* of this deed, so a date nearer 1245 than 1249 is probable for it, which in turn suggests that Giles had succeeded Richard de Blechingley in the mastership by about 1245.

The foregoing interpretation of the Percy benefactions assumes that William's gifts began very soon after Joan's death, about 1233, and were substantially completed before 1242, so that the hospital was obtaining a considerable accession of funds in this period. This seems to be confirmed by the activity of the master, Richard, in the

[1] *Sx.A.C.* XLVII, 5–6.
[2] *Percy Chartulary*, no. 964, also in *Monasticon*, VI, 676, no. ii.
[3] *Sallay Chartulary*, no. 34; *Percy Chartulary*, nos. 450, 952.
[4] There are many references to Wymund's staying at the larger episcopal manors, in the foreign expenses of the manorial accounts of Raleigh's episcopate.
[5] On heart burial in the early thirteenth century see J. H. Round, *Essex Arch. Soc., new series*, XVI, The Heart of St. Roger.

Surrey eyres of 1235 and 1241, when he was party to three final concords. Although the narration of Robert III de Watevill and the jurors in 1258 would seem to give to the first master the credit of bringing the hospital to the strength of eight chaplains, there seems little doubt that it was the second master who was in office throughout the period of the Percy benefactions. Certainly it was he who was in office in 1241, for in that eyre Ralph de Imworth brought an action of nuisance against the master of St. Mary Magdalene's hospital, Sandon, for raising a bank or ditch at Imber to his damage;[1] the jury found for the master, saying that the nuisance had been done by his predecessor. This proves that the Richard of 1241 was the second master, and since the activity of 1235–41 is of a piece it seems that we have in it a master of the hospital who was a sufficiently shrewd administrator to make the most of the accession of wealth brought about by the accident of Joan's death. In the Surrey eyre of 1235 he secured a large estate in the Bramley district.[2] Fuller details of the transaction will be given in a forthcoming edition of the eyre roll by the Surrey Record Society.[3] In brief, John de Fay, a courtier who held Bramley and Puttenham in chief, was heavily indebted to the Jews. In 1229 he conveyed an estate to one of his leading tenants, Roger de Bydon. In 1235, by an enrolled concord and chirographs, whose terms differ somewhat, the prior bought the estate from Roger at a rent of 10 marks yearly so long as Roger lived, and thereafter at the almost nominal rent of 18d. It was a good bargain, for Roger died, in violent circumstances, before 1241. The estate consisted of 200 acres of wood in Burningfold and Witherfold, in Dunsfold; one mark of rent at Cugate, which later litigation shows to have been in Bramley and is perhaps to be identified with Cowgates there; £2 rent at Utworth, in Cranleigh, and Chilworth. The master thereupon leased the Cugate estate to John de Gatesden, a man from a knightly Hertfordshire family who, from small beginnings as a Surrey sheriff's clerk, was rising to be a prominent member of the royal household, and amassing vast estates in Surrey and Sussex. The estate there consisted of the lands and services of four privileged villeins of the ancient demesne manor of Bramley, and by June 1239 Gatesden was involved in a successful dispute with John de Fay about the villeins' services, in the course of which he described the series of conveyances. He was then paying the hospital a rent of 36s. 8d. He still held the estate at his death in April 1262; in 1269 it was said to consist of unspecified assize rents in Bramley, worth 39s. 10½d.[4] Two of the villein tenants of 1229–1239 had been Eylwin de Billinghurst and Geoffrey de Thorncombe; two of the inquisition *post mortem* jurors of 1269 may have been

[1] Eyre, Assize, Trailbaston etc. Rolls: P.R.O. ref. J.I. 1/867, m. 4.

[2] *Ibid.*, roll 864, ms. 1, 3, 7; Feet of Fines before 1509: P.R.O. ref. C.P. 25(1), 225/9, no. 9.

[3] *1235 Surrey Eyre*, note 195. A partial account of the transaction in *Sy. A.C.* XXIII, 62–3, correcting *M. & B.* II, 750, itself requires correction and addition.

[4] *Cal. Inquisitions post mortem, Henry III*, no. 706.

their descendants, being Robert de Billinghurst and Robert de Thorncombe. When John de Fay's sisters and heirs were litigating about their rights with John's widow in 1243, the prior of Sandon appeared as holding 5 marks worth of rent and 104 acres in Bramley;[1] but we have no details of this holding, and it must have covered more of the estate conveyed in 1235 than the mark's worth of rent in Cugate. Nothing is known of any further action by the master about the woodlands in Burningfold and Witherfold. The lease of 1262, already mentioned, must have concerned part of them; from it, it seems that the masters leased out the woodlands in parcels for short terms. The £2 rent in Utworth and Chilworth arose from tenements held by Sir Walter de Utworth, a leading knight of the county who served as steward to the de Clere family (who were honorial barons of the earls of Warenne), as coroner from before 1241 to 1254 and as as deputy sheriff in 1242–1244. In the 1241 Surrey eyre, after a year and a half's instalment had been unpaid, he acknowledged his obligation to the hospital for the rent by a final concord with the master, Richard.[2]

In the conveyancing of 1235 the master was represented by Gilbert the chaplain of Sandon, whom one assumes to have been one of the chaplains of the hospital. Other litigation in the 1241 Surrey eyre shows that a little before that year Gilbert had secured from John de Fay a sixteen-year lease of the considerable estate of a carucate at Shoelands, in Puttenham, on condition that Gilbert payed off a debt of 60 marks owed by John to a Jew.[3] It is possible that Gilbert was acting in this on the hospital's behalf, but as a result of the litigation the contract was abandoned. In the preliminaries of the 1235 conveyance the master was essoined by John de Marwick, in Hascombe, which makes it possible that the hospital already had interests in the district, since essoiners were commonly tenurial connexions of their principals. But this conveyance of 1235 was the first that is known by a master in a royal court: coming so soon after Joan de Percy's death it tempts one to believe that it represented the investment of money from gifts made by, or shortly to be expected from, William de Percy. By letters close dated 14 Dec. 1233, Sandon had obtained exemption from the fortieth levied that year, on the ground that the house was so poor that it depended for its sustenance upon the begging of alms.[4] Too much importance must not be attached to this. The exemption was obtained by the bishop of Winchester, Peter des Roches, who was a considerable patron of the religious houses of his diocese. It covered all four Augustinian hospitals in Surrey; while Reigate and Tandridge may have been no richer than Sandon, St. Thomas's, Southwark, was well endowed. Nevertheless it seems that the effect of the Percy benefactions was to increase the number of chaplains from two to eight, and the activity of master

[1] Inquisitions Post Mortem, Henry III: P.R.O. ref. C. 132/36, no. 19.
[2] Feet of Fines before 1509: P.R.O. ref. C.P. 25(1), 226/11, no. 29.
[3] Eyre, Assize, Trailbaston etc. Rolls: P.R.O. ref. J.I. 1/864, m. 11d.
[4] *Close Rolls, 1231–4*, 290.

Richard in 1235–1241 strongly suggests a remarkable increase in the hospital's revenue.

The third final concord in which master Richard was concerned brings us back to the Watevills.[1] By it, William son of William Pycot, a freeholder of prominence in the Kingston district, paid the master 55 marks for the grant of a carucate at Chessington and Tolworth, to be held at a rent of 44s. and service to the superior lord. The conveyance was grounded on the then novel device of a writ of covenant, which suggests that Pycot's was a newly created tenancy. Chessington was held by the main branch of the Watevills, whose principal seat was in Essex and whose head at this time was William de Watevill, the friend of Walter de Merton. We do not know what mesne tenancies there may have been, but the fact that the estate was on a Watevill fee suggests that it was an early endowment from that family. Not long afterwards master Richard, by an undated deed, reduced the rent to 17s. 4d. in consideration of Pycot's services, and of 20 marks which he had paid "towards the arduous business of our house."[2]

The Watevill connexion is further shown by an entry in the *coram rege* plea roll of 1243 Michaelmas term, under the quinzaine of Michaelmas, whereby the house of Sandon was acquitted of the custody of charters which had been deposited with it by Robert II de Watevill, who had died earlier that year.[3] They had been handed over to the leading courtier and administrator Philip Basset, whose elder brother had extensive interests in the Woking district: those concerning the infant Robert III for delivery to his uncles, Gilbert and Nicholas de Sandford who were themselves related to the Bassets; those concerning Peter de Watevill, a younger brother of Robert II who had estates in Sussex and Herefordshire, for delivery to him. The transaction is a reminder that the family which held the patronage of a religious house could always use it as a safe deposit.

Sandon, like other Augustinian hospitals, was sometimes referred to as a priory. In the evidences cited it is so styled in the final concords of 1235 and 1250 and in one Percy deed (no. 964), and in the Fay litigation of 1243; in all the rest the head of the house is called master. The evidences also shed some light on the dedication of the hospital. In the *Victoria County History* it was assumed that the original dedication was to the Holy Ghost, and that St. Mary Magdalene was a subsidiary dedication, perhaps of the church only. In the Pycot final concord of 1241 and in the litigation in 1241 (about Imber) and 1258, in which masters were defendants, they are said to be masters of the hospital of St. Mary Magdalene.[4] In the Utworth final concord of 1241, in which the master was plaintiff, and in two

[1] Feet of Fines before 1509: P.R.O. ref. C.P. 25(1), 226/11, no. 13.

[2] Merton College, deed no. 1088.

[3] Rolls of the Bench and Court *Coram Rege*, Richard I–Henry III: P.R.O. ref. K.B. 26/131, m. 3.

[4] Feet of Fines before 1509: P.R.O. ref. C.P. 25(1), 226/11, no. 13; Eyre, Assize, Trailbaston etc. Rolls: P.R.O. ref. J.I. 1/867, m. 4; *Ibid.*, J.I. 1/873, m. 10.

deeds that are grants by a master, the style is of the Holy Ghost.[1] This style was also used in litigation in the 1241 eyre when the master successfully brought an action of novel disseisin against Geoffrey de Cruce and a number of his tenants about 40 acres of heath at Burwood, in Walton on Thames.[2] In all four cases it is Richard de Blechingley who is using this style, and in one of the deeds he uses it though in the preceding final concord Pycot, in bringing his writ of covenant, had used the style St. Mary Magdalene. In short, when Richard describes himself and mentions a dedication, either as a plaintiff or in deeds, it is the Holy Ghost. But where others describe a master in bringing writs against him the dedication which they mention is St. Mary Magdalene. Two of these others were neighbours: William Pycot, a man of affairs who was to be for many years steward of Chertsey abbey, and Ralph de Imworth, who was to die fighting on the baronial side at Lewes. The third was Robert III de Watevill, the founder's grandson. The conclusion seems inescapable: the original dedication was to St. Mary Magdalene, but during the mastership of Richard de Blechingley the Holy Ghost was added, no doubt because of a particular devotion either by the master or by William de Percy or someone connected with him. The new dedication was favoured by the religious in the house; the earliest use of it which we have found by a master other than Richard was in the 1271 Surrey eyre when the then (unnamed) master made arrangements for repaying a debt to the prioress of Rusper, Sussex.[3] Its earliest use so far discovered by a known master other than Richard is in a deed of 8 September 1278 whereby brother Geoffrey keeper of the hospital of the Holy Ghost of Sandun' and the brothers of the place made a release of rent at Broomhall in Windlesham to Agnes prioress of Broomhall.[4]

It may be convenient to summarize the information given about the first seven known masters. In addition, among the heads of a number of Augustininian houses who witnessed an undated deed in the Cartulary of St. Thomas's hospital, Southwark, was William the master of the hospital of Sandon;[5] the deed seems to date from some time between 1255 and 1270.

1199/1216—after 1216	Richard de Ripley
after 1216—after 1241	Richard de Blechingley
? *c.* 1245—after 1250	Giles, canon of Newark
after 1250—*c.* 1256	Ives
c. 1256—1258	Thomas of London, canon of Newark
in 1262	Richard le Frank
in 1278	Geoffrey

[1] Feet of Fines before 1509: P.R.O. ref. C.P. 25(1), 226/11, no. 29; *Percy Chartulary*, no. 952; Merton Coll., deed no. 1088.
[2] Eyre, Assize, Trailbaston etc. Rolls: P.R.O. ref. J.I. 1/867, m. 13d.
[3] *Ibid.*, J.I. 1/875, m. 14d.
[4] St. John's College, Cambridge, deed 14/9.
[5] *St. Thomas Chartulary*, no. 446.

XIX

St. Teath's Tithes—1295

St. Teath emerges in the episcopate of bishop Brondescombe (1258-80) as a small collegiate church of two prebends and an endowed vicarage.[1] The great ecclesiastical taxation of 1291 shows the prebends then held by Mr. Osbert de Baggeston (who also held the Warminster prebend in Salisbury cathedral and another living and died about 1304)[2] and Mr. William de Wymundesham (who had been collated on 5 May 1276, still held in 1297, and also held a living in Devon[3]); their prebends had a taxable value of £4 10s each. The vicarage was worth £1. It had been endowed in 1269 with the small tithes, altar offerings and glebe; there appears to be some doubt whether the great tithes at this time remained with the prebendaries or had become appropriated to Exeter cathedral, to whose bishop the patronage of prebends and vicar pertained.[4] The heading and endorsement of the following little document suggests that by 1295 they belonged to Exeter, which regularly farmed them to local men, paying the prebends a fixed amount and retaining the balance to the use of the bishop or chapter. In 1295 the tithes were farmed for a total of £14 3s to eleven local men.

The document is very simple, just listing the name of the manor or estate from whose lands the tithes were due, the person to whom they had been sold and their price, together with the farmer's sureties for his payment. In all, 25 persons are named; four of the farmers also figure as sureties for other farmers while a couple of other men were also surety for more than one farmer.

The names of the estates and the place elements in personal names are mostly readily identifiable. Those of the estates have been given their modern form in brackets. Only three of the names call for comment. Gracelin de Septem Fontibus, who farmed a moiety of the Treligga tithes, was concerning himself in an estate at the other end of the parish from his home, for the name of his family is preserved in the modern Suffenton; an interesting medial form of this name is found in a plea about land in it in the Cornwall eyre of 1284: "Setfontem Maiori juxta Trewrosel".[5] In the same eyre there is an interesting plea brought by Amana relict of John de Rowallan against Richard Carrou of Dounant for dower in a messuage and carucate at "Dounant Rowalan".[6] In the course of the plea a charter was put in evidence that had been made about this estate by John Rowaleyn, who was now dead but whose daughter Maud was living as the wife of John Rosingor. Clearly the Rowallan family had been connected with this estate as the actual tenants on the land for long enough for their name to become associated with it. One estate has defied identification: "Lounant". Though clearly so written, one is tempted to think that Dannon, to give Dounant its modern form, had through subtenancies become divided, one half being known as Dounant Rowallan and the other simply as Dounant, for which "Lounant" is a mistake; but one always hesitates to offer a solution based on putative scribal errors.

No doubt by patient search of unpublished deeds and plea rolls some biographical information could be assembled about most of the persons named. The writer has had time only for an examination of the main roll of the Cornwall eyre of 1284 and of the crown pleas of the Cornwall eyre of 1302. None of the men mentioned served as hundred jurors for Trigg-shire in either eyre. Only one, Henry Kavel, who farmed the New Hall tithes, made a marked impression on these legal records. He was clearly a man of business of considerable local standing. In 1274, acting as bailiff or sheriff's officer he had arrested and imprisoned the abbot of Bodmin under legal process.[7] In the 1284 eyre he stands at the head of six men, all from the St. Teath locality, who were prosecuting an action of prohibition against Thomas de Bodeham, the bishop of Exeter's official, William the vicar of the church of St. Teath and another. His appearance as part of the group, together with his presence as both farmer and surety in our document, makes it likely that he and the others had already been so acting before 1284, that they or those for whom they had gone surety then had failed in some payments, that the bishop had then resorted to his own ecclesiastical courts to enforce payment (a common device) whereupon Kavel and the rest had brought an action in the royal courts to prohibit these proceedings. Henry probably met an untimely end; for he is probably the "Henry Cavel of St. Thethe" whose murder by two local men after a quarrel was reported in the eyre of 1302.[9] Stephen Gracelyn, the farmer of the Hendra tithes, was also concerned in a killing. Some time before 1284 he had killed a man in self defence at "Launomora", taken sanctuary in the church of "Sancta Tetha de Launomora", been imprisoned and then acquitted before the gaol delivery justices but had failed to obtain the necessary royal letters of pardon; so in the 1284 eyre he was again committed to prison until he did this.[10]

The list is written on a small piece of parchment, 9 inches long and tapering from 4½ inches at the head to 4 inches at the tail (23.3 cm. x 11.6-10.6 cm.). The hand is a neat late thirteenth century current hand. The position of the single endorsement at the head, suggests that the membrane was rolled up from the tail, when the endorsed heading would appear as an identification on the small visible portion. The style of this endorsement "Fruits of St. Teath", like the heading, suggests very strongly that the roll formed part of a collection of kindred little rolls. Such a collection would exist at Exeter, where the bishop and chapter possessed a number of appropriated churches.

No reference has yet been assigned to the document, which the writer found recently in one of the still numerous sacks of unsorted matter of all kinds from the mid-thirteenth century onwards in the Public Record Office. Most of the medieval documents in such sacks come from the former Treasury of the Receipt of the Exchequer archives at Westminster. It is hazardous to suggest how this document could have come into the royal archives.

Vendicio decimarum Sancte Tethe anno Regni Regis Edwardi vicesimo tercio.

Trewrosel [Treroosel] venditur Warino capellano pro. Lij. solidis· Plegii Amundus de Trevyhan et Johannes de Trevyly.

Nova Aula [Newhall] venditur pro. xxx. solidis Henrico Kavel. Plegii Stephanus Gracelyn at Amundus de Trevyhan [deleted and replaced by] Stephanus de Trevyhan.

Hendre Maior [Hendra] venditur pro. xxv. solidis Stephano Gracelyn. Plegii Henricus Kavel et Gracelinus de Septem Fontibus.

Tregonet [Trehannick] venditur Hamundo de Trevyhan pro. xxx. solidis. Plegii Willelmus de Sancta Tetha et Johannes Kavel.

Lounant [?] venditur pro. xvj. solidis Stephano Fabro. Plegii Willelmus Russel et Rogerus de Hendr'.

Dounant Rowallan [Dannon] venditur pro. xxvj. solidis. viij. denariis. [Details bracketted] Henrico Textori debet. xiij. s. iiij. d. Plegii Ricardus Avyan et Willelmus Symple; Nichalao Coki debet. xiij. s. iiijd. Plegii Stephanus Gracelyn et Johannes Jocelyn.

Tetha [St. Teath] venditur pro. xl. solidis [Details bracketted] Randolfo Molendinario medietatem pro. xx. s. Plegii Warinus de Trewynan et [blank] Edwardo Fulloni medietatem pro. xx. s. Plegii Rogerus de Karylyan et Christoferus Fullo.

Treluga [Treligga] venditur pro. Lxiij. solidis. iiij. denariis. [Details bracketted] Willelmo de Treverion medietatem pro. xxxj. s. iiij. d. Plegii Ricardus Pelliparius et Ricardus Auxen. Gracelino de Septem Fontibus medietatem pro. xxxj. s. viij. d. Plegii Willelmus de Sancta Tethe et Johannes de Trevyly.

Endorsement: Fructuum Sancte Thethe Anno Regni Regis Edwardi xxiij

NOTES

1. J. Maclean *Deanery of Trigg Minor*, iii, 96; F. C. Hingeston Randolph *Exeter Episcopal Registers* (Brondescombe), 178-9.
2. *Calendar of Patent Rolls* 1292-1307, 264; Joyce M. Horn *Le Neve's Fasti Ecclesiastici*, 1300-1541, iii, 93.
3. Hingeston Randolph, *op. cit.*, 179; *C.P.R.* 1292-1307. 281.
4. Maclean, *loc. cit.*
5. Public Record Office: J. I. 1/112, m. 33.
6. Also J. I. 1/112, m. 33.
7. J. I. 1/112, m. 8d.
8. J. I. 1/112, m. 40.
9. J. I. 1/118, m. 57.
10. J. I. 1/112, ms. 57, 72.

XX

THE PIPE ROLL ORDER OF 12 FEBRUARY 1270

LETTERS patent directed to the treasurer and exchequer barons were issued on 12 February 1270, ordering a change in the way in which the county accounts on the Pipe Rolls were to be made up.[1] Madox gave the text and a substantial translation of the letters patent, together with some examples of the formula entered at the foot of accounts in accordance with the order.[2] He explained that the order was concerned with a new method for the removal of desperate debts from the county accounts: such debts were to be marked 'd' in a particular account and left there, without being copied on to the next account, unless they were eventually cleared; and a formula to say that this had been done was to be entered at the foot of the next and subsequent accounts. He further explained that the terms of this order were carried out, apparently until fresh regulations were made on the matter by the letters close of 23 March 1284 known as the Statute of Rutland or, more correctly, Rhuddlan. Madox said nothing of any earlier methods of removing such debts, nor of any special circumstances about 1270 which led to the formulation of this order. Rather, since this commences the paragraph of chapter xxiii, section 2 which he devoted to Dead and Desperate Debts, he left it to be inferred that until 1270 such debts were not systematically removed and that the order of 1270 was the result not of a particular crisis but of the gradual realization of the futility of a particular practice:

It being the Ancient course to write the Kings Debts in the *Great Roll* afresh every year, in order to charge the sheriff therewith: This became very burdensome to the Officers of the Exchequer concerned in That service; especially where Debts were Desperate or stood long in Charge:

[1] It was enrolled on Patent Roll 54 Henry III, m. 22, being marginated *De statu scaccarii* with a pointing hand as a catcheye. The number '61' was added in the seventeenth century when the abstract of Patent Rolls was compiled at the Tower which was eventually printed in 1802 by the R.C., in which it occurs with this number: *Cal. Rot. Pat.*, p. 43. It was not calendared in *C.P.R., 1266–72* because the text (minor inaccuracies) had been given in 1816 in the R.C. edition of *Rymer's Foedera*, i. 483. At the Exchequer it was entered in the Red Book: *Red Book* (R.S.), iii. 842.

[2] *History of the Exchequer*, 654–5. The text is better than that of the *Foedera*.

And was at the same time of little or no advantage to the Crown. For remedy of this inconvenience a form of a Provision was drawn up . . . and approved.

Since Madox wrote, the order has often been referred to, without being examined afresh; and when it has been referred to it has sometimes been with misunderstanding. To Hubert Hall, discussing the Ordinances of 1323–6 in his preface to the *Red Book of the Exchequer*: 'The existing records of the Exchequer clearly prove that the reforms enjoined since the 54th year of Henry III had been allowed to remain inoperative as late as the Parliament of Lincoln in 1316.'[1] For Miss Mills, permitting the magnetized figure of Peter de Rivaux to attract into its field of force most changes of Exchequer procedure that occurred in the thirteenth century, 'the reform outlined in the statute . . . of 1270 really had its origins in the reforms of 1236. The supposed reforms of 1270 had been the practice of the exchequer for thirty-four years.'[2] It may therefore be useful to fill a small gap in exchequer history by attempting to show why the order of 1270 was needed, what it was designed to do, what it did, and how it fitted into a series of changes that took place between the days of Richard of Ely and those of Bishop Stapeldon.

The order was not concerned with any notable principle of administration but with a single feature only of the audit of the county accounts. It was needed because the Barons' War had rendered acute a problem that had been chronic in Pipe Roll practice since the reign of Richard I. The Pipe Rolls began when the king's casual revenue consisted of fairly large sums owed by a few and when the Exchequers, Upper and Lower, were not institutions but occasions which filled some weeks each year after Michaelmas and Easter; the expansion of royal government in the latter part of the twelfth century led to sums, mostly fairly small, being owed by a great many and made the Exchequers into an institution whose Lower part was open for most of the year for the receipt of cash and whose Upper part took from October to July in auditing county and foreign accounts, thereby reducing proffers and Easter view of account into something of a formality.[3] Richard of Ely says much of the labour of maintaining the accuracy of the Pipe Roll

[1] *Red Book*, iii, p. cccxlvi.

[2] 'The Reforms at the Exchequer', *R. Hist. Soc. Trans.*, 4th ser., x. 127.

[3] 'The Receipt, like the Upper Exchequer, is an occasion rather than an institution': Charles Johnson, Introduction to the *P.R. of 2 Richard I* (P.R.S.), p. xvj. The pioneer account of the changes came with Miss Mills's 'Experiments in Exchequer Procedure (1200–32)', *R. Hist. Soc. Trans.*, 4th ser., viii. 151–70.

and its counterparts, of writing the Exchequer writs and making out the summonses; but he says nothing to indicate that he was aware of a need to restrict to the minimum the number of new debts entered in the sheriffs' accounts. Moreover, the removal of debts from the roll otherwise than by authorized allowance or proof of payment was for him that rare residual problem of Exchequer process, the discovery of a debtor's total insolvency: 'the Treasurer submits to the King that it is useless to write them in the Roll since there is no possibility of the money being recovered'.[1] Nevertheless, in discussing the summonses he reveals a growing problem. Richard of Ilchester had begun the practice of making duplicates of the summonses: 'But . . . the number of debtors enormously increasing so that a whole skin of parchment was scarcely long enough for a single Summons the number of names and the labour involved proved overpowering, and the Barons were satisfied as of old, with the original Summons.'[2] In fact it was about the time that Richard of Ely wrote the *Dialogus* that he and his colleagues had to take the first measures, soon intensified by their successors, to counter the increase in the number of persons from whom the revenue was due by limiting the number of entries in the county accounts on the Pipe Rolls.

They did this in two ways. One was by restricting to the minimum the number of entries to be copied in the county accounts from the subsidiary documents out of which each year's account was made up. The other was by periodically removing from the accounts those debts which had been in them for a long time and which seemed, from a variety of reasons, to be incapable of clearance. One says incapable of clearance rather than illeviable because the matter did not essentially, though it might accidentally, arise from the efficiency or otherwise of the exchequer and sheriffs in collecting revenue. In entering a debt on the Pipe Rolls, the Exchequer assumed, from the information it received or supplied, that a particular person was liable for a particular debt in a particular county or that a debt was due, debtor unknown. In fact the debt might not be owed, or not owed to the Crown, or not owed by the persons to whom it was debited; or when owed it might have been paid, yet persist in the rolls for want of proof of payment. If liability was never formally contested or if it was respited by inaction there would be no decision which could lead to the debt being cleared. Hence the problem was the audit

[1] *Dialogus*, II. ii, ed. Charles Johnson (Nelson's Medieval Classics), 74.
[2] Ibid. II. xviii, ed. Johnson, 115.

problem of clearance, rather than the administrative problem of collection; though of course conditions which made proper collection difficult would increase the problems of audit.

From the latter part of the twelfth century the Exchequer depended for its knowledge about new revenue chargeable in the county accounts upon the information supplied by the chancery, courts of law, and some other branches and officials of the royal administration. Membranes of the Originalia Rolls arrived regularly from chancery throughout the year and in the course of Henry III's reign the estreats from the bench, court *coram rege*, assize and gaol delivery justices, and the exchequer of pleas became regular arrivals also. The principal occasional arrivals were the estreats of forest and common pleas eyres (or the returned summonses, if these estreats had been summoned locally by the justices themselves), lists of tallages, of newly arrentated assarts and serjeanties, of confiscated Jewish debts and so on. The only considerable revenue for which the exchequer did not receive a list seems to have been scutage, whose liability it had to calculate from its own archives, though it naturally received lists of those exempt from the liability or compounding by fines. It is not necessary to discuss the treatment of this varied matter in detail since the task of restricting new matter resolved itself mainly into the treatment to be accorded the Originalia Rolls and the estreats of forest and common pleas eyres.

Here practice diverged sharply. Originalia Rolls were being transmitted by chancery to Exchequer from Richard I's reign if not earlier;[1] and down to 1258 (the Roll for 42 Henry III) it was the practice to transfer every item in the Originalia Rolls to its appropriate county account in the Pipe Rolls.[2] For much of this time, moreover, the Originalia Rolls were not confined to revenue arising through the chancery but included revenue arising from

[1] The early history of the Originalia Rolls has been discussed by H. G. Richardson in his Introduction to the *Memoranda Roll of 1 John* (P.R.S.); the text of the earliest surviving fragment of such a roll, for 7 Richard I, is given in the same volume, pp. 85–88. Two rolls survive from John's reign, most of the later, for 15–16 John, being given in *Rotuli de Oblatis et Finibus*, ed. Hardy (R.C. 1835). The Roll for 11 Henry III is the earliest for that reign, there being another, imperfect, for 17 Henry III. All this is ignored by Powicke, *Henry III and the Lord Edward*, i. 96, who in writing of the reforms of the 1230's believes that the creation of the Originalia Rolls was one of the reforms made in this period.

[2] The few exceptions are of the nature of the single one in the fragment of 7 Richard I (op. cit., p. 86, *Norfolch* and note 12), where a fine of 100 marks was not entered in the Pipe Roll because a larger fine was made for the same purpose in the same roll later on. The notes from part of the Roll for 15–16 John are missing because the left-hand margin is damaged.

other sources; for example many assize and gaol delivery justices sent their estreats to the chancery, not to the Exchequer, where they were enrolled on the Fine Rolls (and thence onto the Originalia) or even forwarded as membranes of Originalia. Between 1259 and 1269 (the Rolls for 43–53 Henry III) this practice was very slightly modified. An increasing, but even at its greatest a very small, number of debts were not transferred to the Pipe Roll but left in the Originalia Roll, to be summoned thence as with the estreats. This treatment of the Originalia Rolls has an importance beyond that of a mere feature of audit practice, for it means that where chancery enrolments are wanting the Pipe Rolls supply the deficiency to a limited extent so that the *Nova Oblata* and sheriffs' expenses in the Pipe Roll assume something of the importance which they have before the chancery enrolments begin.

The treatment of the estreats of forest and common pleas eyres is a different and much longer story, and although nearly half of it lies within the period for which rolls have been published by the Pipe Roll Society, the introductions and subject indexes to these volumes do little to help to elucidate it. The preparation of the summonses from estreats is described by Richard of Ely.[1] The transmission of estreats to the Exchequer is probably as old as the system of provincial visitation by royal justices. Down to the eve of the compilation of the *Dialogus* it was the general practice to enter in the Pipe Roll all the debts contained in the estreats. The smaller debts for which the sheriff answered were often grouped together in a paragraph. But with the increase in judicial visitations after the assize of Clarendon, in a few accounts only, instead of the debts being grouped the sheriff simply answered for so much of the smallest pleas or amercements or perquisites by so many tallies, indicating that several debts had been lumped together and charged to him, without being detailed. There were a few examples of this arising from the visitation of 1175, the sums being mostly small but in the case of Yorkshire amounting to £63 by 103 tallies.[2] In the next year the Exchequer received the

[1] *Dialogus*, II. i, ii. 70, 77–78. Many writers have made the mistake of identifying these *rotuli errantium, rotuli perambulantium judicum* with the plea rolls preserved in the treasury of the receipt. But none of the plea rolls of the central courts and eyres which survive from 1194 onwards show any signs of having been used by the Exchequer for the preparation of summonses or for audit, while the amercements rolls which some contain from 1195 onwards are clearly the justices' own copies of the estreat. Powicke, op. cit., p. 97, mistakenly attributes the origin of the estreat rolls to the reforms of the 1230's.

[2] *P.R. 21 Henry II*, pp. 46–47, 88, 206, 220; 179. These and other italicized references are to the volumes of the P.R.S.

estreats from the justices who had administered the assize of Northampton and taken civil pleas and from their colleagues who had taken forest pleas; these contained more debts than any it had received hitherto. When the summonses from these estreats were audited in the autumn and winter of 1176, Richard of Ely and his colleagues converted the previous very occasional practice into a new formula. After the names of the justices (copied from the estreat roll heading) and the usual entry of partially paid or wholly owing debts, the smallest debts which the sheriff admitted he had received were charged to him in a lump under the heading *De hiis qui totum reddiderunt*; the entry ran, 'The same sheriff renders account of so much of the smallest amercements of the towns and men of such a county, whose names are entered (*annotantur*) in the roll which they (the justices) have delivered into the treasury. Paid so much by so many tallies.'[1] But in at least one case instead of making this summary entry under the *De hiis* heading the writer entered the debts individually as of old.[2] Since Hodgson's edition of the Northumberland accounts to 1272 provides the only printed texts for the whole of the period down to the order of 1270, examples of subsequent developments will mostly be taken from them and from Yorkshire, whose eyres generally produced the largest estreats. So in 1176 the Northumberland sheriff accounted for £10. 13*s*. 4*d*. by 25 tallies and the Yorkshire sheriff for £45. 13*s*. 4*d*. by 81 tallies, while some 28 and 82 owing or partially owing debts were entered individually.[3] The *De hiis* heading continued in general use down to the entries arising from the eyre of 1194, but the word 'smallest' was gradually dropped and in that year was hardly used at all. The Northumberland sheriff then accounted for £15. 3*s*. 4*d*. by 31 tallies and the Yorkshire sheriff for £68. 13*s*. 4*d*. by 159 tallies.[4] The only changes during the next few years, following the abandonment of the *De hiis* heading, was a tendency to bring the summary entry to the beginning of the matter arising from each eyre. But the visitation of 1202 brought a sensational increase in the revenue. The sheriff of Northumberland then accounted for 531 marks 10*s*. 8*d*. by 201 tallies and the sheriff of Yorkshire for £924. 10*s*. 5*d*., by 1,138 tallies, some 130 partially or wholly owing debts being also entered in the

[1] *P.R. 22 Henry II*, pp. 8, 21, 25, 34, 40, 43, 45, &c. The Latin subject-indexes unfortunately ignore such entries.

[2] Ibid. 105.

[3] John Hodgson, *History of Northumberland*, III, iii, col. 25, *P.R. 22 Henry III*, p. 140; ibid. 108–11.

[4] Hodgson, col. 57; *P.R. 7 Richard I*, p. 26; ibid., pp. 92–98.

latter's account.[1] About the same time tallages were being assessed on individuals instead of on boroughs and manors, and the quite separate problem which this remarkable increase in individual debtors posed to the tally cutters of the receipt, and its eventual solution by a *tallia dividenda* struck for the sheriff who in turn struck his own tallies for the debtors, has been discussed by Miss Mills.[2] It is, however, doubtful if the invention saved work in the shires since we do not know if sheriffs had hitherto distributed the Exchequer tallies before they passed their accounts; it is certain that it transferred the burden of tally cutting from the receipt to the sheriff's office; and it is by no means certain that all crown debtors welcomed a sheriff's tally in place of the king's tally. The invention is reflected in the Northumberland accounts when the sheriff answered for the common pleas and forest eyres of 1208, answering for 341 marks 14½*d.* and £118. 17*s.* 7*d.*, no number of tallies being expressed.[3] The account for the Yorkshire eyre of 1208 does not show the same use of the new invention but does foreshadow a further development. In the account for 11 John the only entry under the eyre is the summary entry for £1,100. 9*s.* 10*d.* by tallies; in the account for 12 John there is a further summary entry for £343. 9*s.* 2*d.*, nearly all paid, by 123 tallies, and some 61 partially paid debts are entered individually, followed by a note that the wholly owing debts have not yet been entered in the Pipe Roll: *Debita huius Itineris nondum in Rotulo*.[4] There is nothing to show that this was more than a temporary expedient in a particular case and during the remainder of John's reign the quasi-judicial visitations that took place were not those of the common pleas eyre nor did their estreats present the same problems.

The eyre visitation of 1218–19 formed part of the return to normal conditions and its revenue was, designedly, moderate: the sheriff of Northumberland accounted for £59. 11*s.* 1d. and the sheriff of Yorkshire for £289. 3*s.* 9*d.*, the uncleared debts being apparently all transferred to the Pipe Rolls.[5] As under John they were set out systematically: those on which a part payment had been made were usually set out in columns; those still wholly owing were sometimes set out in columns but more often in para-

[1] Hodgson, col. 85; *P.R. 5 John*, p. 88; ibid., pp. 216–22.

[2] *Experiments in Exchequer Procedure*, pp. 156–7.

[3] Hodgson, col. 105; *P.R. 11 John*, p. 176.

[4] *P.R. 11 John*, p. 139; *P.R. 12 John*, pp. 217–19.

[5] Hodgson, col. 121; P.R. 3 Henry III, rots. 14, 16. These and other non-italicized references are to the original rolls.

graphs; the issues from felons' chattels, debts which had been specially pardoned and debts arising within those liberties whose lords were themselves entitled to the issues of royal justice were all usually entered in paragraphs. The appearance of the issues of a common pleas eyre set out in this way, even from the visitation of 1218–19, may seem a little overwhelming; but we must guard against thinking of the Pipe Rolls, whether at the end of John's reign or the beginning of Henry III's, as being 'clogged with long lists . . . of debts . . . with which the exchequer had utterly failed to cope'.[1] For cope with them it did very speedily. In a few years (and there was often an inevitable time-lag before payment or entitlement to remission could be proved) all but a few bad debts or debts where the Exchequer had itself made mistakes were cleared. But there was obviously need for a change whereby the estreat roll could serve as the main record after the first summons had been prepared, so that the second and subsequent summonses might be made from it. An estreat had a left-hand margin and if this could be used to show distinctively those debts which, for various reasons, had been entered individually on the Pipe Rolls, those whose payment had been proved and charged to the sheriff at first summons, and those which were still owing, the estreat could become the main record, being annotated when the sheriff answered at subsequent summonses to show what debts were then charged to him in lump sums or entered in the Pipe Roll, thereby saving much time, labour, and parchment. This was done when the Exchequer dealt with the revenue arising from the general sessions for novel disseisin and gaol delivery of 1225 and from the common pleas eyres of 1226–8, in accounts audited between the autumn of 1226 and the summer of 1231: before the reforms of Peter de Rivaux, for whom Miss Mills has claimed the change.[2]

The debts in the estreat which, for various reasons, were entered in the Pipe Roll were marked, as they may always have been: 'In Rotulo'; those which the sheriff admitted receiving were marked 't' and charged to him in a lump sum. Those still wholly owing were marked 'd'; if the sheriff admitted receiving them after they had been resummoned then 't' would be prefixed, or if it was necessary to enter them in the Pipe Roll 'In Rotulo' would be prefixed. The formula of 1176 had been changed a little in the ensuing half-century and at the beginning of Henry III's reign there were several variant forms in use, of which the commonest

[1] *Experiments in Exchequer Procedure*, p. 156.
[2] *The Reforms at the Exchequer*, p. 127.

was, perhaps: 'The same sheriff answers for so much of the amercements of men, towns and hundreds whose names, debts and the causes of the debts are entered in the roll which the aforesaid (justices) have delivered into the treasury. Paid so much.' With the entry of the revenue from the visitation of 1225 in the accounts of 10 Henry III this became: 'The same sheriff answers for so much of the amercements of men and towns (and the chattels of fugitives and men hanged) before whose names the letter "t" is placed in the roll which the aforesaid (justices) have delivered into the treasury.' So the sheriff of Northumberland answered for 15 marks 22½*d.* of debts marked 't', by 38 tallies, since the *tallia dividenda* was not invariably used at this date.[1] At the end of the matter from the visitation a note was entered towards the right-hand margin: 'the wholly owing debts (*debita*) of this eyre are not yet in the roll'.[2] There were two other sorts of debts: those on which a partial payment had been made at first summons, known as *parciales* or parcels, and those arising from within franchises whose lords were themselves entitled to the profits of royal justices, known compendiously as *libertates*, liberties. Just at the beginnings there were some variations of practice. The parcels were marked 'p' in the estreat, 't' being added when they were paid; the liberties were left in the estreat and then brought into the Pipe Roll for formal clearance, or brought in on first summons. So when the issues from Martin de Pateshull's last eyres in Norfolk and Suffolk in 1228 were first brought to account in the Roll for 13 Henry III, the sheriff accounted for £825. 5*s.* 6½*d.* of debts marked 't' and paragraphed entries were made of the debts from the liberties of Langley, Sempringham, Bec, St. Albans, the Templars, and the Hospitallers; the note at the end of the matter ran: 'The wholly owing debts (*debita*) and the parcels and the liberties of Ely and St. Edmunds and of the Bishop of Norwich are not yet in the Roll.'[3] Then in the next account the sheriff accounted for £225. 14*s.* 7*d.* of debts marked 't d' and 't p' while the remaining parcels and those from the liberties of Norwich and St. Edmunds were entered, the note at the end running: 'The wholly owing debts (*debita*) of this eyre are not in the roll but in the summons, nor is the liberty of Ely.'[4] But before the end of the account the latter were formally cleared:

[1] Hodgson, col. 144.

[2] The note from Martin de Pateshull's Somerset and Dorset sessions was still in the account five years later: *P.R. 14 Henry III*, p. 45.

[3] P.R. 13 Henry III, rot. 9 d.

[4] *P.R. 14 Henry III*, pp. 157, 90–95.

The same sheriff renders account of 44 marks 4*s*. 8*d*. of the amercements of men in Martin de Pateshull's eyre before whose names is put 'Ely' 'summoned' 'd' in the roll of the same eyre, namely from reeves, men, lands and fees of the bishop of Ely. In cash nil and to the bishop of Ely 44 marks 4*s*. 8*d*. by privilege (*per libertatem*) of the charters of the kings of England. And he is quit.[1]

The Devon account in the same year has a similar payment of £96. 0*s*. 8*d*. from 't d' and ' t p' debts of the eyre of 1228, coupled with the clearance of the rest of the estreat by the entry of the parcels, in columns, and the wholly owing debts, in paragraphs.[2] But the 'p' annotation was not long used. Such debts were removed to the Pipe Roll or left in the estreat: the formal clearance of debts from liberties was abandoned for the most part. Debts cleared on the third and subsequent summonses were indicated by dots combined with 't'. The Yorkshire account for 14 Henry III shows the clearance of £11. 15*s*. 8*d*. of debts marked '.t' from Brian de Lisle's recent forest eyre and of £14. 8*s*. 8*d*. of debts marked '. .t' from the common pleas eyre of 1226–7.[3] It also provides examples of the accounting at first summons of debts marked 't' from the Sussex common pleas eyre of 1229; from the visitation of the Midlands conducted by the regents Segrave and Neville in the summer of 1230; and from several recent forest eyres.[4]

The reduction achieved by the method in full operation may be measured from one of the earliest surviving estreats, from the forest eyre held by Gilbert de Umframvill and his fellows at Newcastle on Tyne in May 1240.[5] The estreat listed some 317 debts totalling some £93. 1*s*. 10*d*.; of this some 309 debts totalling some £91. 19*s*. 10*d*. were accounted for, but it was only necessary to enter two of these and a few lines of summary in Northumberland accounts between 1240 and 1253. Under the heading 'From the Pleas of the Forest by Gilbert de Umframvill and his fellows' in the account for 24 Henry III the sheriff accounted for £75. 8*s*. 9½*d*. of the debts marked 't' (of which there were some 251 in the estreat) and one large debt, for 15 marks, was entered in the Pipe Roll and marked 'In Rotulo' in the estreat. After this came the

1 Ibid., p. 96.
2 Ibid., pp. 17–26.
3 Ibid., pp. 284, 279.
4 Ibid., p. 241; pp. 31, 88, 210, 229, 235, 303, 325; pp. 61, 129, 231, 254, 321 and 219, 253. The subject-index of this volume is inadequate.
5 Like the majority of early L.T.R. Estreats it is in the collection assembled in the nineteenth century from various Exchequer departments known as K.R., Accounts Various: E. 101/534/4.

stock formula: *Debita huius Itineris non sunt in Rotulo.*[1] The heading was repeated in the roll until the account for 31 Henry III.[2] The tailpiece was repeated in its original form as it gradually moved with the heading into the somewhat inchoate mass between the body of the county and the *De Oblatis* section until the account for 31 Henry III and then, with the removal of the heading, it was altered to: *Debita Itineris G. de Umframvill' non sunt in Rotulo*, in which form it remained until its last appearance, in the account for 51 Henry III.[3] The answer to the first summons had left 66 debts in the estreat, all of which were marked 'd'. At the next summons 30 had been collected so to them 't' was prefixed, the sheriff answering for £3. 16*s*. 9½*d*. of 't d' in the account for 25 Henry III; at the next summons 11 more had been collected, to which '.t' was prefixed, the sheriff answering for £1. 6*s*. of '.t d' in the account for 26 Henry III; at the next summons 4 more had been collected and annotated with '. .t', the sheriff answering for 11*s*. of '. .t d' in the account for 28 Henry III; at the next summons the sheriff answered for 6 more to which '. . .t' was prefixed, the sheriff accounting for 5*s*. of '. . . t d' in the account for 29 Henry III; at the next summons 5 more were collected and annotated '. . . .t', the sheriff accounting for 11*s*. 3*d*. of '. . . . t d' in the account for 30 Henry III.[4] This left nine debts, totalling 25*s*., still in the estreat. We do not know how often the estreat was resummoned after that but when the account for 37 Henry III was taken the sheriff admitted receipt of one of these debts, from William son of Gervase of Mitford, for 12*d*. 'In Rotulo' was then prefixed to its 'd' in the estreat and the debt itself was entered on the Pipe Roll, without any reference to the eyre, just below the point which the tailpiece had now reached.[5] The remaining eight debts, totalling 22*s*., were apparently never collected nor were they entered in the Pipe Roll. It is, however, not certain that estreats were generally so left uncleared or whether until the late 1240's it was not the more usual practice, after some six resummons, to remove the few remaining debts to the Pipe Rolls.

So much for the restriction of new matter reaching the Pipe Rolls. The removal of matter already in it presented two different aspects. One concerned debts cleared in a normal way by proof of payment. Down to the eve of the *Dialogus* all debts in an account on which the sheriff subsequently answered when the

[1] Hodgson, col. 193. [2] Ibid., col. 211. [3] Ibid., cols. 211, 213, 268.
[4] Ibid., cols. 196, 199 (= *P.R. 26 Henry III*, p. 16), 204, 207, 211.
[5] Hodgson, col. 228.

contents of that account had been resummoned were normally entered in the new Pipe Roll for clearance. But about the same time that summary entries were first used systematically for estreats a similar entry was used occasionally for the previous year's Pipe Roll. In the Surrey account for 22 Henry II there were entered a considerable number of fairly small debts from the forest eyre of 1176; these were all cleared in the next account but were not again entered, for instead, under the heading elsewhere employed for estreats *De hiis qui totum reddiderunt*, the sheriff accounted for so much 'of the smallest amercements of men for the forest (pleas) whose names and debts are entered in the 22nd Roll'.[1] But this method did not come into general use for many years. In the 1180's it became the practice to annotate the old account at audit when the sheriff was answering on the summons made from it and before the new account was completed. Debts then admitted to have been received were marked 't'; those on which a part payment had been received were marked 'p'; those wholly owing were marked 'd'; debts from liberties whose lords were entitled to them were marked with an abbreviation to denote the liberty, and so on.[2] But generally when the clearance of the debts marked 't' in the old account was made in the new account these debts were not cleared in a summary entry but were entered individually in a paragraphed group. About the beginning of John's reign a further symbol was introduced: '+'. These debts were known as *crusiati* but when so marked in the old account they were normally cleared by assembling them all together in the new account under the heading: *De hiis qui cruisiati sunt in Rotulo precedenti*.[3] A few summary entries were made, as when in the account for 3 John the sheriff of Yorkshire accounted for £20. 3*s*. 9*d*. by thirty-eight tallies 'of amercements . . . entered in the preceding Roll before whose names is written "t" as a sign of quittance'.[4] It was only in the early years of Henry III's reign, when *crusiati* had been abandoned, that summary clearance of entries marked 't' in the old account became normal practice, with the

[1] *P.R. 22 Henry II*, pp. 216–17; *P.R. 23 Henry II*, p. 195.

[2] Cf. Charles Johnson, Introduction to *P.R. 2 Richard I*, p. xix. As Miss Mills pointed out in *Experiments in Exchequer Procedure*, p. 155, the marks were unfortunately not reproduced in the volumes of the P.R.S. Old Series so that the precise origin remains to be investigated.

[3] e.g. *P.R. 4 John*, p. 63.

[4] *P.R. 3 John*, p. 152. Some examples of similar groups and of the debts from which they were assembled, from the Warwick and Leicester accounts of 17 and 21 Henry III, are given in the *Prospectus for . . . a Calendar of Pipe Rolls* (1949), pp. 9, 13–15.

formula: 'The same sheriff accounts for so much of the debts of many persons contained in the preceding Roll before whose names is placed the letter "t".' In the largest accounts several such entries might be necessary, the old account being split up arbitrarily by reference to the various (often obsolescent) headings in it, for convenience of reference. So the Yorkshire account of 13 Henry III was split into three parts and in the account for 14 Henry III the sheriff answered for 23 marks 11*s.* 3½*d.* of debts marked 't' between the headings *De Ammerciamentis* and *De Placitis Foreste*, for 7 marks 3½*d.* of debts marked 't' between the headings *De Placitis Foreste* and *De Amerciamentis per R. de Lexington*, and for 46 marks 4*s.* of debts marked 't' between the headings *De Amerciamentis per R. de Lexington* and *De exitibus foreste per H. de Nevill.*[1]

The other aspect of the removal of debt from the Pipe Roll was the organized removal of desperate debts: as distinct from the removal of individual debts, each on its own merits, described by Richard of Ely. Here development was much more reluctant. But it was done twice under Richard of Ely: in 1182, when debts in the Roll of 27 Henry II (arisen in the past five years or so) were removed and entered in a schedule prefixed to the Roll of 28 Henry II; and in 1183–7, when debts from the Rolls of 29 to 32 Henry II were similarly removed and entered in a schedule prefixed to the Rolls of 33 Henry II.[2] It was done again under John, when many debts which were marked with a special sign in the Roll of 4 John are not found in the next roll, though no schedule of them has yet been discovered.[3] Under Henry III it was done twice, about 1240–2 and between 1258 and 1261. On the former occasion debts from fifteen counties in the Rolls of 24 and 25 Henry III were marked 'in pullo' and entered on separate membranes or *Rotuli Pullorum* of which both Pipe and Chancellor's copies survive.[4] Thus twenty-two Northumberland debts were so removed from the account of 24 Henry III, the oldest having been first entered in 14 Henry III; ten were removed from the account for 25 Henry III, the oldest having been first entered in 4 Henry III.[5] The removal undertaken about 1258

[1] *P.R. 14 Henry III*, pp. 276, 283, 286.
[2] *P.R. 28* and *33 Henry II.*
[3] *P.R. 4 John*, passim; *P.R. 5 John*, Introduction, p. xvij.
[4] L.T.R. Misc. Rolls [E. 370], 2/20, rots. 7, 7 d and (copy) 8, 8 d. The counties are: Berks., Cambs. and Hunts., Devon, Essex and Herts., Glos., Hereford, Kent, Lincs., Norfolk and Suffolk, Northants., Northumb., Notts. and Derbys., Oxon., Somerset and Dorset, Warwicks. and Leics.
[5] E. 370/2/20, rots. 7 and (copy) 8; cf. Hodgson, cols. 192–3 and 195–6.

and 1260–1 concerned the accounts of ten counties in the Rolls of 41, 44, and 45 Henry III; again, both Pipe and Chancellor's copies survive.[1] This removal was probably connected with the baronial attempts at reform or with the royal counter-reforms, since at the same time old estreats were resummoned, the estreat of the Northumberland forest eyre of 1240, already described, being endorsed to show that it was summoned again in 44 and 47 Henry III. The reluctance of this development is not surprising, for these desperate debts were nevertheless the king's debts and their removal in any number too frequently might expose treasurer and barons to obloquy as depredators of the king's revenue. So long as the Exchequer was not too seriously behind in its work it was easier to copy such debts year by year into the summons and the new account: 'the spirit of a great official establishment, with plenty of routine work, is the spirit of leaving alone'.[2]

To sum up the practices which, on the eve and the morrow of the Barons' Wars, obtained in the Exchequer for restricting the number of entries in the county accounts on the Pipe Roll: the entry of new matter from common pleas and forest eyres and some analogous lists was severely restricted; that from the chancery was hardly restricted at all; economy was achieved in the clearance of many paid debts by summary entries which referred back to the details on the previous account; desperate debts were removed in bulk at long intervals by transfer to schedules known latterly as *Rotuli Pullorum*.

It will be useful to indicate the number of county accounts audited during the four decades 1232–72, though naturally forces other than the mere bulk of matter in the accounts, such as the increase of foreign accounts business and the growth of litigation at the Exchequer of pleas, must have helped to reduce the number of sheriffs' accounts which were taken yearly. Since 1236–7, when the Pipe Roll accounts for 20 Henry III were audited, the Exchequer had not been able to take each year the accounts of all the 27 regularly accounting sheriffs.[3] In the first three decades, in which if each sheriff had had his account audited yearly there

[1] E. 370/2/20, rot. 7, 7 d, 9 d and (copy) 8 d, 9 and 13, third membrane, both sets somewhat confusedly arranged. The counties are: Beds. and Bucks., Berks., Devon, Essex and Herts., Hants, Kent, Norfolk and Suffolk, Notts. and Derbys., Oxon., Warwicks. and Leics.

[2] Maitland, *Collected Papers*, ii. 116.

[3] The counties which did not account regularly were Cornwall, Rutland, and Westmorland.

would have been 270 accounts, the position was as follows. In the auditing decade October 1232–July 1242 (accounts for 16–25 Henry III) there were 258 accounts: 248 for one year and 10 for two years, with 2 accounts for a year outstanding at its end. In the next decade, 1242–52 (accounts for 26–35 Henry III), the position was similar, there being 254 accounts: 241 for one year and 14 for two years, with 3 accounts for a year outstanding at its end. In the decade 1252–62 (accounts for 36–45 Henry III) the Exchequer began to fall appreciably behind in its auditing, especially in the disturbed atmosphere after 1258; in the year of reform itself, 1258–9, it had been able to take only 17 county accounts. In this decade there were only 225 accounts: 186 for one year, 35 for two years and 4 for three years, there being 5 accounts for a year each outstanding at its close. In the last decade Lancashire ceased to account regularly on being granted to Prince Edmund, so that between October 1262 and July 1272 there could have been only 260 accounts, for 46–55 Henry III. There were only 134: 67 for one year, 43 for two years, 12 for three years, and 12 for more than three years (representing a total of 62 years), there being accounts from 6 sheriffs for an aggregate of 13 years still outstanding in July 1272. The full details for this decade may be seen in the table at the end of this article.

So much for the back and middle grounds to the order of 1270; we may now move to the foreground. The troubles from 1263 to 1267 had seriously upset the normal functioning of the Exchequer and sheriffs. In many counties there had been rival officials: in most there had been difficulties of collection; the routine summoning of debts had been at times impossible; where money had been collected it may not have reached the Exchequer or have been disbursed in equivalent fashion; where it had done so proof might be lacking. As soon as settled conditions were restored the Exchequer made great efforts at auditing, taking seventeen sheriffs' accounts in 1267–8 and sixteen in 1268–9. But in these accounts much less than the normal amount of old debt had been cleared; very much less than the normal amount of the debts of the several recent years now first entered in the *Nova Oblata* sections had been cleared. So an abnormally large number of debts remained to be copied into the summonses and on to the next account, at an expense of time and labour that inevitably reduced the number of accounts that could be audited. The accounts of those counties represented in the Pipe Rolls of 51 and 52 Henry III, though more closely written, occupied between two and three times as much parchment as the accounts of a decade earlier. Since by September 1269 the Exchequer had audited at least one post-war account for each of the twenty-six regularly accounting sheriffs it might have been thought that in the year 1269–70 it would have set about reducing the trouble-swollen accounts by preparing new *Rotuli Pullorum*. But this would have demanded the copying of a mass of detail once more both for the *Pullus* and, presumably, for a final resummons. An Exchequer able to take barely a half of the sheriffs' accounts yearly had plainly no margin of resources even for such a clearance.

At Michaelmas 1269 days for audit in the Michaelmas term (which lasted until Lent 1270) were given to nine sheriffs.[1] In the Michaelmas quarter the accounts of the first four sheriffs were taken. Three were among the smaller accounts: Northumberland, Shropshire and Staffordshire, Nottinghamshire and Derbyshire; one was among the larger: Bedfordshire and Buckinghamshire. But the fifth, Essex and Hertfordshire, whose account was among the largest, could not even be begun, so its sheriff was adjourned *sine die*. For the Hilary quarter days had been given for two of the largest and one of the smaller accounts: Norfolk and Suffolk, Northamptonshire or Lincolnshire, and Gloucestershire. The first and last were taken up to the *summa* but were not completed. The other could not even be begun. The full effect of the swollen matter was thus now being felt and at this rate the Exchequer would have to resign itself to taking about a third only of the sheriffs' accounts each year, with every possibility of the number diminishing yet more: an impossible position.

On 6 February 1270 John de Chishull, Dean of St. Paul's and apparently a career household and Exchequer official about whom insufficient is known, was appointed treasurer in place of Master Thomas de Wymondham.[2] He put forward a scheme, *quedam forma*, which was read, explained, examined, and approved at a council on 11 February and, as we have seen, was embodied in letters patent issued on 12 February. The patent begins with a preamble summing up the situation and with the names of the more dignified magnates, down to the household stewards, present at the council: 'We have gathered that, because of the lengthy and useless copying of many of our debts each year, the accounts

[1] K.R. Memoranda Roll, 53–54 Henry III (1269–70), *dies dati*, m. 21; accounts, mm. 15–17.

[2] His ecclesiastical career is covered in Newcourt's *Novum Repertorium*, ed. Hennessy, note 45*a*. Tout's *D.N.B.* article deals with his official career from about 1262 onwards but his earlier career remains to be investigated.

of many of our sheriffs and other officers remain unaudited to our great damage; on which account you have provided a scheme by which the matter may in future be corrected.'

There follows the scheme itself, in the form of instructions on the way in which a county account is to be written; its first part simply describes the traditional layout of an account, from the body of the county to the *Nova Oblata*, and need not be repeated for it had not changed in essentials since the conventional headings *Nova Oblata* (for new revenue) and *De Oblatis* (for revenue new in the previous account) had become finally conventionalized about 1198–9.[1] Then comes the new scheme. All the debts in the account are to be demanded diligently from the sheriff in the presence of those taking the account; if the sheriff does not admit that he has received any money on a particular debt, that debt is to remain in the old account and the letter 'd' is to be written in front of it. It is not to be copied onto the new account. At the end of new and succeeding accounts a formula is to be written: 'The debts of divers persons before whose names the letter "d" is placed in such a Roll are to be demanded and summoned each year and afterwards put in a summons and the summons sent to the sheriff with the other summonses.' If the sheriff admits at a subsequent account that he has received one of these debts, then the 'd' is to be taken out and in its place is to be written, 'He answers in the roll of such a year'; the debt is then to be entered and cleared in the later account. The new scheme was brought into operation with the first account taken in Easter term 1270, which was for Devonshire whose audit began on 21 April.[2] An account for that county had been audited in the previous year, so that account, on the Roll for 52 Henry III, was marked 'd' in the appropriate places. None of the debts so marked was copied onto the new account, for 53 Henry III, and at the end of that account the formula laid down in the order was written out, in a slightly modified form: 'The debts of divers persons before whose

[1] Compare the county accounts in P.R. 10 Richard I and 1 John. There is an evident tendency towards convention before 1199 but not the fully conventionalized use of these headings. New matter was entered under *Nova Oblata*; occasionally where revenue came from an estreat or list with its own heading, as with the issues of a common pleas or forest eyre, it might be entered immediately above the *Nova Oblata* heading. In the following year what remained was entered under *De Oblatis*. Thereafter what remained moved up into the somewhat unarticulated mass above. In order to break up this mass to some extent it became the practice under Henry III to retain a few eyre, &c., headings at convenient intervals for years after the relevant issues had disappeared.

[2] K.R. Mem. Roll 53–4 Henry III, mm. 21 d, *dies dati*, and 18, account.

names the letter "d" has been placed in Roll 52 shall be demanded and those on which the sheriff renders nothing shall be summoned when the account is finished, and the summons shall be sent to the sheriff with the other summonses as is provided by the king and council and as is contained in his letters patent in the treasury.'[1] Usually, however, there was not in front of each entry sufficient space in which to put the 'd' without risking ambiguity; so the clerks put the letter above the beginning of each entry and in the accounts taken later in Easter term they wrote 'above whose names' instead of 'before whose names' in the formula, which with that change became standardized. Only sixteen counties had had their accounts audited in 1268–9; for those counties whose previous account had been on a roll other than that for 52 Henry III, reference had to be made to the appropriate account.[2] For a couple of years the clerk who entered the formula knew which was the appropriate roll for each county; but the clerk who made the entries at the end of the accounts on the Roll for 56 Henry III did not, so he left a space for the correct year which was later entered by a colleague.

Debts had been marked 'd' since the closing years of Henry II's reign, while Richard of Ely was yet treasurer. The rule for nearly a century had been that all debts so marked must be entered in the next account unless cleared by entry in a special schedule or *pullus*. Now all debts marked 'd' in a number of selected accounts, namely the last account of each county that was audited before Easter 1270, were to be left there: to be entered in a later account only if and when they were cleared. A select series of accounts had been converted into a sort of *Rotuli Pullorum*. One fears that this break with the past might have scandalized Richard of Ely. It would have pleased his disciple. For to him, as to many a young civil servant after him, eager to point out the desirability for some change in traditional methods, nothing can have been more galling than to be told: 'How right you are. I could not agree with you more. But I am telling you how it is done: not how it ought, perhaps, to be done.'[3] In practice by no means all of the debts on

[1] 'Debita diversorum quorum nominibus preponitur littera .d. in Rotulo Lij singulis annis exigantur et ea de quibus vicecomes nichil inde reddit summoneantur finito compoto, et mittatur summonicio vicecomiti una cum aliis summonicionibus, sicut provisum est per regem et eius consilium et sicut continetur in litteris suis patentibus in thesauro.' Madox gives an example from the Gloucestershire account, begun before but completed after Easter: op. cit., p. 655, note (i). He gives a similar example from the Norfolk and Suffolk account of 55 Henry III, ibid., note (k). A small 'h' is usually added over *per regem* from the beginning of Edward I's reign.

[2] For details see table at end of article.

[3] *Dialogus*, ii. 12, p. 106.

which nothing had been received during the period under audit were marked 'd'. To establish fully the rules which the Exchequer evolved in applying the order would require a study of the accounts of several of the smaller counties as detailed as Miss Mills's edition of the 1295 Surrey account.[1] In general, debts from earls, barons, prominent knights, most religious corporations, counties and towns, all the lesser farms and debts of some size (say above 5 marks) seem to have been left in. The Surrey account is more typical of the general run than that for Northumberland, so some approximate figures from it may be useful as a guide to the sort of relief obtained by the engrosser of the Pipe Roll.[2] The account marked was that for 52 Henry III in which there were some 420 debts between the end of the attermed debts and small farms and the beginning of the *De Oblatis*. Of these, some 256 debts were marked 'd'; about 45 of them were subsequently answered on in accounts ranging between 2 and 35 Edward I. The *De Oblatis* section contained some 98 debts, which were the remains after the first summons of the new revenue for the six years 1262–7 that had been first charged in the *Nova Oblata* of the previous year's account, the first since the troubles. Of these some 65 were marked 'd' and 11 of these were subsequently answered between 3 and 17 Edward I. Thus above the *De Oblatis* section in the next account there were left some 197 debts: a reduction of well over half. Thirteen of the marked debts had been first entered, at least in part, in the Pipe Rolls of John and of Henry III before 1233. Next came three debts that had arisen from William of York's Surrey eyre of 1235.[3] Among several Yorkshire pleas heard in that eyre was one in which the plaintiff defaulted so he and his sureties had been put in mercy. The debt was only transferred from estreat to Pipe Roll in 32 Henry III when one surety had paid his amercement. The other, Ellis son of Paulin of Elvington, still remained in 52 Henry III, to be marked 'd': it is a reasonable assumption that this debt should never have been entered under Surrey but under Yorkshire. Similarly amerced had been a plaintiff and his sureties in a Kingston action; their debt was only entered in the Pipe Roll in 34 Henry III, apparently when the eyre estreat was finally cleared: the debt

[1] Surrey Record Society, xxi.

[2] P.R. 52 Henry III, rots. 15, 15 d, 13. For Northumberland, see Hodgson, cols. 276–85.

[3] Surrey 1235 eyre roll (*J.I. 1/864*), mm. 7 d, 10 d (Gilbert the miller and Gilbert Thridehalf) and 15 d. As with many other eyres of 1234–6 the original summons had been made by the justices, not the Exchequer: Fine Roll 20 Henry III, m. 17.

should have been collected by the Kingston bailiffs rather than the county sheriff. Finally, William de Rukenhall had fined 5 marks to compromise an appeal. His debt, first entered in 22 Henry III, was the earliest in the account marked 'd' to be eventually answered, against the 'd' being noted: 'But Matthew de Hasting' the sheriff answers in Roll 56'. Matthew's answer was to show that William was a Merton priory tenant and Merton had the right to the profits of royal justice arising from its tenants. It is impossible to say how typical these three debts may be of the whole but they do confirm the belief, already advanced, that the persistence of debt in the Pipe Rolls does not necessarily reflect mere failure to collect on the summonses.

By the end of auditing in the summer of 1271, twenty-one counties had been dealt with under the order, as may be seen in detail from the table at the end of this article: immediate relief had been gained. John de Chishull may have intended to use this method only once, and then on revenue which had arisen down to the end of the troubles. But before Edward I had returned to England 'those who hold the place of the king that now is' ordered that the last account of the old reign for each county should be treated in the same way. The new order does not seem to have been enrolled in chancery. We know of it only from the additional formula that now appears at the end of the accounts.[1] The application of the second order differed in one significant respect from that of the first, as may be seen from some approximate figures from the Surrey account for 56 Henry III.[2] There were some 210 debts above the *Nova Oblata* (there being no *De Oblatis* section); of these some 90 were marked 'd' and some 25 of these were eventually cleared in accounts ranging from 1 to 30 Edward I. But the order was also applied to the *Nova Oblata*, or rather, so far as can be gathered, from so much of it as arose from the Originalia Roll; some 38 debts from that source were marked 'd' and of these about 15 were cleared in accounts from 1 Edward I to 3 Edward II. Under both orders, in addition to clearances by transfer to later rolls, a number of debts were cleared by the old estreat method of prefixed symbols, ranging from 't' to about '. . .t', for summary entry in the next few accounts.

[1] 'Et eodem modo fiat de debitis diversorum quorum nominibus supraponitur eadem littera .d. in Rotulo Lvj eiusdem Regis sicut provisum est per illos qui tenent locum Regis qui nunc est.' Madox gives a very late example, from the Northumberland account of 10 Edward I: op. cit., p. 655, note (l).

[2] P.R. 56 Henry III, rot. 27, 27 d; for Northumberland, see Hodgson, cols. 292–9.

Until the Pipe Roll for 2 Edward I the years of the appropriate accounts in which debts had been marked 'd' were accurately entered in the notes at the end of the accounts. Thereafter the sort of thing familiar to those who know something of the work of departmental clerks happens. Because most of the accounts to be referred to happened to be on the Rolls for 52 and 56 Henry III, the notes tend to refer all the accounts with debts marked 'd' to those two Pipe Rolls. This laziness reaches its pitch of absurdity with Westmorland, a county whose account was taken at rare intervals. When its first account since the Barons' War was audited in 1276–7 the note stated that debts in its accounts for 52 and 56 Henry III had been marked 'd': whereas its last previous account was on the Roll for 46 Henry III; and its debts were not marked at all.

Parallel with the application of the two orders the Exchequer had at last changed its treatment of the Originalia Rolls. In the Roll for 54 Henry III there is for the first time a fair number of debts not entered in the Pipe Roll but marked 't'; in the Roll for 56 Henry III, remarkable in another way for having its membranes filed Exchequer-fashion through their heads, the estreat method is first applied in some fullness. Only about half the entries in the Roll for 1 Edward I were transferred to the Pipe Roll; from the outsize Roll of 3 Edward I onwards the majority of entries were left to be summoned from the roll and not transferred to the Pipe Roll. In the early stages of this development notes were entered in a convenient blank somewhere along the right-hand margin of the *Nova Oblata* section to the effect that the debts from the estreats of chancery for the years 54, 55, 56, and so on, had not been entered in the Pipe Roll.[1]

The combined effects of the two Pipe Roll orders and of the estreat treatment of the Originalia Rolls can be readily seen from the table at the end of this article. Despite the interruption caused by political circumstances in 1275, in the audit year October 1277 to July 1278, for the first time for forty years, the accounts, for 5 Edward I, of all the now regularly accounting counties were taken. Moreover these 27 accounts required only 20 rotulets, whereas the 16 accounts on the Roll of 52 Henry III had occupied 27 much more closely written rotulets. The time for emergency measures was now past. The Exchequer was able to return to traditional methods by compiling a further series of *Rotuli Pullorum* in which, unlike those of Henry III's reign, all the regu-

[1] e.g. Dickson, *Northumberland Pipe Rolls 1273–81*, pp. 65, 77.

larly accounting counties were represented.[1] With few exceptions, the debts were all taken from the accounts of 5 Edward I and were marked to show that they were summoned in 7 Edward I.[2] The copies, Pipe and Chancellor's, were filed up with, and in some cases made use of blank spaces in, the rotulets of the Henry III *pulli*. The character of the entries varied. Surrey, with eighteen entries from 5 Edward I, consisted mainly of old issues of county profits, manors, escheats, purprestures, and the farms of Guildford and Southwark that a cautious Exchequer had retained for years after arrangements had been made transferring the revenue from the Crown.[3] Ten more Surrey debts were taken from the Roll of 7 Edward I. In all, five of the debts were subsequently cleared, in 8, 13, and 23 Edward I. The last of the twenty-eight entries was of a mark due from the town of Carshalton for arrears of market perquisites; this was eventually cleared and entered in the *Nova Oblata* of 23 Edward I; another debt similarly cleared and entered had been the first of a batch in the Sussex *pullus*.[4] The fact that in a few counties debts were taken from a later account suggests that the engrosser of the Pipe Roll and his clerks were feeling the need for something more than an occasionally prepared *pullus*.

From what seems to be the Hampshire summons of estreats whose debts were not entered in the Pipe Roll that was returnable at Michaelmas 1282, being issued on 10 July 1281,[5] there are examples of the summonses of debts marked 'd' under both orders and of the debts removed to the *pullus*.[6] This Hampshire example shows forcefully the number of older estreats which were being summoned at this time and the vast quantity of uncleared debts, in this instance approaching a total of three thousand from 44 estreats, that never burdened the Pipe Rolls. In addition to the

[1] E. 370/2/20, mm. 1–6, 9 d (lower part), 10–12, 13 (except part of dorse), 14–15, which include fair copies for Cambs. and Hunts. and for Norfolk and Suffolk made after 1293.

[2] Cambridge and Huntingdon was taken from 1 and 5 Edward I; additions were made from 6 Edward I to Essex and Herts. and London, from 7 Edward I to Glos., Surrey and Oxon., and from 9 Edward I to Northampton. Devon was summoned in 8 Edward I.

[3] E. 370/2/20, mm. 5 and 10.

[4] *Surrey Pipe Roll, 1295*, in entry 116 and entry 127.

[5] E. 101/603/6, to which reference it has been, mistakenly, removed in fairly recent times from the L.T.R.'s and Pipe Office records. Only the first membrane, of debts from Robert Fukes's assize sessions about 1280, has the usual summons top and tail.

[6] Ibid., mm. 11–12, headed 'Debita diversorum quorum nominibus suprapponitur Littera D in Rotulo Lij°'; m. 10, headed 'Debita de D in Rotulo Lvj^to de Comitatu Suh'pt'; m. 13, headed 'Debita pullorum de tempore R. E.'

estreats of the debts marked 'd' and of the *pullus* there were summoned the Hampshire contents of eight estreats of the chancery, 55 Henry III–6 Edward I; of 10 Bench estreats from 1251, 1263, and 1269–78; 3 of common pleas eyres, of 1256, 1263, and 1280; 3 from the Exchequer of pleas, 52–54 Henry III; 3 from the court *coram rege*, 51–53 Henry III; 7 from various assizes justices, 1269–80; and 7 of miscellaneous origin running from Robert Passelewe's forest visitation of 1243, through the justiciar Bigod's assizes in 1259, market amercements in 1260, Jews' debts in 1262, the Hampshire eyre *de terris datis* in 1270, to gaol deliveries under Edward I. There is another, isolated, example of a summons of debts marked 'd' in the Pipe Roll of 56 Henry III, under the regents' order, from Somerset and Dorset.[1]

The next development in the restriction of matter reaching the Pipe Roll came with the letters close of 23 March 1284, known as the statute of Rhuddlan.[2] These provided that the details of the county farm and of the lands formerly part of it but granted away subsequently, which formed the entry at the head of each account and was known conventionally as the body of the county, should in future not be entered in the Pipe Roll but in a separate roll; they provided also that the dead farms and desperate debts should also be transferred from Pipe Roll accounts to a separate roll: the sheriff to be yearly apposed on the contents of both rolls. In fact a single roll, called the Roll of the Bodies of the Counties, was used for both purposes.[3] The bodies of the counties were entered in it as they stood in the account for 11 Edward I and they were omitted from the Pipe Rolls from 12 to 26 Edward I. Then, for no very obvious reasons, they were again entered in the accounts for 27 Edward I and remained in the accounts until about 1311. Edward II issued letters confirming, and enjoining the observance of the provision of 1284;[4] whereupon, from the accounts of 6 and 7 Edward II onwards they were again omitted.[5] The dead and

[1] E. 101/119/7, headed 'Debita diversorum quorum nominibus preponitur Littera D in Rotulo Lsexto'.

[2] *C.C.R. 1279–88*, 294–6. A copy, probably made about 1311, is prefixed to P.R. 12 Edward I.

[3] It is included among the P.R.s: E. 373/129.

[4] The explanatory matter in the accounts says that the confirmation was entered in the *Communia* for 5 Edward II Michaelmas but a search in the two Memoranda Rolls has not discovered it.

[5] Of the regularly accounting counties the bodies for Cambs. and Huntingdon, Essex and Herts., Hants, Hereford, Norfolk and Suffolk, Northumb., Salop, Staffs., Warwicks. and Leics. last appear in the accounts for 6 Edward II and those of the other counties in 5 Edward II.

desperate debts, like the body of the county, were first taken from the account of 11 Edward I. They continued to be removed from subsequent rolls down to various dates between 1315 and 1319; the latest Surrey debts were taken from the Pipe Roll of 13 Edward II.[1] In the process of making the removals the clerks developed a new marginal convention 'but' to indicate entries annotated 'but he answers in the Roll of the Bodies' on their last appearance in the Pipe Roll. Six Surrey debts were so removed in the account of 23 Edward I, a typical year.[2] The notes at the foot of the accounts in accordance with the orders of 1270 and 1273 had in 1284 a phrase added to cover the similar summons of debts contained in the *pullus* and in the Roll of the Bodies of the Counties;[3] but soon afterwards these notes ceased to be entered. The letters close of 1284 also made a ruling on the restriction of new matter to be entered from the estreats, &c. Only debts upon which the sheriff answered at first summons that he had collected something and debts from the Originalia that seemed clear (that is, owed by persons or corporations of such standing that there was not likely to be any difficulty over their eventual collection) were to be entered in the *Nova Oblata*. This ruling, however, was hardly an innovation but a declaration and confirmation of the practice which had obtained over the previous decade once the Originalia had begun to be treated like the rest of the estreats. It did make unnecessary the notes in the right-hand margin of accounts to the effect that the debts in various estreats had not been entered in the Pipe Roll and such notes soon ceased to be made.

It will be obvious, therefore, that Tout was mistaken when, possibly misled by Hubert Hall, he described the statute of Rhuddlan as being 'as ineffective as most medieval legislation was'.[4] On the contrary, during the next forty years the county accounts remained streamlined to an extent that they had never been under Henry III. We have already seen that in the Surrey account of 52 Henry III, when congestion was at its worst, there were over 500 debts in the account down to the end of the *De Oblatis* and that removals under the orders of 1270 and 1273 had reduced them to just over 130 in the account of 1 Edward I. In 23 Edward I there were only some 99; in 34 Edward I there were 94; in 10 Edward II, 89, and in 16 Edward II, 92. The increasing

[1] E. 372/129, rots. 7, 5.

[2] *Surrey Pipe Roll, 1295*, entries 64–65, 72, 79, 99, and 113.

[3] Madox gives an example from the foot of the Sussex account, 12 Edward I: op. cit., p. 655, note (m).

[4] *The Place of Edward II in English History*, p. 195.

bulk of the Pipe Rolls, which under Edward II deterred Tout from using them, was not due to any increase in the uncleared debt in the county accounts but to a diversity of causes of which the chief were: the increase in the number of foreign accounts, which not only filled over a third of the rolls but whose debit balances were transferred to the county accounts; the increasing detail of cleared debt entered in the *Nova Oblata*, of which the Surrey account of 23 Edward I supplies a typical example;[1] and the increasing prolixity of wording that characterizes so many records from the late thirteenth century onwards. But below the comparatively streamlined superstructure of the county accounts lay, in various chests and bags, the bulky Originalia Rolls and the numerous estreats, all containing debts still owing that ought to be and no doubt were summoned. We are necessarily concerned with the accounting problem at the centre but we must not forget the social problem at the periphery, the sheriff's officers, the distrained beasts and corn, the aggrieved villager or country gentleman that made up the levying of old debts. The summoning of old estreats was politically unpopular and not surprisingly one of the acts of the Earl of Lancaster's ascendancy after the parliament of Lincoln dealt with the matter. On 5 August 1316 a general pardon of all amercements and forfeitures incurred before the beginning of 20 Edward I was proclaimed, the sheriffs and Exchequer being ordered to take the necessary steps, including the cancellation of the relevant estreats.[2] It was apparently decided at the Exchequer that the entries in the estreats not covered by the proclamation, such as the fines, the sums due in respect of the chattels of felons, and so on, should be copied out into new rolls, called *compendia* or compendium rolls. The stages whereby the Exchequer implemented the proclamation remain to be fully investigated but William de Everdon, who on 1 June 1318 exchanged the office of treasurer's remembrancer for that of engrosser of the Pipe Roll, was assigned 'to supervise and order the extraction of debts from old estreats up to 20 Edward I and to instruct the clerks in new estreats of the debts arising'; he and four clerks were at work in London from 11 to 31 March 1318 on this and were paid £6.[3] Although most of the estreats have perished, a few that survive bear endorsements indicating that

[1] *Surrey Pipe Roll 1295*, where the *Nova Oblata* fills some 6½ pp. against 7½ pp. of the rest of the account.
[2] *C.P.R. 1313–1317*, 532.
[3] Issue Roll 12 Edward II Mich., 186, m. 7.

they were dealt with at this time. For example, the roll of the 1260 Oxford forest eyre is endorsed: 'The fines owed by this roll have been extracted into a new roll entitled Compendium etc. in the 12th year of king Edward son of king Edward. And all the amercements have been pardoned.'[1] It is also endorsed: 'Summoned in the year 13.' The eight debts remaining from the Northumberland forest eyre of 1240 were all amercements, so that roll is merely endorsed: 'Nothing is due from this roll since all the amercements have been pardoned.'[2] Nothing was prefixed to the old 'd' of first summons against the pardoned amercements but all the debts transferred to the new compendium rolls had 'In Rotulo Compendii' prefixed to their 'd'; there are many examples of debts so marked not only in the few surviving estreats but also in the Originalia Rolls from 43 Henry III onwards. Most of the compendium rolls have perished. The earliest extracts among the few that survive are provided by the compendia of Thurkelby's Somerset common pleas eyre of 1249, of Roger de Clifford's Somerset forest eyre of 1270, and of the Bench from 1252 Michaelmas to 1263 Trinity.[3]

This work was therefore already in hand before Bishop Stapeldon became treasurer: whereupon it was intensified. In the long vacation of 1320 William de Everdon with three clerks, along with the treasurer's remembrancer with two clerks, supervised and arranged the work of a team of eleven clerks, led by one each from the treasurer's remembrancer's and the controller of the pipe's office, who put in a total of 532 clerk-days, the total expenses coming to £15. 10*s*. 8*d*. exclusive of parchment, which at this time and for the next few years was being bought in exceptionally large quantities.[4] No more work of this sort was done until after the promulgation of the Cowick ordinances on 14 June 1323. As is well known, these ordinances began with a statement of the Exchequer barons' overriding responsibility for the audit of accounts and then defined in detail the responsibilities of the engrosser of the Pipe Roll and of the two remembrancers.[5]

Only some of the sections concerned with the work of the engrosser and treasurer's remembrancer concern us. Section 2 reiterated the established rules whereby the items to be transferred from the estreats were limited to the wholly and partially paid

[1] E. 101/119/4; another example is the estreat of the Shropshire forest eyre of 1250: E. 101/533/16.

[2] E. 101/534/4, m. 1 d.

[3] E. 101/119/2.

[4] Issue Roll 13 Edward II, East., 191, m. 7.

[5] *Red Book*, iii. 848–907.

debts, those arising from within franchises[1] or some yearly accruing items. Section 4 set up a new record, the Exannual Roll, to which all desperate debts, except the arrears of farms, were to be transferred; such debts were to be marked in the Pipe Roll whence they were removed and were not to be restored to a later roll unless wholly or partially paid. Section 5 provided that the debts in the Exannual Roll as well as the debts in the now superseded Roll of the Bodies of the Counties were to be summoned and—an echo of the orders of 1270 and 1273—a formula was to be entered at the foot of the accounts as a reminder that these debts were to be apposed and those cleared were to be restored to the appropriate Pipe Roll. As a preliminary to all this Stapeldon, or perhaps Everdon, had a neatly arranged transcript made of the by now very untidy Roll of the Bodies.[2] The main series of the Exannual Rolls, destined to continue into the nineteenth century, was begun with debts taken from the accounts in the Pipe Rolls of 15 or 16 Edward II, varying with the counties.[3] The first batch of entries followed the practice of the Roll of the Bodies, which merely mentioned the roll from which debts were taken after the first debt. But with the extracts from 16 Edward II onwards the matter was arranged under distinct headings: 'Debts extracted from the Roll of such a year.' The extraction from the first accounts was ruthless: 60 of the 92 debts from the Surrey account of 16 Edward II were so removed.[4]

In dealing with the treasurer's remembrancer, who was responsible for keeping estreats and making the summonses, section 32 of the ordinances provided that all estreats should be sought out and a list of them compiled and maintained up to date, while section 33 provided that all old estreats should be examined and the debts in them which had not been paid, allowed, or pardoned should be entered in new estreats and resummoned. This led in the long vacation of 1323 to a renewal of work on the estreats far more extensive than that of 1318 and 1320. Again under the supervision of the engrosser, William de Everdon, 23 clerks,

[1] Special instructions on the treatment of debts from franchises, over which the practice of Edward I's time had been harsher than under Henry III, had been laid down in letters of 17 February 1321: *Red Book*, iii. 970–2.

[2] The vagaries of modern listing have called this Exannual Roll [E. 363] 2, instead of 1.

[3] E. 363/1 and 3. These form two parts of one roll in which the various county lists run to the end of Henry IV and include abstracts from some foreign accounts. A succession of Public Record Office *Guides* has wrongly ascribed these earliest Rolls to Edward I.

[4] E. 363/1, m. 41.

apart from his own staff, were engaged for varying periods between 10 August and 29 September 1323 at a total cost of £18. 11*s*., exclusive of parchment;[1] though it is reasonably certain that their work included the transcription of the very large Roll of the Bodies and of the considerable first extracts in the Exannual Roll. Some of the surviving estreats bear endorsements, similar to those of 12 Edward II, with the dates 17 Edward II or September 17 Edward II, indicating that they were among those dealt with in the long vacation of 1323.[2] In the long vacation of 1324 there was again great activity. Part was no doubt concerned with the general array of records still proceeding: *pro arrayando diversa officia*. Part was expressly concerned with 'making estreats of the king's debts from his own time and those of his ancestors'.[3] It was again superintended by William de Everdon, since 18 June an Exchequer baron, with another baron present part of the time and with the new engrosser, William de Stowe (who had been Everdon's clerk since 1318 or earlier) and three subordinates and thirteen other named clerks with nine unnamed subordinates, including the keeper of the tallies, six auditors of foreign accounts, two clerks from the king's remembrancer's office and one from the controller of the pipe: at a cost of £21. 14*s*. 6*d*. There was also a further payment of 55*s*. 6*d*. to unnamed clerks who between 10 June and 7 August were writing *compendia* for a total of 222 clerk-days.[4]

By the winter the work on the estreats seems to have been practically completed so that John de Chisenhale, previously one of the additional auditors of foreign accounts, was on 12 November 1324 appointed to keep all estreats.[5] He evidently examined the documents now brought to his custody, for on most of the estreats that have a note of the making of a compendium roll there occurs the note: *Examinatur per Chis'*.[6] He was succeeded on 3 February 1326 by Hugh de Colewyk, who had been among the named clerks engaged on the work in 1324, when he had two unnamed assistants.[7] He took oath to keep the estreats and make the

[1] Issue Roll 16 Edward II, East., 202, m. 7.

[2] Estreats of the Northants. forest eyre of John Biset (*c*. 1240), E. 101/533/23; of assizes taken by Martin de Littlebury, 1268, E. 101/119/6; of Oxfordshire forest eyre of 1240, E. 101/119/1.

[3] Issue Roll 17 Edward II, East., 1/207, m. 12.

[4] Ibid., m. 13.

[5] Madox, op. cit., p. 731, citing L.T.R. Mem. Roll 18 Edward II, Mich. *Communia*, rot. 4.

[6] e.g. E. 101/119/1, 4, 6 and 533/16.

[7] Madox, loc. cit., citing 19 Edward II, Hil. *Communia*, rot. 4*a*.

summonses. On 20 February he was paid 5*s*. 6*d*. for buying a chest to put the estreats in and soon afterwards he was paid 40*s*. for making a calendar of the headings of all the estreats existing in the Exchequer.[1] A torn fragment of this calendar survives.[2] So, with the appointment of Chisenhale and Colewyk, the custody of the estreats and the duty of making the summonses was removed from the office of the treasurer's remembrancer to become the responsibility of a specially designated officer who became known as the Clerk of the Estreats and whose office long remained separate from but a link between the offices of the treasurer's remembrancer and of the Clerk of the Pipe.[3] We have seen that section 33 of the Cowick ordinances provided for the summons of the new compendium rolls and it may be that the clerks who were at work between 10 June and 7 August 1324 on *compendia* were writing out these summonses for the one known example of such a summons that survives issued over Walter of Norwich's *teste* on 25 July 1324 to the sheriff of Surrey and Sussex, being returnable at Easter 1325.[4] It gives a clear picture of the magnitude of the work just accomplished and of the accumulation of estreats that had existed, for it summoned the contents of some 75 compendium rolls, made from at least as many estreats. These included 25 Bench estreats for periods between a term and a year ranging from 1251 to 1292; 20 estreats of common pleas eyres ranging from the Surrey eyre of 1229 to the last eyre held for either county, that of Sussex in 1288; 5 estreats of forest eyres between 1240 and 1270; 7 estreats of gaol delivery justices and 7 of assize justices from the later years of Henry III to about 1291; 4 *coram rege* estreats from Hengham's time; a single Exchequer of pleas estreat for the year 1290 Mich.–1291 Mich.; and 7 miscellaneous estreats ranging from those of assizes and special sessions held by the baronial justiciars Bigod and Despenser in 1258–60, through the Sussex eyre *de terris datis* of 1268, to inquests into various offences between the 1240's and 1291. Under some there was only a single entry, or one or two; but from the Sussex and Surrey eyres of 1263, on the eve of the worst of the troubles, there were 133 and 63 respectively, due very largely from sheriffs and bailiffs. There were very large numbers from other common pleas and forest

[1] Issue Roll, 19 Edward II, Mich., 217, m. 14 and 19 Edward II, East., 218, m. 3.

[2] E. 101/681/10.

[3] Tout, *Place of Edward II*, p. 349, note 1 mistook Colewyk for a treasurer's remembrancer, ignoring what Madox had assembled about the origins of the Clerk of the Estreats, and misdated his appointment by a year.

[4] E. 101/681/14.

eyres and the total number in the summons is close on a thousand. These, moreover, are all debts not covered by the proclamation of 1316, suggesting that there may have been at least a similar number of pardoned amercements in the cancelled estreats; they come from estreats of before 1292; and they include nothing from the Originalia Rolls. In addition, while some of the estreats must have provided entries for the compendium rolls of many other counties, such as those of the central courts, or assize justices, and common pleas eyres (with until 1272 an extensive foreign pleas side), there must have been many estreats of central courts that provided no Surrey or Sussex material, as well, of course, as many estreats from common pleas and forest eyres, assizes after the development of circuits, gaol deliveries, and various special sessions that contained matter for only one or a few counties. The work on estreats, for which the executive credit seems certainly to be due to William de Everdon, formed only one part among the many of the great array conceived by Bishop Stapeldon that ranged from the compilation of the Gascon and Stapeldon calendars to the recovering and labelling of all the older plea rolls. The array, alike in conception and in its execution by various subordinates, was magnificent both as a piece of administration and as record keeping; but like the ordinances of 1323–6 it still awaits exhaustive study.

To conclude. The Pipe Roll order of 1270, repeated in 1273, was an attempt to deal with a critical phase, caused by the troubles since 1263, in a problem of the audit of county accounts that had been chronic since the later years of Henry II. The order could not, nor was it intended that it should, solve the basic problem: but it successfully resolved the crisis; thereby enabling the Exchequer to resume and to develop established practice, in the course of which the principles of the order were applied in fresh ways. The problem of too many entries in the county accounts on the Pipe Rolls that exercised the minds of Exchequer officials for a century and a half now beset the officers of the Pipe Roll Society as they consider the publication of the Rolls of Henry III. The solutions adopted to restrict entry of matter in the county accounts need to be understood by all those who use the Rolls in which the different practices obtained, because they limit the matter which is to be found. The need which bygone engrossers of the Pipe Rolls felt to lighten their labour of transcribing numerous debts on which little or no action took place for many years might point the need for a publication of the rolls in calendar form, such as it was proposed in 1949 should be undertaken by the Public Record Office. The proposal has been laid aside. It is, however, encouraging that it should have been revived in a limited way by a local society; and entirely appropriate that in succession to the century-old work of Hodgson and Dickson it will soon be possible to follow the course of all essential matter in the Northumberland Pipe Roll accounts down to 1298.[1]

[1] *Archaeologia Aeliana*, 4th ser., xxxii, xxxiii.

EXPLANATION OF TABLE (*see opposite*)

This table sets out the county accounts on the Pipe Rolls from 45 Henry III to 5 Edward I. The numbers given are those of the rotulet or dorse of the rotulet on which the account for each county begins. A dash indicates that there is no account for a particular county on the given roll, in which case the next account covers the period since the last. The calendar year is that of the Michaelmas at which the accounts ended. The audit took place between that Michaelmas and the following July; the accounts were filed from the bottom or highest rotulet numbers to the top or lowest numbers roughly in the order in which they were taken.

Accounts with debts marked 'd' under the orders of 1270 and 1273 are denoted by figures in bold type thus: **16.** Accounts in which the note is first added to say that this has been done under the order of 1270 are denoted by an asterisk, thus: 4*; accounts in which the note is first added to say that this has been done under the order of 1273 are denoted by an obelus, thus: 13†.

The method was not applied to the Westmorland account on the Roll of 46 Henry III although the notes were appended to that county's account on the Roll of 4 Edward I; nor was it applied to the Lancashire account on the Roll of 46 Henry III, for the next account for that county was on the Roll of 12 Edward I and was treated under the rules of the Statute of Rhuddlan. It was not applied to Rutland whose few accounts in this period are not shown.

Table of County Accounts on the Pipe Rolls 45 Henry III (1261)–5 Edward I (1277)

Regnal and Calendar Years	45 1261	46 1262	47 1263	48 1264	49 1265	50 1266	51 1267	52 1268	53 1269	54 1270	55 1271	56 1272	1 1273	2 1274	3 1275	4 1276	5 1277
Bedfordshire and Buckinghamshire	9	18	2	8 d	..	..	22	..	**16 d**	1*	..	**10 d**	13†	1	7	2	16 d
Berkshire	12	20	..	14 d	..	..	24 d	**16**	..	12*	..	**14**	14†	..	15	21 d	9
Cambridge and Huntingdon	8	17	4	..	..	..	5	**4**	..	4*	17	**6 d**	5†	4	8 d	19	6
Cumberland	16 d	10 d	..	..	..	..	**3 d**	..	3*	..	**16**	..	..	15†	..	1 d	10
Devon	4	..	7	12	..	..	..	**9**	11*	..	..	**17 d**	18 d†	2 d	..	1	19
Essex and Hertfordshire	7 d	7	..	7 d	2	9	13	**22 d**	6*	..	8	**5 d**	10†	3	9	4	13
Gloucestershire	..	16	..	..	11	**2 d**	..	..	4*	..	3 d	**24**	18†	7	17	6 d	7
Hampshire	10	19	8	9	7	5 d	8 d	**8**	..	6*	16 d	**14 d**	3†	17	3	12	1
Herefordshire	15	..	..	..	..	..	..	**11 d**	..	2*	..	**25**	..	9 d†	11	5	9 d
Kent	..	5	7 d	..	9 d	6	..	**23**	..	..	7 d*	**3**	8†	13 d	11	15	8
Lancashire	..	10	..	..	..	..	..	..	..	..	..	..	..	..	..	..	..
Lincolnshire	14	5 d	..	4	6	..	**11**	..	10*	..	10 d	**10**	..	5†	13	17	20
Lincolnshire and Middlesex	17	11	6	10	3	11	18 d	**27**	8 d*	8	13 d	**26 d**	17 d†	14	19	7 d	19 d
Norfolk and Suffolk	5	15	5	..	..	..	21 d	26	**14 d**	15*	4	**20 d**	11†	11	18	9 d	12
Northamptonshire	..	12	3	..	..	3	2	**7 d**	..	16*	5	..	1†	10 d	2	13	2
Northumberland	13	7	..	..	..	..	26	..	**20**	..	18*	**23 d**	..	..	4†	9	16
Nottinghamshire and Derbyshire	11	2 d	..	13	..	12	..	..	**18 d**	..	**19***	..	9†	..	..	3	5
Oxfordshire	12	1 d	..	14	..	..	25	**13**	..	13 d*	..	**15**	15 d†	..	16 d	21	10 d
Shropshire	2 d	..	..	..	..	..	6	..	**20 d**	..	..	..	17 d*†	..	5	10	17
Staffordshire	1 d	..	..	..	..	..	4 d	..	**19 d**	..	..	..	16 d*†	..	5 d	10 d	17 d
Somerset and Dorset	18	..	9	..	..	..	..	**12**	..	18 d*	..	**7 d**	..	15†	1	16	3
Surrey	19	..	..	..	..	..	23	**15**	..	9 d*	15 d	**27**	12†	14 d	14	18	4
Sussex	19 d	..	..	..	..	..	9 d	**14**	..	8*	14 d	**27 d**	12 d†	14 d	14	18 d	4
Warwick and Leicester	..	8	..	..	4	..	..	**19**	..	7*	..	**8**	2†	..	6	7	14
Wiltshire	8 d	13	..	11	10	5	..	**18**	..	4 d*	12	**18 d**	15†	..	16	11	18
Westmorland	..	10 d	..	..	..	..	..	..	..	..	..	..	..	..	..	17*†	6 d
Worcestershire	16	9	..	10 d	..	**10**	..	..	..	18 d*	**10**	..	..	..	19†	..	8 d
Yorkshire	2	3	..	2	..	..	**16**	..	..	11*	..	**22 d**	4†	6	10	20	15

INDEX OF PERSONS AND PLACES

INDEX OF SUBJECTS

Most legal and administrative subjects are arranged in groups, the main groups being: Courts of law; Criminal and other offences; Officials; Procedure and process; Records and manuscripts; Writs.